D0813207

This book is to be returned
the last date stamped

F -

The English Press in the Eighteenth Century

Jeremy Black

CROOM HELM
London & Sydney

© 1987 Jeremy Black
Croom Helm Ltd, Provident House, Burrell Row,
Beckenham, Kent BR3 1AT
Croom Helm Australia, 44-50 Waterloo Road,
North Ryde, 2113, New South Wales

British Library Cataloguing in Publication Data

Black, Jeremy
    The English press in the eighteenth century.
    1. Press—England—History—18th
    century
    I. Title
    072   PN5116

ISBN 0-7099-3924-8

Printed and bound in Great Britain by Mackays of Chatham Ltd, Kent

Contents

Trip to Scarborough, the manager in affliction, *and* no song no supper. The royal nuptials, slack rope vaulting, *and* the King and cobler. East India stock, board and lodging, *and* kitchen utensils. The fugitive, Earl Macartney's embassy to China, *and* a schoolmaster wanted. Pleasures of imagination, a simple exposition of St Athanasius's creed, *and* a chaplaincy for sale. Treasury chambers, transparent orrery, *and* every man his own gardener. Irish poplin warehouse, view of the prophecies, *and* three letters to Mr Pitt. Pocket peerage of Great Britain and Ireland, the impenetrable secret, *and* the whig-club. Independent freeholders, to sail for Philadelphia, *and* John Hunter's infallible preventative. Foreign wines, sea bathing, *and* national calamities. Rheumatic Tincture, reports of cases, *and* the history of antient Greece. Sketch of the last campaign, a capital collection of pictures, *and* paper hangings for the spring trade. Poems in the Scottish dialect, Nipple Liniment, *and* board and lodging for a lady. Law of corporations, patent watches, *and* repertory of arts. Essence of pearl, a servant out of livery, *and* book-keeping at leisure hours. A desirable farm, treatise on tithes, *and* the next presentation to a valuable rectory. The travellers at home, thirty guineas bounty, and England preserved.

Hodge-podge: or, the first page of a Daily paper, *Leeds Mercury*, 9 May 1795

To Sarah

Acknowledgements

I am grateful to a large number of friends, colleagues, archivists, librarians and owners of manuscripts without whom it would have been impossible to write this book. It is not possible to name more than a small number of those who have helped. I owe much to Her Majesty the Queen, the Duke of Northumberland, Earl Walde-grave, Lady Lucas, the trustees of the Wentworth Woodhouse Collection and John Weston-Underwood for permission to consult their papers. Peter Borsay, Grayson Ditchfield, Michael Harris, David Hayton, Derek Jarrett, Maurice Milne, David Pearson and Peter Thomas read earlier drafts of all or part of this work and their comments have been of the greatest assistance. This book owes much to the kind hospitality of the Warden and Fellows of Merton College, Oxford. Professor Fleury rendered great assistance in Paris. A large number of friends aided the course of research, especially by providing invaluable hospitality. I would particularly like to mention Peter Bassett, Richard Berman, John Blair, Tony Brown, Jonathan Dent, Robert Gildea, Anthony Gross, Dan and Stella Hollis, Harold James, James Kellock, Max King, James Lawrie, Jeremy Mayhew, William Salomon, Peter Spear, Mark Stocker, Alan Welsford and Paul Zealander. My parents were as ever extremely helpful. Richard Stoneman has been an exemplary publisher. The Staff Travel and Research Fund of Durham University and the Twenty Seven Foundation provided useful assistance. The secretaries in the Durham department, particularly Wendy Duery, displayed great patience in coping with my drafts. The book is dedicated to Sarah for being herself.

Abbreviations

Add.	Additional Manuscripts
AE	Paris, Quai d'Orsay, Archives des Affaires Etrangères
AN	Paris, Archives Nationales
Ang.	Angleterre
AST.LM.Ing.	Turin, Archivo di Stato, Lettere Ministri, Inghilterra
BL.	London, British Library, Department of Manuscripts
Bodl.	Oxford, Bodleian Library, Department of Western Manuscripts
C(H)Mss.	Cholmondely (Houghton) Manuscripts
Chewton	Chewton Mendip, Chewton House, papers of James, first Earl Waldegrave
CJ	*Commons Journals*
Cobbett	W. Cobbett, *Parliamentary History of England from . . . 1066 to . . . 1803* (36 vols., 1806–20)
CP	Correspondance Angleterre
CRO	County Record Office
CUL	Cambridge, University Library
EHR	*English Historical Review*
HHStA	Vienna, Haus-, Hof-, und Staatsarchiv
HJ	*Historical Journal*
L	Lucas papers
LJ	*Lords Journals*
PMLA	*Publications of the Modern Language Association of America*
PRO	Public Record Office, State Papers
RA	Windsor Castle, Royal Archives, Stuart Papers
Rawl.	Rawlinson letters
Sheffield	Sheffield City Library, Wentworth Woodhouse papers
SRO	Edinburgh, Scottish Record Office
TRHS	*Transactions of the Royal Historical Society*

| Weston-Underwood | Iden Green, Kent, house of John Weston-Underwood, papers of Edward Weston. |

Note on Currency

Prices are given in eighteenth-century British units of currency. £1=20 shillings (sh)=240 pennies (d). Therefore 6d=2½ new pence, 1sh=5 new pence.

Note on Dates

Until the 1752 reform of the calendar Britain conformed to Old Style, which was eleven days behind New Style, the Gregorian calendar used in most of the rest of Europe. Until the reform all dates given are Old Style apart from those marked (ns). The convention by which the English New Year began on 25 March has been ignored, and I have given it as starting on 1 January.

Preface

Upon the whole, if I cannot boast of having produced edifying strains of morality, dissertations of sound indefeazable criticism, and papers of exquisite mirth and humour, I hope, at least, the whole plan has been conducted with a strict regard to decency, and without any offence against virtue or good manners.

Arthur Murphy, *Gray's Inn Journal*, 21 September 1754

This book seeks to provide a general introduction to the eighteenth-century English press. In a work of this length it has not been possible to cover all aspects of the subject. Such a task, demanding knowledge of a wide range of disciplines, has not been attempted for many years, and studies of the press have tended to be of two types. The first, devoted to the press and politics, is predominantly metropolitan in its interests, the second, concentrating on issues of production and ownership, largely so. The most recent study of the London press, the excellent thesis of Michael Harris, to be published as *London Newspapers in the Age of Walpole: A Study in the Origins of the Modern English Press*, treats metropolitan developments as crucial.[1] There has been no attempt to build on the interesting studies of the provincial press in the first half of the century produced by Cranfield and Wiles. This work seeks to treat London and provincial papers side by side. Provincial papers took most of their news from London publications and the organisation of this news was dictated by the arrival of the London posts. London newspapers circulated in the provinces. And yet provincial printers were not simply scissors and paste men. They produced readable, interesting and, in some cases, campaigning newspapers. Several provincial papers enjoyed justified fame. Across much of Britain the press was a matter of provincial papers. It is dangerous to discuss the political or social influence of the press without considering these papers. Most specialist papers were of course metropolitan. The first number of the opposition weekly the *Yorkshire Freeholder*, published in York in 1780, claimed, 'A periodical essayist, printing his lucubrations at the distance of two hundred miles from the metropolis, will undoubtedly be thought a literary phenomenon.'[2] The *Country Spectator*, which was published in Gainsborough in 1792–3, made similar claims. In terms of newspaper publication provincial papers were singularly unvarying: no dailies, Sundays or evening papers, none devoted largely to economic or literary news. However, the generalist provincial papers developed markedly during the century, particularly in ending the monopoly of London opinions in their columns, and it is impossible to consider the press without discussing them. For reasons of space I have concentrated on English newspapers.

Historians have selected various events and dates as marking the arrival of the modern British press. The decision that this book would be devoted to the eighteenth century does not entail any suggestion that 1800 was a crucial date. The press of the 1800s was very similar to that of the preceding decade both in London and in the provinces. New newspapers were being founded on both sides of the divide. Montrose had its first periodical in 1793, Greenock and Arbroath in 1799 and Inverness in 1807. There was no break in terms of circulation or technology. The decision to end with the century reflects rather a need to limit the scope of the study and a scepticism concerning the idea of crucial dates in this period. Historians discussing the press of the eighteenth and early nineteenth centuries stress change and modernity and make much of the great expansion in the number of copies produced in the country. However, this was often a matter of more of the same, and a reader of eighteenth-century newspapers might be forgiven for stressing continuity rather than change. Newspapers, being recognisable, are seen often as a 'modernising' force and a sign of the modernity of the eighteenth century, while the newspaper form itself is regarded as becoming modern. All these assumptions can be questioned.

A flexible approach to the problem of definition has been adopted. There are several possible bases for differentiating between newspapers and other periodicals, including frequency of appearance, size, content and payment of stamp duty. Joseph Frank defined a newspaper as being printed, appearing at regular and frequent intervals and concentrating on current events.[3] That might appear a reasonable definition and yet journals that are widely accepted as newspapers did and do not devote themselves to current affairs only. Items characteristic of eighteenth-century magazines can be found in abundance in the newspapers of the period. The distinction between the two is more one of size and frequency than of content. Essay-sheets, journals devoted to a single essay and bereft usually of news and advertisements, are not regarded by some as newspapers. Rae Blanchard argued that Steele's tri-weekly the *Reader*, a Whig propaganda sheet of 1714, which was printed on stamped paper of newspaper half-sheet size, was not a newspaper for this reason.[4] However, as with magazines, there is a continuum, not a sharp break, in the case of essay-sheets. Any rigid definition ignores the fluid nature of the eighteenth-century press, titles changing their format, content or frequency of publication. All sought a common goal; as the *Country Spectator*, a weekly magazine-type journal, pointed out in 1792, 'To find readers is the first object with every man, who offers his labours to the Public.'[5] It is best to adopt a pragmatic approach,[6] and this has been done in this work. By concentrating on journals appearing at least once a week most magazines have been excluded. They did not report much news, other than providing monthly summaries. Essay papers appearing at least weekly have, however, been included as their prime rationale was commenting on the news.

The organisation of this book is thematic and within individual chapters an analytical rather than a chronological approach has been adopted. This is particularly the case with the two chapters devoted to the press and politics. In the space available any chronological account could only be a very abbreviated and superficial one. Instead certain themes have been selected for consideration. The subject of this book is too big for any one work of this length. If readers are encouraged to turn to the originals, preserved in a large number of libraries across Britain and available increasingly in microfilm editions, its purpose will have been achieved.

Notes

1. There is an interesting discussion by Harris in his introduction to *The Press in English Society from the Seventeenth to the Nineteenth Centuries* (1986).
2. *Yorkshire Freeholder*, 20 Jan. 1780.
3. J. Frank, *The Beginnings of the English Newspaper 1620–1660* (Cambridge, Mass., 1961), p. 1.
4. R. Blanchard, *Richard Steele's Periodical Journalism 1714–16* (Oxford, 1959), p. xvii.
5. *Country Spectator*, 9 Oct. 1792.
6. Harris, *The London Newspaper Press, 1725–1746* (unpublished PhD thesis, London, 1973), p. 3.

1 Development of the Metropolitan Press

The lapsing of the Licensing Act

We writers of essays, or (as they are termed) periodical papers, justly claim to ourselves a place among the modern improvers of literature. Neither *Bentley* nor *Burman*, nor any other equally sagacious commentator, has been able to discover the least traces of any similar productions among the ancients: except we can suppose, that the history of *Thucydides* was retailed weekly in six-penny numbers; that *Seneca* dealt out his morality every Saturday; or that *Tulley* wrote speeches and philosophical disquisitions, whilst *Virgil* and *Horace* clubbed together to furnish the poetry, for a Roman Magazine.

George Colman, *Connoisseur*, 14 February 1754

. . . certainly if the Parliament had at the Revolution,[1] looked upon the Liberty of the Press as so essential and sacred a Part of the Liberties of the Kingdom, as this Gentleman[2] and indeed almost all Writers have endeavoured to represent it, they would have cleared it of all Restraints that were laid upon it, as they did every other branch of publick Liberty. If the Press had ever been consider'd as the proper instrument to restrain the excesses and correct the misbehaviour of men in power, would it not have been claim'd and asserted in the Declaration of Rights, that was made to the Prince and Princess of *Orange* upon presenting them the Crown, in which all the Rights and Liberties of the subject were particularly enumerated and expressly demanded? But there is not one Syllable in jt, as I can find, relating to the Liberty of the Press; that was a Thing not so much as dreamt of in those days.

Daily Gazetteer, 6 January 1738

The forceful reminder by the *Daily Gazetteer*, the leading newspaper supporting (and indeed subsidised by) Walpole's Whig ministry in the later 1730s, that the framers of the Revolution

Settlement of 1688–9 had neither evoked nor enforced the 'Liberty of the Press', however defined, was an accurate one though largely forgotten. In 1762 the *Briton* saw 'the liberty of the press' as a 'consequence of the Revolution'. However, as the *Daily Gazetteer* pointed out, the legislation of the later Stuarts for controlling the press was maintained and in 1693 revived. The 1662 'Act for preventing the frequent Abuses in printing seditious, treasonable, and unlicensed Books and Pamphlets, and for regulating of Printing and Printing Presses' had lapsed in 1679 at a time when Charles II's control of Parliament had been tempered by the excitement generated by the Popish Plot, an exposé whose intoxicating rumours and slanders owed their propagation in great part to unregulated presses. Revived by James II in 1685, this Act was renewed in 1693 by a Parliament engaged in supporting William and Mary against the exiled James and his patron Louis XIV of France. Governments that take power through violence often maintain the apparatus and follow the methods of those they have discredited and replaced. In the case of William III, a Stuart by blood and an autocrat by disposition, this was far from surprising. Though the United Provinces (modern Netherlands), where William represented the monarchical component in the government, enjoyed the freest press in Europe this owed nothing to him. It was made a capital offence in the United Provinces to accuse William of aspiring to sovereignty and John Roth, one pamphleteer who continued to do so, was declared insane and confined for 14 years,[3] a method of control happily absent from eighteenth-century British ministerial supervision of the newspapers.

The Printing Act of 1662, renewed in 1693, was far from permissive. Based on the theory that the freedom to print was hazardous to the community and dangerous to its ruler, a threat to faith, loyalty and morality, the Act sought to limit both the right and the ability to print. Printing was strictly limited to the master printers of the Stationers Company of London and the university printers. Only twenty of the former were permitted and vacancies were filled by the Archbishop of Canterbury and the Bishop of London, who were troubled enough by the dissemination of heterodox opinions not to support a relaxation in the control of printing. Only four founders of type were permitted and vacancies were again filled by the two senior clerics. All master printers and founders were obliged to provide sureties of £300 not to engage in illegal printing. The number of apprentices, journeymen and presses per printer was regulated. The printing of material offensive to the Christian faith, the Church of England, any officer of the government or any private person was prohibited and a licensing system established to enable pre-publication censorship. The Secretaries of State were given authority over publications dealing with 'affairs of state'. This authority was delegated in 1663 to Sir Roger L'Estrange, who undertook it in return for the profitable patent for the exclusive publication of 'all narratives or relacons not exceeding two sheets of paper and all advertisements, mercuries, diurnals, and books of public intelligence'. Existing newsbooks were suppressed to make way for L'Estrange's. The competing schemes of Joseph Williamson, one of the Under-Secretaries, led to the breaching of L'Estrange's monopoly with the publication of the *Oxford Gazette* in November 1665. This became the *London Gazette*, (or *Gazette* for short) the following year when the Court returned to London after the plague and L'Estrange sold his monopoly to Williamson. The Scottish Privy Council discouraged the printing of news relating to Scotland, and it was not until the Union and the abolition of the Council that the situation altered there.[4]

The *Gazette* was not the sole means of spreading news. Though the trade and advertising newspapers set up after the Fire of London of 1666 contained no political news,[5] this was not the case with the manuscript newsletters. The lack of domestic news in the *Gazette* led readers who wanted political, and, in particular, parliamentary news to turn to newsletters.[6] It was not until the Popish Plot that the *Gazette*'s monopoly in printed news was breached. Public excitement, political commitment and the expiration of the licensing provisions in 1679 led to a sudden proliferation of unlicensed newspapers. The first of these appeared on 3 December 1678, edited by Henry Care or Carr. The full-title made clear the didactic nature of the work:

The Weekly Pacquet of Advice from Rome: or, The History of Popery. A Deduction of the Usurpations of the Bishops of Rome, and the Errors and Superstitions by them from time to time brought into the Church. In the Process of which, The Papists Arguments are Answered, their Fallacies Detected, their Cruelties Registred, their Treasons and seditious Principles Observed, and the whole Body of Papistry Anatomized. Perform'd by a Single Sheet, coming out every Friday, but with a

continual Connexion. To each being added, the Popish
Courant: or, Some occasional Joco-serious Reflections on
Romish Fopperies.

The introduction in the first number, addressed 'To all true
English Protestants, but especially those of the Cities of London
and Westminster', made clear the educational nature of the work
and the hope that its form and cost would enable it to reach an
extended readership:

> Though I doubt not but you have generally been so well
> Educated, as to understand the grosser Tenets of the
> Apostasiz'd Roman Church, and look upon them with just
> Abhorrence; Yet possibly some of you, (especially the Younger
> or more Mechanick sort) may not have had leisure or
> opportunity to inspect the whole of that Mystery of Iniquity; or
> to know how to answer their Emissaries when privately . . .
> they shall seek to undermine your Faith with specious, but
> fallacious Arguments. To give you a thorough insight into the
> Doctrines and Practices of that dangerous Party, that none may
> be sillily seduc'd for want of due warning, or defensive Arms,
> shall be the scope of these successive sheets . . . Not in the least
> intending hereby to intrench on the Province of our Reverend
> Divines . . . but only to furnish meaner Capacities with such
> familiar Arguments, as every Judicious Christian ought to have
> at hand . . . This good Design may possibly seem contemptible,
> by being Attempted in a Pamphlet-course; but 'tis considered,
> though there be good Books enow abroad, yet every Mans
> Purse will not allow him to buy, nor his Time permit him to
> read, nor perhaps his Understanding reach to comprehend
> large and elaborate Treaties. This Method is therefore chosen,
> as most likely to fall into Vulgar hands, and more agreeable to
> their circumstance, who have most need of such Assistances.

For their penny a week readers were promised the use of
mockery to obtain the paper's ends, and the following number
carried an advertisement accordingly:

> These are to give notice to all that think themselves concerned,
> that there will shortly be exposed to sale by drops of Holy-
> water, a couple of convenient Halters, Consecrated at St.

Tyburn, put up at five Nobles a-piece, to advance a French Crown each bidding. There likewise may be had a choice second hand Coffin ready seasoned, and fit for use. If any frugal Gentleman have a mind to it, let him repair to the new appointed Colledge of Priests and Jesuits, near Pye-Corner, and they may know further.

The *Popish Courant* of 24 January 1679 reported 'From the Laboratory of the Inquisition — A Catholick Pill to purge out Christianity'. Many of the characteristic features and devices of the eighteenth-century press were already present and fully developed. Eighteenth-century newspapers were characterised by a paranoid mentality, rigid convictions and a style that exploited humour: mock-advertisements, fictional creeds, such as that in the *Popish Courant* of 16 May 1679, and fake-prophecies. The *Popish Courant* of 15 August 1679 carried one, supposedly dating from Roman times, that attacked the Catholics and commented on contemporary politics. Each issue of the *Weekly Pacquet* began by stating what it was to contain, as some of the essay papers were to do the following century. In 1679 the publisher of the paper, Langley Curtis, produced a collected edition. In the preface he stressed the need for zeal and truth in the fight with Catholicism: 'You have need of knowledge, because your Enemy is subtle to deceive; and of Zeal, because your Contest is of the greatest Importance in the world.' Curtis also rejected criticism of the nature of his work 'as if Sense and Reason were confin'd to Folio's, and could not be delivered but in vast cumbersome Tracts'.

The preface to the second collected volume, which appeared in 1680, returned to the same theme. Ignorance was a peril, 'the Mother and Nurse of Romish Devotion'. Attacking it through a newspaper was likely to be the most effective method, 'that it might the better and more easily fall into the hands and hearts of the middle or meaner Rank; who having not time nor Coin to Buy or peruse chargeable, tedious, and various Books, might readily and cheaply be furnished here with a General Scheme of Popery'.

The upsurge in press activity during the Popish Plot and the Exclusion Crisis was unwelcome to the government. It brought back memories of the collapse of Charles I's personal rule and the virulent press of the 1640s. By the end of 1679 more papers were being published than at any time since 1649.[7] A Tory press directed against the opposition Whigs was founded, 'a whole kennel of

Popish Yelpers',[8] including such papers as *Heraclitus Ridens*, the *Observator* and the *Weekly Discovery*. However, Charles II wished not to conduct a propaganda war but to terminate one. As the 1662 Act had lapsed Charles turned to his judiciary to ascertain his regulating powers under the prerogative, and was rewarded with the opinion that the crown could, without seeking parliamentary assistance, prohibit 'the printing and publishing of all news-books and pamphlets of news whatsoever not licenced by His Majesty's authority'.[9] A proclamation was accordingly issued and prosecutions for seditious libel conducted in the common-law courts with Chief Justice Scroggs directing that juries were only competent to determine whether the defendants had published the libel; judges alone could decide whether it was seditious. The *Weekly Pacquet*, prosecuted by George Jeffreys, received the benefits of Scroggs's attention. As the preface to the third volume of the collected edition noted, Care was 'Jayl'd, inform'd against, and Convicted too, tho nothing of the Fact charg'd, much less any Criminal matter, prov'd; (for where Malice prosecutes, and Self-interest sits Judge, and sordid Ignorance is of the Jury, who may not be Condemn'd) . . .'. Scroggs ruled that the paper should cease publication, 'meer Arbitrary Will and Pleasure' according to Care, and Care, deserted by his printer, found it impossible to continue unless he changed the title. In July 1680 he produced the first number of the *New Anti-Roman Pacquet: or, Memoirs of Popes and Popery since the Tenth Century* accompanied by the *Pope's Harbinger By way of Diversion*. Charles's limited control over Parliament enabled Care to return to his original title on 3 December 1680, when Parliament, then in session, attacked Scroggs for his ruling. However neither Care's paper, nor any other unlicensed political one, was destined to survive. Charles II used his personal rule to stamp out the Whig newspapers, whilst James II supplemented his brother's use of the seditious libel method by having Parliament revive the Printing Act in 1685. Certain of governmental stability and support, the officials of the Stationers Company and the 'messengers of the press', officials of the Secretaries of State who searched for evidence of illegal printers, sought to enforce the law. The Stationers Company, which had played a major role in controlling printing in furtherance of ministerial views and its own monopoly, dealt with Richard Baldwin, the Whig publisher of the *Protestant Courant* in 1682.[10] The ministerial success in stamping out Whig newspapers forms an interesting contrast with the position the following century. The press in the 1680s was of course newer, smaller, confined to London, with a less-developed distributive network, smaller financial resources and without the loyalties of a long-established readership. However, much of the difference can be explained by a contrast in governmental attitudes. No eighteenth-century ministry sought to suppress the press with the thoroughness and vigour of Charles II and James II. The Civil War, the Popish Plot and the Exclusion Crisis engendered a fear and a desire for action in ministerial circles that was to be matched neither by the fears generated by, and thanks to, Jacobitism, nor by those associated with the French Revolution. Eighteenth-century ministries, in common with the political nation, were more accustomed to the expression of various opinions, often antagonistic, in the press. In part no doubt the growth of the press led to a change in governmental attitudes. The greater maturity of these attitudes in contrast to the paranoia and hyperbole of opposition rhetoric and propaganda, can be best appreciated when compared to the actions of seventeenth-century ministries. The relatively limited nature of eighteenth-century legal and extra-legal action against the press is then clear.

None of these developments was obvious at the time of the Glorious Revolution. Although the Printing Act of 1662 was still in force a series of newspapers appeared, benefiting from public interest in national politics, and the disruption of the agencies which supervised printing. On 12 December 1688 alone three papers were founded. All the surviving newspapers were favourable to William of Orange.[11] Whether there were attempts to publish Jacobite newspapers in this period, for which no copies survive, is unclear. The strident Whiggism of the surviving newspapers is obvious. The *London Courant* condemned the policies of James II's government: 'Some Corporation Troopers, who lately for a competent number of Guineas advance to mount and accoutre themselves, and a Guinea per diem constant pay, besides all expences in their journeys born, upon an Expedition against the Test and Penal Laws, invaded Charters, Liberties of Freemen . . . are now taken up.'

The same paper used the report of a procession, the arrival of William of Orange at St James's Palace, to make political points, a technique that was to be a commonplace one for eighteenth-century newspapers in their coverage of celebrations and demonstrations. The Prince arrived, attended by a great number of persons of Quality in Coaches and on Horseback, while multitudes of people of different ranks crowded the High-ways, echoing their Joys from all hands in the loudest acclamations of welcome, which was more entirely testified by the cheerfulness and serenity that sat in all peoples Countenances, to whom either true Religion or Liberty are of any value, all such ascribing their deliverance from Popery and Slavery to the courage and conduct of his Illustrious Highness, next to the Providence and Power of the Almighty. Nor were the exterior testimonies of ringing of Bells, Bonfires at night, etc. wanting to testify a general satisfaction at the coming of his Highness.

The papers carried reports of support for William's invasion, making success appear inevitable, and began to usurp the *Gazette*'s function of printing official announcements. The *London Mercury* printed a summary of William's declaration for the better collecting of the public revenues.[12] William himself was adept at using the printing press for his own purposes.[13] Partly no doubt because he appreciated the possibilities of the press William moved to revive the machinery of press control. The Stationers Company and the Messengers were instructed to seize unlicensed works. This reflected more than William's own views. The Convention Parliament prohibited the printing of reports of its proceedings and barred the public from its debates. William's campaign had results. The newspapers failed to report on the elections to the Parliament and gave little information about its proceedings. Richard Baldwin found himself in trouble with both the Secretaries of State and Parliament in 1690–1 despite his unimpeachable Whig credentials.

The lapse of the Licensing (Printing) Act in 1695 has recently been thoroughly investigated.[14] It is clear that the lapse did not spring from a general desire for the emancipation of printing. Instead it was felt that the existing system for the supervision of printing was inadequate and that a new one had to be created. The system was under stress for two significant reasons. The volume of unlicensed material in circulation, a problem that had affected L'Estrange, was high. This owed much to Jacobitism. Jacobite material could not be assimilated or controlled by the licensing system, and the nature of the Jacobite threat in the 1690s, aided by France and active in diabolical conspiracies, led to more awareness of the defects of the system. The second major problem was that the kaleidoscopic nature of British politics in the early 1690s, and, in particular, William III's wish for mixed ministries containing both Whigs and Tories, made the task of the licensers a very difficult one. Two were dismissed for licensing pamphlets judged unacceptable and others were threatened with legal action.[15] The activities of the licensers were criticised in the Lords in 1693 when the Act was renewed. In February 1695 a Commons committee was set up to prepare a new regulatory Bill that would avoid the defects of the existing system. A Bill was drafted and given a first reading, but it was killed for a variety of reasons: the opposition of the Stationers Company, which objected to the provision ending their monopoly, opposition in the Lords, divided opinions in the Commons, and a lack of parliamentary time, a reason that killed many Bills in an age when Parliament sat for only a few months in the year. Sessions tended to end in a confused rush and legislation over which Commons and Lords were in disagreement in mid-April stood little chance of becoming law.

The lapsing of the Act did not signal the end of all interest in press censorship. Parliamentary limitations of royal and ministerial authority during the reign of William III were not always permanent. The Triennial Act of 1694 was to be replaced by the Septennial Act; part of the Act of Settlement was repealed. There was a fluidity in constitutional arrangements that did not correspond to the views of later Whig zealots on the immutable perfection and completeness of the Revolution settlement.

Fredrick Siebert suggested that a significant aspect of the Revolution settlement was the relinquishment by the crown of all prerogative rights governing the press. However, Astbury has revealed that prerogative powers were still an issue after the lapsing of the Licensing Act and that the legal advice taken on the validity of the use of general warrants empowering the messengers of the press to suppress seditious books, pamphlets, and newspapers and to arrest those engaged in their production, was positive.[16] The ambiguity of the new situation and the unforeseen lapsing of pre-publication censorship were probably responsible for the introduction of a new 'Bill for the regulating of Printing and the Printing Presses' that autumn when a new Parliament assembled. A host of complaints from interested parties, such as the bishops, the universities and the Stationers Company, led to serious delays, and the Commons rejected a resolution to revive the Licensing Act in March 1697.[17] This was not the end of the matter. For the next two decades proposals were mooted and pamphlets written calling for the revival of some form of Licensing Act. The issue was raised in Parliament in 1698, 1702, 1704, and 1712. In 1702 Archbishop Tenison's attempt to revive the licensing system was rejected by the Lords on the third reading, whilst the Commons ordered 'that a Committee be appointed to consider of methods for preventing libels and scandalous papers'.[18] In 1704 a Tory Bill for restraining the press, supported by both Secretaries of State, was considered in Parliament, and pamphlets published on the subject.[19] Several of Queen Anne's speeches to Parliament, composed by her ministers, deplored the licentiousness of the press, and in 1712, in response to a royal message to the Commons calling for new legislation,[20] a Bill was drafted calling for the registration of all printing presses and of the names and addresses of all authors, printers and publishers.[21]

The failure of these successive measures may have owed something to a conviction among some parliamentarians that the press was beneficial. Whether parliamentarians, who had access to newsletters, really needed newspapers in order to stay informed is open to question. Some may have been influenced by the liberal sentiments of intellectuals, such as John Locke, who had sought to influence parliamentary consideration of the topic in 1693–5. Pamphlets on the subject were specifically addressed to parliamentarians.[22] Party politics were involved. The tellers for the majority on the renewal of the Licensing Act in 1693 were both Tories, and one, Simon Harcourt, was to be Lord Keeper at the time of the 1712 legislation. The tellers for the minority were a Whig and an independent Tory. In 1703 the Tory writer Charles Davenant warned that 'the liberty of the press will be the ruin of the nation and I must confess anything that doth but look like an appeal to the collective body of the people is of very dangerous consequence to the constitution'. Prominent Tories supported legislation in the winter of 1703–4. The Tory-dominated Convocation of Canterbury called for legislation in 1711. The High-Tory almanac of George Parker attacked the Whig press:

What Reams of Scandalous and impious Lies,
Were daily Published, to Corrupt the Crowd.[23]

The close Tory association with the call for revived controls ensured that the best opportunities for such legislation were during periods of Tory power, the early 1700s and 1710–14, which were indeed the periods when attempts were made. The importance of other issues, such as the management of the War of Spanish Succession, must have detracted from consideration of the press. Alan Downie has suggested that the attitude of Robert Harley, the dominant figure in the 1710–14 Tory administration, was crucial, particularly in ensuring that in 1712 taxation, the first Stamp Act, rather than the reimposition of pre-publication censorship, should be government policy. Downie attributes Harley's decision to his understanding of the value of the press as a means of propaganda.[24] One might supplement this view by pointing out that comparatively little about the 1712 legislation is known, that the context of national indebtedness produced by war should lead to a stressing of the fiscal considerations in Harley's mind, and that the experience of attempts to revive pre-publication censorship since 1695 might well have encouraged many politicians to abandon interest in the idea and the pragmatic Harley to settle for his fiscal scheme. The problems that had afflicted pre-publication censorship in the early 1690s could scarcely have encouraged politicians active in that period, such as Harley, to revive the system, while the existing machinery of seditious libel and breach of privilege was more effective. The Stamp Act did not end ministerial expressions of concern over the press. The need for action was stressed in the Queen's Speech of 1713 and the Commons Address of March 1714. However it was clear by then that short of some major upset there would be no general censorship of the press. Possibly a peacetime Tory ministry under someone other than Harley encouraged by clerical and royal pressure over the dissemination of heterodox opinions would have acted. The cry of the 'Church in Danger' was a potent one, as the Sacheverell affair had revealed, and it was probably the best approach for the revival of general censorship. However, in 1714 the Tories were pushed into the political wilderness by their own ambiguity towards the Hanoverian Succession and the exploitation of this by the Whigs.

Whig religious sensibilities were less acute than those of the Tories. Even though the Whig ministries encountered several serious crises, including Jacobite invasions in 1715, 1719 and 1745 and a serious Jacobite conspiracy in 1723, all exacerbated by Jacobite publications in England and each more serious than any domestic problem encountered by Queen Anne's Tory ministers, they made no attempt to move from their specific weapons for dealing with seditious works to a more general supervision. The years after 1714 were to witness a debate over the role of the press in the political system rather than one over the means to suppress it.

A spate of new titles

At present both city, town and country, are over-flow'd every day with an inundation of news-papers . . .
St. James's Weekly Journal, 31 October 1719

. . . the Vegetation of News-papers within these last six Months has been of the Mushroom Kind; and many of them, no Doubt, enjoy full as precarious an Existence.
Advertisement for a new magazine the *Treasury* in *Berrow's Worcester Journal*, 28 December 1769

A Gentleman in the Temple, who used to amuse himself with reading all party papers, finding it difficult now from the arguments alledged on both sides, to decide between them, made use of the following curious experiment: He one day took the occasional papers, and putting them into two scales, found that the liberty side, as he supposes by mere weight of argument, preponderated so greatly, that it made the other kick the beam, and so settled his opinion.
Reading Mercury, and Oxford Gazette, 8 January 1770

The lapsing of the Licensing Act was followed by a considerable growth in the press. There had been several licensed newspapers in 1689–94, besides the *Gazette*, but nothing comparable in number to the spate of new titles thereafter. A day after the Act lapsed on 3 May 1695 Richard Baldwin recommended his *Historical Account*, and three days later the *Flying Post* appeared. The following month saw the appearance of the first tri-weekly, the *Post Boy* and in October the *Post Man* followed. These three tri-weeklies were to dominate the press for many years. The 1704 estimate of 44,000 newspapers published weekly put the *Post Man* second at 11,600 and the *Post Boy* third at 9,000.[25] The first successful daily paper, the *Daily Courant*, began publication in March 1702, and the first successful colonial paper, the *Boston*

News-Letter, started two years later. Though the earliest extant copy of a provincial newspaper, the *Bristol Post-Boy*, dates from 1704, it is probable that the first provincial paper was the *Norwich Post*, starting in 1701 and followed by the Bristol paper a year later. The numbers of papers grew until the first major blow, the first Stamp Act of 1712, put several out of business. However, there was no permanent decline. In 1717 one paper noted, 'It having been for some time observ'd, that many papers are obtruded upon the publick on Saturdays'.[26] It became a commonplace for new papers in their first number to refer to the large size of the existing press. The first number of the *Old Post-Master*, a tri-weekly that appeared in 1696, noted, 'So many news papers (or so called) are daily published, that it would seem needless to trouble the world with more.' The *Wednesday's Journal* commented in 1717, 'We see so many Pretenders to Journals setting up every day.'[27] Two years later the first number of the *Daily Post* promising to be impartial, another convention of opening issues, observed, ''Tis the misfortune of the town to have much news, but little Intelligence . . .' The *British Observator*, which first appeared during the Excise Crisis of 1733, a good time for a new paper, admitted that 'it is grown a general complaint that there are already such a glut of newspapers and of weekly pamphlets'. In 1737 the first number of *Common Sense* commented on 'the present great number of my weekly brethren, with whom all people, except the stationers and the Stamp Office, think themselves already over-stocked'. The *New Weekly Miscellany* of 1741 accepted that it was imprudent to start a new paper, 'at a time when public newspapers are so numerous, and mankind in general think themselves too wise for instruction', but it declared its uniqueness, 'my chief force against irreligion, schism, and enthusiasm'. The prospectus for the *Star* in 1788 observed, 'It has long been a subject of complaint, that the number of Morning Prints tend rather to confound than to inform.'[28]

Whilst new papers made excuses, established ones passed comment. Complaining in 1722 that 'the town is eaten up' with too many papers, the *St. James's Post* called on its readers to support it as an old-established paper and promised that it would satisfy them. The *Weekly Journal* commented on 'the multitude of new papers lately started up, and which come out weekly', the *Whitehall Journal* on 'the great load of their weekly lumber, wherewith they oppress the town', the *Freeholder's Journal* on 'the crowd of papers that incumber the town, and make the tables of our coffee-houses look like the counters of a Pamphlet-shop', the *English and French Journal* on 'news writers, wherewith this country abounds more than any other in Europe' and the *Weekly Journal or, British Gazetteer* that 'there is not a place under the sun that is so fruitful of scribblers of all denominations and qualifications, as this famous City of London'. R.H., writing 'amidst this great dearth of news' from London in the peaceful spring of 1724, claimed 'there are 24 newspapers for the 24 hours in the day, nine or ten for every week, six or seven for every month'. *Oedipus: or the Postman Remounted*, a good instance of the more exotic names chosen for some papers, stated in 1730, 'There is almost every day new papers coming out, as well as old ones continu'd and improv'd.' Three years later the *Hyp-Doctor* noted, 'The article of Public Papers is now swell'd to a considerable size: and among them, the political is not the least considerable.'[29]

These comments represent a convention that reflected a sense of continuous activity and expansion in the press. And yet, despite this expansion, the number of papers at any one time was more modest than these claims would suggest. The Stamp Tax returns printed by Henry Snyder for August 1712 and May 1714 both list 12 London newspapers. Michael Harris has estimated the number of London weeklies and essay sheets published in 1746 as six, with the same figure for the number of tri-weeklies and dailies. In 1760 London had four dailies and five or six tri-weeklies. A decade later there were at least five dailies, eight tri-weeklies and four weeklies published in the capital. In 1783 London possessed nine dailies and ten bi- or tri-weeklies. By 1790 the figures were 13 morning, one evening, seven tri-weekly and two bi-weekly papers; by early 1792 the number of dailies had risen to 14 and by the end of the year 16. In 1811 the total of papers in all categories published in London was 52, a number swelled by Sunday newspapers, the first of which, the *British Gazette and Sunday Monitor* was started in about 1779, and all of which were illegal due to sabbatarian legislation.[30]

The best estimates for the number of papers in print at any one time are those given hesitantly, for there are large gaps in the surviving material. R.H. claimed in 1724 that 'the curious collector may by the help of his binder fill two or three yards of shelf every year with the news of it only'. His list included some of the American, European, Irish, Scottish and unstamped newspapers, but accepting that, even the best endowed of modern American libraries would find it difficult to fill the yards.[31] There are no known surviving copies of some newspapers that are known to have existed from references to them elsewhere, and in many more cases even the aggregated surviving runs are incomplete. The problem is exacerbated by the paucity of material on the press. Stamp Tax material is incomplete, while the records of the printers and booksellers who ran the press have largely failed to survive. There are no national licensing or distribution records, and the surviving records of advertisers are sparse. Some reports by government informers and other agents have survived, but they are patchy in the extreme. At least the surveillance of the opposition press, and in particular the seizure of office papers and the questioning of staff, has produced some material on the opposition press. However this source is less valuable after the 1730s when the intensity of surveillance diminished. Records of payments by the ministry or by political groups are also of value. Nevertheless, particularly for shortlived and unsuccessful papers, information is lacking, and new pieces of information often extend the known run of newspapers. The Stamp Tax receipts showed that the *Night Post*, an obscure tri-weekly whose known run was July 1711 to January 1712, continued until at least November 1713.[32] It is still possible that hitherto unknown newspapers may be discovered.

It is clearly necessary to be wary of stating a supposedly de-finitive figure for the number of newspapers at a particular date. Despite this it is obvious that the numbers of newspapers do not match the figures that would be anticipated from details and claims of the foundation of new papers. The reason is a high mortality rate, that has received very little consideration. As far as the sources are concerned most newspapers do not end; they flicker out. For every newspaper whose definite final number is known there are many, both London and provincial, which are known to have continued after their last surviving number and/or whose last surviving number gives no clue as to the subsequent fate of the paper. Even when the final number survives it is frequently the case that there is no statement to explain the demise of the paper.

The causes of the ending of a paper clearly varied. Given the rudimentary nature of the organisation of many, particularly pro-vincial, newspapers it is apparent that personal factors played a role. Alongside those papers that failed due to an inability to gain sufficient circulation there were others whose end can be traced to the death or retirement of a printer. The *Hyp-Doctor* claimed that 'the life of a paper is as uncertain as his, who gives life to it'. Again there is a difference between the collapse of an old-established and once-successful newspaper, and the failure of a new paper struggling without success to break into an already occupied market. Robert Haig has produced an excellent study of a newspaper in the former category, the *Gazetteer*. This paper, founded in 1735 as the government-subsidised *Daily Gazetteer*, enjoyed in 1790 an average daily circulation of approximately 1,650. It was one of the three most popular London morning papers and it was in no need of any subsidy; the average annual dividend on the paper from 1783 to 1794 was slightly more than 13 per cent. In 1797 the paper was ended largely due to an uncorrected management failure in 1793–4 when the paper was allowed to drift without a real 'conductor', a firm editor who could ensure the maintenance of the readership. By concentrating on the advertisements the proprietors neglected the circulation which ultimately proved fatal for the continuance of the former, most of which were placed on a very short-term basis in the eighteenth century.[33] There were other factors that helped to harm or to end long-established papers. Internal feuds, such as that which led to the production of two competing *Craftsman*, were of considerable importance.[34] Relationships between printers, proprietors and editors were both fluid and personal and there was no real concept of the copyright of a newspaper title so that disputes could spawn two newspapers of the same or similar title. For the same reason a new paper could attempt to usurp some of the market of an existing one by usurping its title. A rival *Flying-Post* was founded in 1714, the *Monitor* (1762), *General Evening Post* (1770), *Morning Post* (1776) and *Star* (1789) being among those which followed suit.[35] The *York Courant*, an opposition newspaper, that frequently reprinted the front-page essays of the *Craftsman*, was confused by the split in the latter and explained to its readers, 'There being at this time a misunderstanding between the Proprietors of the Craftsman, which has divided the paper into two, we shall suspend the printing thereof 'till we are fully assured which of the Publishers has the best right to that title . . .'[36]

The decisions of political sponsors and subsidisers could also be fatal. In 1735 two well-established titles, the *Daily Courant* and *Free Briton*, the first 'a paper of note'[37] since its foundation in

1702, were terminated when the ministry decided to concentrate its efforts, subsidies and talents on a new paper, the *Daily Gazetteer*. When other newspapers that are either known or suspected to have been subsidised end it is possible that the decision was taken by the sponsor. Announcing in 1723 that it would end with the session, despite continued high demand, the *St. James's Journal* stated that its function of defending the ministry was no longer necessary in 'the present happy calm which is spread over all His Majesty's affairs, . . . I have been long tired with the want of opposition'.[38] Political factors also lay behind the ending of several papers suppressed or harassed by the ministry. A certain degree of attention could bring publicity and help sales, but, particularly in the case of Jacobite papers, the extent of ministerial action permitted by the law could be fatal. Though *Mist's Weekly Journal* was continued as *Fog's Weekly Journal* in 1728, Nathaniel Mist found it prudent to flee to France. George Flint produced a series of papers in the mid and later 1710s — *Weekly Remarks and Political Reflections*, *Robin's Last Shift*, *The Shift Shifted* and *Last Shift* — but they were cut short by government action.

Due to the absence of reliable or frequent circulation figures it is difficult to establish with any precision the reason for the demise of some long-established papers, but a sense of exhaustion, that may have been reflected in lower sales, is discernible in some. After the death of its founder Abel Roper in 1726 the *Post Boy* seems to have flagged. In 1728 it felt it necessary to defend its coverage against attacks, and in 1728 and 1729 claims about its low sales were made, albeit by a rival. *Fog's Weekly Journal* emulated the new-found political passivity and the ill-health and death of Mist in 1737. The printer of the paper John Purser sought to keep it going, but he failed, probably because he had nothing distinctive to offer in contrast to the energetic new *Common-Sense*.[39]

The activities of rivals was clearly a factor in the fortunes of papers. The last issue of Francis Clifton's Tory *Weekly Medley: or, The Gentleman's Recreation*, founded in 1718, carried a letter to the readers:

Having gone thro' with every point, that I intended to handle when I first undertook this paper, I now intend to lay it aside . . . such artifices have been used underhand to obstruct the publication of them, that when these papers have been asked for, they have been hid and refused by those persons whose business it was to vend them, and others exposed to sale in their room; and large returns have been often made by them, when there was a general complaint, that the number printed was too small to satisfy the demands of the town for them. I should be glad to say that profess'd Whigs only had a hand in endeavouring to hide works from the publick, that laid open all the vile aims of Presbyterian and Whiggish principles more at large than has ever yet been done in any treatise now extant; but some, who pretend themselves Tories, were the men most industrious in procuring the concealment thereof from publick eyes, partly out of malicious, and partly out of mercenary views . . .[40]

The previous year Clifton had complained about his fellow-Tory Mist's *Saturday's Post*,[41] and had warned readers of his London tri-weekly the *Oxford Post or the Ladies New Tatler*,

concerning Read the Whig journalist . . . I'm credibly inform'd this Grand pirate printer designs to invade my right, by printing and publishing a paper by the name of the Oxford Post, as also that he'l put at least the two first letters of my name to it, and get the same figure at the frontispiece; I have therefore only this to beg that my readers will give themselves the trouble of looking that my name be right spelled and at full length, at the bottom of the first and last page, for if one letter thereof differs from this present paper you may assure yourselves the whole is spurious.[42]

In 1722 James Pasham's new *Northampton Journal* was lacerated by the *Northampton Mercury* as ungrammatical, derivative and 'fit to wrap up Drugs, and keep shirts clean', though at least this ensured its immortality as no copies and no other references to the newspaper are known. In a similar fashion our knowledge of the ministerial London newspaper the *Public Ledger* in 1767–8 is dependent upon hostile papers such as the *Monitor* and the *Middlesex Journal*.[43] How much the opposition of the already well-established *Mercury*, which only referred to two issues of the *Journal*, led to the demise of the latter is unclear. Probably Northampton could only support one newspaper in the early 1720s: no other one was founded there in the first half of the century, apart possibly from a shortlived imprint of *Jopson's*

Coventry Mercury in 1743.[44] The rivalry of existing papers was clearly a problem that new ones had to surmount, particularly in the provinces, where the market was more restricted and the prime means of distribution an expensive circuit of agents and newsmen that had to be established fast to ensure advertising and circulation revenue, but that could only be justified by a speedy rise in sales. In London the distribution system required less organisation, and could be better matched to the sales of the paper. For a new paper in London distribution was less of a problem and less of a cost. The difficulty was rather persuading existing outlets to accept the paper. Getting a paper advertised could be a problem. The *Publick Register: or, The Weekly Magazine*, an interesting attempt to bridge the often hypothetical gap between newspapers and magazines, attributed its termination to having to pay Stamp Duty and to 'the ungenerous usage I have met with from one of the proprietors of a certain monthly pamphlet, who has prevail'd with most of the common newspapers not to advertise it'. The *Hyp-Doctor* complained of a difficulty in getting the paper advertised as it was without 'a junto of booksellers to puff it about the shops, and grace it with a circular testimonial in their other papers and pamphlets'.[45] More frequent were complaints about the unwillingness of shops or hawkers to sell papers and of coffee-houses to buy them. A flysheet advertising *Heraclitus Ridens* noted,

> Some persons have complain'd, that either through the negligence of the hawkers, to whom the name of it may be difficult to be cry'd, and the unwillingness of such as keep coffee-houses, and other publick places of resort, to add to their former charge, they have not been able to come at the sight of it.[46]

The cost of subscribing to so many papers made the coffee-houses unwilling to automatically accept new papers. This was probably very serious for a new paper for two reasons. It deprived them of a stable market that did not need to be served by hawkers. Possibly more serious was the impact on potential advertisers of not being certain that a paper would be read in the coffee-houses, the sphere in which each copy was likely to be most intensively read. In 1721, a new paper called the *Projector* reported that the author of this paper being inform'd, that it cou'd not, tho' given, be suffer'd to lye on the coffee-tables has inquir'd, and finds that the coffee-men have met in form, and agreed to receive no new papers. The confederates in excuse pretend expence, that papers given at first, are not always given, and that some coffee-men are at 150 1 per ann. charge or more for papers of all kinds.[47]

Financial motives appear to have been more significant than political ones in leading to the exclusion of papers, though Tories were accused of stealing Whig material from coffee-houses in 1712 and a decade later the ministerial *Whitehall Journal* claimed that it was kept out of public places by opposition pressure. Scots were accused of removing papers critical of the Earl of Bute from London coffee-houses in 1762. The *Morning Post* claimed in 1784 that it was being removed by political opponents.[48] Several papers referred to the coffee-houses as deluged by newspapers. In 1721 the first number of the *Daily Journal* stated,

I do not in the least doubt, but that 'twill surprize a vast number of people, to see a News-paper come thrusting itself into the Coffee-Houses, which are already so over-stock'd with them, that there is never a Politician, not even of those who smoke you three or four pipes of the best Virginia at a sitting, in one of those Intelligence-Shops, who has Time or Patience enough to read them over.[49]

The end of the 1720s was to witness a full-scale quarrel between the coffee-houses and the newspapers, the former claiming saturation and complaining of the cost.[50] Given this situation it is easy to appreciate why new publications were regarded as a threat. An advertisement for the *Court and City Magazine*, a new monthly that appeared in the winter of 1769–70, declared, 'Publications of this kind are already very numerous; but their Number alone cannot render a new one unnecessary. No Wood is so thick but it may admit of planting another Tree; no Garden so full that it may have Room enough for another Flower.'[51] This elysian image of the world of print was far from accurate. Isaac Thompson and William Cuthbert, in the flysheet that set out their plans for the *Newcastle Journal*, declared, 'We have no design to enter into the service of a party, nor to set ourselves up in opposition to any present paper, or publisher of news . . .' The already established *Newcastle Courant* saw things differently and attacked the *Journal*.[52] The *St. James's Journal* complained that journalists 'look upon every new Author, that starts up among them, as one who is endeavouring to snatch the Bread out of their Mouths . . .' and argued that this was unnecessary, because it claimed 'there are idle people enow in England to take off twice the present number of Journals and weekly Lucubrations of all kinds'.[53] The large number of newspapers that failed to establish themselves or to survive, the largely static nature of the provision of news, at least in terms of numbers of titles, for much of the century in London and the provinces suggests that the *St. James's Journal* was wrong, that there was no large untapped market for the press. At least initially nearly all newspapers were part of a general printing business. It was therefore relatively simple for printers to test a market by setting up a newspaper, and, if it failed, they could concentrate on their other activities. This lack of specialisation, and, in particular, the relatively low investment required by a printer when founding a paper, helps to explain the large number of titles launched and abandoned. It also suggests that the potential market was fairly well explored, particularly in London where there was a large number of printers. A saturated market ensured a competitive atmosphere and a large number of failures, 'the prodigious number of Coffee-House papers that have of late appear'd like comets, with a pompous entrance, but short continuance'.[54] Some papers that ended were continued under a different name, Mist's *Weekly Journal: or, Saturday's Post* (1716–25) becoming Mist's *Weekly Journal* (1725–8), when it changed its form after the Second Stamp Act, and then *Fog's Weekly Journal* (1728–37). The last number of the tri-weekly the *St. James's Post* announced that its publisher would in future publish the *Daily Journal*.[55] However, most papers that ended did so in defeat not transformation. Competition for a market perceived with accuracy as relatively limited in its extent and fickle in its nature underlay the rivalry between papers. Defoe wrote of 'a Paper War. This is another Kind of Manufacture, which I believe we need not apprehend will go out of Fashion, since, while there are Printing-Presses, there seems to be some assurance that we shall never want Authors to quarrel, or Subjects to quarrel about'.[56]

Newspaper rivalry was an economic imperative that ignored political affiliations. Mist and Clifton attacked each other, the *Craftsman* competed with *Common-Sense* and the *Champion*. The

Times complained about the *True-Briton*'s speedier access to government-supplied foreign news in the 1790s. Whatever their politics newspapers, other than the essay-sheets such as the *Hyp-Doctor*, *Monitor*, *Briton*, *North Briton* and *Gray's Inn Journal*, which did not print any, competed for advertisements. The number of these increased during the century, in both the London and the provincial press, at a rate that probably exceeded the growth in readership. Thus for newspapers, in competition for advertisements and readers, rivalry was natural. Political rivalry was overt, the *York Gazetteer* declaring that it was founded 'to correct the weekly poison of the *York Courant*',[57] and could help sell papers. The *Flying-Post* introduced an attack on the opposition *True Briton* in 1723 by commenting that it 'may be no ill entertainment to the Publick in this great scarcity of news'.[58] Uncertain of their market, newspapers diversified, improved and stressed the quality of their contents. It was on those that they were dependent.

Notes

1. Glorious Revolution of 1688.
2. *Craftsman*, an opposition newspaper.
3. S. B. Baxter, *William III* (1966), pp. 130–1; for a contrary view on William, W. L. Sachse, *Lord Somers* (Manchester, 1975), p. 98.
4. F. S. Siebert, *Freedom of the Press in England 1476–1776* (Urbana, 1965), p. 292; J. G. Huddiman, *The King's Journalist* (1923); P. Fraser, *The Intelligence of the Secretaries of State and their monopoly of licensed news, 1660–1688* (Cambridge, 1956); M. E. Craig, *The Scottish Periodical Press 1750–1789* (Edinburgh, 1931), p. 1.
5. Siebert, *Freedom of the Press*, p. 295.
6. J. B. Williams, 'The newsbooks and letters of news of the Restoration', *EHR*, 23 (1908), p. 274; *Publick Occurrences Truly Stated*, 6 Mar. 1688.
7. R. B. Walker, 'The Newspaper Press in the Reign of William III', *Historical Journal*, 17 (1974), p. 692; Bodl. Ms Tanner 37 f. 41a.
8. Preface to vol. 3 of collected edition of *Weekly Pacquet* (1682); *Popish Courant*, 12 Sept. 1679; *Mercurius Anglicus*, 10 Oct. 1681.
9. J. Walker, 'The Censorship of the Press during the reign of Charles II', *History*, 35 (1950), p. 228; T. Crist, 'Government Control of the Press after the Expiration of the Printing Act in 1679', *Publishing History*, 5 (1979), pp. 49–77.
10. L. Rostenberg, 'Richard and Anne Baldwin, Whig Patriot Publishers', *Papers of the Bibliographical Society of America*, 47 (1953), p. 9.
11. L. G. Schwoerer, 'Press and Parliament in the Revolution of 1689', *Historical Journal*, 20 (1979), p. 567.
12. *London Courant*, 22 Dec. 1688; *London Mercury*, 22 Dec. 1688, 7 Jan. 1689.
13. L. G. Schwoerer, 'Propaganda in the Revolution of 1688–89', *American Historical Review*, 82 (1977), pp. 854–8.

14. R. Astbury, 'The Renewal of the Licensing Act in 1693 and its Lapse in 1695', *Library*, 5th ser., 33 (1978), pp. 296–322; A. Downie, 'The Growth of Government Tolerance of the Press to 1700', in R. Myers and M. Harris (eds), *Development of the English Book Trade, 1700–1899* (Oxford, 1981), pp. 45–50.

15. Astbury, 'Licensing Act', p. 298.

16. Siebert, *Freedom of the Press*, p. 300; Astbury, 'Licensing Act', pp. 317–18.

17. Astbury, 'Licensing Act', pp. 317–22.

18. L. Hanson, *Government and the Press, 1695–1793* (Oxford, 1936), pp. 8–11; *LJ* 17, 22; *CJ* 13, 699; F. Gregory, *A Modest Plea for the Due Regulation of the Press* (1698).

19. D. Defoe, *An Essay on the Regulation of the Press* (1704); J. A. Downie, 'An Unknown Defoe Broadsheet on the Regulation of the Press?', *Library*, 5th ser., 33 (1978), pp. 51–8; M. Tindal, *Reasons against Restraining the Press* (1704).

20. *CJ* 17, 28.

21. J. A. Downie, *Robert Harley and the Press* (Cambridge, 1979), p. 150.

22. Astbury, 'Licensing Act', pp. 304–14; *A Letter to a Member of Parliament, Showing, that a Restraint on the Press is Inconsistent with the Protestant Religion, and dangerous to the Liberties of the nation* (1698).

23. Davenant, *A Dialogue Between a Member of Parliament . . . or, Remarks . . . Upon the Liberty of the Press* (1703), p. 5; J. M. Thomas, 'Swift and the Stamp Act of 1712', *PMLA*, 31 (1916), pp. 255–6; Parker, *Ephemeris* (1713), unpaginated.

24. Downie, *Harley*, p. 195.

25. J. R. Sutherland, 'Circulation of Newspapers and Literary Periodicals, 1700–1730', *Library*, 4th ser., 15 (1934), p. 111.

26. *St. James's Post*, 6 Sept. 1717.

27. *Old Post-Master*, 23 June 1696; as the full title proclaimed this was a supplement to a Saturday paper, a common form in the 1710s, *Wednesday's Journal being an Auxiliary Packet to the Saturday's Post*, 25 Sept. 1717.

28. *Daily Post*, 3 Oct. 1719; *London Evening Post*, 12 Dec. 1729; *Parrot*, 25 Sept. 1728; *British Observator*, 10 Mar. 1733; *Common Sense*, 5 Feb. 1737; *New Weekly Miscellany*, 18 July 1741; *National Journal*, 22 Mar. 1746.

29. *St. James's Post*, 2 Feb. 1722; *Weekly Journal, or Saturday's Post*, 28 July 1722; *Whitehall Journal*, 26 Mar. 1723; *Freeholder's Journal*, 18 May 1723; *English and French Journal*, 12 Sept. 1723; *Weekly Journal: or, British Gazetteer*, 17 Aug. 1723; *Flying Post*, 2 May 1724; *Oedipus*, 5 Mar. 1730; *Hyp-Doctor*, 7 Aug. 1733.

30. H. Snyder, 'The Circulation of Newspapers in the Reign of Queen Anne', *Library*, 5th ser., 23 (1968), pp. 222, 225; M. Harris, *The London Newspaper Press c. 1725–1746* (unpublished PhD thesis, London, 1974), p. 30; I. Christie, *Myth and Reality in Late-Eighteenth-Century British Politics* (1970), p. 314; A. Aspinall, 'Statistical Accounts of the London Newspapers during the Eighteenth Century', *EHR*, 63 (1948), pp. 220–3; P. D. G. Thomas, 'The Beginning of Parliamentary Reporting in Newspapers, 1768–1774', *EHR* 74 (1959), pp. 624–5; A. Aspinall, *Politics and the Press c. 1780–1850* (1949), p. 6; L. Werkmeister, *A Newspaper History of England, 1792–1793* (Lincoln, Nebraska, 1967), p. 19; J. Ehrman, *The Younger Pitt* (1969), p. 605.

31. *Flying Post*, 2 May 1724.

32. Snyder, 'Circulation', *Library*, p. 212.

33. *Hyp-Doctor*, 7 Aug. 1733; R. L. Haig, 'The Last Years of the *Gazetteer*', *Library*, 5th ser., 7 (1952), pp. 242–61.

34. S. Varey, 'Printers as Rivals: The Craftsman, 1739–40', *Library*, 6th ser., 2 (1980), pp. 220–2.

35. This happened to the *St. James's Evening Post* in December 1715; see also, *Original Weekly Journal*, 9 Mar. 1717; *St. James's Post*, 6, 9 Sept. 1717. There were two rival editions of *Common-Sense* in 1737.

36. *York Courant*, 16 Jan. 1739.
37. Thomas Brodrick MP to his brother Alan, Lord Chancellor of Ireland, 13 June 1724, Guildford, Surrey CRO, Brodrick Mss. 1248/b, f. 37.
38. *St. James's Journal*, 18 May 1723.
39. *Post Boy*, 7 May 1728; *London Evening Post*, 17 Dec. 1728, 25 Nov. 1729; J. Black, 'An Underrated Journalist; Nathaniel Mist and the Opposition Press during the Whig Ascendancy', *British Journal for Eighteenth-Century Studies* (forthcoming); *Weekly Remarks*, 3 Mar. 1715.
40. *Weekly Medley*, 23 Jan. 1720.
41. *Weekly Medley*, 19 Sept., 3, 10 Oct. 1719; *Oxford Post*, 27 Jan. 1719.
42. *Oxford Post*, 6 Jan. 1719.
43. *Northampton Mercury*, 9, 16, 23 (quote) July 1722; J. Black, 'A Missing Northampton Newspaper', *Northamptonshire Past and Present* (forthcoming); R. R. Bataille, 'Hugh Kelly's Journalism', *Journal of Newspaper and Periodical History* I, 3 (1985), p. 10.
44. R. M. Wiles, *Freshest Advices. Early Provincial Newspapers in England* (Columbus, 1965), p. 463.
45. *Publick Register*, 13 June 1741; *Hyp-Doctor*, 7 Aug. 1733.
46. Undated flysheet, c. 1718, Bodleian Library, Nichols collection; *National Journal* 29 Mar. 1746.
47. *Projector*, 17 Feb. 1721.
48. *Flying-Post*, 2 Dec. 1712, quoted in *The Spectator*, D. F. Bond (ed.) (Oxford, 1965) I, lxxxv; *Whitehall Journal*, 4 Dec. 1722; Bodl. Firth b18, No. 127; *Citizen*, 29 June 1754.
49. *Daily Journal*, 24 Jan. 1721; *Freeholder's Journal*, 18 May 1723.
50. Anon., *The Case between the Proprietors of News-Papers, and the Subscribing Coffee-men fairly Stated* (1729).
51. *Reading Mercury and Oxford Gazette*, 1 Jan. 1770.
52. *Proposals . . .* , 22 Jan., *Newcastle Journal*, 7 Apr. 1739.
53. *St. James's Journal*, 1 Nov. 1722.
54. *Original Weekly Journal*, 4 Apr. 1719.
55. *St. James's Post*, 31 Jan. 1722.
56. [Defoe], *Manufacturer: or, The British Trade truly Stated*, 1 June 1720.
57. *York Gazetteer*, 15 Dec. 1741.
58. *Flying-Post*, 12 Sept. 1723.

2 'As Full as an Egg': Balancing the Contents of the Press

In the Nature of a Newspaper, *'non datur vacuum'* — A Newspaper must be as full as an Egg: — It is not like many other daily Vehicles or Stages, which frequently go off half empty, and sometimes without any Passengers at all, but is obliged to set out at the appointed Time, and *must* be cram'd full, Outside and Inside, Before and Behind, Top and Bottom; nay, if there is but *one* empty Place, you are sure to be overset. Since this is the case with those political Vehicles, Newspapers and there exists an absolute Necessity of Plenitude, 'tis no Wonder that the conductors of those Machines are not very scrupulous or nice in the Choice of their Company; but rather than suffer any Vacancy, they imitate the great Man's Servants in the *Parable*, who went out to the Streets and Highways, collecting the Old and the Young, the Lame, the Blind, the Good, and the Bad; in short, whomsoever they could get to make up the Number of Guests.
Berrow's Worcester Journal, 30 November 1769, anonymous
letter

Sir, I have often observed, that there is not so inconsistent, so incoherent. so heterogenious, although so useful and agreeable a thing, as a public newspaper: The very ludicrous contrast in advertisements, the contradictory substance of foreign and domestic paragraphs, the opposite opinions and observations of contending essayists, with premature deaths, spurious marriages, births, bankrupticies, etc. etc. form a fund of entertainment for a world of which it is in itself no bad epitome.
Reading Mercury, and Oxford Gazette, 31 July 1780, letter from
W.C.

There are great similarities between the newspapers published after the lapse of the Licensing Act and those that appeared a century later. This is not very surprising. The technology of newspaper production and distribution and of the transmission of news and advertisements to the press had not altered. News was still obtained in the same fashion and produced without the benefit of illustrations or maps. The contents of the newspapers were similar. Again this is far from surprising. Despite a fascination with new or newly popular forms and devices, whether umbrellas or turnpikes, balloons or steam engines, magazines or foreign travel, the age was a deeply conservative one, eager to support God and the king, despite the actions of prelates and monarchs. Deeply religious, wedded to a conservative social structure and an oligarchic political system, the political nation defended all three against the French Revolution, just as it had earlier refused to act in response to the paranoid pleas of the 'radicals', pre-Wilkite or otherwise. A major change in the content of the press was not to be expected, though there is a further reason for the similarities in the press in 1695 and a century later. Britain was at war with France, and not winning: the press was dominated by the conflict and by its ramifications, for its impact was general. War and international affairs did not only affect statesmen and coffee-house politicans; the merchant scanning for information about privateers, the farmer eager for news of the effect of war on the corn trade, shared their concern. As Britain was at, or close to, war for most of the period 1689–1721 and from 1792 onwards, it is best to compare the newspapers of the 1720s and 1783–91 in order to appreciate changes over the century; not that these periods were free from the fear of war, military preparations for conflict taking place and being discussed in 1725–30, 1787, 1790 and 1791, just as they were in other years of peace, such as 1731, 1734–5, and on several occasions in the 1760s and 1770s.

The most obvious difference was the increase in the physical size of the newspapers and the smaller type. In essence, however, the reader was given more of the same. The news was still predominantly political, the reports derivative, anonymous and impersonal. Events, rumours and manifestos were printed rather than interviews. Most items were short, without explanation or introduction, and there was a relative absence of pieces providing background information. There are several readily apparent differences between the papers of the 1720s and 1780s. There were more advertisements in the latter and they occupied both a larger and a more prominent proportion of the papers. In place of newspapers striving to emulate essay-sheets by devoting their entire first page to an essay there were papers whose first page contained many advertisements. Political news was no longer so dominated by the affairs of Europe. Instead colonial affairs and those of the newly independent United States of America were discussed, while during the session there were regular, lengthy reports of parliamentary debates. In general there was more non-political news, particularly items devoted to social habits and fashions. Literary, particularly theatrical, news had become a regular feature, and there was more economic news, though nothing approaching the percentage of non-advertising space devoted to it in modern 'quality' British newspapers. The activities of criminals were still a popular topic, while sporting news, virtually absent in the 1720s, was regularly carried by the 1780s, with much news of horse racing, boxing, cock fighting and cricket. Provincial newspapers printed more local news, and both they and the London press carried more items from other areas of Britain, a product of the development and better distribution of the provincial press. The *Leeds Intelligencer* referred to items in the *Cambridge Chronicle*, *Ipswich Journal* and *Freeman's Dublin Journal* between October 1781 and the following April. On 17 March 1789 the *Leeds Mercury* used the *Newcastle Chronicle* as a source for reports about disorders by Tyneside miners. The conspicuous variety of the newspapers in the 1720s, some carrying essays, but many not, some keen to comment on the news, others only relating it, some heavily derivative, others striving for a distinctive content and/or style, was still a feature in the 1780s, as was the division of the press into dailies, bi- or tri-weeklies and weeklies. This variety makes a statistical content analysis questionable, as does both the difficulty of assessing which items were copied and the serious problems of categorising much of the material in the absence of any agreed guidelines. An item on the corn trade in 1766 could be regarded as 'economic' or 'political', as it was a matter of great controversy then. Similarly several sexual scandals were discussed and exploited for political ends. It is not clear whether much of the correspondence printed in the press did not originate from it.

The proportion of newspapers devoted to advertising might seem to be an obvious subject for statistical analysis, but a careful reading of news items both in the London and the provincial press would suggest that many of these had been paid for, and it is known that prominent individuals paid to have puffs inserted. Newspapers frequently stated that they could not accept items from contributors, often essays or letters, unless they were paid for as advertisements. A failure to charge did not excuse a paper from the attentions of the Stamp Office, keen to receive the duty on advertisements.[1] Presumably many contributors did pay, but while it is clear that the notice of say a sale of tea was paid for, it is not so clear in the case of letters on economic topics or medical and sporting items.[2] As many newspaper proprietors, particularly in the provinces, had interests in particular medicines, often being local patentees, many medical items can be regarded as inserted for their benefit. The information about cream of violet soap that appeared in several issues of the *World* in late 1791 under the headline 'Interesting to Ladies' is an instance of what was almost certainly advertising material masquerading as news.[3]

If statistical analysis is fraught with difficulties, there are also major problems in establishing the principles and methods of editorial selection, for there has been no study of eighteenth-century editing. This clearly varied by paper, and the problems of editing a London or a provincial, a daily or a weekly paper were not identical. The prospectuses or first issues of newspapers provide some indication of what was considered desirable, as do subsequent comments and those of rivals. Aiming to gain the widest possible readership, papers tended to stress the variety of what they had to offer. William Foster inserted at the beginning of the issues of his 1709 daily the *Miscellany* a manifesto, 'The smallest as well as greatest Occurrences shall be mentioned . . . you may also expect from us, as Occasion shall serve, what concerns Trade, Manufacture, and Remittance of Mony from one part of the World to another.' The fourth issue stated, 'When we have no other Occurrences which are worthy of public Notice . . . we shall endeavour to bring into our Language some memorable Action of the Antients, which is new to those who have only our Mother-Tongue.' The *Weekly Packet*, founded three years later, announced in its full title that it was a 'Methodical Collection of the most Material Occurrences in Matters of State, Trade, Arts, and Sciences'. The *St. James's Post*, founded in 1717, made clear its intention of confronting the opposition press in its pages,

> in which it is propos'd to give a clear and faithful recapitulation or abstract of the weeks news, in such connexion with regard to place, time, and fact, as may make together an useful history; and to each of which will be subjoin'd due remarks upon those vermin of the press, who are yet retain'd in the cause of our enemies . . .

The *Wednesday's Journal*, founded in 1717 to supplement Mist's *Weekly Journal*, which appeared on Saturday, stressed the demand of the readers for a mid-week paper and also the extent of available material:

> We find the variety of publick occurrences is indeed so great that a paper once a week cannot discharge the quantity; several things will not keep cold, and the substance of them is lost before the week comes about, so that our readers are not fully informed and diverted, as they may and ought to be . . . there is sufficient matter, both of foreign and domestick news, to supply two papers, and to make them entertaining too.

The *Whitehall Evening Post* emphasised the importance not only of giving 'intelligence, but that all this intelligence be calculated for the publick good'. Francis Clifton, who announced his intentions in the title of his paper, the *Weekly Medley: or, the Gentleman's Recreation*, claimed to offer the reader something different in the shape of a judicious evaluation of the news:

> Whether a general peace, or a more general war than has appeared already is likely to overspread all Europe, is a deliberation at this Juncture, which employs the most considering heads. The huntings of one Prince, and the hawking diversions of another; the death of one General, and the wounding of another; the marriage of a Princess, and the equipage and entertainments of an Ambassador, are the shining trifles, which common News-Mongers count to be sublime; but the other more solid point is the view of an historian. Look we then with a narrow searching eye into the confirm'd and known authentic passages of the present times in the different nations, and from thence let us after making judicious comparisons, judge whether their several interests will probably run so far on in amicable links as to constitute one whole and solid chain, of agreement . . .

His conclusion was that peace was still distant, a rebuttal of the claims of the ministerial press, which led him to share with Mist in the accusations of being pro-Spanish. In 1720 Clifton reported an engagement near Gibraltar and returned to his theme of the historical, and thereby both accurate and lasting, methods that should be followed:

I would be exact in this so particular a relation, and not have it said by my enemies, that I altered anything, and wrote it with partiality either to one side or another, a thing, which pursuant to the duty incumbent upon me, as I stand distinguished by the name of an historian from the common herd of news writers, I have diligently avoided giving reason of my being suspected or accused of, tho' some inveterate persons have falsely charged me with unnaturally taking the part of the Spaniards.[4]

In 1721 the *Daily Journal*, in its introduction, announced that it had settled an extensive correspondence abroad and at home and had determined to launch a paper because it was 'sure of receiving the best Advices both Foreign and Domestick' and because there were not enough papers to satisfy the demand for advertising space. The author warned readers who sought papers '*not so much for the News as the Stile*, or rather the Party-Reflections of their Authors', not to bother with his impartial product. A newly launched weekly, the *London Mercury*, shortly afterwards attacked the *Flying Post* for political partisanship and commented on the difficulty of pleasing all readers, the ideal goal of the non-partisan press:

> We must confess, that to render a Journal acceptable to every-body, is one of the most difficult things in nature; for if it is inclining to one party, it displeases another; and if to none, it then becomes very often indifferent to all. Others are fond of an agreeable style, copious subject, and exact manner of argument, and yet among these there are men of such different learning and taste, that what seems admirable to the one, is rendered most insipid to the other. However, surely none can find fault with transactions ingenuously and faithfully deliver'd, contrary to that malignant manner partially made use of by contending writers, who so far from rendering things as they really are, very often thro' their prejudice veil the truth with a cloud of obscurity.[5]

Nathaniel Mist, who stamped a distinctive style on his papers far more than most other proprietors,[6] used them as a platform in a very personal and often discursive fashion, and often commented on his own activities. In 1721 he stressed the role of the paper in political education, providing a 'recapitulation of the occurrences of the whole week, with comments, explanations and annotations on all the ambiguous parts thereof, for the use of young politicians'. Commenting the following year on 'the multitude of new papers' Mist declared that pen and ink and the title of a journal were insufficient. Like Clifton, Mist sought to exalt the craft of the newspaper:

> There are certain other ingredients necessary towards the carrying on a paper with success . . . such as a tolerable judgment in the affairs of the world, and the interests of nations, a love of truth, and the settling a good correspondence abroad and at home, for certain and early intelligence. These . . . are the orderly parts of a Journal, and with those supports it may be as profitable and pleasant as a good history; since it is in effect the History of the present Times, which I conceive is as necessary for men to know as the transaction of a thousand years past.

In 1723 Mist with justice referred to the variety of his work: 'This Paper always begins with some entertaining Essay, either upon the Times, or else the Behaviour and Follies of Men, and the rest is a fair and impartial History of the whole World for a Week', a good example of the inaccuracy of some of the claims of impartiality so often made by the eighteenth-century press. The following year he made an interesting comparison of his paper with the theatre, and stressed the pedagogic character of his work, echoing the *Spectator*, which had set the model for the use of humorous essays to improve morality. Mist wrote that he modelled his journal on the playhouse in 'mixing the profitable with the pleasurable', a theme he returned to in 1726, adding 'as we well know, that curiosity is mix'd in the Nature of Man, we shall take care to gratify that of all ages, sexes, and conditions: To which purpose, subjects serious, moral, and political, as well as essays on pleasures, gallantry and ridicule, shall, by turns, have a place in this paper'. The moral theme was extended to the political sphere:

> The whole aim and design of the following papers, has been to censure and correct those monstrous vices and corruptions, which have of late so openly shewed themselves in all public affairs, as well as to ridicule the little follies and impertinences

of fops, coquets, prudes, pedants, and coxcombs of all sorts, whose affected airs often disturb the harmony of all polite conversation . . .[7]

In 1727 the *Craftsman* stressed its 'private intelligences' for foreign affairs and its impartiality, Thomas Gent the accuracy, comprehensiveness and impartiality of his *Original York Journal*, the *London Evening Post* its accuracy and economic news, and the *Evening Journal* the need for a tri-weekly on those evenings hitherto without papers as they were not post days, in order to fill the 'chasm', enable rapid advertising, provide 'hints for discourse' and 'as matters require it . . . explain what may occur either in history or geography'.[8]

In 1733 the introduction to the *British Observator* claimed to discover a dissatisfied section of the newspaper-reading public:

The middle part of mankind, with respect both to fortune and sentiments, complain of all the journals now in being . . . They dislike such in general as carry a political letter in the front, they want not to study politics, tho' they are inclined to see how the world goes, and therefore would willingly part with a florid period for an important paragraph, choosing news rather than conjectures; and desiring to meet with facts instead of speculations . . . Our constant care shall be to procure the best foreign advices, to digest them into a proper method, and to cloath them with a convenient style . . .[9]

Essays were clearly an issue in Newcastle that summer, for the *Newcastle Courant*, at the time the sole newspaper in the north-east, stated,

Some persons having of late express'd a dislike to the room which weekly letters take up in this paper; and also of the subjects they are writ on: we therefore in answer to the first objection, crave leave to inform them, that they only supply the place which useless paragraphs would take up; and as to the latter, we presume that no one has reason to be displeased with any affair they treat on, since the press is open to all those who use their antagonists with good language, and have the least colour of justice on their side . . .

Twelve years later the same paper began an essay by announcing, 'The scarcity of news, and the desire of informing our readers of what they indeed, as well as every individual, ought to know, obliges us to insert the following enquiry into the disappointment at Fontenoy.'[10]

In the same period that a number of advertisers were being launched in London without any essay, the provincial press continued its commitment to the form. This probably reflected a number of factors, the as yet fairly limited nature of advertising in the provincial press, the ease of reprinting an essay from a London paper, the political commitment of a number of provincial papers, such as the *York Courant*, that was most readily expressed by reprinting essays from prominent London opposition weeklies, and the sense that newspapers ought to provide more than simply a number of isolated news items. If Addison had sought in the *Spectator* to bring 'philosophy out of Closets and Libraries, Schools and Colleges, to dwell in Clubs and Assemblies, at Tea-Tables, and in Coffee-Houses',[11] then William Cuthbert and Isaac Thompson could propose 'a short essay, letter, or discourse, on some useful subject, art, or science'. They would have agreed with Mist that a newspaper was 'a Paper of Entertainment' and 'a Paper of Intelligence', but they saw the entertainment not as humorous moralising, but as a stiff course of secular improvement:

As a news-paper is an historical rhapsody, or register, of civil, political and natural occurrences, and the present state of things; it therefore generally lays before the reader, in the compass of a few pages, a scene of the whole world, and presents him with a multitude of very distant and different countries and people; and on this account, it is necessary for every one, who would read to any purpose and satisfaction, to have competent knowledge of Geography and Natural History: We therefore propose that our first Introductions shall chiefly contain a description and account of the whole earth and seas, according to the best authors, and latest discoveries and observations; which will give our readers a distinct view . . . of all remarkable countries; with the manners, languages, arts, governments, arms, religions, and ceremonies of their inhabitants.

They did this and people read the paper.[12] Another provincial enlightener Andrew Hooke explained his intentions in his newly launched *Oracle: or, Bristol Weekly Miscellany*. He promised to translate foreign news from the European papers himself, in order to ensure accuracy, and to devote attention to trade and commerce. The *Hull Packet*, launched in May 1787, announced, the following New Year's Day, that it had succeeded in its purpose of conveying 'early and useful information' and improving the mind.[13]

The *Daily Post* solicited information from 'both sides of the question' in order to give the 'best information', whilst Henry Fielding in the *True Patriot* stressed his 'particular correspondents', and offered, like Mist, a useful and entertaining performance.[14] The *London Evening Post* claimed that one reason for the increase in its cost in 1762 was to render the paper 'more useful, instructive, and entertaining'.[15] Several newspapers in the century, such as the *Craftsman*, *Westminster Journal* and Mist's papers, published their leading essays in book form. This yielded additional profit and enhanced their claim to serve a historical purpose, to be journals of record, not as the *Gazette* was with its recital of facts, but rather by clarifying and solving the problems of the age; for eighteenth-century papers did not discuss without purpose or conclusion. Many of these essays were political, but non-political essays, in the *Spectator* tradition, were also reprinted. In 1767 a selection of the 'Babler' essays, printed since 1763 in *Owen's Weekly Chronicle*, were published in book form. The *London Chronicle*, an ordinary tri-weekly founded in 1757, and neither an essay paper nor a campaigning political paper with a prominent essay, offered readers a free general title and index to encourage them to bind the paper and preserve it. The *Universal Chronicle* did the same the following year.

The didactic function of print was readily apparent. As the century progressed more public bodies inserted injunctions and notices. In 1767 the *Leeds Intelligencer* benefited from an order by the Quarter Sessions for the insertion of an abstract of a new Act for regulating the public highways.[16] Junius, the anonymous assailant of George III's ministries, who used the *Public Advertiser* from 1769 to 1772 to advertise and trumpet his message, which was then reprinted in other newspapers,[17] wrote of 'the glorious Business of instructing and directing the people . . .'. A standard letter from the publisher John Almon announced in 1779 the forthcoming appearance of a new daily paper, the *London Courant*, scheduled to start on the first day of Parliament:

The principal design of this undertaking is to furnish the public with early and authentic intelligence of every public transaction, both at home and abroad; for which every known channel of communication has been opened, nor will any pains or expence be spared to discover others, as well as to preserve every source of information. At the same time no attention will be wanting, to prevent the insertion of any articles of falsehood, malignancy and private scandal. In the conduct of this publication, it shall be a fixed principle to meddle with no private character of either sex: But public characters in public stations will be treated with freedom yet always with liberality.[18]

The *Newcastle Chronicle* indicated its scope in 1787 with its extended title, 'Or, Weekly Advertiser, and Register of News, Commerce, and Entertainment — Open to all Parties, and influenced by none'. The following year the advertisements for the daily London evening paper, the *Star*, offered

the occurrences of the present day . . . the transactions of the next . . . the debates in Parliament . . . drama and the opera and every fashionable place of public amusement . . . strictures on commerce, the fluctuation of the funds, literary discussions, public trials, discoveries and improvements in the arts, sciences, and even in dress.

The notices for the *Independent Chronicle: or, Freeholders Evening Post* in 1769 were similarly expansive. *Bell's Weekly Messenger*, a Sunday that first appeared on 1 May 1796, announced that it would seek 'to render the Messenger hereafter a welcome visitor at the Sunday breakfast-table of every person who wishes to be informed or amused'.[19]

With so much that could be offered, and a potential readership of varying interests, the process of selection was clearly of importance but, bar occasional notices in the newspapers, there is very little information on this. As newspapers increased in size the potential material that could be included also grew, with more foreign, colonial, London and provincial papers to derive items from, a growth in advertisements, the development, albeit seasonal, of regular parliamentary reports, and, thanks probably partly to the magazines, a greater awareness of the range of non-political news that readers sought and that could be provided. The editorial task was therefore one of selection, often arbitration, given the limited space in newspapers, which could not be readily contracted or expanded as late twentieth-century papers can be, both because of the nature of the Stamp Duty, which was linked, however imperfectly, to size, and because the limited capacity of each printing unit would necessitate the provision of additional units. It was easiest for a weekly to expand its size, particularly if the printing press was not being used, as it often was in London, to also print other newspapers. The *Reading Mercury, and Oxford Gazette*, one of the more interesting provincial papers of the late eighteenth century, did so in 1771, providing readers with an occasional additional sheet, free and without advertisements, and therefore untaxed, whenever there were sufficient items that were felt to be of interest. Initially episodic, by 1773 these sheets were being numbered as a Miscellany. On 16 March 1781 the printer of the *Leeds Intelligencer* produced a single sheet supplement, four days before its next issue was due, reprinting a *London Gazette Extraordinary* on Admiral Rodney's capture of St Eustatia. He made clear his ministerial sympathies by heading it 'Rodney's Pill for the Discontented!'[20] Such an expedient was highly unusual, and it is unclear whether it was profitable. A provincial printer could probably assess with greater ease how far the expedient of a free-sheet would help to retain his readership, as that of provincial papers tended to include a reasonable number of subscribers, whose personal links with the proprietor may have been closer than in the metropolis, and as the habit of writing to the newspapers was well-developed, judging by many of the surviving papers.

The provincial press was always under challenge, not so much from improved distribution methods for London newspapers, but from the increased density of the provincial network, as new papers emerged to test markets, and existing ones sought to expand their circulation, a process aided by their weekly character. In some areas the geographical distribution of newspaper production was remarkably static. In the north-east Newcastle remained the only centre, bar a brief attempt to produce a paper at Darlington in 1772–3. Durham and Sunderland lacked their own paper. Elsewhere the picture tended to be one of increased competition. The *Northampton Mercury* had more agents in 1800 than in 1720 but the farthest was now at Birmingham: East Anglia, Staffordshire, Lincolnshire, Derby, Nottinghamshire and Gloucestershire were no longer served by agents. The *Reading Mercury* was certainly under challenge in the 1770s, particularly in

Hampshire, and this may have led to the appearance of the *Miscellany*. Such an expensive device was not generally suitable and was not really practicable for dailies. Varying the type must also have been expensive. The entire issue of the *Original York Journal* of 3 October 1727 was set in a smaller type to enable the inclusion of a long account of coronation ceremonies. Experience also showed that a more frequent appearance was unlikely to be successful. Provincial papers tended to be weeklies. More frequent publication was probably discouraged by their extended distribution systems and possibly by the relatively saturated nature of the market, particularly in light of the Stamp Acts. In the first half of the century only the Canterbury-based *Kentish Post* appeared regularly more than once a week. Geoffrey Cranfield suggested that this was due to a geographically restricted circulation, but as little is known about the bi-weekly it is possible to speculate only. The prosperity of Kent, and the absence of local competing papers — none in the Channel ports, only shortlived ones in Maidstone — may also have been of importance. Attempts in London to produce midweek supplements to weeklies, which usually appeared on Saturdays, tended to be shortlived, though tri-weeklies could become dailies, either with a similar title, the *Post Boy* becoming the *Daily Post Boy*, or by the proprietor founding a completely new paper.[21]

Most editors (and the word should be used without suggesting that this was a distinct function or individual) could not therefore spread the news over more space. Instead they had to select what to insert. They had to do so without being sure what existing and potential readers wanted. There was a certain amount of correspondence sent by readers and presumably the proprietors of coffee-houses and similar establishments, and hawkers and others involved in distribution made known their views. However, the predominant impression is one of editors uncertain of the balance to strive for, facing criticism, particularly when they delayed advertisements in order to insert other material, and tending to conform to the established pattern both of layout and of content. The *Weekly Register*, in its issue of 20 February 1799, printed a letter from 'An Arminian':

> I have often thought that the situation of an editor of a periodical work is, of all others, the least enviable. His readers are composed of the learned and the illiterate, social and de-

mure, liberal and bigotted, Christian and Infidel, Calvinist and
Arminian etc. Whether he be wise and consistent, or foolish and
unprincipled, it is impossible for him to give universal satisfaction: he has as many judges as readers, and they all claim an
equal right to think highly of their peculiar opinions.

Provincial papers tended to at least mention editorial selection
as they usually sought to explain which London papers they were
reprinting items from and why. The *Newcastle Weekly Mercury*
devoted half a page in February 1723 to an item on scandal, dogs
and squabbles after announcing, 'The following letter of Cato we
have inserted in our paper, for the entertainment of our readers,
and think it will be much more acceptable than so many pages of
insipid news; we shall for the future give Cato's political letters a
place in our weekly paper.' The *York Courant* stated in 1739,

> In our choice of political papers, we shall always prefer those
> which appear most deserving the attention of the public; and
> therefore propose to print sometimes the Craftsman and
> sometimes Common-Sense, not doubting but as they are both
> engaged in the same common cause of liberty and their country,
> they will be equally agreeable to our readers.

The *Northampton Mercury* introduced the first Duke of
Marlborough's obituary by explaining that there was 'nothing new
of Foreign Affairs'. The *Newcastle Journal* devoted space in two
issues to a parliamentary attack on the ministry by the Duke of
Argyll which replaced the usual geographical essay: 'It is thought
proper by many impartial persons that our readers ought not to be
deprived of satisfying their curiosity with the perusal of it.' The
balancing of political and non-political items was as much of a
problem as that of advertisements and the rest of the paper.[22]

Letters printed in provincial papers throw some light, though
the practices of anonymity or of using initial or pseudonymous
names makes it unclear whether these letters were not sometimes
written by the editor. In 1728 J.D.'s request to Thomas Gent that
as there was 'no very great news stirring' he would insert 'the
Horse Doctor's harangue to the credulous mob' was successful.
Five years later another reader pressed the *Newcastle Courant* for
hard news: 'By no means let a rapsody upon the Test Act, jostle
the Emperor and his dominions out of your Courant, or a song on

a Grotto take place of a speech in Parliament.' In 1775 the *Reading Mercury* printed a letter that looks like a plea from the editor for material. Having discussed the varied interests of readers, divided into the literary and political orders and 'the admirers of fun', those who supposed the paper deficient in particular respects were asked to supply items: 'A modern newspaper is not to be considered as the production of a single person; but is maintained, like other public foundations, by such contributions as the generosity of a charitable public shall continue to raise.'[23] Six years earlier *Berrow's Worcester Journal* had printed an essay commenting on the transformation of newspapers from being 'dry Registers of Common Intelligence' to the 'Annals of History, politics and Literature' with nearly every paper 'now a Magazine'.[24]

Comments from correspondents were not a monopoly of the provincial press. An unsigned letter in the *Flying Post* in 1717, which accompanied an account of the astronomical and musical clock in St James's Street, accepted that the accent might seem to some to be 'foreign' to the paper's 'agreeable miscellany of news and politics. I persuade myself that many of your news readers who have the least taste of curiosity will be more diverted with an account of this wonderful machine, than with a dry foreign story'. The following month Mist introduced a facetious journal of a trip to the Baltic with a letter from its supposed author, Simon Forecastle, complaining about an absence of news about ships. The same paper printed a letter from Antidialecti in January 1720 attacking the profanity of discussions on religion in coffee houses and a letter from Timothy Trifle the following month saying that he read papers in order to rail at them and that he expected to be imposed upon by newspapers, as they only sought the readers' money. In 1727 Cassio sent Mist a love poem in February as he expected springtime wars to crowd the paper later.[25] In 1720 Chints offered Wilkins's *London Journal*, which had been complaining of plagiarism by other papers, a letter suggesting that Jacobite sympathies lay behind the weavers' riots against the wearing of calicos, 'to make your paper something more worth reading than others are, as there may be something extraordinary in it, which other papers cannot come at an understanding of'. On the same day an unsigned letter urged the *Weekly Journal* to 'sometimes digress from the dry relations of news, just as it comes warranted to you by foreign prints, and advices, though I allow that to be the proper business of a news-writer; and take a little freedom upon suitable occasions of recapitulation and reflection'. Philalethes, urging the weeklies to insert material on the liberal arts and sciences in 1722, differentiated them from the 'Gazetteers and common daily News-Papers' which had nothing to do with anything other than 'the usual occurrences of things that is commonly called news'. An anonymous letter on inoculation was introduced that July with the reflection that times of peace forced the press to diversify its contents in order 'to furnish out bright pieces to hit the genius of the times . . .', and later in the year a letter in the *Freeholder's Journal* suggested that there could be too much politics even for 'an English Palate'.[26]

The various tastes of readers were commented on in a London item in the *Original Mercury* in 1727: 'Some are high, some low, some neither: others complain of having too much foreign news, or too much domestic: one is displeased at an ingenious excursion, another in love with it.' The *Daily Journal* was praised the following year by Britannicus for behaving like a weekly, distinguishing itself 'from the other Daily Papers, by inserting now and then, a short essay, of a more spirited nature than the dry repetitions of old intelligence, new-modell'd'. The *Westminster Journal*, an opposition weekly, announced in 1742 that in response to readers' requests it would occasionally provide 'a kind of Miscellany; which will be an amusing relief to those, who have not gravity or patience enough to go through a long essay, but would have a little mirth, as well as much wisdom'. Writing towards the end of the Seven Years' War Oliver Goldsmith urged the *Public Ledger*, a daily founded in 1760, to include an account of new publications as more interesting 'than a journal of battles or negociations, an elopement, or a broken leg, the marriage of a celebrated toast, or the adventures of a mad cow'. In 1785 a correspondent sent the newly-founded *Daily Universal Register* an attack on the fashionable 'West-End Sheets', such as the *World* and the *Morning Post*: 'Newspapers were originally intended for the conveyance of important intelligence, which concerns the public in general. If so, what have we to do with the ridiculous disputes of whimsical ladies, or the infamous assurance of bullies and swindlers, at public places and gaming houses?'[27] If the contrast between dailies, being heavily political, and weeklies, becoming increasingly diversified and more like magazines with additional news, remained true throughout the century, it was nevertheless the case that even papers with a strong political slant

had to include other material. This was particularly the case when
the posts from the continent were delayed by wind,[28] and less so
when they brought the same news as the previous post, and/or
reflected a quiescent international situation.[29] From the 1760s
parliamentary news and domestic extra-parliamentary political
action, particularly the conspicuous agitation which sought
publicity consciously, made this a less serious problem.[30] The
American rebellion, unlike previous eighteenth-century wars,
witnessed a tolerated vociferous domestic agitation in favour of
the external enemy, and thus when the posts from America failed
the press could consider the domestic debate.

The problems created by attempting to sustain a regular supply
of fresh news doubtless played a part in encouraging diversification, but they should not be exaggerated. The greater
volume of advertisements as the century progressed helped to fill
space; parliamentary reports were rarely short, there were more
papers to derive items from. Magazine-type material was not
without its problems, and it was doubtless more difficult to obtain
attractive theatrical and social reports or essays that were interesting and amusing than it was to transcribe news reports. There
was also a clear feeling, displayed in some of the correspondence
(contrived or otherwise) printed, that the job of the dailies was to
print news, and in particular political information. In their domestic news dailies also went for brief items of information, largely
crime and 'the private concerns of particular families', the
elopements, marriages and deaths of the great.[31]

Similar items of course appeared in the weeklies. There was a
continuum of content between the different types of newspapers,
with the significant exception of the essay papers that carried no
news or advertisements. 'Deaths, executions, and discoveries of
the most shocking, audacious, and unheard of villainies' could be
'read over a whole page in a Weekly Journal' as much as in a
daily.[32] As neither type nor title dictated a specific content, however much the latter might lead to a particular political stance,
editors were pushed back to their sense of what the readers
wanted, a sense sharpened by an awareness of the relatively rapid
turnover of the press. There were clearly some serious disputes
within newspaper managements over the issue of content. A recent study of Arthur Young and the *Universal Magazine* in 1762
has detected a tension between what the readers apparently
wanted and the solemn, heavy pieces that Young thought they

should be given, which ended with the purchase of the magazine by booksellers, and the lowering of its tone. John Taylor, the editor of the *Morning Post*, was sacked as a result of a dispute in 1790.[33] However, the scarcity of relevant surviving material makes it difficult to discuss the subject. Both in London and the provinces discussions between proprietors, printers and editors were probably largely verbal, and whereas business arrangements and financial transactions might be committed to paper and encapsulated in legal documents, the nuances of editorial selection were not readily expressed thus.

Newspaper authors were aware that they were 'obliged to conform to the prevalency of fashion, as well as men of dress and gaiety, and change the scheme of their writings according to the taste of the public',[34] but this taste proved surprisingly constant. Lord Tyrawly, Envoy Extraordinary in Lisbon, angry with the British press for reporting illegal gold imports from Portugal, lashed out in 1738, 'If these people could be confined to the accounts of highway men, and horses stolen or strayed, their papers would be every bit as diverting and instructive to the generality of their readers.'[35] Tyrawly had had no home leave since his arrival in 1728, but his comment cannot be dismissed, no more than the discernment of one of the three groups of newspaper readers in 1775 as those

> belonging to both sexes, who delight in no particular track of information, but examine the public prints with the laudable design of annihilating a certain portion of time in that tedious age — a day of idleness. These are great admirers of fun (as it is called) and usually attach themselves to strange anecdotes, odd advertisements and casualties . . .[36]

This was a rather jaundiced view. It was not only the idle who delighted in humour, no more than it was only precocious and presumptuous tradesmen and coffee-house politicians who read about politics.[37] Humorous stories, verses and epigrams were frequently printed in the press as were numerous jokes. The humour by modern standards is often cruel: excremental jokes or verses directed against cuckolds[38] were commonplace. Clearly they reflected popular interests. It is difficult to accept that only the idle wished to read Mist's account of kissing,[39] whilst the elopements and sexual scandals of the great were covered in great degree, helped by the often lurid nature of adultery cases in the House of Lords.[40] The discovery of an admiral's wife in a Charing Cross brothel in 1771 was as good copy as the Countess of Eglinton's adultery in 1788 and Lady Abergavenny's in 1729. Robert Trevor wrote from London in the latter year, 'Private persons have not escaped the notice and censures of our licentious press; nor can even the grave bury poor Lady Abergavenny's shame, every sillable of whose name, and every particular of whose life are hawked about the streets as articulately as old cloaths etc.'[41]

Addison included in the *Spectator* the tale of the sexual tempting of an immobilised gallant, and the *Newcastle Chronicle* indicated the perils of categorisation by including among its preponderantly political foreign news an amusing account of Viennese disturbances occasioned by moves against prostitution. A correspondent of the *Reading Mercury* attacked women who wore cork round-abouts complaining that 'cork rumped devils' were harder to play with. The perils of provincial culture were brought home to a woman who had been to see a performance of the Shakespeare Jubilee Ode on Leominster when she came home to find her husband embracing their servant, an episode that helped to provide an amusing tale. The often earthy nature of newspaper reports can be seen in a report in the *London Mercury* in 1721:

A certain Last-maker in Butcherhall-Lane being resolved to divert himself after a new Method, ran into the Sign of the Three Birds, and call'd for the Landlady, who immediately attending, he call'd her a Bitch and fell a laughing. The Woman, surpriz'd to know his meaning, stood mute, while Dick persisted in his Tone, calling her Bitch, and Bitch of Bitches, and as she kept such a House, ought to stand the Censure of her customers; the Woman, who was infinitely above the sawcy Language of his scandalous Tongue, resenting his ill Manners by calling him Rascal. Dick to prove to the contrary before 40 People, pulls down his Breeches to stand Search. The Gentlewoman of the House absconded with great Confusion; but a lusty Butcher Woman broiling her Supper, having more Courage than the former, she swore she would try the Event, and Catches fast hold by his Trickstaff with a pair of Stake Tongs with which she was turning her Meat, and shook him while he roar'd out like a Bull, and ran away as fast as he came, and hath been seen no more. The Woman swore she believ'd he was a Rascal by her manner of feeling; but whither she be a competent judge I cannot well determine.[42]

'The Taste of the Times is wholly turned to Joking', wrote Lady Mary Wortley Montagu in 1738,[43] and, besides the humorous items in general newspapers,[44] some papers specialised in humour, such as Henry Playford's *Diverting Post*, a weekly that appeared from 1704 to 1705, which printed a lot of ribald poetry, John Henley's *Hyp-Doctor* of 1730–41, and Popping's *Growler: or, Diogenes Robb'd of his Tub*, which anticipated Henley's extraordinarily picturesque knockabout style, and declared in 1711, 'Men nowadays do not read cursory papers so much to improve themselves, as to gratify their appetites, according as they are delighted in scandal and reflexion; by which means, the pen is become the bubble of the rabble.'[45]

Humorous stories and a ribald style were criticised, and discussion over style was closely linked to debate over content, although of course the two were not really separable. Criticism was frequent, part of the continual rivalry between newspapers that was always kept in front of readers. Papers felt it necessary to proclaim their superiority; the reader could not be relied upon to make up his own mind. Clifton's *Medley* attacked the style and content of Mist's *Weekly Journal*. He accused it of being lewd, claimed that Mist understood neither politics nor how to describe them and mocked 'his domestic fables of assaults upon stage-coaches, and skirmishes of highwaymen'. Referring to Mist's 'vast success among the lower class of readers', the *Medley* claimed that it had promised never to appeal to Mist's readers by printing puns, conundrums, and *double entendres*, and that it dealt with people of sense. It was however to be Clifton who went to the wall.[46] In 1724 Benjamin Hoadly, the Whig bishop of Hereford, expressed his suspicions of the declamatory, dictatorial and pathetic styles and formulated what some would have seen as a Whig theory of religion, 'appealing to the passions, is talking to children; for among men they either are, or ought to be, under the conduct and guidance of reason'.[47] The success of Hoadly's approach may be questioned. His 'Britannicus' essays in the *London Journal* have recently been charitably described as 'often prolix',[48] and the series was to end in another five months. Shortly before its termination the *Daily Courant* condemned the opposition press for following the low tone and seeking the popularity of the buffoon and in particular attacked the *Craftsman*:

It is a point fully settled among honest and reasonable people, that in respect of things of real importance to mankind, a person who discourses on them with a sincere intention of doing good by declaring truth, will always make use of serious arguments, and keep closely to the subject he undertakes to elucidate. Wit, raillery and joking are proper ingredients in popular essays; and when exerted on proper topics, entertain the mind agreeably at the same time that they inform the understanding. But then these talents ought not to be continually employed, and the same turn of style, and quaintness of expression, made use of in explaining a theological or political proposition . . .[49]

Lady Wortley Montagu found her printer throw 'in a little Bawdy' to make her newspaper sell and another printer reject a 'moral Paper' as unprofitable.[50] In 1762 the former diplomat Guy Dickens wrote to his son from London, 'We are split into factions and parties, whose scribblings are full of such low abuse and scurrility, that they make liberty degenerate from a blessing into a curse.'[51] Some newspapers justified levity as a means of getting their message across,[52] and they probably did help in making what was often fairly recondite information more generally accessible. It was not the humorous accounts of domestic accidents that are significant in this context, but rather the attempts to absorb political news into the more homely and popular language, images and style that characterised the other sections of the papers. In 1726 Mist discussed Anglo-Dutch relations in a way that was easy to understand using the image of two men on a board at sea. The Jülich-Berg dispute, an inheritance quarrel of labyrinthine complexity, was described in the *Champion*, in 1740:

To be cudgell'd for The Dutchies of Bergue and Juliers, situated, as may be seen in the map, very conveniently for an appendage to the dominions of many great Princes. The Kings of Poland and Prussia, . . . are already on the list of champions . . . the Emperor will be call'd upon to see fair play.

The same year the *Newcastle Journal* reprinted an item that encapsulated the opposition's critique of the ministry's conduct of the war with Spain: 'A gentleman, last week, asking the news, was answered, another embargo is to be laid on all the shiping: To which he merrily reply'd, "I hope then 'twill be taken off the men of war".' Ben Budge's letter to George Grenville over the Wilkes affair printed in *Berrow's Worcester Journal* was highly colloquial, while a London account of a new Welsh thread-spinner, reprinted in Newcastle in 1787, introduced its technical details with the observation that sufficient thread was spun daily in Holywell to encircle the world, an apt image of what was felt to be the capacities of technology and industrialisation.[53] The argument that opposition newspapers sought to 'democratise' the tone and content of the press and that ministerial papers resisted would be a seductive thesis, but it is too simplistic. It is true that some opposition figures, such as Mist and Wilkes, sought to broaden the appeal of opposition propaganda, but the same was true of certain ministerial publicists, such as Fielding and Henley. The Earl of Chesterfield, whilst still an officeholder, complained that a ministerial pamphlet lacked 'strength and spirit' and that the opposition 'attack with invectives, and should be answer'd in the same manner; and we should not content ourselves with reasoning, with enemies that fight with poison'd arrows besides that all reasoning is thrown away upon the people they are utterly incapable of it'. Chesterfield's letter suggests that those works that dispensed with an appeal to 'reason' should not necessarily be seen as 'popular' in any sense of praising the reading public. It is also of interest to the scholar of the opposition press as Chesterfield was closely associated later with *Common-Sense*.[54]

Opposition papers did not always seek a popular style. Clifton vaunted the reflective nature of the *Weekly Medley*, the *Crafstman* rarely emulated the vigorous idioms of Mist's papers, and its leading essays were often philosophical or intricate. The *North Briton*'s discussion of British politics in terms of the history of Lady Wiseacre's family, a device that had been used on numerous occasions already, was dismissed by the *London Chronicle* as 'an allegory not very intelligible to common readers'.[55] Junius's penultimate letter, addressed to Lord Chief Justice Mansfield, bored his readers and was a serious flop.[56] Vindictive satire, such as the *Craftsman*'s attacks on Walpole and Junius's on the Duke of Grafton, was readable and interesting, an accessible form of political propaganda, but all too often the opposition used lengthy essays whose tone of high seriousness and moral outrage became repetitive and whose vindictive abuse could not compensate for a general humourlessness. This was true of many of the essays of the

Craftsman, the *Monitor* and the *North Briton*. George Colman's remark in 1775, 'I have even been assured by my friends, that the people of this country will not at present read any article in a newspaper longer than a paragraph',[57] was a comment not only on the impact of much of the political press, but also on the style and content of many newspapers. It can be substantiated by the low circulation figures of such essay-papers as the *Review* and the *Briton*.[58]

To appreciate the press and the problems of editorial selection in the period it is necessary to dispense with the idea that closely argued, reasoned discussions of political theory or sophisticated examples of literary analysis represent the goal that newspapers pursued, or should have done. Many scholars would support the *British Journal*'s attack on the inability of other papers to distinguish between important and trivial news. Shipley commented that the *Weekly Register* of the 1730s 'suffered from a split personality: part miscellaneous, part political'.[59] These views are questionable. The newspapers were not written for the benefit of political theorists or literary scholars. The editors of the period had an extremely difficult task to fulfil, without the support that their descendants have enjoyed. That so many chose not to use lengthy essays probably reflected an awareness of their readership. As Goldsmith observed in 1761, 'The effort is now made to please the multitude, since they may be properly considered as the dispensers of rewards.'[60]

Notes

1. *Reading Mercury and Oxford Gazette*, 15 Feb., 19 Sept. 1768, 3 Sept. 1770, 25 Jan. 1773; *Newcastle Chronicle*, 17 Nov. 1787; *St. James's Chronicle*, 29 Dec. 1763.
2. *Reading Mercury and Oxford Gazette*, 28 Nov. 1768, item on Oakingham plays. *London Daily Post*, 5, 17 Jan. 1743. For money being sent to pay for the insertion of a paragraph on the misfortunes of a local cleric, *Leeds Intelligencer*, 1 Apr. 1766; *Jackson's Oxford Journal*, 24 Apr. 1773, ad. in news; *St. James's Chronicle*, 31 May 1764 re letters on plays.
3. *Reading Mercury and Oxford Gazette*, 16 July 1770, remedy for 'weakness of sight'; *York Herald*, 9 June 1792, item from *Lincoln Mercury*.
4. *Miscellany*, 17 Mar. 1709; *St. James's Post*, 6 Sept. 1717; *Wednesday's Journal*, 25 Sept. 1717; *Whitehall Evening Post*, 30 Dec. 1718; *Weekly Medley*, 3 Oct. 1719, 16 Jan. 1720; *Honest True Briton*, 21 Feb. 1724.
5. *Daily Journal*, 24 Jan. 1721; *London Mercury*, 11 Feb. 1721.
6. Though not as much as Henley in the *Hyp-Doctor*.
7. *Weekly Journal*, 24 June 1721, 28 July 1722, 29 Apr. 1723, 29 Feb. 1724;

Mist's Weekly Journal, 22 May 1726; *A Collection of Miscellany Letters, selected out of Mist's Weekly Journal* III (1727), dedication.

8. *Craftsman*, 13 May, 22 Sept. 1727; *Original York Journal*, 13 June 1727; advert in *St. James's Evening Post*, 28 Nov. 1727; *Evening Journal*, 1 Dec. 1727.

9. *British Observator*, 10 Mar. 1733; *Morning Herald*, 15 Aug. 1782.

10. *Newcastle Courant*, 30 June 1733, 27 July 1745.

11. *Spectator*, 12 Mar. 1711; *London Evening Post*, 12 June 1762.

12. *Proposals*, 22 Jan. 1739; *Mist's Weekly Journal*, 22 May 1726.

13. *Oracle*, 24 July 1742; *St. James's Chronicle*, 28 Jan. 1766: Philo-Cachinnus.

14. *Daily Post*, 15 Aug. 1745; *True Patriot*, 4 Mar. 1746.

15. *London Evening Post*, 30 Mar. 1762; *Citizen*, 20 Apr. 1757.

16. *Leeds Intelligencer*, 8 Sept. 1767; *London Evening Post*, 30 Sept. 1762.

17. Numerous examples include *Berrow's Worcester Journal*, 28 Dec. 1769, 8 Mar., 5, 19 Apr. 1770; *Reading Mercury and Oxford Gazette*, 30 July 1770, 4 Feb., 15 Apr. 1771.

18. Junius to John Wilkes, 18 Sept. 1771, *The Letters of Junius*, J. Cannon (ed.) (Oxford, 1978), pp. 423–4; Almon to Dear Sir, 6 Nov. 1779, BL. Add. 20733.

19. Proposals for an Evening Newspaper, 22 Apr. 1788, advertised in numerous other newspapers, e.g. *Newcastle Courant*, 26 Apr. 1788, *Reading Mercury*, 9 Oct. 1769; *Public Ledger* in 1777 declared itself 'a Daily Political and Commercial Paper, Open to All Parties, but influenced by None'.

20. The following, not a complete list, have been examined: *Reading Mercury*, 15 Apr. 1771, 21 Sept. 1772, 26 Apr., 17, 31 May, 21 June, 25 Oct., 15 Nov. 1773.

21. J. Feather, 'Cross-Channel Currents: historical bibliography and *l'histoire du livre*', *Library*, 6th ser., II (1980), pp. 10–11; G. A. Cranfield, *The Development of the Provincial Newspaper, 1700–1760* (Oxford, 1962), p. 46.

22. *Newcastle Weekly Mercury*, 2 Feb. 1723; *York Courant*, 6 Feb. 1739; *Northampton Mercury*, 18 June 1722; *Newcastle Journal*, 7, 14 June 1740.

23. *Original Mercury*, 5 Mar. 1728; *Newcastle Courant*, 3 Mar. 1733; *Reading Mercury*, 21 Aug. 1775. The *Gentleman's Museum*, a new monthly, made the same request in its advertisements, *Reading Mercury*, 23 July 1770.

24. *Berrow's Worcester Journal*, 9 Nov. 1769; *London Evening Post*, 23 Jan. 1762.

25. *Flying-Post*, 12 Feb. 1717; *Weekly Journal*, 2 Mar. 1717, 23 Jan., 6 Feb. 1720; *Mist's Weekly Journal*, 11 Feb. 1727.

26. *London Journal*, 2 Jan.; *Weekly Journal*, 2 Jan. 1720; *Applebee's Original Weekly Journal*, 10 Feb.; *Post Man*, 26 July; *Freeholder's Journal*, 31 Oct. 1722.

27. *Original Mercury*, 19 Dec. 1727; *Daily Journal*, 2 Apr. 1728; *Westminster Journal*, 4 Dec. 1742; *Public Ledger*, 19 Aug. 1761; *Daily Universal Register*, 17 Jan. 1785; *Cirencester Flying-Post*, 5 Apr. 1742; *St. James's Chronicle*, 23 Jan. 1766; *Protestant Intelligence*, 27 Feb. 1725.

28. *St. James's Post*, 13 Sept. 1717; *St. James's Evening Post*, 27 Jan. 1722; *St. James's Chronicle*, 27 Dec. 1763.

29. *Weekly Journal*, 16 Feb. 1717; *St. James's Post*, 6 Mar. 1717; *Freeholder's Journal*, 31 Jan. 1722; *Applebee's Original Weekly Journal*, 27 June 1724; *Fog's Weekly Journal*, 1 Feb. 1735; *Weekly Miscellany*, 22 Feb. 1735.

30. J. Brewer, *Party Ideology and Popular Politics at the Accession of George III* (Cambridge, 1976), pp. 166–78; Brewer, 'Commercialization and Politics' in N. McKendrick, J. Brewer and J. H. Plumb, *The Birth of a Consumer Society* (1982), pp. 253–60.

31. *Fog's Weekly Journal*, 14 Feb. 1736. Such items were often attacked: *Craftsman*, 21 Oct. 1727; *True Patriot*, 5 Nov. 1745; Horace Walpole to Horace Mann, 27 Jan. 1743, *Mann–Walpole Correspondence* II, W. Lewis (ed.) (1955), p. 148.

32. *Mist's Weekly Journal*, 14 May 1726.

33. R. Bataille, 'Arthur Young and the *Universal Magazine* of 1762', *Library*, 6th ser., 6 (1984), pp. 284–5; J. Taylor, *Records of My Life* (1832) I, 270.

34. *Cirencester Flying Post*, 5 Apr. 1742.
35. Tyrawly to Newcastle, 22 Aug. (ns) 1738, PRO. 89/40.
36. *Reading Mercury*, 21 Aug. 1775.
37. J. Black, 'Political Allusions in Fielding's "Coffee-House Politician"', *Theoria*, 62 (1984), pp. 52–4.
38. *St. James's Chronicle*, 28 Mar. 1767.
39. *Mist's Weekly Journal*, 24 July 1725.
40. *Gentleman's Magazine* 40 (1770), p. 314; *Newcastle Chronicle*, 3 Feb. 1787; *London Chronicle*, 9 Feb. 1788.
41. *Reading Mercury*, 27 May, 3 June 1771; *Newcastle Courant*, 12 Jan. 1788; Trevor to Stephen Poyntz, 21 Dec. 1729, BL. Althorp Mss. E3; *Westminster Journal*, 15, 22 May 1773.
42. *Spectator*, 13 June 1711; *Newcastle Chronicle*, 27 Jan. 1787; *Reading Mercury*, 20 Jan. 1777; *Berrow's Worcester Journal*, 13 Sept. 1770; *London Mercury*, 11 Feb. 1721.
43. *Nonsense of Common-Sense*, 14 Feb., *Weekly Miscellany*, 21 Apr. 1738.
44. The forms of humour were very varied. Jokes were reprinted from jestbooks, *Country Tatler; or the Daily Pacquet*, 3 Sept. 1739, humorous articles printed, *Reading Mercury*, 18 Oct. 1773.
45. G. Midgley, *The Life of Orator Henley* (Oxford, 1973), pp. 216–28; *Growler*, 15 Feb. 1711. The fake advertisement in that issue attacking two senior clerics is a superb example of a device later to be used with great effect by the *Craftsman* and other papers, *Craftsman*, 16 Jan. 1727, *London Chronicle*, 18 Dec. 1762.
46. *Weekly Medley*, 19 Sept., 3 Oct. 1719; *Senator*, 12 Mar. 1728.
47. *London Journal*, 1 Aug. 1724; *An Address to Friends and Foes* (1754), p. 4.
48. R. Browning, *Political and Constitutional Ideas of the Court Whigs* (Baton Rouge, 1982), p. 69.
49. *Daily Courant*, 9 Feb., 15 June, 9 July 1734.
50. *Nonsense of Common-Sense*, 17 Jan. 1738.
51. Guy to Gustavus Dickens, 15 Oct. 1762, Gloucester CRO, D 4582/3/19.
52. *Champion*, 22 May 1740; *Select Letters taken from Fog's Weekly Journal* (2 vols., 1732) I, xii; R. I. Cook, *Jonathan Swift as a Tory Pamphleteer* (Seattle, 1967), pp. 112–13; *St. James's Chronicle*, 4 Jan. 1766.
53. *Mist's Weekly Journal*, 2 Apr. 1726; *Champion*, 19 Apr. 1740; *Newcastle Journal*, 19 July 1740; *Berrow's Worcester Journal*, 30 Nov. 1769; *Newcastle Chronicle*, 27 Jan. 1787.
54. Chesterfield to George Tilson, 2 Feb. (ns) 1731, PRO. 84/311; J. Black, 'Fresh Light on Ministerial Patronage of Eighteenth-Century Pamphlets', *Publishing History*, 19 (1986), p. 56.
55. *North Briton*, 18 Dec. 1762; *London Chronicle*, 18 Dec. 1762.
56. *Junius*, Cannon (ed.), p. 320.
57. *Gentleman*, 12 July 1775.
58. Snyder, 'Circulation', p. 209; M. Peters, *The Monitor 1755–1765* (unpublished PhD thesis, Canterbury, New Zealand, 1975), p. 45.
59. *British Journal*, 14 Dec. 1723; J. B. Shipley, *James Ralph: Pretender to Genius* (unpublished PhD thesis, Columbia, 1963), p. 298.
60. *Public Ledger*, 22 Aug. 1761.

3 Holding up the Truest Portraits of Men's Minds[1]

> The following letter of JUNIUS we thought too remarkable to be omitted, notwithstanding its extraordinary length obliges us to postpone the inserting several Advertisements, etc.
>
> *Berrow's Worcester Journal*, 28 December 1769

Editorial selection, although a difficult problem, helped to produce a rich variety in the contents of the newspapers, especially in those of London. For most papers the preponderance of national and international news is clear, and this will be dealt with in a subsequent chapter. While political news was regarded as an essential aspect of most papers, this was not true to anything like the same degree for any other items, bar advertisements. The variety in non-political news is difficult to chart as it is unclear how far it reflected the interests of readers, the availability of items and the activities of competitors. Newspapers made reference to the inclusion of items in order to please their readers, but such claims have to be handled with care: not all papers would have been willing to admit that they had nothing else free and convenient to include, or that they were emulating rivals. All though sought readers. The 'Advertisers', papers which made clear, not least through their titles and layouts, that their prime rationale was as advertising sheets, needed readers in order to ensure advertising revenue. Papers that depended on political subsidies could not expect to enjoy them unless they were read, either directly or through excerpting by other newspapers. Thus all editors were determined to provide a product that would be consumed, contents that people wished to read.

Advertisements

> . . . there is a great deal of useful learning sometimes to be met with in Advertisements; I look upon mine to be a kind of Index of All Arts and Sciences, they contain the Advices both from

51

the learned and unlearned World; Fools, and Philosophers may there meet with equal Matter to divert and amuse themselves. — What can be more edifying to a Beau or a Coquet than to read of the extraordinary Effects of the right Italian Cream, the finest Cosmetick in the World for the Improvement of the Complexion, or the Vertues of the true Chymical Washballs for the Hands . . . there is not an Arcanum, or new Discovery in Physick, but is there spoke of . . . it is certain, that in a great and populous City like this, where the Inhabitants of one End of the Town are Strangers to the Trade and Way of Living of those of the other, many Things which prove of singular Use and Benefit could never be known to the World by any other Means but this of advertising; . . .

Mist's Weekly Journal, 22 May 1725

The volume of advertising in the press greatly increased during the eighteenth century. Many early newspapers had very few advertisements. The *London Courant* of 22 December 1688 had none at all. The *London Mercury* of the same day had one, by a London doctor, that of 7 January 1689, three, two advertising books and one seeking information concerning the theft of a white gelding. The *Evening Post* of 1711 had more advertisements: eight, seven of them selling printed material, in the issue of 4 January enough to fill two columns, a quarter of the paper, on 9 January, 13 per cent in that of 11 January. However, much of the paper was empty. Partly this probably reflected the habit of leaving space in tri-weeklies, particularly early in the century, for those sending them to rural corrrespondents to add material of their own, but in the case of the *Evening Post* it is difficult to escape the impression that there simply was not enough material for the paper. All the issues from 4 January to 3 February 1711 were at least 30 per cent blank and several were 40 per cent or over. The *Weekly Packet* of 1 January 1713 contained only one advertisement: one and a half of its four pages were blank. By the 1720s most papers carried more advertisements, five in the *London Mercury* of 11 February 1721, three in the *Newcastle Weekly Mercury* of 2 February 1723. The *Newcastle Courant* of 25 September 1725 carried 22 advertisements occupying 37 per cent of the paper. It did not require many advertisements to start to fill an appreciable portion of a newspaper. The *Leeds Mercury* carried seven, eight and ten in its issues of 11, 18 July and 1 August 1738, but the last constituted about 16 per cent of the paper. Over half the *York Courant* of 6 February 1739 was occupied by advertisements, and unwilling to lose revenue by omitting them, the paper's size was increased.[2] Those bored by a leading essay on tithes in the issue of 17 March 1747 could turn to no less than 38 advertisements occupying 46 per cent of the paper. The *Oxford Gazette* offered a similar percentage on 26 November 1753.

Not all papers, however, were so successful. The *Birmingham Journal* of 21 May 1733 carried only five advertisements: for the products of a Stourbridge glazier and two Birmingham cloth warehouses, for the sale of an ass at Lichfield and for horses for covering in Warwickshire, the last a form of advertisement that became increasingly common during the century. The *Hereford Journal* of 11 September 1739 contained two notices of property to let, both in Herefordshire, and four notices of books for sale. Seven surviving issues of the *Kendal Weekly Mercury* from 1735 to 1747 contained 47 advertisements with little real increase in the number per issue. A month's issues of the *Cirencester Flying-Post* in 1742 contained only 11 advertisements. The *Hull Courant* carried none for several issues in 1749.[3]

Complicating the position were the advertisements for printed matter and medicines. The printers of newspapers often acted as local agents for these in the provinces, whilst in London many newspapers were owned by booksellers. It is by no means clear how far advertisements of these items were paid for and Cranfield has suggested that they may have been paid for in kind.[4] Whatever the position they did not have to be solicited, as others had to be. They were an important, sometimes dominant, feature of the advertisements in all papers, and successful newspapers could feel that they restricted the number of other, more directly profitable advertisements. A leading London opposition newspaper, *Old England: or, The Broad Bottom Journal*, informed its readers in 1746, 'Old England having lately increased in the sale, encourages the Gentleman concerned to give it, for the future, better paper; and in order to make room for other Advertisements . . . the Medecinal Advertisements shall be, occasionally confined to the last page.'[5] The biggest advertisement in the *Leeds Mercury* of 11 July 1738 was for Daffey's Elixir, a cure-all sold by the printer as by many other provincial printers in the country. In the next issue the largest advertisements were for the same Elixir and for *Spadacrene Anglica: or, The English Spa*, a book printed by James Lister, the printer of the paper. This interest probably inspired the inclusion in the issues of 25 July and 22 August of items from York and London praising the spa at Scarborough. Though the *Kendal Weekly Mercury*, printed by the bookseller Thomas Ashburner, only included seven advertisements of goods sold by the printer in the seven issues discussed above, they occupied a disproportionately large space. In the issue of 11 April 1741 over half the space devoted to advertising was occupied by one item providing details of five books sold by Ashburner. The *Penny London Post, or The Morning Advertiser* of 6 January 1749 carried an advertisement by the printer for the printing of hand bills and shop bills. The government-subsidised *Daily Courant* revealed a similar feature. Of the six advertisements in its issues of 4 September and 9 October 1734 one was inserted by the Admiralty and one by the Customs. Books played a large part in the *Cirencester Flying-Post* printed by the bookseller Thomas Hill. The issue of 29 November 1742 carried an advertisement beginning, 'At the Printing-Office aforesaid, Gentlemen etc. may be served with any new books; and that they may be acquainted with what Books are printed we shall insert an Account of them Weekly', a notice which was indeed repeated.

The unspecialised nature of most newspapers in terms of business organisation was such that advertisements could serve a very useful purpose even if very few were carried. The profits on some books and medicines may well have been considerable. The three-volume work on Charles XII and the allegorical romance *Celenia and Adrastus* advertised by Ashburner on 11 April 1741 sold for 15 and 5 shillings respectively. He clearly regarded advertisements as important and when his newspaper, for reasons that are unclear, came to an end in 1749, Ashburner produced a flysheet with a proposal for publishing a new weekly, the *Agreeable Miscellany*:

> Since declaring my intention of discontinuing the NEWS-PAPER, some persons have justly observed, that the circulation of advertisements or hand-bills would in some degree be cut off, to remedy which I have, by the advice of several gentlemen, etc. determined to publish a weekly paper . . . should this work meet with encouragement . . . the distribution of advertisements, hand-bills etc. will be made very extensive, by being sent along with it to all neighbouring towns, villages, etc. so consequently will be of great advantage in the sale of estates, houses, timber, etc. or letting any property.[6]

As the volume of advertising increased it probably became more important for a paper to ensure that it was in the top tier of advertisers in order to obtain more business. Walker, in his important study of advertising in London newspapers, has demonstrated the particular 'advertising profile' of different periodicals. Cranfield has suggested that from about 1740 onwards three distinct tiers of provincial newspapers emerged, defined by the number of their advertisements per annum.[7] This was possibly of great importance from the point of defining regional dominance within the urban network. The preponderant position of Newcastle in the regional economy of the northern four counties of England was expressed in the relative or complete failure of other centres to establish viable newspapers. However much Ashburner may have been satisfied with his advertising it was scanty by Newcastle standards and this state of affairs existed partly probably because Cumbria was, and remained throughout the century, within the sphere of the Newcastle press. The list of towns in which the *Newcastle Journal* named agents in 1739 where the paper was delivered and subscriptions and advertisements accepted included Cockermouth, Carlisle, Whitehaven, Penrith, Appleby, Kendal, Lancaster, Sedbergh, Brough, Kirkby Lonsdale and Kirkby Stephen. The ability of the paper to name agents contrasted with the habit in some papers of simply claiming that agents existed in particular towns or counties. The advertisements in the *Newcastle Journal* substantiated this picture of a newspaper able to serve local society and the Cumbrian economy. Many of the advertisements relating to Cumbria, such as those for the Carlisle races, were no doubt partly inserted to attract Newcastle interest, but they also suggest that Cumbrian advertisers thought it worthwhile to attract local purchases by advertising in the Newcastle press. The ability of that press to obtain many advertisements reflected and in turn helped to ensure its regional dominance. A clear example of this is provided by a contrast between the circulation of the *Newcastle Courant* in 1771 and that of the *Darlington Pamphlet* the following year. Four consecutive issues of the former in October and November reveal the percentage occupied by advertisements as averaging 63 per cent.[8] The fifth issue of John Sadler's *Darlington Pamphlet*, a weekly that sought to evade the Stamp Tax, which appeared on 19 June 1772, carried eight advertisements. The issues of 26 June and 3 July had three each, one more than that of 10 July. Fourteen per cent of the issue of 19 June was occupied by advertisements, though the following issue contained less than 4 per cent. By 4 September the number had risen to seven and by 30 October, recovering from the harvest recessional, to nine.[9] By the time the paper was cut short on 20 November, as the result of its discovery by the Commissioners of the Stamp Duties, it had achieved a number of advertisements that was satisfactory by the standards of the first three decades of the century. However, Sadler was trapped by the limited circulation and local nature of the paper. That ensured a local advertising base which in turn limited the total number of likely adverts. Those of 19 June 1772 originated in Darlington, Stockton and Hartlepool only. Richmond appeared in the issue of 3 July and places in southern Durham and North Yorkshire thereafter, but the geographical dominance of Darlington was obvious. Though an advertisement for Matthew Raine's *English Rudiments*, a school grammar book written by a local vicar, included booksellers in Newcastle, Sunderland, Durham and Thirsk,[10] there is little to suggest that the paper was read so far afield or that advertisers in those towns thought it worth advertising in either to attract Teesside or local custom. From 24 October 1743 the *Cirencester Flying-Post* carried a notice under the title:

As several persons, upon being informed in how many different places this paper is dispersed, may perhaps be inclined to advertise herein, or may be so kind as to communicate to us articles of intelligence, etc. Here follows a list of the several counties, (through most of the principal towns in which this paper is regularly distributed,) viz. Berkshire, Dorsetshire, Glamorganshire, Gloucestershire, Herefordshire, Monmouthshire, Northamptonshire, Oxfordshire, Radnorshire, Somersetshire, Warwickshire, Worcestershire, and Wiltshire.

The evidence of the paper suggests otherwise. Most of the advertisements were inserted by the printer, advertising medicines and books that he had for sale. The list of places inserted in the issues up to 26 April 1742 where advertisements for the newspaper were taken in named agents only in Tetbury, Stroud, Bristol, Chepstow, Wotton-under-Edge and Minchinhampton.

In contrast a successful newspaper would circulate over and receive advertisements from a large area. The Chester paper,

Adam's Weekly Courant, carried North Wales and Staffordshire advertisements in 1738. The *Preston Journal* of 24 September 1742 carried advertisements referring to Lancaster, Chester, Warrington, Liverpool, Manchester and Wigan, the *Weekly Worcester Journal* listed agents in Bridgnorth, Stafford, Stourbridge, Shrewsbury, Evesham and Warwick. Increasingly successful provincial papers carried advertisements inserted by London firms as in the *York Courant* of 16 January 1739, an attempt by London businessmen to penetrate provincial markets via the already existing urban provincial hierarchy. This was part of the growing integration of the press nationally, with provincial papers being regularly obtainable in London. Advertisements for the *York Courant* were taken in by London coffee-houses. In December 1767 the *Bristol Gazette* named three London coffee-houses where it could be seen and included London in the list of places where advertisements were taken in. The list also mentioned Taunton, Wells, Bath, Bridgwater, Exeter, Sherborne, Worcester, Gloucester, Wotton-under-Edge, Cirencester, Devizes, Birmingham, Liverpool, Usk, Abergavenny, Pembroke and Haverfordwest, and the paper used the argument of its extensive circulation to justify its calls for more advertisements. The general success of the Bristol press can be measured by the delay in establishing newspapers in South Wales.[11]

There was a notable increase in the volume of advertising in the second half of the century. The four-page twelve-column *York Courant* of 17 March 1747 with 38 advertisements occupying 46 per cent of the paper had become a six-page eighteen-column issue by 1761. The issue of 7 July 1761 carried 116 advertisements, occupying 74 per cent of the paper. The physical dominance of advertisements was also more striking. All of pages 3–6 of the paper were occupied and this was true of over half of the four-column front page of the issue of 2 January 1776, as it was of such London papers as the *Gazetteer and New Daily Advertiser*.[12] The *Oxford Gazette* of 10 January 1767 and *Leeds Intelligencer* of 17 October 1769 each devoted 34 per cent of their space to advertisements, the *Kentish Gazette* of 21 January 1772 28 per cent, the *Gloucester Journal* of 5 June 1780 77 per cent, the *Newcastle Chronicle* of 6 January 1787 56 per cent, the *London Chronicle* of 1 and 3 January 1788 and the *Newcastle Courant* of 12 January 1788 25 per cent. The number of advertisements was also impressive, particularly as each often contained a mass of information. The *Leeds Intelligencer* above carried

25, the *Newcastle Chronicle* 52, and the *Newcastle Courant* of 12 January, 2 and 23 February and 8 March 1788 an average of 82.5

The importance of advertising can be further suggested by the large number of papers, both London and provincial, that included the term advertiser in the title. A primarily political paper such as the *Champion* had a sub-title *Evening Advertiser*. Asquith has recently claimed that there was 'relative decline of the newspapers' importance as advertising mediums, which had developed with the publication of Junius' essays in 1769 and the full coverage of parliamentary debates in 1771', and that this was reflected in the omission of the word advertiser from sub-titles.[13] Clearly however this cannot be used as a measure of the importance of advertising, as fashion must have played a role in the choice of titles and sub-titles. Some new newspapers, such as the *Star and Evening Advertiser* or the *Bristol Gazette and Public Advertiser*, included 'advertiser' in their sub-titles. The two largest circulation morning papers in London in 1789 were the *Daily Advertiser* and the *Gazetteer and New Daily Advertiser*.[14] It is far from apparent that there was any decline in the importance of the press as an advertising medium. Junius's essays only lasted three years and the newspapers of the 1770s and 1780s very rarely devoted as large a proportion of their space to political essay material or to parliamentary news, itself seasonal, as their counterparts in the first half of the century had done.[15] Neither was sure of a place on the front: in general advertisements had displaced political essays. This process did not mean that advertisements always displaced other items. The British press could not act as some of the Jamaican press did. The *Royal Gazette*, floating on very extensive official advertising, regularly produced an eight-page *Additional Postscript*, besides its habitual eight pages. The *St. Jago Gazette* and *Cornwall Chronicle* also benefited greatly.[16]

British newspapers did not always accept advertisements. The introduction to the *Daily Journal* referred to the difficulty of getting advertisements inserted speedily, which may reflect a practice of printing off the advertisements first, and to papers demanding higher prices on the pretence that they were full. In 1725 Mist blamed the second Stamp Act, and the consequent reduction in the size of his paper, for the drop in advertisements printed and suggested that this lessened the appeal of the paper. The following year however he printed a letter supposedly from a reader expressing a wish to be entertained rather than to read 'a tedious repetition of nauseous (though perhaps to you profitable) advertisements'.[17]

In 1728 the *Craftsman* announced,

> We hope that none of our readers will take it amiss, that we have of late admitted so great a number of advertisements into this paper; since we can assure them, that we are resolved never to postpone any diverting essays, or any material articles of foreign or domestic news on that account: But as we found that they increased upon us every week (which must be allowed to be of some use to the town as well as profit to us and the Government,) we have put ourselves to a considerable expence by enlarging our paper and widening the columns for that purpose, without encroaching on the entertainment of our readers.[18]

Fog's Weekly Journal praised the reading of advertisements in 1736:

> I look upon them as pieces of *domestic* intelligence, much more interesting than those paragraphs which our daily historians generally give us, under the title of home news . . . the advertisements are filled with matters of great importance, both to the great, vulgar, and the small.

A condescending attitude was adopted by the *Comedian, or Philosophical Enquirer*, a London magazine, in 1732: 'I cannot see the great advantage which an inferior tradesman can reap from the study of newspapers, unless it is from the advertisements; which seem the parts designed for his perusal.' A different view of their readership was revealed by an advertisement for the *General Evening Post* the following year which noted 'a list of estates to be sold in all parts of the Kingdom will be inserted on proper occasions'.[19]

The *Reading Mercury*, which omitted advertisements for reasons of space on several occasions, printed a letter from an unnamed correspondent, who could have been the editor, attacking 'the impolicy and excessive cruelty . . . of imposing an additional tax upon news-papers' on the grounds of the value of advertisements, a view not commonly advanced in discussions of the Stamp Acts.

> The great variety of advertisements which make their daily appearance is a proof of their utility to all ranks of people. The merchant, the artist, the mechanic, have all recourse to news-

papers; commerce is extended; the liberal sciences promoted,
and all mutual intercourse in the ordinary connections of trade
maintained and supported very principally by newspapers;
houses and lands are purchased and disposed of by means of
news-papers; offenders against the laws of their country are
apprehended and brought to justice, and the peace and
welfare of individuals preserved, entirely by news-papers. The
public offices of London, great companies, and other societies
established for the public good, are severally connected with,
and their stability or credit promoted by, news-papers. All
public charities are under indispensable obligations to newspapers, but none more so than that establishment for the relief
of the King's troops serving in America; the 'Luxurious'
News-papers having raised for that charity upwards of
eighteen thousand pounds.[20]

The extent to which these claims were justified is unclear.
Clearly press advertising was a powerful tool for those seeking to
inculcate, elicit or manipulate consumer demands.[21] Papers were
widely available and consulted at coffee-houses and taverns,
places where commercial transactions took place and particularly
important because of the general absence of specialised offices in
many commercial, industrial and agricultural businesses and because of the practice of handling most transactions through
meetings. Advertisements were part of a system of intelligence,
not isolated curiosities. The *Public Advertiser* in 1753 carried
beneath its title the notice,

The principal pawnbrokers within the bills of mortality have
agreed to take in this daily paper; and if any lost or stolen
goods shall be advertised in it, they will, to their utmost,
endeavour to secure the property for the owner, and to bring
the offender to justice. NB. Advertisements of things lost or
stolen, will be taken in by Mr. Brogden, Clerk to Justice
Fielding, at his office at the said Justice's in Bow-Street where
all persons are desired to send immediate notice of any
robbery, burglary, or theft committed; by which means they
may often hear of their goods and the thief, without
advertising at all; or if not, their advertisements will be drawn
up in the most conspicuous manner, and forwarded directly to
the press.

Fifteen years later the paper announced,

> The extensive sale of The Public Advertiser (joined to the
> *Variety* of Channels through which it passes) has always been
> the means of detecting so many robberies, and of apprehending
> so many offenders, that it may be proper to give this public
> notice, that, for the future, all informations of this kind, sent to
> Bow-Street, will be constantly inserted in this paper: and if such
> informations are properly attended to, by pawnbrokers, . . .
> few robberies will escape detection.[22]

In 1777 the *General Advertiser, and Morning Intelligencer* recorded a process that may well have been more general, organised
either by individual newspapers or by proprietors of places of
resort, such as coffee-houses, 'that part of the paper allotted for
advertisements . . . is daily stuck up in every public place
throughout London and Westminster'. This was also true of the
London Gazetteer in 1749.[23]

The effectiveness of eighteenth-century advertisements is a
question that cannot be answered: millions of pounds are expended on a similar question today with little success. However,
the advertisers presumably thought that they would obtain a return for their investment, more 'Anti-Venereal Pills' sold as a
result of the *Review* in 1709, increased attendance at the concerts
and balls held in Colchester and Long Melford, advertised in the
Colchester Journal: or Essex Advertiser in September 1739. As
most advertisements, other than those for medicines and printed
matter, were paid for, the decision to advertise was presumably
based on an expectation of a reasonable return.

Advertisements were made subject to taxation in 1712, at the
rate of one shilling each, a duty renewed in 1743, and doubled in
1757.[24] In 1789 the duty was set at three shillings. These increases
helped to push up the price charged for advertisements. In 1724
the *York Mercury* and *Leeds Mercury* charged two shillings each,
but advertising rates rose in general after the Stamp Act of 1725,
though duty on advertisements was not increased. Cranfield discovered no case in which this led to a decrease in the number of
advertisements in the provincial press, and it appears to have had
little impact on the London press, contrasting with the first Act,
which definitely hit advertising in the latter.[25] Possibly some newspapers felt that there was reasonable flexibility in the price

advertisers would pay, and displaced some of the burden of added duty onto them, rather than to readers in 1725, whilst other papers followed the trend in prices. The *Taunton Journal*, a new paper founded in 1725, charged one and a half pence per issue, in contrast to the usual charge after the 1725 Act of 2d but asked 3sh 6d for each advertisement on its first appearance, with a 2sh charge for each subsequent entry. In 1730 the *Leeds Mercury* raised its comparable prices to 2sh 6d and 2sh but in 1734 the *Daily Courant* felt able to accept 'advertisements of a moderate length, and which require no preference, or particular character' at 2sh. Possibly this reflected the advantages of a government subsidy, but in 1738 both the *Daily Post* and the *London Daily Post*, which did not benefit from ministerial largesse, charged the same price.[26] The tax increase in 1757 led many newspapers, such as the *Oxford Gazette* to rise the price to 3sh 6d, whilst the *London Evening Post* cited the 1757 increase five years later as part of the deterioration in its financial position that had forced it to increase the price of the paper.[27] 3sh 6d was clearly regarded as an acceptable price as John Slater charged it for entries in his illegal, untaxed *Darlington Pamphlet* in 1772.

Luxury products, such as tea, coffee, wine, medicine and printed matter were best able to absorb the costs of advertising, presumably because the percentage cost of the advertisement was low, and the profits in selling the products high. They dominated the advertisements of goods for sale whilst commonplace products, such as ordinary foodstuffs or beer, were rarely advertised, in contrast to the position today. There was clearly less need to encourage consumption of everyday products, the individual sales outlets were too small-scale to justify advertising and the newspaper was not the most effective way of notifying the often rapidly altering availability or price alterations of products that were often local and frequently sold in markets. The newspaper was rather an effective means of advertising for products imported into a region whose availability was unpredictable and whose potential purchasers had often to be persuaded that it was fashionable to consume. William Smythies of Colchester, advertising his ability to sell Spa, Pyrmont, Bristol, Bath and Scarborough bottled waters, was announcing the arrival of these imported products and suggesting that water should be drunk bottled.[28]

Not all advertisements were for items for sale. Advertising could be used to make a point, often, though not always, political. An example that illustrates what was felt to be the importance of newspaper advertising appeared in the *Newcastle Chronicle* of 24 March 1787:

> The advertisement inserted in our last week's paper, offering the stock of Mr. Punshon in Chester-le Street, to sale, was, we find, sent us by some malicious, lurking villain, doubtless with an intention to injure the business or credit of the tradesman to whom it relates, by a most base and unprecedented imposition; the author of which, we hope, will soon be detected, and branded with a due share of public infamy; and, if possible, of public punishment. Few crimes betray a greater depravity of heart, and it is a matter of regret that the laws of our country will not admit of the perpetrator's being tried as a criminal, on whom a capital punishment might be inflicted . . . the printer of this paper hereby offers a reward of ten guineas . . .[29]

A London grocer had the same problem with the *World* in 1791.[29] National and regional struggles could be waged through press advertisements, and mock advertisements, making a political point, such as those carried in the *Craftsman*, added a further twist. In 1767 the *Public Advertiser* printed a fake advertisement purportedly by a dealer in public offices for men seeking places.[30] In 1781 the late surveyors for the Parish of Wokingham used an advertisement to attack a decision by the JPs to remove a signpost.[31] Economic controversies, such as those over the siting of turnpikes, were often conducted by means of essays inserted as advertisements, declarations of intentions to stand, appeals for support and news items inserted for payment.[32] It is not always easy to determine what was paid for, and whether items from the party supported by the paper were inserted free. The printer of the aggressively partisan *York Courant* announced in 1741 that he would insert 'any advertisements relating to the present contested Election, come it from what quarter it will . . .', and did so. Accounts of electorally convenient charity carried as news items may well have been paid for. The same was possibly the case for partisan accounts of electioneering, such as those supporting Henry Hartley printed in the *Reading Mercury* in 1776. In 1780 the same paper announced, 'An Anti-modern Courtier, A Friend to Liberty, etc. and several other Pieces are received; but cannot be inserted without the customary compliment attending essays, calculated to answer electioneering purposes.'[33] The Grey interest actively used the press in the Northumberland election of 1786.[34]

Advertisements could readily serve for commenting on national politics. In 1711 the Austrian envoy Count Gallas used the *Gazette* in order to condemn British foreign policy, a rare feat. He achieved this 'by getting an advertisement inserted by surprise'.[35] In 1730 the *Daily Post Boy* carried an advertisement attacking the Anglo-French alliance:

> This Day is published . . . *Remarks on the Proceedings of the French Court, from Charles VIII, to . . . Lewis XIV.* Shewing what little regard has been had to the faith of Treaties . . . Proper to be compared with the present Times, and to be perused by all True Englishmen . . .[36]

Advertising was sometimes criticised particularly for the puffing of worthless products, an accusation that the methods for validating new medicines made particularly apposite. The press lent itself readily to quackery. In 1741 the *Publick Register* announced,

> All possible care will be taken to render this pamphlet authentic, useful, and entertaining. And whereas one fourth part at least of all the papers that are now extant, is filled with quack advertisements and other impositions on the public; to prevent the like in this, and to give room for matters of more importance, no advertisements will be admitted, but such as relate to books and pamphlets.

In 1759 Dr Johnson attacked irresponsible and inaccurate advertisers.[37] It is indeed possible to find many ridiculous items, particularly among the medical advertisements, their claims constituting an eighteenth-century system of comprehensive insurance. However, advertisements are a form that did and do not dictate particular standards, and alongside the continued presence of medical advertisements, such as Dr Walker's Genuine Jesuit Drops in the *Leeds Intelligencer* of 11 November 1766, their supporting testimonials, and occasional illustrations of, for example, voided stones, can be found an increasing number of advertisements inserted by organisations, many of them official. One of the functions of the *Gazette* was extended to most other papers. A bewildering variety of organisations inserted material. Two types of material increasingly inserted were notices about criminal activity, by the 1780s a major feature of the advertisements in many newspapers, and information about economic matters, particularly lobbying for new projects. Advertisements for societies for agricultural improvements rubbed shoulders with notices from the Quarter Sessions or announcements about local education. The Commissioners for Charitable Uses for Essex advertised in *Pilborough's Colchester Journal* in April 1739; Bristol churches began to use the press to advertise sales of church land in the 1740s. In the following decade Bristol charitable societies advertised their meetings in the papers, since as one advertisement noted this was more efficient and less time-consuming than dispersing printed notices by hand. *Berrow's Worcester Journal* drew the attention of its readers in 1770 to militia advertisements.[38]

Developments in advertising mirrored the general expansion of the press: increases in size and cost and a growing diversification in contents, both in London and in the provinces. The benefits offered by advertising were varied, and it helped to increase the value of the press to many groups, whether book advertisers, who paid quite considerable sums,[39] Bradford hatmakers seeking to preserve their monopoly of hat sales from the mercers, or those unaware of the dangers of copper cooking utensils.[40] Newspapers were used to advertise the meetings of joint-stock companies, notices of lottery draws and appeals for lost property. The relationship between the press and advertising was intimate, well represented by the fact that so many newspapers were owned by booksellers and that in 1794 the Licensed Victuallers Association founded the *Morning Advertiser* in order to help their advertising. Thomas Robe proposed to use this relationship to the benefit of the ministry with his 1727 scheme for suppressing opposition newspapers by attracting their advertisements to a new daily paper, a new evening post and a new weekly journal, which were to constitute the press. He envisaged a ministerially sponsored and cheap *Daily Advertiser* with several officials to take in advertisements:

It is evidently true that the certain, excessive profits arising from advertisements, are the great support of the proprietors, writers and printers of newspapers and chiefly promote the sale of them . . . It is further evident that the advertisements,

published in the different papers at present is the chief reason
with most houses both private and public for their taking in so
many. And that in case of a general Advertiser they would
gladly decline such a useless expence . . .[41]

As with the press, no regulation of advertisements was to take
place. Given the difficulty of enforcing the Stamp Act, with both
entire newspapers unstamped and some established ones not
paying sufficient duty, it is probably just as well that no further
regulation was attempted. The relatively limited authority and
weak power of central government could hardly have encouraged
any attempt at control. Regulation would probably have been for
fiscal reasons. However spurious they may have seemed it is
difficult to see anyone prohibiting advertisements for Bartlett's
Inventions for the Cure of Ruptures or Dr Saunders' Golden
Spirits of Scurvy-Grass.[42]

Economic news

They write from Newcastle, that the gentlemen of Northumberland being sensible, that whatever corn may be spar'd for exportation out of this Kingdom, above what is necessary for
subsisting our own people, is clear gain to the public wealth of
the nation; and that, on the contrary, whatever corn is imported, is so much real loss . . . a petition therefore from that
county is designed to be presented to the Parliament, for the
amendment of the law which relates to the importation of
foreign corn: But as the success thereof will much depend upon
the joint and hearty interest of the gentlemen of that county,
and others concerned, a general meeting has been agreed upon,
to concert proper measures for obtaining the end aforesaid . . .
Norwich Mercury, 29 January 1732

The economic news carried by the press still awaits systematic
study. It was not a new development of the eighteenth century, for
in the 1660s London newspapers had been produced carrying no
political news and simply containing advertisements and news of
trade. Papers that were primarily devoted to economic news continued to exist thereafter. It was not however the custom for
newspapers to be owned by large companies, though the *British*

Mercury of the 1710s was published by the Sun Fire Insurance Company. In 1781 the *Aurora and Universal Advertiser* was launched with the support of leading London hoteliers. In 1696 the coffee-house keeper, Edward Lloyd, published a tri-weekly *Lloyd's News*, which contained a lot of shipping news, though it ceased the following year as a result of contentious items in the political and religious sphere. *Proctor's Price-Courant*, the *City Intelligencer*, *Robinson's Price-Courant* and *Whiston's Merchants Weekly Remembrancer* were published in the following reign. In 1718 the *Weekly Packet, with the Price Courant* was founded, and in 1721 the *Exchange Evening Post. Freke's Price of Stocks* was a journal of the 1720s.[43] Economic matters also played a major role in papers that did not specialise in them. In 1720 the *Weekly Miscellany for the Improvement of Husbandry, Trade, Arts and Sciences*, a paper that ran for about two decades, was founded. Two years earlier the *York Mercury* had started with the sub-title, *or a General View of the Affairs of Europe, But more particularly of Great Britain: with useful observations on trade*. In 1739 appeared the *Citizen, or, The Weekly Conversation of a Society of London Merchants on Trade, and other Public Affairs*. Three years later the *Cirencester Flying-Post* serialised part of the *Trade and Commerce of Great Britain considered*.

Shipping and grain were the early staples of economic news in the press. The *Supplement to the Weekly Journal* promised readers in 1716 that it would provide them with information of ships arriving at and leaving London, and in so doing it was providing a service common to many papers. In 1737 the *Daily Gazetteer* thought it worthwhile to carry a large notice announcing 'the ship news which hitherto has been inserted in the Daily Journal, will for the future be continued in this paper'. Later that year the 'port news' in the paper, the list of ships' movements, included information from Elsinore, Amsterdam, Liverpool, Portsmouth, Bristol, Falmouth, Plymouth and Southampton. In 1791 the *Evening Mail*, a tri-weekly, announced,

In order to comply with the requests of several of our commercial readers, particularly those concerned in the shipping, we shall in future give a complete list of the arrivals of vessels at the different out ports of our kingdom, as well as foreign stations, instead of confining it, as heretofore, to the arrivals made known on the mornings on which the Evening Mail is published. This amendment, together with a faithful, though necessarily concise, abstract of the news of the day received by the foreign mails will, we trust, make this paper the most correct and perfect evening print that is now published.

Shipping news, with its accumulation of foreign, provincial and London items, symbolised the role of the press in the circulation of information. In 1744 the *Daily Advertiser* printed a report which it had received, via Edinburgh, from Berwick of the nearby wreck of a South Carolina ship. Shipping news continued to be of great importance in the London press for the rest of the century. This was true both in peace and war. In wartime the press provided details of ships taken by privateers.[44] It also became of great significance for the provincial press. In 1740 the *York Courant* gave a list of ships stranded in the Humber by ice, but most shipping news related not to accidents or events,[45] but to the regular listing of shipping movements, the accounts of Hull and Liverpool movements and imports and exports printed in York, or those of the coasting trade recorded by the *Darlington Pamphlet*. The latter paper also provided details of the arrival of whalers and sealers at Newcastle and Hull.[46] In 1788 the *Newcastle Courant* reprinted sections of the Sound List giving details of British ships, their captains, loads and routes.[47] The previous year the *Newcastle Chronicle*, commenting on the punishment of ships' masters for falsely describing the size of their crews, noted in italics, 'Let masters and owners of vessels take notice of this, that such as have been guilty of the like frauds, may not share the same fate.'[48]

Shipping reports were found largely in newspapers produced near the sea: information on inland navigation did not approach the amount of space devoted to the location of canals. Reports on grain prices were found in most newspapers. The prices invariably mentioned were those at Bear Key, the Bear Quay in London where grain was landed and where a major corn market had been established. These prices and the value of the leading London stocks were carried by many of the newsletters used by early provincial papers as a major source of information. As the century progressed more markets tended to be cited and the information given on the grain situation became more diversified and sometimes more fully discussed. In 1723 the *Reading Mercury* reported the price of grain at the markets of Reading, Basingstoke and Bear Key, but the *Newcastle Weekly Mercury* only gave the last.[49] Five years later the *Original Mercury* commented on Hull prices while the *Newcastle Courant* used newsletters as a source for some of its reports on the harvest, and also cited prices at Bristol, Hull, London and York. In 1729 prices in Warwickshire and Worcestershire were printed in the paper under London bylines.[50] The same byline was used for reports on the situation in South Wales in the *Norwich Mercury* in 1732. Five years later the *Reading Mercury* cited prices in the markets at Guildford, Reading, Farnham, Newbury, Henley and Gloucester, while *Pilborough's Colchester Journal* was but one of the newspapers that reported on grain exports in the 1730s.[51] The riots over grain movements in 1740 and the controversy over exports to France, with which Britain was at war, in 1748 led to extensive discussion of the corn situation in the press.[52] 'Philalethes', writing in Newcastle, condemned many of the reports, 'those prejudices and mistaken notions which may have been so industriously spread among the vulgar (who are too apt implicitly to give way to any report which best agrees with their inclinations) . . .', challenged the accuracy of the reports of the Newcastle disturbances printed in the *Daily Advertiser* and other papers, blamed the rain and portrayed the grain markets as nationally linked and dominated by the metropolis: 'London (which place governs the value of all grain in England) . . . all the markets in England have a natural dependence on each other, and expect a mutual assistance.'[53] This dominance was further displayed by the *Cirencester Flying-Post* in 1744 deriving a report of agrarian conditions in nearby Herefordshire from London.[54] By 1757 however the *Oxford Gazette and Reading Mercury* could comment on the news itself:

> We think it very improbable that a vessel should be now lying in the River Thames, taking in her loading of wheat for the Isle of Wight, as mentioned in one of the London papers; because we are well informed that there is at present great plenty of wheat in that island . . .

The paper commented on an essay by A.B. by cross-referencing to another item, an increasing though far from common habit in the press: 'This writer treats the farmers with too much tenderness; for the present high price of corn seems chiefly owing to their artful management . . . see the article from Bath . . . in the preceding page.' The *Public Advertiser* provided details of grain prices in Salisbury, Warminster and Devizes.[55] Five years later the *London Chronicle* linked Guildford, Farnham and Kent prices to grain exports, while the *Newcastle Chronicle* in 1787 provided both a description of the condition of the London markets, as opposed to a mere list of prices, and details of the bleak local harvest. In January 1796 the *St. James's Chronicle* carried its monthly report on agriculture, a regular feature of the press in the period, but added a qualification in brackets:

> We cannot help intimating that we have some hesitation to place anything like implicit faith in the above report. The present high price of corn arises from complicated causes, of which though a real scarcity seems, in some degree, to form a part: yet the evil is undoubtedly increased by private avarice: and we are convinced that absolute legislative restrictions would be far preferable to any palliative recommendations.

By the 1790s London papers which in no way specialised in economic news, such as the *Express* and the *Telegraph*, were providing in every issue nearly a column of information on London markets ranging from the price of butter and hides to that of tallow and sugar. By 1774 the *Kentish Gazette* was regularly providing half a column of comparable London material, while *Bonner and Middleton's Bristol Journal* in 1795 reported grain prices at Chipping-Norton and Reading.[56]

Increasingly in the second half of the century space was devoted, both in the news and advertisements sections, to the propaganda of agricultural improvement. New practices were described, pernicious ones discouraged; yields and machinery, weight and enclosure became topics of discussion. In 1766 the Society for the Encouragement of Arts, Machines and Commerce advertised a prize of £20 for the best machine for slicing turnips. In 1772 the *Darlington Pamphlet* carried tips on potato cultivation from Carlisle and remedies for cattle infections, the latter a common theme in the press.[57] The *Newcastle Chronicle* urged the need to bury cattle in order to prevent their acting as the source of infection, the *Newcastle Courant* printed information of the cultivation of flax and the use of beet for cattle, the latter translated from a French source. In 1790 the *Sheffield Advertiser* claimed that every article which relates to the improvement or advantage of Agriculture, cannot but prove highly serviceable to the community at large. As such, we thankfully accept to publish the following method of keeping rooks and crows off corn land. Added to the evident probability of its universal success, a respectable Yorkshire farmer has found it to answer the intention on his own grounds.

Earlier that year the paper had urged the protection of birds' nests as a long-term solution to problems with grubs and caterpillars and had warned of the dangers of letting pigs drink the liquid in which turnip greens had been boiled.[58]

New developments in industry and mining were also followed with interest. Particular attention was devoted to details of new machinery. In 1772 the *Darlington Pamphlet* reported,

We hear from Nottingham, that an ingenious mechanic has just invented a machine with which a girl of ten years of age may spin several threads . . . from the simplicity of its construction and its being easily managed, cannot fail being a considerable advantage to the Yorkshire Manufactories both in the linen and woollen way.[59]

The press provided singularly little criticism of new developments in industry and technology, a marked contrast to the position over agriculture where enclosure and the free market in grain, livestock and wool aroused strong feelings, such as the dispute over a local enclosure recorded in the advertisements of the *Newcastle Courant* in 1743. Reading her newspaper at breakfast the popular playwright Hannah Cowley noticed a report of the ceremonies at the marking out of the boundaries of a village to be built for the purpose of introducing Lancashire manufactures. An opponent of industrialisation, she was led by this item to write her poem the *Scottish Village*, published in 1786. There was little comparable in the press. Industrialisation did not attract much discussion largely because it was not a topic of frequent press criticism. A letter from 'a friend to both Poor and Rich' in the *Leeds Intelligencer* of 6 December 1791 supported the use of machines in Leeds dressing-shops:

As to the right which every Englishman has to use the best implements he can invent in the performance of his business, I need not say much it is a right by nature, as well as by law; and whenever an ignorant and deluded populace have attempted to rob men of that right, they have always become the victims of their own injustice and folly.

Developments in transportation aroused considerable controversy in the second half of the century that were well expressed in the press, partly because of disputes between conflicting interests. Indeed these similar disputes in such fields as corn exports and pricing policies suggest the need for a revision of Cranfield's portrayal of the mid-century provincial press as one that was singularly unperturbed by local disputes. He claimed that provincial printers had no local policies to propound or local reforms to urge 'because as yet there had arisen none of those social and economic issues which were to assume such alarming proportions towards the end of the century'.[60] Clearly the position varied by paper, *Jopson's Coventry Mercury* being less willing to follow majority opinion than *Aris's Birmingham Gazette*,[61] but strongly held opinions over local issues were increasingly noticeable, particularly during the late 1760s.

The as yet restricted development in the editorial commentary and local essays of the provincial press of the 1720s and 1730s and the limited interest of the London press led to a somewhat episodic coverage of the often bitter prominent labour disputes of the period that affected in particular the West Country cloth industry. Isolated pieces of news were printed with relatively little comment. *Farley's Bristol Newspaper* presented an interesting picture of social justice in 1727: 'They write from Devonshire, that the poor weavers in several parts of the country, for want of employment, or other subsistence, go about in small parties and raise contributions on the alehouse keepers . . . by putting the laws in execution against them, for drawing in unsealed or too little measures.' Other papers provided some details of pay and conditions in the cloth industry. Some attention reflected the use of reports of economic decline for political purposes.[62]

By the second half of the century the situation was different. The larger size of newspapers, the ending of the front-page essay in nearly all of the press and the whole-page essay in most of it, and its replacement by a series of short essays, usually of between one half and two columns in length, devoted to a variety of topics, permitted a more frequent discussion of local issues. Dramatic changes, such as turnpiking and canal-building provided subjects, writers and reader interest. Proposals to link the North and Irish Seas by a Calder – Mersey canal touched off a controversy in the *Leeds Intelligencer*. Canalisation schemes in the Thames Valley system led to disputes as did the road network in the area and the attempt by York to prevent the construction of a bridge at Selby.[63] Many items were clearly inserted as advertisements but in some disputes the opinions of the printers are clear, and in others their willingness to insert particular items suggests their interest in propounding particular views. The printer of the *Leeds Intelligencer* was probably not being too controversial when he condemned the worrying of sheep and lambs by dogs in 1766.[64] His involvement in the major controversy over the price of food later in the year was more significant. The paper launched a comprehensive attack on many aspects of food distribution, particularly the provision of urban markets and corn exports.[65] The views of the printer were clear. Accompanying the printing of the Assize and Weight of Bread set by the Mayor, was a note from the printer, 'The bakers may observe by the above order that bread of all kinds or denominations soever, supposed to be superior to wheaten-bread, must be of the same weight and size of wheaten.'[66]

The need to oblige distillers to use malted grain only was stressed in the *Public Advertiser* in 1757. The printer of the *Oxford Gazette and Reading Mercury*, who chose in 1767 to transpose his title, to the future delight of indexers, was bitterly opposed to the system of food distribution and printed a number of pieces attacking it. They varied in tone. In May 1767 readers were assured that the previous week

a very fine leg of veal was purchased at Newbury Market by a gentleman of this place at 3 and a half per pound. — Query, What reason can the butchers of this place assign for keeping up that article at the exorbitant price of 5d per pound, since the distance between the two places is no more than 17 miles?

The following month the criticism had a historical perspective: 'In our next and subsequent papers will be inserted an order of the Chancellor of Oxford, made in the reign of Queen Elizabeth, to prevent forestaling, regrating etc in that city.' In January 1768 the approach was more specific:

By the present state of the tolls at two different gates near this town, a *great* farmer with his *great* waggon, whose wheels roll a surface of 16 inches, can bring to market with six horses in *one day* as much corn for *three-pence* through one gate, as a *little* farmer with narrow wheels and three horses can bring through the other in *four days* for *five shillings*; and if the *great* farmer's expence of horses and servants be set at 10s per day, and the *little* farmer's at 7s the difference to the latter in bringing the same quantity of corn will be no less than twenty-two shillings and nine pence; a burden, which in its consequences tends to enhance the price of corn, to discourage the *little* farmer from coming to market, and to compel him to throw up his lands to the *great* engrossers.

Fish also attracted the attention of the paper in 1768:

This day a cart loaded with mackerel arrived here from Worthing in Sussex; which, according to custom, were engrossed by the fish-people, and by them retailed at the *moderate prices* of four-pence, and three-pence each . . .
— Query, Whether the prudent and benevolent scheme of the Chamberlain of London, for raising a subscription to grant premiums to those who bring a certain quantity of mackerel to Billingsgate, might not, if set on foot by some public-spirited Gentleman of this borough, tend very much to the better, more regular, and cheap supply of that and every other kind of fish in our market, and, consequently be serviceable to the poor inhabitants in general?[67]

Three years later the contrast between the price of bread at Henley and Reading led to condemnation, a denial, and criticism of the failure by successive mayors to set an assize of bread. A 'public address' to the mayor was published calling for action.[68]

Berrow's Worcester Journal was sympathetic to the rioters of 1766. The high price of grain was blamed on the failure to prohibit exports and on the manipulation of the market by profiteers. One item referred to 'the present *artificial* scarcity'. The paper criticised the refusal of most bakers to give value for money, referred to reports of nefarious dealings and called for a prohibition of grain exports.[69] However, their anonymous corrrespondent in Cirencester reported on the disturbances there in a far less favourable fashion.[70]

The active involvement of the provincial press in local disputes came more from printing, often for money, submitted material than from comments by the printer. The growing role of these disputes in the press was partly a testimony to the wider circulation of the newspapers. The Hampshire correspondent who warned that the hill farmers were angered by the poor care of their sheep in the lowlands during the winter, was presumably of the opinion that this would advance his case, a confirmation of a sort of 'Hob's' letter that year about the reading of papers by farmers.[71]

More significant however was information and discussion about national economic developments. Partly this reflected the increased prominence of economic lobbying. Public lobbying in newspapers and pamphlets had been significant in the first half of the century, particularly when, as with the Anglo-French commercial negotiations of 1713 and those between Britain and Spain a quarter of a century later, they were politically controversial. Many of the more significant lobbying interests, the Bank of England, the East India Company, the Russia Company for example, preferred to operate largely in private, benefiting from their close links with the Whig ministries of Walpole and Pelham. In the second half of the century there was more press lobbying, as economic interests that had not hitherto appreciated the value or gained access to the press did so, as the close relationship between long-lasting ministries and powerful chartered companies weakened and as economic issues, particularly trade with America and the position of the East India Company, were pushed to the forefront of domestic politics. Aside from the time of the South Sea Bubble, when very lengthy reports had been printed, press accounts of the great commercial companies had been only occasional in the first half of the century. The situation was to be very different in the second half. 'Why should the landed interest ingross the attention of the ministry to the neglect of the manufactories of our land?' asked Benevolo in the *Leeds Intelligencer*, and the press provided an opportunity for economic lobbies to articulate support and express their views.[72] Some campaigns, such as those to prohibit wool exports, had a long history. In the early eighteenth century, the cloth manufacturing lobby, supported by parliamentary legislation, had sought to keep British wool prices low and foreign cloth manufactures weak by preventing the export of wool. Irish and British wool producers, unsuccessful, on the whole, in Parliament, indicated their views by smuggling vigorously. Pieces in the press attacking wool exports were a constant feature throughout the century.[73] William Bennett noted in Abbeville in 1785, 'I expected from the accounts of our newspaper writers to see the hills about it covered with flocks of our English sheep, the wool of which they were to work into the finest cloths, and to undersell us at every market. What I did see was very contrary to this idea . . .'[74]

Sir James Lowther, the developer of Whitehaven and an MP, was well aware of the role of the press in economic lobbying, and he kept a close eye on it:

They are now busy stirring about the iron project as you may see by the inclosed advertisement in the prints . . .

I was glad to see the paragraph in the enclosed and other newspapers today about the Newcastle coals for people fancy the coal owners have the profit of the high prices. I will advise them to put in such remarks for we want nothing but writing freely to show the vast benefit and indeed necessity of taking off the coast duty to help the manufacturers . . .

You will see by the inclosed *paragraph in the newspaper* today what envy and spite there is against the coal trade at Whitehaven for its being in one hand . . . I have drawn the inclosed paper as from one about Newcastle to his friend at London about the coal trade. If you think some such paper would do good to be printed in the newspapers at Dublin as taken from some of the London papers . . . Nothing can make people here comprehend that the trade at Newcastle is better in the hands of 30 great coal owners than in 2 or 300 little ones . . .

There is some malicious body is putting in *paragraphs in the news* to hurt the trade of Whitehaven. I wisht Mr. Younger today to call on the printer to try to find out the meaning of it.[75]

It is probable that many paragraphs devoted to economic news were obtained by this method. In 1768 the London booksellers published a notice announcing their abandonment of the practice of binding in leather, due to problems of cost and availability. It was printed in some newspapers, doubtless as a result of the close links between the two. The same year *Berrow's Worcester Journal* called for neighbouring counties to emulate Gloucestershire Quarter Sessions' move to enforce weights and measures, whilst *Lloyd's Evening Post* attacked profiteering by the sellers of candles. Lobbying over the coal trade attracted the attention of the Newcastle press, which kept readers in touch with relevant developments in London. Editorial selection clearly played a role in the presentation of material, one essay being rejected in March 1787 because of its uncompromising nature.[76] The press devoted attention to economic lobbying, partly as a result of payments, partly because it was news in its own right. Whether enlarging the dock at Hull, resisting new taxation on tobacco, debating the Anglo-French commercial treaty of 1786 or proposing parliamentary regulation of the price of sugar, the cause of particular interests received much attention.[77] This was part of the process by which the volume of newspaper space devoted to economic news and information increased. The growth in advertisements was an integral part of the development. Advertisements did not simply offer items for sale. They also offered units of economic production and exchange: shops, farms, warehouses, industrial sites. Advertisements not only offered services; they also sought them as organisations put out work to tender, such as masonry work for Liverpool pier in 1738 and solitary cells in York Castle in 1789.[78] Advertisements provided details of goods and documents lost and found, the basket with new pewter in left at the Three Cups Inn in Colchester in 1739, and vital information on bankruptcies; not that this information was only presented in advertisements. The *Public Advertiser* of 13 January 1757 carried a 'public notice' inserted by the Master Hatters warning that they would act against embezzlement by sub-contractors.[79] Newspapers provided information on the condition of the economy. The state of particular trades and industries was mentioned, such as stagnation in the Yorkshire woollen industry in 1726, the success of the Bristol woollen cloth fair of 1731, and a denial of reports of stagnation in the Gloucester pin manufactory in 1766.[80] Rumours of alterations in taxation were mentioned,[81] as were the activities of fraudsters, local and national, such as attempts to counterfeit the coinage or banknotes and men claiming false credit.[82] At the local level newspapers and their distribution systems could help in the conduct of economic affairs, not least by also serving as the distribution system for medicines and printed matter. An advertisement for a Leicestershire farm in 1716 urged 'enquire at the Mote House in Wigston, or Francis Edwards, the messanger that carries the news from Stamford to Litchfield'. Personal correspondence refers to sending cash 'by the Newsman'.[83] Details of legislation, of meetings of chartered companies and of those entitled to act in certain functions, such as brokers of the City of London, were provided.[84] John Pilborough, printer of the Colchester newspaper, offered for sale *The Compleat English Tradesmen* and informed his readers that it was 'very necessary to be perused by Tradesmen, of all Denominations'.[85] The press was used in 1772 to bolster confidence in the financial system, then afflicted by the crash of several prominent banking houses, though some papers were not very responsible. The *Darlington Pamphlet*, which warned readers to 'be extremely cautious of trade' nevertheless reported attempts to support the credit of the Glasgow and Newcastle banks. The *Reading Mercury* reported,

> We are glad to find, that at last some person has had spirit to check the indecent liberties, taken by some of the printers of the public papers, in mentioning houses of the first credit having stopped, without the least foundation for such reports; and we are authorised to inform the public, that the Court of King's Bench has, this day, at the insistence of the Carron Company, granted a rule to shew cause why the printer of the Morning Chronicle should not have an information granted against him, for the scandalous paragraph relative to that company in this day's paper.[86]

The press could also be of value in providing information about foreign trade. In the *Spectator*'s dream of Public Credit, one of the most effective instances of the use of a dream in order to make a political point, Addison wrote of seeing a virgin on a throne of gold at whose feet sat

> a couple of secretaries, who received every hour letters from all parts of the world, which the one or the other of them was perpetually reading to her; and, according to the news she heard, to which she was exceedingly attentive, she changed colour, and discovered many symptoms of health or sickness.[87]

The dependence of foreign trade on war and contingencies such as the early onset of Baltic ice or the loss of galleons in West Indian hurricanes, led to a great interest among the mercantile community in news from abroad, and the press was well placed to serve this as a result of its drawing on foreign newspapers and the access of London newspapers to information from the private correspondence of leading merchants. The news could have political consequences: 'Some have been very busy in spreading and aggravating a report of the seizure of some English merchants effects in the ports of Spain, giving thereby uneasy apprehensions to some timorous people, and prejudicing the public credit . . .'[88]

News of the activities of foreign powers was essential for merchants. In 1787 those of Newcastle were assured that the report of a Russian prohibition in trade to or from Russia in non-Russian ships was false, and that if there was an Anglo-French war, British ships in French ports would not be seized. They also learned of the total failure of the Portuguese vintage.[89] The role of foreign news in economic decisions was satirised in the *Corn Cutter's Journal* in 1734. Readers were entertained with the account of a discussion in a chop-house between Pestle, an apothecary who read the *Craftsman* and *Fog's Weekly Journal*, and Anchovy, an oilman, who advised, 'Lay in a stock of rhubarb, for fear the Persian should push on his advantage over the Turk. I bought an hundred jars of Lucca oil, the other day, for my part, upon the strength of Don Carlos having declared his majority.'[90]

Easy to satirise, the consideration of foreign news for economic information seems to have been widespread among newspaper readers.[91] Newspapers stressed their economic information and it could be tentatively suggested that its relative importance increased during the century as a possible result of the increased provision of literary, humorous and social items by the magazines. The *London Evening Post* devoted much of its attempt to publicise its contents in 1762 to its economic news, offering

> an exact table of the current price of merchandize . . . an account of the arrival of British ships at, and their departure from the several ports of the habitable world . . . the several courses of exchange, the prices of gold and silver, of stocks of corn at the Corn Exchange . . . and of other articles of a like nature. All notices given in the Gazette, with lists of bankrupts, and such other matters as may be useful to the public.[92]

Several 'provinces of intelligence': crime and sport

> 'Tis observable that our newspapers seem to have each their province of intelligence, the Daily Post being most in the secrets of

custom-house officers, the London Daily Post of Justices of the
Peace, the Daily Advertiser of foreign ministers, and the Daily
Gazetteer of our own.

Champion, 1 May 1740

Crime

Silver spoons, lap dogs, horses, negroes, bank notes, old
blankets, diamond rings, pointers, pocket books, capes, muffs,
and trash, meet the eye in every page, in the several predi-
caments of stolen, strayed, eloped, lost, run-away, missing, etc.

Reading Mercury, 17 October 1768

Accounts of the actions of criminals not only served to excite
readers, they also provided warnings to those fearful of attack.
News of the arrest of Thomas Coker, a notorious East Anglian
robber, could permit readers to sleep more safely in their beds.[93]
Those who might break the law, either deliberately, as by
poaching, or inadvertently, as by failing to pay duty for riding
horses, could be warned of the consequences.[94] Readers could be
alerted to the activities of criminals, such as the Durham swindler
who sold shovels he had borrowed in 1788, or the man selling
imitation watches in Sheffield two years later. In 1778 the *Reading
Mercury* ended an account of an Andover robbery by announcing,
in a different type, 'As the above villains may possibly be lurking
in this neighbourhood, these descriptions, if attended to, may be
the means of bringing them to justice . . .' The papers clearly
thought these warnings of value. A report in the *Leeds Intelligencer* on convictions at Wakefield for false weights and
measures was followed by a comment from the editor, 'Would it
not be right to have the names of these offenders published?' The
press was used to publishing advertisements and notices from
those seeking criminals, such as the reward offered by the Mayor
of Worcester in 1766 for the identity of blackmailers who had
threatened to light fires, or advertisements from local associations
against crime. John Styles has recently produced an excellent
study of this topic.[95]

However, interest in a good story seems to have played as large
if not more of a role in the preference for inserting details of
criminal activities. This is apparent when one considers the
frequency of such accounts in the foreign items printed. The *St.
James's Evening Post* offered in 1722 a story of wedding mayhem

at Modena inspired by the activities of the bridegroom's rival that led
to a general carnage. A decade later the *Derby Mercury* offered 'an
account of a woman called La Grande Catin who was lately hanged at
Paris' — a beautiful young woman who turned to crime after being
seduced and abandoned. The *Darlington Pamphlet* reported on the
execution of a Portuguese mass-murderess in 1772, the *Reading
Mercury* drew its readers' attention to its account of a mass-poisoning
in Amsterdam two years later and the *Newcastle Chronicle* offered the
murder of President Bardy in Paris, a tale of sex and violence, in
1787.[96]

Most reports were domestic in their origin. Many were written in an
exciting manner, particularly accounts of attempted jailbreaks and
highway robberies.[97] Some papers, such as *Applebee's Original
Weekly Journal*, were renowned for their crime reporting, and there
was much in the cheap London press of the second quarter of the
century. However, it would be a mistake to suggest that the subject
was the province of a particular section of the press. Interest was
general. Papers reported the activities and punishment of criminals
elsewhere in the country,[98] and drew attention to their own reports.
The *Reading Mercury* often contained notices mentioning long
accounts on their back page.[99] The lives of villains and their trials were
frequently discussed. The *Leeds Intelligencer* of 10 April 1781, a
period of wartime activity, devoted nearly two columns to a York
murder trial.[100] Interest was clearly considerable. Minor crimes were
often reported; crime tended to share with accidents the local news
section of early provincial papers.[101] *Causes célèbres* were discussed at
length. The alleged abduction of Elizabeth Canning and the subsequent legal action led to the production of *Canning's Farthing Post*,
a two-column, four-page work printed on poor paper that lasted for 65
numbers. There were regular reports on assizes and executions. Most
reports were unsympathetic to criminals, 'this sort of cattle', in the
words of one correspondent,[102] but highwaymen were sometimes
presented as glamorous figures and the cruelty of punishing 'honest
industrious' men for minor crimes, such as killing a hare,
condemned.[103] Celebrated pickpockets, such as the famous
Barrington of the 1780s, were treated as amusing rather than sinister
figures. Though criticism of the lengthy coverage of crime was
sometimes expressed,[104] most readers of the press throughout the
century would have been able to remark, as the Earl of Essex did in
1735, 'I see frequent murders and robberies mentioned . . .'[105]

Sport

The Earl of Essex had also remarked in his letter of 1735 on reports of cricket matches. One significant area of increased reporting in the press in the second half of the century was sport. The limited notices of and advertisements for horse races, which had dominated the occasional references to sport in the first half of the century, were replaced by lengthy advertisements, sometimes highlighted by illustrations, and by notices for and results of a variety of sports. The *Sheffield Advertiser* of 31 August 1792 devoted nearly a column to the results of a local cricket match, while the *Oracle* of 26 July 1796 printed individual scores in a Wiltshire match. The *Newcastle Courant* of 19 July 1788 provided information on the Durham, Hexham, Morpeth and Newcastle races. The activities of famous sportsmen, such as the leading pedestrians, were reported. Vivid accounts of boxing matches became a feature, particularly with the development of a star system round boxers such as Mendoza. Spectacular events, such as the development of ballooning, enjoyed similar prominence. Sport inspired correspondence, such as the letter on a new way to score at cricket printed by the *Reading Mercury* in 1773 or the controversy over a local match reported two years later, and anecdotes and information concerning betting, a popular topic in the press for all spheres of life ranging from matrimony to international politics.[106] As with much of the press reporting of domestic news it was the human interest and therefore often the exceptional items that attracted attention. In 1766 *Berrow's Worcester Journal* carried a long account of a race between two local butchers, both of whom had been naked.[107] The greater prominence of sport was reflected in the article headings of papers such as the *Oracle* and the *World* in the 1780s, with cricket or boxing featuring more often. Specialist periodicals were founded. In 1733 appeared the fortnightly *Historical List of all Horse-Matches Run*, and in 1769 for four pence an issue the *Racing Calendar*, another fortnightly complete with advertisements, could be purchased during the season.

The *Weekly Register* divided the readers of newspapers into seven groups in 1798: Interested, Anxious, Curious, Hasty, Idle, Party and Judicious.[108] All could find something in the press, both London and provincial. The variety of material in the newspapers, something not always glimpsed in books devoted to the press and politics, helped to make them an attractive product. Their appeal depended also however on several factors unrelated to content, particularly on cost and distribution.

Notes

1. 'Their newspapers, those pretty little modern histories, hold up to us the truest portrait of their minds . . .', *Reading Mercury*, 17 Oct. 1768.
2. *York Courant*, 13 Mar. 1739; *Western Flying Post*, 4 Feb. 1793.
3. *Kendal Weekly Mercury*, 3 May 1735, 6, 17 Nov. 1739, 12 Apr. 1740, 11 Apr., 30 May 1741, 26 Sept. 1747; *Cirencester Flying-Post*, 25 Oct., 15 Nov. 1742. All advertisements in the *Reading Mercury* of 21 Feb. 1737 were for printed matter. C. W. Chilton, *Early Hull Printers and Hull Booksellers* (Hull, 1982), p. 118.
4. Cranfield, *Provincial Newspaper*, p. 233; P. S. Brown, 'The vendors of medicines advertised in eighteenth-century Bath newspapers', *Medical History*, 19 (1975); Brown, 'Medicines advertised in eighteenth-century Bath newspapers', *Medical History*, 20 (1976).
5. *Old England*, 27 Dec. 1746.
6. Flysheet, 8 Apr. 1749, Kendal Library.
7. R. B. Walker, 'Advertising in London Newspapers, 1650–1750', *Business History*, 15 (1973), pp. 120, 123; Cranfield, *Provincial Newspaper*, p. 210.
8. S. M. Bosher, 'Three Years of the *Newcastle Courant*', *Direction Line*, 5 (1977), p. 19.
9. 17 July: 3, 28 Aug.: 4, 13 Nov.: 7.
10. *Darlington Pamphlet*, 19 June 1772. Black, 'Eighteenth-Century Journalism in the North-East: the *Darlington Pamphlet* of 1772', *Durham County Local History Society Bulletin* (forthcoming).
11. *York Courant*, 2 Jan. 1776; *Bristol Gazette*, 24 Dec. 1767. For Yorkshire advertisements in the Newcastle press, *Newcastle Courant*, 2 Mar., 6 Apr. 1734, *Newcastle Journal*, 7 Apr. 1739, and an assumed Yorkshire readership, *North Country Journal*, 6 Mar. 1736. For Staffordshire and Flintshire advertisements in the Chester press, *Adam's Weekly Courant*, 15 Nov. 1738. Advertisements for bleaching of linen in Roxburghshire and for Manchester races, *Newcastle Journal*, 26 Apr., 3 May 1740.
12. *Gazetteer*, 11 Aug. 1770, 12 adverts/53 per cent of front page.
13. I. S. Asquith, *James Perry and the 'Morning Chronicle' 1790–1821* (unpublished PhD thesis, London, 1973), p. 331.
14. *Gazetteer*, 10 Sept. 1789.
15. The Junius letter reprinted in the issue of *Berrow's Worcester Journal* of 28 Dec. 1769 did however occupy 33 per cent of the issue.
16. R. Cave, 'Printing in Eighteenth-Century Jamaica', *Library*, 5th ser., 33 (1978), p. 194.
17. *Daily Journal*, 24 Jan. 1721; *Mist's Weekly Journal*, 22 May 1725, 14 May 1726.
18. *Craftsman*, 2 Mar. 1728.
19. *Fog's Weekly Journal*, 14 Feb. 1736; *Comedian*, Aug. 1732; *Norwich Mercury*, 13 Oct. 1733.
20. *Reading Mercury*, 29 Apr. 1776, 6 Aug. 1781; *Westminster Gazette*, 28 Dec. 1776.
21. The most valuable work on this is McKendrick, Brewer, Plumb, *Consumer Society*; *Owen's Weekly Chronicle*, 22 July 1758.
22. *Public Advertiser*, 26 June 1753, 4 Nov. 1768; *Citizen*, 20 Apr. 1757.

23. *General Advertiser*, 16 Aug. 1777.
24. J. Feather, 'The English Book Trade and the Law', *Publishing History*, 12 (1982), p. 54. It was difficult to 'determine what is one advertisement, or more', *Newcastle Courant*, 23 Feb. 1788.
25. Cranfield, *Provincial Newspapers*, p. 225; Walker, 'Advertising', *Business History*, p. 119; Bond, *Spectator*, I, lxx.
26. *Daily Courant*, 5 Sept. 1734; Bond, *Spectator*, I, lxx.
27. *London Evening Post*, 30 Mar. 1762.
28. *Colchester Journal*, 15 Sept. 1739. For Barbados citron-water, *London Mercury*, 11 Feb. 1721.
29. *Newcastle Chronicle*, 24 Mar. 1787; *World*, 9 Nov. 1791. For the inaccurate announcement of the letting of a tithe and glebe in Hampshire, *Reading Mercury*, 10 Feb. 1772.
30. *Craftsman*, 1 May 1727, 13 Sept. 1729; *Public Advertiser*, 4 Feb. 1767.
31. *Reading Mercury*, 15 Oct. 1781.
32. J. F. Quinn, *Political Activity in Yorkshire, c. 1700–1742* (unpublished M.Litt dissertation, Lancaster, 1980), p. 410; *Post Boy*, 17 Nov. 1722; *Reading Mercury*, 11 Jan. 1768, 12 Feb. 1776; *Western Flying Post*, 3 Sept. 1792.
33. *York Courant*, 20 Oct. 1741; *Reading Mercury*, 11, 18 Jan. 1768, 19 Feb. 1776, 2 Oct. 1780; *Jackson's Oxford Journal*, 11, 18 Nov. 1775.
34. Mr Davidson to Duke of Northumberland, 14 June, W. Charleton to Duke, 25 June 1786, Alnwick Castle, Y.V. Id.
35. Tilson to John Chetwynd, Envoy Extraordinary in Turin, 2 Nov. 1711, Stafford, CRO. D 649/8/7/14.
36. *Daily Post Boy*, 18 Mar. 1730.
37. *Public Register*, 3 Jan. 1741; *Idler*, 20 Jan. 1759.
38. I owe this information to the kindness of Jonathan Barry. For the advertising of tithes to let, *Newcastle Journal*, 7 Apr. 1739; *Berrow's Worcester Journal*, 7 June 1770. E. C. Black, *The Association. British Extraparliamentary Political Organization 1769–1796* (Cambridge, Mass., 1963), p. 270.
39. St John's College, Oxford, Rawlinson Mss. 268, 10, 18, 20 May, 25, 26 July, 19 Nov., 23 Dec. 1727, 24 Feb. 1728, 11 Sept., 4 Nov. 1732, 20 June 1735.
40. *York Courant*, 17 Mar. 1747; *London Chronicle*, 17 Jan. 1788.
41. Robe's proposal, 17 Mar. 1727, CUL. C(H) Mss. papers 75/la.
42. *Review*, 14 May 1709; *Cirencester Flying-Post*, 15 Mar. 1742.
43. F. Martin, *The History of Lloyd's* (1876), pp. 65–76; C. Wright and C. E. Fayle, *A History of Lloyd's* (1928), pp. 21–4; Snyder, 'Circulation', p. 213.
44. *Supplement*, 4 Jan. 1716; *Daily Gazetteer*, 12 Apr., 11 Oct. 1737; *Evening Mail*, 3 Jan. 1791; *Daily Advertiser*, 9 Oct. 1744; *Public Advertiser*, 26 June 1753; *Oracle*, 24 July 1795.
45. Such as the account of a fur-trading voyage to eastern Labrador in the *Darlington Pamphlet* of 4 Sept. 1772.
46. *Darlington Pamphlet*, 19, 26 June, 3, 10 July 1772.
47. *Newcastle Courant*, 26 Apr. 1788.
48. *Newcastle Chronicle*, 24 Mar. 1787.
49. *Reading Mercury*, 2 Sept., *Newcastle Weekly Mercury*, 2 Feb. 1723.
50. *Newcastle Courant*, 4 May, 1, 8, 15 June, 6, 13 July, 31 Aug. 1728, 6, 13 Sept. 1729; *Original Mercury*, 3 Sept. 1728.
51. *Norwich Mercury*, 1 Jan. 1732; *Reading Mercury*, 21 Feb. 1737; *Pilborough's Colchester Journal*, 19 May 1739; J. Black, 'Grain Exports and Neutrality', *Journal of European Economic History* 12 (1983), pp. 593–8.
52. *Craftsman*, 24, 31 May 1740; *Newcastle Journal*, 17 May, 5 July 1740; *London Evening Post*, 30 Dec. 1740; *Jacobite's Journal*, 23, 30 Jan., 27 Feb., 14, 28 May 1748.
53. *Newcastle Journal*, 19 July 1740.

54. *Cirencester Flying-Post*, 9 Jan. 1744.

55. *Oxford Gazette*, 9, 16 May 1757; *Public Advertiser*, 6 Jan. 1757; *Kentish Gazette*, 14 Dec. 1774.

56. *London Chronicle*, 18 Mar. 1762; *Newcastle Chronicle*, 17 Mar., 17 Nov. 1787; *St. James's Chronicle*, 7 Jan. 1796.

57. *Berrow's Worcester Journal*, 16 Jan. 1766; *Darlington Pamphlet*, 13 Nov., 26 June, 4 Sept. 1772; *Reading Mercury*, 1 Jan. 1770. For hints on killing crows and rats, *Berrow's Worcester Journal*, 25 Sept. 1766.

58. *Newcastle Chronicle*, 15 Dec. 1787; *Newcastle Courant*, 15, 29 Mar. 1788; *Sheffield Advertiser*, 4 June, 26 Mar., 23 Apr. 1790.

59. *Darlington Pamphlet*, 30 Oct., 4 Sept. 1772; *Newcastle Chronicle*, 19 May 1787; *Leeds Mercury*, 24 Jan. 1795; *Oracle*, 24 July 1795.

60. *Newcastle Courant*, 20 Aug., 3, 10 Sept. 1743; Cranfield, *Provincial Newspaper*, p. 257; *Westminster Journal*, 30 Mar. 1771, 18 Jan. 1772.

61. J. Money, *Experience and Identity. Birmingham and the West Midlands 1760–1800* (Manchester, 1977), pp. 54–6.

62. *Farley's Bristol Newspaper*, 27 May 1727; *Pilborough's Colchester Journal*, 5 May 1739; *Cirencester Flying-Post*, 17, 31 May 1742, 11 July 1743.

63. *Leeds Intelligencer*, 8, 15 July, 5 Aug., 23 Sept. 1766; *Oxford Gazette*, 14 Feb. 1757, 18 May, 26 Oct. 1767; *Reading Mercury*, 15 Jan., 23, 30 Apr., 7 May, 3 Sept., 5 Nov., 31 Dec. 1770, 25 Feb., 11 Mar. 1771, 3 Feb. 1777, 25 Apr. 1785; *Leeds Intelligencer*, 2 Mar. 1790; *London Evening Post*, 6 Jan. 1778; *Berrow's Worcester Journal*, 17 Apr. 1766; *Sheffield Advertiser*, 21 Sept. 1792.

64. *Leeds Intelligencer*, 6 May 1766.

65. *Leeds Intelligencer*, 14 Oct., 18, 25 Nov. 1766, 8 Sept., 3 Nov. 1767; *Westminster Journal*, 17 Sept. 1774.

66. *Leeds Intelligencer*, 25 Nov. 1766; *London Evening Post*, 20 Feb. 1762.

67. *Public Advertiser*, 19 Jan. 1757; *Oxford Gazette*, 11 May, 1 June 1767; *Reading Mercury*, 11 Jan., 13 June 1768.

68. *Reading Mercury*, 30 Sept., 7 Oct., 4 Nov. 1771.

69. *Berrow's Worcester Journal*, 13, 27 Feb., 28 Aug., 4, 11, 18, 25 Sept., 6, 13 Nov. 1766.

70. *Berrow's Worcester Journal*, 18, 25 Sept., 9 Oct. 1766; A. J. Randall, 'The Gloucestershire Food Riots of 1766', *Midland History*, 10 (1985), pp. 74–5, 88.

71. *Reading Mercury*, 16 Oct., 6 Mar. 1769.

72. *Evening Post*, 21 May, 13, 15 Oct. 1720; *Whitehall Evening Post*, 31 Dec. 1720, 3, 5, 7 Jan. 1721, 20 Jan., 10 Mar. 1722; *Public Advertiser*, 8 Apr. 1773; *Morning Chronicle*, 11, 10 Apr. 1787; *Leeds Intelligencer*, 3 Nov. 1767.

73. *St. James's Evening Post*, 15 Feb. 1729; *Leeds Intelligencer*, 9 Sept. 1766; *Oxford Gazette*, 25 May 1767.

74. Bennett journal, 27 Oct. 1785, Oxford, Bodleian Library, Ms. Eng. Misc. f. 54.

75. Lowther to John Spedding, his Whitehaven agent, 3 May, 8, 10 Nov., 13 Dec. 1740, Carlisle, Cumbria RO. D/Lons/W.

76. *Reading Mercury*, 23 May 1768; *Berrow's Worcester Journal*, 11 Feb. 1768; *Lloyd's Evening Post*, 1 July 1768; E. Hughes, *North Country Life in the Eighteenth-Century. The North-East, 1700–1750* (1952), p. 176; *Newcastle Chronicle*, 10 Feb., 10 Mar., 26 May, 17 Nov. 1787; *Newcastle Courant*, 22 Mar. 1788.

77. *Morning Chronicle*, 1 Jan. 1787; *Newcastle Chronicle*, 27 Jan., 24 Feb. 1787; *Newcastle Courant*, 29 Mar., 19 July 1788; *London Chronicle*, 10 Jan. 1792; *Berrow's Worcester Journal*, 16 Jan. 1766.

78. *Adam's Weekly Courant*, 27 Dec. 1738; *Leeds Intelligencer*, 24 Feb. 1789.

79. *Pilborough's Colchester Journal*, 3 Feb. 1739; *London Mercury*, 11 Feb. 1721; *Newcastle Journal*, 5 Jan. 1740; *York Herald*, 9 June 1792.

80. *Leeds Mercury*, 18 Oct. 1726; *Newcastle Courant*, 20 July 1728, 21 Aug. 1731; *Berrow's Worcester Journal*, 16 Jan. 1766.

81. *Cirencester Flying-Post*, 15 Mar. 1742; *Newcastle Chronicle*, 27 Oct. 1787.

82. *Darlington Pamphlet*, 17 July 1772; *Newcastle Chronicle*, 20 Jan., 7 Apr., 18 Aug. 1787.

83. *Stamford Mercury*, 21 June 1716; J. Wallace to Honoured Madame, 10 May 1727, Gosforth, Northumberland CRO. ASW/10/24/6.

84. *Newcastle Chronicle*, 20 Jan., 24 Nov. 1787; Duke of Newcastle, Secretary of State for the Southern Department, to Lord Harrington, his Northern counterpart, 23 June 1732, PRO. 43/82, enclosing *Daily Courant* of 19 June; *London Chronicle*, 25 Dec. 1762.

85. *Pilborough's Colchester Journal*, 3 Feb. 1739.

86. *Darlington Pamphlet*, 26 June, 10 July 1772; *Reading Mercury*, 29 June 1772.

87. *Spectator*, 3 Mar. 1711.

88. *St. James's Post*, 8 Oct. 1718; *Newcastle Courant*, 13 Sept. 1729.

89. *Newcastle Chronicle*, 16 June, 27 Oct., 10 Nov. 1787.

90. *Corn Cutter's Journal*, 8 Jan. 1734.

91. Brigadier Warring to William Leathes, 13 Aug. 1723, Ipswich, East Suffolk CRO. HA 403/1/3.

92. *London Evening Post*, 30 Mar. 1762; M. Morineau, *Incroyables gazettes et fabuleux métaux. Les retours des trésors americains d'après les gazettes hollandaises* (Cambridge, 1985).

93. *Colchester Journal*, 22 Sept. 1739.

94. *Colchester Journal*, 1 Sept. 1739; *Newcastle Courant*, 2 Feb. 1788.

95. *Newcastle Courant*, 2 Feb. 1788; *Sheffield Advertiser*, 11 June 1790; *Reading Mercury*, 26 Oct. 1788; *Leeds Intelligencer*, 28 Nov. 1786; *Berrow's Worcester Journal*, 23 Jan. 1766; *Newcastle Courant*, 5 Jan., 3 May 1788; *Darlington Pamphlet*, 30 Oct. 1772; J. Styles, 'Sir John Fielding and the Problem of Criminal Investigation in Eighteenth-Century England', *Transactions of the Royal Historical Society*, 5th series, 33 (1983), pp. 127–49.

96. *St. James's Evening Post*, 20 Mar. 1722; *Derby Mercury*, 25 May 1732; *Darlington Pamphlet*, 4 Sept. 1772; *Reading Mercury*, 2 May 1774; *Newcastle Chronicle*, 17 Feb. 1787.

97. *Pilborough's Colchester Journal*, 4 Nov. 1738, 10 Feb. 1739; *Darlington Pamphlet*, 17 July 1772.

98. *Leeds Mercury*, 8, 15 Aug. 1738; *Newcastle Journal*, 10 May 1740; *Cirencester Flying-Post*, 23 May 1743; *Darlington Pamphlet*, 4 Sept. 1772.

99. *Reading Mercury*, 18 May 1767, 16 Apr. 1770, 9 Apr. 1781.

100. *Original Mercury*, 9 Jan. 1728; *Newcastle Journal*, 26 Apr. 1740; *Berrow's Worcester Journal*, 23 Oct. 1766; *Reading Mercury*, 17 Feb. 1777; *Newcastle Chronicle*, 28 Apr. 1787; *London Chronicle*, 12 Jan. 1788.

101. *Pilborough's Colchester Journal*, 4 Feb., 24 Mar., 20 Apr., 26 May 1739; *Darlington Pamphlet*, 3 July, 13 Nov. 1772; *Adam's Weekly Courant*, 27 Dec. 1738.

102. *Northampton Mercury*, 9 July 1739.

103. *Reading Mercury*, 10 May 1773.

104. *Mist's Weekly Journal*, 14 May 1726; *Original Mercury*, 2 July 1728.

105. Essex to his agent Thomas Bowen, 26 Aug. (ns) 1735, BL. Add. 60837.

106. *Reading Mercury*, 21 June 1773, 17, 24, 31 July 1775. For a letter on walking for wagers, *London Chronicle*, 16 Feb. 1788.

107. *Berrow's Worcester Journal*, 6 Feb. 1766.

108. *Weekly Register*, 11 Apr. 1798.

4 Sources and Distribution; Cost and Circulation

We have given such a variety of accounts in our late papers, relating to the affairs of Persia, Turkey and Russia, that our readers have great reason to suspect they are of our own coining, unless we inform them, that we have faithfully transmitted to them the freshest advices we receive and the most credible.

Freeholder's Journal, 20 February 1723

Sources

Time, which is always the greatest enemy of news mongers, is the bright testimony which stands on the side of an historian. Newswriting consists in gleaning up as many paragraphs as possible, consistent or inconsistent, from the fruitful harvest of scattered reports, dated at such a time, and from such a place; whose mushroom credit sprouts this evening and dies before that hour next morning.

Weekly Medley, 17 October 1717

The major source of press reports was items in other newspapers. London newspapers took a lot of information from foreign and other London newspapers; provincial papers borrowed from their London colleagues. In 1787 one London paper, the *World*, claimed, 'If the admirers of The WORLD, who look into our paper one day, will take the trouble of looking into other papers on the following days, they will find our matter and intelligence copied into all.' However, the situation was not simply one of little fleas feeding off greater ones. All newspapers were part of a far from enclosed system of information in which they, in common with printed matter, such as books and magazines, and unprinted matter, such as newsletters and merchants' correspondence, served as common sources. Newspapers took material from magazines and vice versa. In 1744 'at the request of a great many of our readers' the *Newcastle Courant* reprinted from the *Gentleman's Magazine* George Berkeley's praise of the therapeutic virtues of tar water. On 2 January 1798 the *Morning Post* printed an extract of a pamphlet on taxation published the previous day. London newspapers reprinted items from the provincial press, though only to a limited extent compared to the reverse procedure. Under the headline 'Country News', the *Middlesex Journal* reported in 1769 the discovery of a Roman coin in York. In 1788 the *London Chronicle* inserted a piece concerning the use of coloured glass for the frosting of cakes 'from one of the country papers, as we conceive it to be very interesting, and a matter of most serious importance'. The lengthy article in the *Oracle*, a leading London paper, of 2 February 1795 on the effects of thaw and frost in the various regions of the country was presumably drawn from the provincial press.[1] Foreign newspapers took material from London newspapers and newsletters. The flow of information and opinion was varied and relatively unstructured.

A major source of foreign news was foreign newspapers, particularly the French-language Dutch papers which benefited from the relatively unconstrained nature of the press in the federal United Provinces and from an excellent network of informants that owed much to the Huguenot diaspora. French and Dutch works were freely available in London in Queen Anne's reign,[2] and were probably available in other towns, though there is an absence of reliable information on the subject. Hooke's *Oracle* stressed its direct access to Dutch newspapers, presumably implicitly criticising the other Bristol papers: 'Monday's post brought us the Amsterdam Gazette . . . with the following advices.' The *Oracle* was closely linked with the St Michael's coffee-house 'where the original foreign Gazettes from which our intelligence is taken with their English translations, may be seen'. James Payzant, a clerk in the office of the northern Secretaryship of State, was asked in 1742 to forward the *Gazette d'Amsterdam* to a Derbyshire reader.[3] Some, but not all, papers acknowledged debts to foreign newspapers, the *Exchange Evening Post* of 1721 mentioning the *Amsterdam Courant*, *Amsterdam Gazette*, *Hague Courant* and *Leyden Gazette*.[4] Similar reports often appeared in several papers, suggesting a common unacknowledged source.[5] Some papers acknowledged a foreign source for items other papers reprinted without acknowledgement.[6] Foreign papers were not solely used as a source of political news. The *Daily Gazetteer* began an essay on politeness in 1735 with the notice,

> To render our paper still more generally entertaining, we shall sometimes make a digression from politics, and insert essays on miscellaneous subjects. Accordingly, in the present want of foreign intelligence, we shall begin with the following remarks, taken from a paper called the Dutch Spectator . . . published at Amsterdam.[7]

Foreign reports were not accepted uncritically, and suggestions were made that some news credited as coming from abroad was in fact written in London.[8] The juxtaposition of contradictory accounts from foreign newspapers[9] encouraged caution in accepting their statements, and some foreign newspapers were regarded as anti-British.[10] In 1784 a London item in the *Reading Mercury* warned,

> The editors of English newspapers should be very cautious in copying articles, particularly accounts of the disposition of the country, from the Irish papers, the printers of which are exasperated by the late act respecting the press. They magnify a common tumult into a rebellion, and insinuate the most alarming hints on the slightest marks of dissatisfaction.[11]

The highpoint in borrowing from the foreign press occurred during the French Revolution and subsequent Anglo-French conflict, with lengthy quotations from French newspapers and British newspapers establishing agents at Dover in order to forward material. The services of translators were however required long before the decapitation of Louis XVI: Defoe served Mist in this capacity. The need to translate speedily probably helped to encourage the copying of articles from a few papers, particularly initially those that were established or written by foreigners, especially Huguenots such as Abel Boyer, J. De Fonvive, and Denis de Coetlogan. Samuel Buckley, who ran the *Daily Courant* and later the *Gazette*, was reputed to know Latin, French, Dutch and Italian, and to translate for the press. It would have been unrealistic to expect provincial papers to subscribe to and translate foreign papers when they could rely on the London press. Not of course that the latter was infallible, as the *London Chronicle* noted in 1762:

> The account in some of the papers last week (taken from the Amsterdam Gazette) of an attempt made by the English on the island of Eustatia with considerable loss, was owing to a mistake in the translation. Maritinco was the place meant to be attacked, and the news only came from Eustatia.[12]

Newspapers were keen to demonstrate that their sources were best. This was amply shown by the title of Wilkins's new paper of 1719, the *Thursday's Journal; with a weekly letter from Paris, and another from Genoa*. It announced, 'We have letters from Paris, Genoa, and Leghorn, written by English correspondents settled in those places, at our own expence, which is more than any author in the world ever had before, or any present writer whatsoever can pretend to.' Two years later the introduction to the *Daily Journal* claimed

> Nothing can be more tiresome than a perusal of all the papers, since, whoever has seen two or three of 'em, has seen them all . . . correspondence is chargeable, and though every one desires, yet has no one taken care to be better informed than his neighbour news-monger. They have built a superstructure upon a scanty foundation, and therefore we not only find the same news penned by different authors, but often the very same story, and almost *verbatim*, in one individual paper, in the several articles perhaps of Paris, Naples, Hamburg, Dresden and Rome; so that the poor reader . . . must take up with soup for breakfast, soup for dinner, soup for supper, and soup for breakfast again. That I might not be guilty on this common fault, I have taken care to settle as good a correspondence as possibly I could, and that not only abroad, but also within His Majesty's dominions, and especially at Edinburgh and Dublin.[13]

Wilkins's paper did not last, but the *Daily Journal* developed a reputation as a paper of 'good credit for its foreign intelligence . . . which has given the public many fine pieces of foreign correspondence, that we have not seen in any other paper, and which we presume therefore are not brought by the common vehicles'. In 1789 John Bell's new London daily, the *Oracle*, announced an exclusive foreign correspondent in Hamburg and that it had taken over 'the channels of intelligence' that had distinguished the foreign reporting of the *World*. In 1799 the *True Briton* claimed that it had 'opened new sources of information both in Ireland and on the Continent'.[14]

Aside from foreign newspapers and newsletters and plagiarism, the principal sources employed for foreign news were ship news, diplomatic reports, the correspondence of London merchants, accounts from travellers and items offered by foreign diplomats. When Thomas Robinson, the envoy in Vienna, wished to indicate the habitual unreliability of flying reports from the distant frontiers of Wallachia he compared them to 'ship news in England'.[15] Ship reports were reasonably uncontentious when it came to describing Italian antiquities or the effects of very cold air in the Bay of Honduras.[16] More serious were reports of political developments. Such reports were sometimes inaccurate, but newspapers were sceptical of unexpected news, whether it be a Spanish declaration of war on Portugal in 1718, French military preparations in 1723 or the surrender of Gdansk in early 1734.[17] War led to an increase in ship news: information about foreign naval movements,[18] dramatic accounts of conflicts with privateers,[19] and reports sent from British warships.[20] Particular coffee-houses, such as Lloyd's, often served as a transmission point for ship news, the *Oracle* of 11 February 1795 printing naval news that had been received at Lloyd's the previous day. Demand for foreign news naturally increased during wartime, and this presented problems for the press, particularly of the verification of news from a distance at a time when diplomatic and some commercial links were severed. The only means of verification was to wait for the next post, particularly as this was what the government had to do and as a result newspapers printed much material of whose accuracy they were uncertain.[21] The importance of ship news during the war with France in the 1790s led to the development by several newspapers of links with correspondents in Channel ports, particularly Portsmouth, Plymouth and Falmouth. These correspondents were unnamed, but were probably the named agents of the papers in the ports that were a notable feature of several newspapers in the period. The *Courier and Evening Gazette* of 3 January 1795 began a report of the likely capture of the Oporto convoy by the French, 'Our Falmouth Letter contains the following important intelligence, which was communicated to our correspondent by the captain of an Oporto ship.' One interesting aspect of ship news was that it did not correspond necessarily to the usual source for foreign news, London. Some reports appeared first in other seaports; Newcastle, in particular, often received items of Baltic and German news.[22] In 1743 news of a Swedish uprising was based on an Edinburgh report from a ship arriving at Leith from Sweden. Much of the American news published in the *Leeds Intelligencer* in 1781 was taken from the Liverpool press.

In his panegyric on the Royal Exchange, Addison had compared merchants to ambassadors and noted that the trading world was held together by 'a good correspondence'. This correspondence often served as a source of reports of foreign news, though the individual source was rarely named, whether it was the Barcelona merchant warning a Leeds correspondent in 1794 on the need for exporters to have consular certification or the Le Havre captain writing to an Edinburgh ship-owner on the absence of any grain shortage in coastal France in 1789.[23] The degree of credibility they received varied, but they could be preferred to other sources:

> The account of Savey-Bey-Oglou's being routed, and flying from his castle is certainly true; there being a great many letters to Turkey merchants in London, which came directly from Smyrna, that confirm that account; therefore the news which came by yesterday's Dutch mail, and published in the papers of this day, of the said Bey's gaining considerable advantage over the Turkish troops, is very old and stale, comes round about by Petersburg, and meets with no manner of credit.[24]

Count Watzdorf, the Saxon Envoy Extraordinary in London, was inclined to believe the report of the signature of an Anglo-Austrian treaty at Vienna in 1731 because it was based on letters several substantial merchants had received from their Viennese correspondents. He informed Augustus II of Saxony-Poland that merchants often discovered the news first because they spared no expense to ascertain it and were often compensated by the impact of this news on the public funds. The merchants' information was accurate but premature in 1731. George II's speech to Parliament in January 1734 was speedily printed in the Amsterdam press thanks to being transmitted by express to the local stockjobbers.[25] Such information, true or false, permitted stockjobbing. The fabrication of news in Change Alley in order to influence the funds was frequently alleged in the press. Mist referred to 'our stockjobbing politicians, who can throw 40,000 men aboard of a fleet and land them in the heart of the Kingdom before the Government can raise a man to oppose them'.[26] Specific instances of attempts to influence the press for stockjobbing purposes are harder to discover, though accusations were frequent.[27] In 1787 false reports of French troops marching towards the United Provinces were spread.

Because of the availability of diplomatic archives more information survives of the role of diplomats in supplying material.[28] The British ministry could also be a source of information about foreign countries. Particularly significant in this context was the *Gazette*. This was the most widely circulated newspaper in 1705–7, but thereafter there was a decline, sales dropping in 1717 to what has been termed 'a mere 2,500', though that was still probably far greater than the circulation of most other newspapers. Ragnhild Hatton revised the suggestion that 1714 constituted a last attempt to get more regular and more vital news for the *Gazette* to 1718. The general impression is therefore that the *Gazette* became insignificant in the late 1710s and there has been no detailed study of it later in the century to enable a revision of this view.[29] In fact it is apparent from the diplomatic papers that further attempts were made by the ministry to ensure regular reports by diplomats for the benefit of the *Gazette*.[30] Diplomats obliged.[31] Nevertheless the appeal of the *Gazette* was not what it had been in the 1710s. In 1723 Tilson referred to Buckley's 'consumptive gazette', and feared that 'his gazettes will be for old women, large letters, to be read without spectacles'.[32] Buckley had to badger Delafaye for material for the *Gazette*, complaining of 'the greatest want of materials'.[33] In 1729 Delafaye wrote that 'one of our common newspapers, I think the *St. James's Evening Post*' had the same information as the *Gazette*, which made the latter 'less outshine the rest of those papers'.[34] In 1769 Lord Weymouth, Secretary of State for the Southern Department, appealed to British diplomats to send material, because the reputation of the *Gazette* was sinking and the sale contracting on account of the small amount of foreign news supplied.[35]

As diplomats often knew no more than what was in the press,[36] and as other newspapers developed their foreign sources it was not surprising that the *Gazette* did not enjoy a monopoly of foreign news. It may also have suffered from its style, described accurately as 'laconic' in 1730, and from its avoidance of interpretative material. A journal of brief items, accounts of ceremonies and notices, it presented material favourable to the ministry, such as addresses supporting the American policy of the government in 1776,[37] but not in any persuasive or argumentative fashion. 'Nothing ever offensive in our *Gazette*' observed Horatio Walpole in 1737, and Charles Townshend noted in 1758 that it was habitually 'an authentic paper of government, designed to check the intelligence of other papers'.[38] As such it suffered from a concentration of government efforts, particularly in financing, employing talented writers and expanding circulation, on more provocative ministerial papers. Its concentration on foreign news had detrimental effects when peace caused a slackening of interest in this sphere. Nevertheless the continued role of both regular and extraordinary issues of the *Gazette* in providing information for other newspapers is notable. It was of particular value in wartime,[39] when reports disseminated by competing powers encouraged reliance on the *Gazette*.[40] In 1781 the publication of the *Reading Mercury* was delayed and advertisements omitted due to the wish to include material from the *Gazette*. The non-arrival of the *Gazette* in the London post was often reported in the provincial press.[41]

The *Gazette* also served for the publication of notices and as a journal of record. It could be used to print notices to officers to repair to their posts in 1719, to deny reports of a Spanish attack upon Gibraltar the following year and to provide information on the progress of the plague in France in 1721. It could equally serve to refute denials of the death of the Duke of Orleans in 1723, to provide information for ministerial newspapers, such as the *True Patriot* in 1746, and to warn about cattle distemper the same year. It was used as a source of material for accounts of ceremonies and lists of bankrupts.[42] It was clearly read widely. The Scottish divine Robert Wodrow was put out by the *Gazette* not being free from the false reports about the Glasgow riots of 1725 found in the rest of the English press. In 1728 the York readers of the *Original Mercury* were referred for an account of a royal ceremonial to the *Gazette*. The *Sherborne Mercury* and the *Salisbury Journal* arranged relays of messengers to convey the *Gazette* to their offices. Fielding's fictional Mrs Western read and expounded the paper to Parson Supple. The Elector of Bavaria had it sent regularly to Munich in 1788. *Berrow's Worcester Journal* referred in

1766 to public disquiet that the *Gazette* did not contain a renewal of the prohibition on the export of corn.[43] The *Gazette* did not therefore retain the prominence it had enjoyed in the 1700s, but it cannot be ignored as a significant source of material for the rest of the press.

The correspondence of individuals other than merchants also played a role in the provision of foreign news. Travellers were cited as sources, as were soldiers fighting abroad. In 1787 the *Leeds Mercury* printed a letter on the Dutch civil war 'just received by a gentleman in York, from a person of distinction in Holland'.[44] The Newcastle press often printed letters sent to individuals from relatives or correspondents abroad. In 1742 the *Newcastle Courant*, aware that the discovery of a new passage to the East Indies was 'look'd upon as very useful to the trade of England, as well as to all Europe', was certain that the printing of two 'letters from a gentleman on board one of the two ships that were sent to discover the said passage, will be satisfactory, as well as entertaining, to our readers'. The previous week a Newcastle item in the same paper had begun, 'According to a private letter from a bombardier in the British train of artillery in Flanders, it consists at present of . . .' Two years later it printed a letter from a correspondent on HMS *Rochester* in Leghorn to his brother in Whitehaven, and in 1745 a letter received in Newcastle from a correspondent at Fontenoy.[45] The *Whitehall Journal* received lengthy accounts from Switzerland in 1722 concerning religious disputes. Thus, whether the source was the Portuguese Ambassador or a strong report 'upon Change', there was no shortage of material, and it was often quicker than that provided by the ministry.[46] By modern standards sources were inadequately identified, all too many being like the report on Anglo-Russian relations in the *Leeds Intelligencer* of 22 February 1791 that began 'a letter just received at Hull from Petersburgh, says'. There was often controversy over the sources used, even if the paper did not claim correspondents in the afterlife as Mist did in 1728, but the large number of 'state whispers' in circulation in Europe made the task of reporting accurately a difficult one.[47]

Excusing himself for contentious items 'Doctor' Gaylard, an employee of Mist, claimed in 1722, 'The home news is generally taken from the publick papers, or sent in by correspondents.' These indeed seem to have been the principal sources of the press, though in addition the role of 'collectors of news' must be mentioned. Possibly Mist was referring to these when he claimed in 1722, 'I have my secretaries, my spies, and agents, and . . . also make use of informers for a better intelligence.' These news-gatherers probably forwarded 'town talk', hanging around coffee-houses and propounding particular political views. Edward King, arrested in 1717, was mentioned as having a correspondence with Jacobites in France; Jones, arrested the following year, was accused of forwarding a forged letter from a Secretary of State to the Spanish envoy. *Applebee's Original Weekly Journal*, which had attacked the use of rumour as a source in 1723, four years later condemned papers 'whose only excellencies consist in their pro- pagating, and improving, with art and subtlety, every factious story, and idle rumour, they can glean up in coffee-houses, and other places of public resort'. Delafaye noted in 1730, 'I have talked to our Whitehall letter man about his idleness in writing everything he has without better authority for it than towntalk, and he has promised me to be more cautious.'[48]

Borrowing material from other papers was commonplace. The provincial press was utterly dependent on it and newspapers could be delayed if the post from London was late. The sources cited were often extensive, the *Kentish Post* of 11 February 1742 mentioning ten, including the *Gazette*, London dailies and tri-weeklies and a London newsletter. Newsletters had been very significant as a source in the first four decades of the century, but the expansion of the press appears to have lessened demand for them and they were always an expensive product. The dominance in the 1730s of the pro-ministerial *Wye's Letter* within the field of the newsletter may have hastened their demise. Most provincial papers in the second quarter of the century had opposition sympathies and presumably therefore pre- ferred to reprint material from the *London Evening Post*, *Craftsman*, *Champion* and *Westminster Journal*, the staple sources for papers such as the *Cirencester Flying Post*. Initially newsletters had been more outspoken and less constrained by supervision, but this advantage over the newspapers was not apparent by the 1720s other than in the reporting of parliamentary news, which several magazines offered the following decade. In one sense newsletters, like the *Gazette*, were a victim of a growing sophistication in the rest of the press. However, while the *Gazette* benefited from the institutional support of government notices and diplomatic information, the newsletters were devoid of institutional support and heavily de- pendent on the life of their writers.

The layout of the provincial press reflected the importance of information from London. In most towns the London post arrived thrice weekly and the papers were divided into sections according to the days on which the post arrived. News in these sections was printed separately and there were only very occasional references from one section to another. The role of the posts encouraged the development of the London tri-weekly papers, called Evening Posts and produced on the post days. The posts left London in the evenings. These papers dominated the news in the provincial press, ousting the newsletters, a process that owed something to the vigour of the opposition *London Evening Post*, founded in 1727 and 'consecrated to the service of faction'.[49] The foreign news in the *Caledonian Mercury* of 16 April 1751 came from the *London, General* and *Whitehall Evening Posts*, while the *Ipswich Journal* of 2 January 1762 relied heavily on tri-weeklies. This dominance was not really shaken during the century, even though the despatch of posts from London became more frequent, as William Bingley pointed out when he launched his *Independent Chronicle; or, Freeholder's Evening Post* in 1769. In 1741 Ralph Allen renewed the farming of the posts on the understanding that the number of London post days for Cambridge, King's Lynn, Great Yarmouth, Bath, Bristol and Gloucester would increase from three to six. In 1787 John Palmer, who had recently inaugurated a mail-coach system, created a 'newspaper office' that made an everyday evening paper commercially plausible.

Correspondents were the other major source of domestic news. Newspapers solicited letters[50] and claimed to receive large numbers. The *Leeds Intelligencer* could not find room for all the accounts sent in of celebrations for George III's recovery.[51] Many took an essay form, but some provided items of information, such as the Durham colliery explosion and the Chester gaol escape reported in the *Leeds Intelligencer* in 1767. 'A private letter' to a Darlington gentleman, who presumably communicated it to the paper, brought news of the 1772 financial crisis in London, and a traveller going overland from Yorkshire to Edinburgh reported on popular unrest over corn exports in 1740. The account of a riot at Leicester against a new machine for spinning worsted carried by the *Leeds Mercury* in 1787 came from 'our informant', who had just left the town. Eight years later the paper's account of prices in North Yorkshire was based on a letter received from there by a Leeds merchant.[52] Newspapers did not accept everything that

they were sent, despite the claim made in 1761 by Lord Bute's
chief propagandist, Dr John Campbell. Items were often rejected
as excessively personal, poorly written or over-lengthy. In 1771 for
example the *Bristol Gazette* announced,

> We have received the piece signed *One of the Public*. — But as
> we desire not to have anything to do with the disputes between
> *Humanus*, *Spectator*, *Probus*, *etc* (it being vastly disagreeable to
> many hundreds of our country readers, who are totally un-
> acquainted with the affair) we hope the author will not take it
> amiss that its not inserted, as we constantly endeavour as much
> as possible to avoid entering into any personal dispute what-
> ever.

The *Morning Chronicle*, a London daily, listed fourteen letters
received in its issue of 8 January 1787, and seven items in that of 2
April 1787. In the former it stated, 'We do not think the subject
treated of by the writer who signs himself NO CYNIC fit for
discussion in a public newspaper, which is open to the perusal of
every beardless boy.' On 16 April 1787 it announced 'a variety of
essays, letters, etc. are unavoidably omitted for want of room',
and promised to print ten items as soon as possible.[53] However,
much material from correspondents was printed, ranging from a
humorous tale of Northumbrian mayhem caused by a woman
accepting three suitors to correction of a false report of a death by
suicide, from a song on the Earl of Rockingham attending York
races to a debate over the national debt.[54] What was unclear is
how far these items were genuinely independent. George Colman
described in 1763 a fictional encounter in Oxford with Mr Folio, a
St Paul's bookseller who asked him to supply 'a few occasional
paragraphs to send up to the Ledger, and Lloyd's Evening Post'.[55]
The two types of principal source were not even completely separate: at times readers drew attention to items in other papers.[56]

   The sources used by eighteenth-century papers reflected a newspaper world that was less sophisticated and less capitalised than
that of a century later. Borrowing from other newspapers and
using correspondents, even if the latter were paid by the line, was
substantially different from a developed system of particular
correspondents or agencies. The crucial differences were in the
reporting of foreign news by London and London news by provincial papers. Though individual correspondents, such as John

Bell of the *Oracle* who went to the Flanders front in 1794, were used, particularly in the coverage of the French Revolution, the practice at the end of the century was still essentially the same as that at the beginning. Newspapers relied on other papers, a cheaper, more comprehensive and not necessarily less reliable method. There were even occasional echoes of an earlier age. In 1734 the *Daily Post Boy* carried an item from Dublin on the death of the Duke of Berwick in the Rhineland:

> The account of the Duke of Berwick's death was preceded here, by something very uncommon; it having been publicly discoursed of as news on the sea coasts of Fingal, above 10 days before the pacquets arrival which brought the account of it, and is said to have been taken from the mouth of a kind of seer.[57]

Distribution

> For a considerable time past it has been sent express, and circulated at the same price and the same day that it is published in London, by agents purposely fixed, in the towns of Bath, Bristol, Portsmouth, Gosport, Oxford, Birmingham, Cambridge, Southampton, Isle of Wight, Winchester, Brighthelmstone etc. and great numbers are daily sold in all these places. This is the first time that a daily newspaper printed in London, has met with so extensive a circulation . . . will be extended . . . advertisements, news taken in at all places above.
> *General Advertiser, and Morning Intelligencer*, 16 August 1777

Sales were a crucial factor in the profitability of the vast majority of newspapers, the principal exception being certain essay-sheets launched for particular political campaigns, such as the *Old Whig*, *Patrician*, *Plebian* and *Moderator*, all published in 1719 during the controversy over the Peerage Bill. An extensive and dense distribution system was essential for permitting adequate sales. A certain number of newspapers were always purchased at the printing offices of the papers, which tended therefore to be near the centre of towns. The *Independent Chronicle* charged ½d less to those who called to collect it on the evening of production. The

General Evening Post simply noted in its colophon in 1743 that it was 'Sold by J. Roberts, in Warwick-Lane, where Advertisements and Letters of Intelligence are taken in'. To maximise the number of potential direct purchases provincial papers usually appeared on market day. Other methods of distribution involved cost and this presumably restrained the desires of some printers to extend the range of their circulation. Keen to secure a stable demand and some working capital newspapers encouraged subscribers, usually offering quarterly rates. The printer of the *Flying-Post* promised to regularly send it to readers who sent in their name and address, while the *York Courant* offered delivery in 1739 at two shillings a quarter. These papers could be delivered easily by the 'flat-cap couriers' referred to by one writer. Most towns were sufficiently small to enable swift delivery by messengers, who could also supply coffee-houses and other places of public resort. This could be supplemented by hawkers and by the newspaper shops which delivered in London in the early eighteenth century. The *Evening Post* announced in 1710 that it was sold 'by the Booksellers' and at 15 named London coffee-houses. In 1748 the *Remembrancer*, a weekly, referred purchasers to newsmen. Like the *Evening Post*, it said nothing about country sales. The *London Advertiser and Literary Gazette*, a new paper launched in 1751 that named agents in London, Oxford and Cambridge, asked potential readers to order it from 'any of the Hawkers'. In 1762 the *Gazetteer* opened a new distribution office in the eastern part of the City. Nine years later the *Middlesex Journal* asked potential subscribers 'either in Town or Country' to apply to the printer. Concerned about tardy delivery by its distributors and newsmen the recently launched *World* asked readers to provide information in 1787. Two years later the *Oracle* claimed that Bell's attempt to make 'the regular newsmen happy' by distributing the names of 700 'regular customers' had failed as they had sold many in the streets instead of delivering them. *Bell's Weekly Messenger*, a Sunday launched in 1796, was distributed by the 'horn boys', hawkers who added a horn to their customary accomplishments. The *Edinburgh Herald*, a triweekly, offered different rates in 1790 depending on whether it was collected, delivered in Edinburgh or sent out by post.[58]

There were several means of distribution outside the printing town, but they can be reduced to two types, those under the control of newspapers and those, such as the Post Office, when reliance had to be placed on others. Most provincial newspapers swiftly established a system of newsmen and agents who distributed the paper as widely as possible. These men, such as John Atkinson, the Alnwick barber, were also responsible for accepting advertisements. The *Reading Mercury* of 21 February 1737 named agents in Eton, Newbury, Basingstoke, Winchester and Salisbury. The *Sheffield Advertiser* named agents in 23 towns in 1761 and 19 in 1790. On 16 January 1773 the *Newcastle Journal* claimed that the circumference of its circulation area was nearly 600 miles. The *Manchester Weekly Journal* announced in 1724, 'All persons may have any small parcels carried to any town in Lancashire, Cheshire and Yorkshire, by my men, that carries the newspapers through these counties . . . at reasonable rates.' By 1798 the *Bury Post* had 53 agents. In 1787 the *Leeds Mercury* named agents in Leeds and 28 in other towns, six of which had more than one agent.[59] This system was not without its problems: agents could be difficult,[60] newsmen negligent, and the weather a frequent problem. In 1742 the printer of the *Cirencester Flying Post* announced,

> I am much obliged to those good-natured gentlemen who informed me of the negligence of the newsman in not constantly supplying them, and approve of the man they were pleased to send; I am determined that all my customers shall be punctually served, and shall take it as a favour if all gentlemen would do the same, when they are not served in any other news-man's walk.[61]

This distribution system was not the principal one employed by most London papers. Around London it was probably of considerable importance, although there is little information on this. In 1743 the *Universal Spectator* reported the arrest of John Moore for hawking unstamped newspapers 'about the towns of Deptford, Greenwich, Woolwich, Lewisham, Dartford, etc. He keeps several servants to serve such of these places as he does not serve himself'. The paper noted that his method was to 'carry many papers unstamped among a few that are stamped'. The *Gazetteer* announced in 1763 that it was 'delivered to any part of the Town or places adjacent'. The belated development of the press in Hertfordshire, Buckinghamshire, Bedfordshire and Surrey and its limited early development in Essex and west Kent can be attributed to the role of the London press in obtaining both readers and advertisements. Attempts to establish papers in Maidstone were very shortlived. Little is known about the distribution of London newspapers elsewhere in the country through local agents. Michael Harris has suggested that this was not widespread, though it is the case that particular provincial printers clearly acted in this capacity. The Nottingham printer, George Ayscough, advertised that he took in subscriptions 'for all the weekly and monthly papers'. Later in the century more efforts appear to have been made to ensure a rapid and wide circulation for the London press and in 1792 the proprietors of the *Gazetteer* even decided to open a circulation depot for the paper at Bath. The spurious *Star* had a Bath agent in 1789, the *Evening Mail* named one two years later and the *Oracle* had in 1795 Mr Dawson in Bath, 'who receives regularly by express, and distributes a very considerable number of this paper on the first day of its publication'. If they had agents outside London, playing a role in distribution, most papers appear to have had only a Bath agent. The *Courier* named agents where orders and advertisements were taken in Nottingham and Edinburgh, but it is not clear whether they played any role in distribution. In 1779 *Bingley's London Journal. A Weekly Political, Commercial, and Literary Paper* named country agents in Aylesbury, Lincoln, Worksop, Derby, Chesterfield, Sheffield, Manchester, Warrington, Liverpool, Chester, Berwick and eight Irish towns, the last reflecting family connections. It was also sold 'by all the news and pamphlet sellers, and penny postmen in and ten miles round London'.[62]

The majority of London papers reached the provinces through the Post Office, particularly as a result of the reduction of costs through the franking system. Members of Parliament and the six Clerks of the Roads at the General Post Office enjoyed free access to the postal system, a privilege that papers benefited from at a price. The *London Packet*, an evening tri-weekly, asked potential subscribers to send their addresses to the printer or to the Clerks of the Roads. The *Evening Mail* mentioned the newsmen and the Clerks in January 1791, as did *Lloyd's Evening Post*. In May 1796 *Bell's Weekly Messenger* promised delivery 'at any place within ten miles of London by the Penny-Post Letter Carriers and Newsmen, at Sixpence each, without requiring any additional expence on account of the express carriage out of town'. Not all papers were delighted with the service. In 1796 the *St. James's Chronicle* admitted frequent complaints from country readers about irregular delivery through the Post Office. The post was also used by provincial papers. In 1798 the *Iris, or Sheffield Advertiser* claimed that it was sent post free to any part of England, Scotland or Ireland. From about 1792 the Post Office provided free distribution of papers. The post was not without its problems for the opposition press as orders were sometimes given to restrict their circulation. In 1728 the *Craftsman* had to therefore advise readers to 'employ coachmen, carriers, watermen, etc. as best suits their convenience'. In 1797 the *Telegraph*, a London opposition paper, noted complaints that the Post Office had been altering addresses on papers sent through the post.[63] The role of the post was amply displayed in the title of a weekly of 1715, the *London Post . . . with room left to write into the country, without the charge of double postage*. Newspapers survive with endorsements revealing that they were sent through the post. White Kennett, the Dean of Peterborough, received the *Evening General Post* in 1716 whilst at his deanery. The newspaper itself revealed a curious geographical perspective, its title including a map that made the North of England smaller than the West Country and put London nearly half the way up England. The post also delivered London papers to distant corners of the country, Sir John Swinburne of Capheaton in Northumberland paying the Post Master for 'the news from London' in the 1740s. Papers were sent through the post not only by retailers but also by private individuals. In 1731 John Drummond, the London agent of the Earls of Morton, who dominated the Orkney Isles, sent Lord Aberdour 'the newspapers, which I desire you'll send to Coll. Charles and let him send it to Capt. Seaton, and let him send them to Mr. Ewing'. This was possibly a regular circulation network. Six years later Aberdour was sent the newspaper accounts of George II's good reception as he passed through the City of London, by his father George, Earl of Morton.[64] How far this resulted in a national readership for the London press is unclear. In 1731 the *Craftsman* was accused of possessing 'a murmuring trumpet, which blows a political rumour in a few minutes from Berwick to Cornwall'. Mist printed a vast estimate of his provincial readership in 1720.

Specific references to London papers being read elsewhere are not common. In 1720 the *Weekly Journal or, British Gazetteer* printed a letter that mentioned its being taken in several Buckinghamshire towns, and the *St. James's Weekly Journal* printed a letter from Devon that referred to its arrival there by the 'carrier'. Mist printed a letter from a Bristol reader in 1726 and the *St. James's Post* one from a Nottingham correspondent in 1717. The *General Evening Post* was referred to as a source of information for a Scottish earl in 1734, the *London Evening Post* as the only paper received in Carmarthen twenty years later.[65] However, the London press had less to offer than the provincial papers in some respects. The latter had lower delivery costs, and were as weeklies, cheaper. The provincial paper could summarise the views and information of several London newspapers, a function also performed by magazines. London magazines rather than London newspapers tended to advertise in provincial papers and provincial printers often served as the agents for these magazines.[66] The impact of the London press in the provinces was largely an indirect one, obtained through magazines and the provincial press. The increase in the space devoted to local news, a feature also of the American press,[67] did not lead to an abandonment of the practice of regularly reprinting a large amount of material from the London press, *Berrow's Worcester Journal* for example taking many items from the *St. James's Chronicle* in the late 1760s. The influence of London was often stressed by contemporaries, but eighteenth- century production and distribution technology and costs ensured that it was generally forced to operate through intermediaries.

Cost and circulation

Let the Stamp-Office be your Register, there let it appear how many readers he may be supposed to have.

Weekly Journal, 30 August 1718

It is a singular circumstance, but a real fact, that the Liberty of the Press, has grown stronger from every attack on it; and that the situation of news-papers has become more and more flourishing in proportion to the increase of the duties imposed on them. Like camomile, they have thriven by being trod upon; and in order to carry the weight of double taxes on their shoulders, they have risen from dry registers of common intelligence into the annals of history, politics, and literature.

Berrow's Worcester Journal, 9 November 1761

The circulation of the press increased during the eighteenth century. James Sutherland calculated the total weekly circulation in 1704 as 44,000 copies. Henry Snyder has calculated the comparable figure for the five weeks after the passage of the First Stamp

Act in 1712 as 67,000 or 78,000, and for five weeks in the summer of 1713 as 46,000,[68] an annual figure of 2,400,000. Snyder's figures, based on the stamp duties, are questionable as he admits. Much depends on the quantity of unstamped papers, while the oscillating nature of sales, both between and within the seasons,[68] induce further caution. The figures for newspaper stamps issued in 1750, 1760 and 1775 were 7.3, 9.4 and 12.6 million respectively. Samuel Paterson claimed in the *Templar and Literary Gazette* sales of 200,000 newspapers weekly in 1773, an annual sale of 10.4 million. Lutnick gave the average daily sale of all 17 London papers in 1775 as 41,615 and 45,422 for the same 17 in 1780, with annual figures of 15.2 and 16.6 million. He quoted a contemporary estimate made in 1782 of 25,000 papers published daily in London. Lord North claimed in 1776 that 12.23 million papers were sold annually. The average daily sale of London morning papers in 1794 was estimated at 1,500, an annual figure of 550,000. Seven million stamps were issued for London papers in 1801, 9 million for provincial.[69] The population of England and Wales was approximately 5.5 million in 1695, of Britain 7.75 million in 1750, 9.4 million in 1780 and 10.7 million in 1801. How many of these read the papers or were aware of their contents is unclear. Contemporary estimates both of the number of readers in the country and the number of readers per individual paper varied widely. Addison claimed twenty readers to every paper as a 'modest computation', a figure supported by Paterson, but others gave figures such as 5 and 40.[70] It is necessary to caution against the use of this multiplier that has been made by certain scholars and was made by some contemporaries, such as Paterson. To simply multiply the number of papers read by the multiplier and assume that this represents even approximately the total readership of the press is fallacious. Instead it is clear that some people read more than one paper. This is clear in the case of some subscribers. Thomas Pelham of Stanmer, spending the summer of 1726 at his Sussex seat, received more than one paper from London.[71] The complaints that were made about the overloading of coffee-houses with too many papers and of readers sated with news suggest that at least in that milieu one is dealing with individuals reading many newspapers. As from 1725 onwards most were only four pages long, and a certain number throughout the century were essentially two-page essays, it was not difficult to read several newspapers at one sitting. It is true that the absence of headlining would have hindered skimming, but readers not interested in advertisements or essays, most of which swiftly revealed their topics, could have read fast. Thus alongside those features of newspaper consumption that encouraged widespread dissemination, such as reading aloud, borrowing in places of public resort, circulating among friends and renting from hawkers, must be placed the suggestion that the increase in circulation was partly due to individuals reading more papers.

The circulation figures of individual successful papers did not rise as sharply as the general trend. Successful early eighteenth-century papers, such as the *Spectator, London Journal, Freeholder's Journal, Craftsman* and *Mist's Weekly Journal* could hope to sell between 8,000 and 12,000 copies per issue, figures rarely exceeded in the period 1760–90. In its issue of 4 April 1795 the *Leeds Mercury* claimed a circulation of 1,500, a figure no greater than that of a successful provincial paper 50 years earlier. Circulation was naturally affected by the ability to obtain particular scopes. *Wye's Letter* reported in 1730, 'The Daily Journal having published the mystery of the Freemasons, which it seems was found in writing among the papers of one of the brotherhood deceased, and people believing it to be genuine, several thousands of the said papers have been sold in this city and suburbs.' Henry Sampson Woodfall was able to sell more copies of his *Public Advertiser* when he obtained the letters of Junius. That daily commonly sold 3,000 copies before Junius was heard of,[72] and it is in the sphere of dailies that circulation figures altered. The prominent newspapers of the first half of the century were weeklies and tri-weeklies, and the dailies did not compare to those later in the century, which had, apart from anything else, more content and far more advertising to offer the reader.

Cost was probably a major factor restricting readership. The price of newspapers rose faster than the rate of inflation and they remained an expensive product, a situation exacerbated by the growth in the importance of dailies. The statistician Gregory King calculated in 1695 that a craftsman's family spent only ten shillings per head less than it earned during a year. In the mid-eighteenth century London bricklayers earned at best 21 shillings a week, while bodice-makers earned at worst seven. It was estimated in 1754 that a workman's lodgings in London would cost him one shilling a week, and his food a further five. The wages of a mason's labourer in London remained fixed at 2 sh a day for more than 50

years after 1731, and at Oxford the pay of a builder's labourer
stood at approximately 1sh 3d a day from 1700 to 1770. From 1700
to 1790 the daily rate of bricklayers, masons and plumbers in
London never fell below 2sh 6d or rose above 3sh. Ten shillings a
week was the normal wage of a furnace keeper in the north
Lancashire iron industry up to 1755. In the mid-1780s the normal
daily rate for unskilled workers was 12d in Lancashire, 14d in
Oxfordshire and 24d in London, and by the late 1780s, 20d, 16d
and 24d.[73]

Newspapers were therefore outside the pockets of many workers, particularly once successive Stamp Acts pushed their prices
up. Before the first Stamp Act of 1712 many newspapers cost 1d,
but thereafter many rose in price to a penny ha'penny, though the
Manchester Weekly Journal sold for 1d in 1724 and in London the
Penny Post: or, Tradesman's Select Pacquet appeared at the same
cost in 1717. The 1725 Stamp Act led most papers to increase their
cost to 2d, though some, such as the *Taunton Journal, Daily
Journal, Daily Advertiser, Champion, General Advertiser,
Cirencester Flying-Post* and *General Evening Post* continued at a
penny ha'penny. Weeklies tended to stick to 2d, the price charged
by Mist, who definitely sought a popular style, and Fielding's *True
Patriot* was untypical in costing 3d in 1745. The Stamp Act of 1757
led most papers to increase their price to two pence ha'penny,
though the *London Evening Post* delayed doing so until 1762. The
Monitor considered its price of 2d sufficiently attractive to carry
the notice 'Price Two-Pence' at its head throughout its life. The
North-Briton in contrast cost two pence ha'penny. The *Darlington
Pamphlet*, which attempted to evade stamp duty, only charged 2d
in 1772. In 1776 Lord North increased stamp duty, in order,
according to some commentators, to curtail the circulation of the
press.[74] Most papers increased their price to 3d, further increases
following in 1789 and 1797 when the tax was raised again so that
the newspaper stamp which had stood at a ha'penny for half a
sheet in 1712 and one penny ha'penny per paper in 1776 was three
pence ha'penny by late 1797. Duty was the principal cost of the
press, the financial margins of newspapers being too tight to
permit them to absorb increases, and successive increases in duty
led to higher prices for newspapers. In the case of the *Ipswich
Gazette*, which sold for 2d in 1725, the price rose to two pence
ha'penny in 1757, 3d in 1776, three pence ha'penny in 1789, 4d in
1792 and 6d in 1797. The *Leeds Intelligencer* increased its price to

3d in 1777, to three pence ha'penny in 1789, 4d in 1793 and 6d in 1797. Other papers, ranging from the *Times* to the *Hull Advertiser and Exchange Gazette* displayed similar changes. The *Morning Post and Gazetteer* carried a notice in 1798:

Price in 1783, 3d
Taxed by Mr Pitt, 3d   Price 6d.

How far circulation would have risen without duty is unclear. It would presumably have led to fewer newspaper failures such as those that followed the 1712 Act, and to more papers being founded, but it would not have prevented intense competition that would have produced serious financial pressures of its own. Illiteracy rates would have constituted an eventual constraint. However the major expansion in the press in the early nineteenth century suggests that eighteenth-century growth did not tap all the available readership, particularly outside London. It is rarely profitable for an industry to exist so that it taps all available demand. By depressing demand stamp duty may have served to encourage a situation of saturation in the market, particularly the metropolitan market, at certain junctures, as indeed did possibly competition between newspapers, the arrival of summer and the ending of wars.[75] Thus, particularly at the level of the individual newspaper, the picture was not necessarily one of a progressively increasing, still less profitable, market. Many proprietors could perceive through the hyperbole and rhetoric of the influence of the press, actual or deserved, the realities of competition or bankruptcy.

Notes

1. *World*, 12 Jan. 1787; *Newcastle Courant*, 23 June 1744; *Middlesex Journal*, 28 Oct. 1769; *London Chronicle*, 22 Jan. 1788.

2. M. Harris, 'Newspaper distribution during Queen Anne's reign. Charles Delafaye and the Secretary of State's Office', *Studies in the Book Trade* (Oxford Bibliographical Society, 1975), pp. 143–4. Dutch papers received information illegally from officials, James Dayrolle, Resident at The Hague, to Viscount Townshend, Secretary of State for the Northern Department, 18 Jan. (ns) 1729, PRO. 84/306.

3. *Oracle*, 12 June, 14 Aug. 1742; Richard Davenport to James Payzant, 14 May 1742, PRO. 36/58; *Devon RO*. 63/2/11/1/22.

4. *Exchange Evening Post*, 10 Feb. 1721; *Post Boy*, 7 Jan. 1720; *London Mercury*, 3 May 1722.

5. For a piece stating that Spain would not accept peace unless Gibraltar and

Minorca were returned to her, *London Evening Post*, 18 Mar., *Evening Post*, 18 Mar., *Post Man and Historical Account*, 18 Mar., *Daily Post Boy*, 18 Mar. 1729. Same Hague letter in *Whitehall, General* and *Evening Posts* of 12 July 1735. For complaints about plagiarism, *Post Boy*, 21 Sept. 1727, 7 May 1728; *London Evening Post*, 12 Dec. 1727, 16 Feb., 10 Aug. 1728; *Nonsense of Common-Sense*, 14 Feb. 1738; *Champion*, 10 Apr. 1740.

6. The Nantes murder in *St. James's Evening Post*, 21 May 1723 and *Weekly Journal*, 25 May 1723.

7. *Daily Gazetteer*, 24 Oct. 1735.

8. *Weekly Medley*, 8 Nov. 1718; *Champion*, 12 Apr. 1740.

9. *General Evening Post*, 7 Nov. 1734; *St. James's Chronicle*, 11 Apr. 1769. On contradictory reports, *Weekly Packet*, 16 Feb. 1717.

10. *London Chronicle*, 12 Jan. 1760. For an attempt to discredit the Dutch press, Mist to James Edgar, Secretary to the Pretender, 23 Jan. (ns) 1734, RA. 167/178.

11. *Reading Mercury*, 2 Aug. 1784; *Newcastle Journal*, 15 Aug. 1752.

12. *Weekly Journal*, 8 Nov. 1718; *London Chronicle*, 23 Mar. 1762.

13. *Thursday's Journal*, 10 Sept. 1719; *Daily Journal*, 24 Jan. 1721; *Craftsman*, 13 May 1727; *General Evening Post*, 4 Apr. 1734; *Newcastle Journal*, 2 Feb. 1754: London items of 17, 19 Jan. On the use of foreign correspondents, Asquith, *Perry*, pp. 18–22.

14. *Weekly Miscellany*, 7 July 1733, 2 Feb. 1734; *Oracle*, 5, 10 June 1789; *True Briton*, 1 Jan. 1799; *Owen's Weekly Chronicle*, 12 Dec. 1761; *Westminster Gazette*, 4 Jan. 1777.

15. Robinson to Harrington, 1 Nov. (ns) 1730, PRO. 80/69; Sir Charles Wager, First Lord of the Admiralty, to Admiral Norris, 1 Oct. 1734, BL. Add. 28156; Robert Trevor, Secretary of Embassy at The Hague, to Benjamin Keene, Envoy Extraordinary at Madrid, 17 Oct. (ns) 1737, BL. Add. 32796; Stanier Porten, Secretary of Embassy at Paris, to Lord Shelburne, Secretary of State for the Southern Department, 20 Aug. 1767, PRO. 78/273.

16. *Post Boy*, 13 Dec. 1718; *London Chronicle*, 19 Jan. 1788.

17. *Weekly Journal*, 22 Feb. 1718; *London Journal*, 16 Mar. 1723; *Newcastle Courant*, 2 Mar. 1734; *Worcester Post Man*, 21 Feb. 1734.

18. *Weekly Medley*, 9 Jan. 1720; *Newcastle Journal*, 30 Aug. 1740, 10 July 1742; *London Chronicle*, 23 Jan. 1762.

19. *Evening Post*, 22 Feb. 1711; *Newcastle Courant*, 10 Apr. 1742, 12 Dec. 1747.

20. *Whitehall Evening Post*, 11 Nov. 1718, 15 Jan. 1720; *Post Boy*, 7 Jan. 1720; *Newcastle Journal*, 15, 22 Mar., 10 May, 14, 21 June, 18 Oct. 1740, 28 June 1746; *Reading Mercury*, 31 July 1780.

21. *Reading Mercury*, 10 Nov. 1777; *Universal Spectator*, 31 July 1742.

22. *Newcastle Courant*, 31 July 1742, 2 July 1743.

23. *Spectator*, 19 May 1711; *Leeds Mercury*, 6 Sept. 1794, 21 July 1789; *Flying Post*, 15 Nov. 1718; *Mist's Weekly Journal*, 28 Aug. 1725; *Farley's Bristol Newspaper*, 24 June 1727; *Daily Post Boy*, 13 June 1735; *Daily Gazetteer*, 8 Apr. 1737; *Craftsman*, 15 Sept. 1739; *Newcastle Journal*, 20 Sept. 1740; *St. James's Chronicle*, 24 July 1800.

24. London item in *Northampton Mercury*, 30 Apr. 1739.

25. Watzdorf to Augustus II, 27 Mar. (ns) 1731, Dresden, Hauptstaatsarchiv, Geheimes Kabinett, Gesandschaften 2676 I. The treaty was signed on that day; Dayrolle to Harrington, 2 Feb. (ns) 1734, PRO. 84/338.

26. *Weekly Journal*, 16 Feb. 1717.

27. *Original Weekly Journal*, 22 Feb. 1718; *Manufacturer*, 25 May 1720; *Wye's Letter*, 30 Oct. 1722, 18 May 1727, 30 Apr., 1 July 1728, 7 Jan. 1731, 25 Aug. 1733, 3 Oct. 1734, 21 June 1739; *St. James's Evening Post*, 30 Mar. 1723; *Northampton Mercury*, 2 Dec. 1723; *London Journal*, 28 May 1726; *Mist's Weekly Journal*, 11 Mar. 1727; *Craftsman*, 13 May 1727; *Stanley's Letter*, 29 June 1728; *St. James's*

Evening Post, 1 Apr. 1729; John Couraud, Under-Secretary in the Southern Department, to Earl Waldegrave, Ambassador at Paris, 27 July 1739, Chewton; *Champion*, 8, 10 May 1740; *Newcastle Journal*, 22 Mar., 17 May 1740; *London Chronicle*, 18 May 1762, 17 Jan. 1788; *Berrow's Worcester Journal*, 30 Nov. 1769; Alexander Straton to Sir Robert Murray Keith, Envoy Extraordinary in Vienna, 7 Jan. 1783, BL. Add. 35527; *Western Flying Post*, 26 Dec. 1791.

28. *Post Boy*, 3 Sept. 1717; Count Gyllenborg, Swedish envoy in London, to Baron Gortz, Swedish minister, 4, 10 Nov. 1716, PRO. 107/1B; Count Bothmer, Hanoverian minister, to Lord Cadogan and Charles Whitworth, British envoys at The Hague, 9 Sept. 1718, BL. Add. 37369; Chavigny, French envoy in London, to Chauvelin, French foreign minister, 28 Aug. (ns) 1733, AE. CP. Ang. 381; De Löss, Saxon envoy, to Augustus III, 11 Jan. (ns) 1735; Charles Jenkinson to George Grenville, 9 June 1761, *Grenville Papers*, W. J. Smith (ed.) (4 vols., 1852–3), I, 363; Earl of Halifax, Secretary of State for the Northern Department, to Edward Weston, Under-Secretary and Writer of the *Gazette*, [17 Dec. 1762], Weston-Underwood; Baron Vieregg, Bavarian minister, to Count Haslang, Bavarian envoy in London, 24 Dec. 1778, 28 Feb. 1779, Munich, Bayerisches Hauptstaatsarchiv, Bayr. Ges. London 257.

29. Snyder, 'Circulation', pp. 216–19; Sutherland, 'Circulation', pp. 114–15; R. M. Hatton, 'The "London Gazette" in 1718: supply of news from abroad', *Bulletin of the Institute of Historical Research*, p. 108; P. M. Handover, *A History of the London Gazette, 1665–1965* (1965).

30. Circular letter from Lord Carteret, Secretary of State for the Southern Department, 11 Feb. 1723, draft copy, PRO. 92/31; Francis Colman, Secretary in Vienna, to Tilson, 4 Mar. (ns) 1724, PRO. 80/51; Weston to Robinson, 28 July 1728, BL. Add. 23802; Weston to Lord Tyrawly, Ambassador in St Petersburg, 16 Mar. 1744, BL. Add. 23630; Earl of Holderness, Secretary of State for the Northern Department, to Charles Hanbury-Williams, Ambassador in St Petersburg, 19 Aug. 1755, Newport, South Wales, Public Library, Hanbury-Williams papers.

31. John Molesworth, Envoy Extraordinary in Turin, to Carteret, 30 Mar. (ns) 1723, PRO. 92/31; Colman to Townshend, 17 Feb. (ns), 10 Mar. (ns), 7 Apr. (ns) 1723, 5 Apr. (ns), 31 May (ns), 28 June 1724, Colman to Tilson, 5 Sept. 1723, PRO. 80/51; Charles Holzendorf, secretary at The Hague, to Tilson, 2 July (ns) 1728, PRO. 84/301; Waldegrave to Townshend, 3 July (ns) 1728, PRO. 80/61; Waldegrave to Tilson, 22 Oct. (ns) 1729, Chewton; Tilson to Robinson, 14 July 1730, BL. Add. 23780; Abraham Castres, Consul at Seville, to Delafaye, 20 Oct. (ns) 1731, Keene to Delafaye, 23 Aug. (ns) 1731, PRO. 94/108; Colman, Resident in Florence, to Delafaye, 26 Apr. (ns) 1732, PRO. 98/84; Robinson to Weston, 28 Apr. (ns) 1736, BL. Add. 23853; Onslow Burrish, Minister to various German states, to William Chetwynd, Under-Secretary in the Northern Department, 23 May (ns), 10 July (ns) 1747, PRO. 81/96; George Aust, Senior Clerk in Northern Department and Deputy Writer of the *Gazette*, to Keith, 27 Oct. 1789, BL. Add. 35541.

32. Tilson to Delafaye, 1 Oct. (ns), 2 Nov. (ns) 1723, PRO. 43/5.

33. Buckley to Delafaye, undated, PRO. 35/65 f. 234, 35/68 f. 99, 115.

34. Delafaye to Tilson, 24 June 1729, PRO. 43/78; Aust to Keith, 27 Oct. 1789, BL. Add. 35541.

35. Handover, *Gazette*, p. 57; Edward Owen, printer of the *Gazette*, to Weston, 12 Mar. 1757, Weston-Underwood.

36. Harrington to Guy Dickens, Secretary at Berlin, 31 Aug. 1733, Dickens to Harrington, 6 Feb. (ns) 1734, PRO. 90/35–6.

37. Tilson to Robinson, 14 July 1730, BL. Add. 23780; *Newcastle Courant*, 3, 24 Feb., 11 May 1776; Horace Walpole, *Memoirs of King George II*, J. Brooke (ed.) (3 vols., 1985), II, 290.

38. Walpole to Trevor, 8 Apr. 1737, Aylesbury, Buckinghamshire CRO., Trevor papers, vol. 7; Townshend to mother, Viscountess Townshend, 1 Aug. 1758, BL. Add. 63079.

39. *Weekly Packet*, 29 Nov. 1718; *Whitehall Evening Post*, 15 Jan. 1720; *Daily Gazetteer*, 11 Aug. 1737; *Newcastle Courant*, 7 Aug. 1742, 1 Jan., 28 May 1743; Owen to Weston, 19, 20 May 1757, Weston-Underwood. For complaints about the *Gazette's* lack of domestic news in 1667, J. B. Williams, 'The newsbooks and letters of news of the Restoration', *EHR*, 23 (1908), p. 274.

40. *Gentleman's Magazine*, 40 (1770), p. 388.

41. *Reading Mercury*, 8 Jan., 6 Aug. 1781; *Newcastle Courant*, 23 July 1743.

42. Meeting of Lords Justices, 21 May 1719, PRO. 43/61; *Whitehall Evening Post*, 22 Sept. 1720; *Northampton Mercury*, 2 Dec. 1723; *Newcastle Courant*, 22 Mar. 1746, 2 Mar. 1776; *Reading Mercury*, 24 Feb. 1772; *York Herald*, 9 June 1792.

43. R. Wodrow, *Analecta* III (Edinburgh, 1842), p. 223; *Gazette*, 8 Oct. 1728; L. E. J. Brooke, *Somerset Newspapers 1725–1960* (no place, 1960), p. 10; H. Fielding, *Tom Jones*, R. Mutter (ed.) (1966), p. 264; Vieregg to du Fossey, Bavarian agent in London, 27 Aug. 1788, Munich, Bayr. Ges. London 261; *Berrow's Worcester Journal*, 18 Sept. 1766; *Bonner and Middleton's Bristol Journal*, 18 Sept. 1779.

44. *Leeds Mercury*, 10 July 1787, 11 Oct. 1794; *Post Boy*, 7 Sept. 1717; *Worcester Post-Man*, 6 May 1720; *Daily Universal Register*, 1 Feb. 1785.

45. *Newcastle Journal*, 19 Jan., 29 Mar., 26 July 1740; *Newcastle Courant*, 20, 27 Nov. 1742, 28 July 1744, 25 May 1745, 30 Apr., 9, 16 July 1743, 24 Feb., 10, 17 Aug. 1776.

46. *Whitehall Journal*, 20 Nov. 1722; *General Post Office Letter*, 18 May 1727; *Gazetteer*, 2 Sept. 1770; *Newcastle Journal*, 29 Mar. 1740.

47. *Craftsman*, 21 Oct. 1727; *Fog's Weekly Journal*, 28 Sept. 1728; Viscount Perceval to Daniel Dering, 19 Nov. (ns) 1725, BL. Add. 47031; Shelburne to the Earl of Rochford, Ambassador in Paris, 6 May 1768, PRO. 78/275.

48. Gaylard to Townshend, undated, PRO. 35/34 f. 161; *Mist's Weekly Journal*, 25 Aug. 1722; *Weekly Journal*, 9 Mar. 1717; *Original Weekly Journal*, 9 Mar. 1717; *Whitehall Evening Post*, 25 Sept. 1718; *Applebee's Original Weekly Journal*, 17 Aug. 1723, 9 Dec. 1727; Delafaye to Waldegrave, 19 Oct. 1730, Chewton; *Whitehall Evening Post*, 8 Nov. 1718.

49. *Owen's Weekly Chronicle*, 7 Oct. 1758, 12 Dec. 1761; *Daily Courant*, 5 Sept. 1734; G. A. Cranfield, 'The *London Evening Post*, 1727–1744', *Historical Journal*, 6 (1963), pp. 20–37.

50. *London Mercury*, 11 Feb. 1721; *York Courant*, 17 Mar. 1747; *St. James's Chronicle*, 1 Jan. 1801.

51. *Leeds Intelligencer*, 12 May 1789; *Westminster Journal*, 4 Dec. 1742.

52. *Leeds Intelligencer*, 7 Apr. 1767; *Darlington Pamphlet*, 26 June 1772; *Newcastle Journal*, 28 June 1740; *Leeds Mercury*, 11 Dec. 1787, 26 July 1795.

53. Brewer, *Party Ideology*, p. 224; *Bristol Gazette*, 18 Apr., 25 July 1771; *Leeds Intelligencer*, 24 June 1766; *Oxford Gazette*, 2 Feb. 1767; *Berrow's Worcester Journal*, 1 Feb. 1770; *Reading Mercury*, 8 Jan. 1776; *Newcastle Chronicle*, 24 Feb. 1787.

54. *Newcastle Chronicle*, 21 Apr. 1787; *Reading Mercury*, 23 Sept. 1776; *Leeds Intelligencer*, 3 Dec. 1765; *St. James's Post*, 6, 8 Mar. 1717.

55. *St. James's Chronicle*, 7 July 1763.

56. *Leeds Intelligencer*, 26 May 1767.

57. *Daily Post Boy*, 26 June 1734.

58. *Flying-Post*, 14 Dec. 1728; *York Courant*, 16 Jan. 1739; *Original Weekly Journal*, 1 Mar. 1718; *Evening Post*, 21 Jan. 1710; *London Advertiser*, 4 Mar. 1751; Haig, *Gazetteer*, pp. 53–4; *Middlesex Journal*, 1 Jan. 1771; *World*, 3 Jan. 1787; *Oracle*, 3, 4 June 1789; *Aberdeen Journal*, 5 Jan. 1748.

59. *Newcastle Courant*, 8 Jan. 1743; *Manchester Weekly Journal*, 1 Oct. 1724; A. Sterenberg, 'The spread of printing in Suffolk in the eighteenth century', in M. Crump

and M. Harris (eds), *Searching the Eighteenth Century* (1983), p. 38; *Leeds Mercury*, 10 July 1787.

60. *Leeds Mercury*, 15 Aug. 1738.

61. *Cirencester Flying-Post*, 16 Aug. 1742; Werkmeister, *London Daily Press*, pp. 256–7; *Evening Mail*, 5 Jan. 1791; *Oracle*, 29 Jan. 1795; *Courier*, 1 Jan. 1795.

62. *Universal Spectator*, 18 June 1743; Harris, *Newspaper Press*, p. 50; *Weekly Courant*, 18 Oct. 1739; Haig, 'Last Years', p. 249.

63. *St. James's Chronicle*, 14 Jan. 1796; *Craftsman*, 2, 30 Nov. 1728; *London Evening Post*, 31 Oct. 1754; *Telegraph*, 3, 12 Jan. 1797.

64. *Evening General Post*, 10 July 1716, copy in All Souls Library; Swinburne accounts, 27 July 1742, 28 June 1744, Gosforth, Northumberland CRO. ZSW 455; Drummond to Aberdour, 8 May 1731, Morton to Aberdour, 15 Jan. 1737, Edinburgh, Scottish Record Office, GD. 150/3476/11, 74; Ad. By A. Norman, *Westminster Gazette*, 7 Dec. 1776.

65. *Norwich Mercury*, 13 Mar. 1731, item from *Daily Courant*; *Weekly Journal*, 30 Jan. 1720; *Weekly Journal or British Gazetteer*, 2 Jan. 1720; *St. James's Weekly Journal*, 19 Jan. 1720; *Mist's Weekly Journal*, 4 June 1726; *St. James's Post*, 6 Mar. 1717; Earl of Haddington to Earl of Marchmont, 5 Feb. 1734, HMC. *Polwarth Manuscripts* V, 81; *Connoisseur*, 7 Mar. 1754; *St. James's Chronicle*, 22 Mar. 1764.

66. *York Courant*, 13 Mar. 1739; *Cirencester Flying Post*, 15 Mar. 1742. The preface to the *Gentleman's Magazine* of 1753 referred to many of our correspondents residing 'in remote counties'.

67. R. L. Merritt, 'Public Opinion in Colonial America: Content Analysing the Colonial Press', *Public Opinion Quarterly*, 27 (1963), pp. 361–2.

68. Sutherland, 'Circulation', p. 113; Snyder, 'Circulation', p. 215.

69. Snyder, 'Circulation', p. 215; I. R. Christie, *Myth and Reality in Late Eighteenth Century British Politics* (1970), p. 313; R. Rea, 'A Sour Note in the Hymn to Liberty: Samuel Paterson and "The Templar"', in D. H. Bond and W. R. McLeod (eds), *Newsletters to Newspapers: Eighteenth-Century Journalism* (Morgantown, West Virginia, 1977), p. 176; S. Lutnick, *The American Revolution and the British Press, 1775–1783* (Columbia, Missouri, 1967), pp. 2, 14; *Cobbett*, 18, 1320; A. R. Wadsworth, *Newspaper Circulations, 1800–1954* (Manchester, 1955), p. 7; Aspinall, *Politics and the Press*, p. 350.

70. Spectator, 12 Mar. 1711; Rea, 'Paterson', p. 176.

71. Grey Longueville to Pelham, 28 June 1726, BL. Add. 33085.

72. *Wye's Letter*, 18 Aug. 1730, in *Newcastle Courant*, 22 Aug.; *Junius*, Cannon (ed.), xv.

73. W. A. Speck, *Stability and Strife. England 1714–1760* (1977), p. 55; T. S. Ashton, *An Economic History of England: The 18th Century* (1955), pp. 218–26, 232–4.

74. *St. James's Chronicle*, 4 May 1776; Lutnick, *American Revolution*, p. 4; *Westminster Gazette*, 28 Dec. 1776; for bitter attacks on the 1757 increase, *Citizen*, 5, 6, Apr., 28 May, 1 June 1757. *The National Journal*, reduced its price to 1½d on 13 May 1746 to match the prices of competitiors.

75. Christie, *Myth and Reality*, p. 314; Cranfield, *Provincial Newspapers*, p. 67; *North Briton*, 4 May 1771. End of *Plain Dealer* with the session, 1764. 'This dead Time of the Year,' *Weekly Register*, 4 Sept. 1731.

5 The Press and the Constitution

The King is exceeding delighted with his reception at Portsmouth. He said to a person about that he was convinced he was not so unpopular as the newspapers would represent him to be.

> Sir Joshua Reynolds to the Earl of Grantham, 1773[1]

I apprehend Sir your reason for declining my paper is an account of the articles I have inserted in favour of Opposition. These articles Sir have every one of them been admitted only on the footing of advertisements. And I could not refuse them. You know Sir how I am surrounded with members who voted on that side, which are my customers . . . I have however received letters of thanks for my introducing so many articles in favor of Mr. Pitt which I have done gratis, and which as a worthy Baronet writes me more than preponderates against the other articles, which will do no harm but to the seditious etc. etc. . . . I shall be happy Sir to insert anything you or any other friend of Mr. Pitts may send . . . without any fee.

> Thomas Wood, printer of the *Shrewsbury Chronicle*, 1789[2]

Public opinion and the political system

. . . cannot agree with you that the threats of your Yorkshire patriots over a bottle need disturb the sleep of any past, or present minister.

> Lord Beauchamp, 1770[3]

A full-length re-examination of the relationship between the press and politics in the eighteenth century is urgently required, in order both to illuminate work on British politics and better to understand the press. Particularly necessary is a clarification of the political impact of the press. In a single chapter it is only possible to draw attention to a few features of the problem and to pose

113

some questions, but one may hope that a debate can be initiated and further work on the subject encouraged.

For most of the 1960s and 1970s eighteenth-century scholarship, in reaction to the preceding years of Namierite ascendancy and in response to contemporary intellectual and political fashions, stressed aspects of the period that were readily conducive to inter-pretations emphasising the role of the press. The century was presented in a progressive and secular light and disproportionate emphasis was placed on signs of radicalism. This reflected a tendency to concentrate on urban, particularly metropolitan, de-velopments and opinions. The openness of the political system was stressed and particular attention devoted to crises, such as 1710, 1733, 1739, 1753 and the 1760s when events 'out of doors' could be argued to have had considerable political influence. Important work with this emphasis continues. However in recent years scholarship based on a different analysis has been produced. Attention has been directed towards the strength of religious sentiment, the continued predominance of the aristocracy and the conservative nature of political and social ideology. Furthermore, it is possible now to argue that the stress on urban activities has led to an undervaluation of rural conservatism, and that historians have neglected the interests of the bulk of the population.

This work has important implications for the study of public opinion and for the consideration of the political impact of the press. These topics are usually treated as one, an understandable attitude that may however be misleading. In addition there is a tendency to discuss the subject over a long time-span. This does not reflect the nature of eighteenth-century press activity. Whereas most modern newspapers possess considerable longevity, many of the eighteenth-century papers that concentrated on politi-cal topics did not last for very long. The transient nature of publications was often referred to, and many political papers were founded to fight particular battles and then ended, often at the termination of a parliamentary session. This process was en-couraged by the role of political sponsorship. In order to appreciate the political role of individual papers or of the press in general it is therefore necessary to consider particular political conjunctures, and this is just as relevant for newspapers that lasted for some time such as the *Craftsman* and *London Evening Post*. It is probable that a stress on specificity is going to be one of the key developments in eighteenth-century historiography. This does not have to mean a return to Namierite analysis. Rather it is going to be necessary to consider the impact of public opinion and of the press in a much more detailed fashion. Attempts to assess the impact of the press in a given political conjuncture clearly require far more detailed knowledge of the political affiliations of particular newspapers and of the nature of newspaper debates. The latter were often autonomous, and newspapers with similar political opinions could attack each other, as Clifton's *Weekly Medley* and Mist's *Weekly Journal or Saturday's Post* did in the late 1710s.

The 'openness of the political system to outside pressures' is not necessarily the best way of treating the role of the political press: that is to say, those newspapers that discussed politics and advocated particular policies, rather than simply reporting without comment of nor reporting at all. For in many senses the press and the amorphous pressures, interests and opinions understood by the term public opinion were part of the political system itself. Propaganda, the expression of opinion in an attempt to persuade, was used by most political groups. Some politicians were less adept or interested than others — Godolphin lacked the skills of the Junto or Harley — but propaganda was not simply the recourse of opposition groups. In Britain, as on the Continent, governments adopted the medium of print to serve their purposes and used to that end the particular forms that were available: the most significant at times of tension being the sponsored press.

Had eighteenth-century Britain been a bi-partisan society starkly divided by comprehensive party ideologies then there would have been only a limited role for the press as an agent of persuasion. One Whig newspaper claimed in 1713 that 'a good Tory will no more dip into a Whig Treatise than a Roman Catholick into Tillotson's sermons'. However, important as party divisions were, and significant recent work has highlighted the vitality of the Tory party under George I and George II, there were periods, such as the Whig Splits of 1717–20 and 1725–42, when major divisions within existing parties confused the image of a neat bi-partisan structure.[4] Furthermore they forced groups of politicians to support their claims to be the stalwarts of party orthodoxy, and they touched off active quests for support at Westminster and in the political nation. Divisions within party groupings tended to conflate two of the major purposes of the political press, that of persuading non-supporters, not all of whom were, *pace* the idea of a 'Divided Society', opponents, and of urging supporters to help towards particular goals. When parties were divided and the result of these divisions uncertain many papers tended to be founded and politics played a major role in the press.[5] The late 1710s was a good instance of this. The press as an agent of persuasion could be regarded as important not only when parties were divided but also when issues emerged that did not correspond to views already clearly expressed or recently discussed. Such issues also necessitated the definition of party views for the benefit of supporters, and it could be suggested that a reason for the tendency to discuss politics in terms of overall adversarial views was to encourage readers to interpret all issues from a partisan viewpoint.

The imprecision of terms used by the press was sometimes referred to in print. Attacking the opposition press Lady Mary Wortley Montagu wrote in 1738, 'Reams of publick papers . . . have been filled with dissertations upon the word *Liberty*, which has been wrested to great variety of purposes, without one definition of the true signification.' In 1762 the *North Briton* asked 'Who has with any precision defined the words faction or patriot?' 'Plautius' in a thoughtful essay on tyranny in the *London Chronicle* in 1776 complained about a lack of precision in terminology and defined his own terms with care, adding, 'It might be well, perhaps, if contending parties would adopt something like this mode of candidly examining matters at this time of day, it might reduce empty declamations . . . and save oceans of *ink*, and perhaps even seas of *blood*, to this divided empire.'[6] These comments were justified, but such caution was all too rare, and an imprecision in terminology characterised the press discussion both of British politics and of the role of the press and of public opinion in the political system. It would be mistaken to assume that journalists should share the miseries of lexicographers, but this imprecision could be related to something more significant, namely the ambiguities of eighteenth-century political ideology, ambiguities reflected in and partly expressed by a number of loaded phrases that sprang from, but did not define the Revolution Settlement. The complexities of this ideology have recently been ably considered,[7] but there has been as yet no systematic study of the relationship between the press and political, constitutional and ideological concepts. The press discussed such ideas frequently in its own pages, and itself constituted a subject for them, never more so than in the vexed question of the role of public opinion, for it was in that issue that the political role of the newspapers was largely considered.

Though political history that explains everything simply in terms of the activities of the Duke of Newcastle and five others, is rarely written these days and was less common in the past than is generally supposed, it is nevertheless all too easy, as this writer knows all too well, to search volume after volume of political correspondence between leading politicians without finding any reference to anything that could be even tenuously described as public opinion. Additional volumes yield references to newspapers, but only in terms of items to be subsidised and manipulated, occasional problems in contrast to those represented by borough-mongering. Officials and politicians sometimes referred to the press only in order to question its impact. Reports that Queen Anne was ill and the ministry split led George Tilson, then Under-Secretary to Bolingbroke, to claim in 1712 'we are lye proof here now, and scarce mind them'.[8] The diplomat Charles Whitworth, who was later to enter Parliament, wrote from The Hague in 1719, 'The Gazetts continue to be impertinent from time to time, but I know no better way than to leave them to their own folly, and to be convicted by the apparent falsity of their accounts.'[9] Lord Perceval noted in 1722, 'Never was a dead Parliament so abused in pamphlets and newspapers; but this is all that party have for it.' The same year Tilson, still an Under-Secretary, doubted the effectiveness of Jacobite propaganda and denied that 'because the mob is poisoned, women and parsons rail, and the grumblers put about libels and ballads, that therefore the whole nation will join and take up arms in favour of the Pretender'.[10] George Lyttelton, later a prominent opposition Whig, wrote an attack on the *Craftsman* whilst on the Grand Tour in 1730. He argued that the paper was sufficiently ridiculous for publicity to guarantee its ineffectiveness: 'The reasoning of those Gentlemen is so false, that in order to ridicule their notions it is only necessary to set them in a strong light, and bring their separate absurdities together.'[11]

Faced with French complaints about British publications in 1772 Viscount Harcourt assured the French foreign minister 'that people were so inured to abuse, that it had almost lost its sting', whilst the Earl of Rochford noted 'how impossible it is for Government to prevent them and of how little consequence they are in this country'.[12] Although most foreign envoys tended to argue that the press was of great significance this view was not shared by all. The Saxon De Löss, sending a translation of the *Craftsman* of 2 February 1734, wrote that it was worthy of attention as it indicated opposition attitudes, but added that the ministry was not greatly disturbed by these criticisms, as it was accustomed to them and certain of parliamentary support. The French Ambassador Cambis similarly argued in 1738 that the ministry would not deviate at all from their policies despite the criticisms of the *Common-Sense* he was forwarding.[13] Newspapers sometimes questioned the effectiveness of the press, though usually that of newspapers of a different viewpoint. The *Daily Courant* claimed in 1737 that Walpole was as little moved by the *Craftsman* 'as the winds with the cry of mariners', whilst in 1769 *Berrow's Worcester Journal* informed its readers, 'It will in general exhaust whole Rivers of Ink, and wear out a thousand Paper-Mills, to write out a bad Minister, unless other Circumstances concur to accelerate his Downfall.'[14]

Alongside these rebuttals of the role of the press and the more telling failure of many politicians to mention it must be placed the willingness of political groups to sponsor newspapers, the weight of political coverage in the press and the conviction of many, not least a large number of newspapers, that the press did and/or ought to have political influence as the epitome of public opinion, however defined. Possibly it is misleading to dignify the frequent reiteration of this conviction and the more occasional qualifications of it by the term debate. As with so many other eighteenth-century, and indeed modern, controversies there is little sense of exchange of opinion or development in ideas. However, the debate is of interest as it was largely in relation to their political role that newspapers both discussed themselves and were discussed by others. This may have led to a misplaced emphasis in historical studies on eighteenth-century newspapers. Compared to the study of their political coverage there has arguably been insufficient attention devoted to other items that they carried and to their business organisation. It is the heavyweight political papers, such as the *Craftsman*, *Monitor* and *North Briton*, and their essays that have attracted most scholarly attention, despite the fact that some of these papers, such as the *Monitor*, had only a low circulation. The tri-weeklies and 'Advertisers' were usually more widely read, but their political coverage did not generally take the form of opinion, or, if it did, as with the *London Evening Post*, the items were often very short. That did not necessarily make them less effective, and Cranfield suggested that the *London Evening Post* was more influential than the *Craftsman*. Certainly the verses in the former were shorter and easier to grasp than the essays in the latter. Verses were no doubt better suited for reading or singing aloud, though some appear very flat.[15] That verses were reprinted often in the provincial press suggests that they were regarded as an accessible form of political comment.[16]

Possibly a concentration on the essay form of political discussion has led to a misunderstanding of the range and effectiveness of political comment. However there is no doubt that political controversy inspired most discussion of the role of the press, though there were debates over the value of printing in other spheres, such as religion, that may well have influenced attitudes to the role of the press.[17] Much of what was written in the late seventeenth century concerning the political role of the newspapers related to discussions over the regulation of the press. There were many warnings of the dangers presented by newspapers, not only from Tories. In 1688 the *London Courant* discerned a Catholic plot to sow dissension among Protestants.[18] The principal pressure for regulation of the press after the lapsing of the Licensing Act came from Tories, and it is because of this that Alan Downie highlighted the significance of Robert Harley, who, as first minister in the Tory government of 1710–14, manipulated party pressure for a restrictive system of press controls and produced instead a modest tax and a number of effective ministerial papers.[19] It is possible that a reason for Harley's attitude was a certain complacency about the position of the Church of England appropriate in one of nonconformist background, and differing from High-Tory concern about the press.[20] The disinclination of the Jacobite court to support major propaganda campaigns in Britain and their relative lack of interest in the press[21] may have stemmed from similar attitudes. Traditional Tory attitudes about the press were indeed expressed in some newspapers. In 1718 *Heraclitus Ridens* used the form of a dialogue, often one suspects in the hands of witty writers such as Henley more effective than the essay, to question ministerial claims on foreign policy, but then added 'Peace and War are the Prerogatives of the Crown' and suggested that it was best to say nothing.[22] Such an argument did not find favour with Tory newspapers, obliged to maximise their readership due to a relative absence of sponsorship, and determined to attack the Whig ministries of Georges I and II. *Mist's Weekly Journal* expressed views that would not have been out of place in a Whig paper in the 1680s:

> When private men observe the face of public affairs to appear with a cloudy and distempered look, they have by our constitution, a right to reason upon the conduct of our ministers; for it is often the only means by which the sense of the people can be convey'd to the ear of the Prince . . . English men have always looked upon it as part of their right to speak and write upon public affairs . . . There is nothing that concerns the attention of a private man so much, as the actions of persons in the administration of public affairs.[23]

The ambiguity of the Whig inheritance was highlighted in the period 1714–60. Whig success in surmounting a series of obstacles — Jacobite conspiracies, general elections, Whig splits, the South Sea Bubble — and in accommodating various interests — the Hanoverian aspirations of the monarchs, the reversionary interests of George II and III as Princes of Wales, the ecclesiastical views of the Church of England hierarchy — ensured that the ministerial Whigs could consider their political position with little fear of being forced to go into opposition. Reed Browning has recently shown how they justified their stance on the issue of public opinion against the background of a political theory that centred on the overthrow of James II. His work is restricted substantially to the arguments of five individuals, and requires an additional study of ministerial newspapers and parliamentary speeches.[24] Those Whigs who went into opposition had to face the corresponding problem of attacking a Whig ministry that claimed to represent traditional Whig beliefs, whilst defining their own position with respect to the largest opposition group the Tories. Both ministerial and opposition Whigs sought to assume the identity of Whiggery by claiming its inheritance, a desire that helps to account for the large role played by history in the political essays carried by the press. Recent history and in particular the Glorious Revolution was used to establish legitimacy, Whigs rushing to the defence of William III.[25] History ancient and modern was used both to discuss general issues of constitutional importance[26] and particular topics of political debate,[27] such as foreign policy which could best be understood by reference to Edward III, Elizabeth and Oliver

Cromwell.[28] It was not surprising that the historical skills of writers and newspapers, particularly the *Craftsman*, became the topic of abuse.[29]

History did not cease to be a tool of newspaper debate in mid-century. The press attack in early 1753 on the manner in which the future George III was being brought up referred to the way in which the country had been governed under the first two Stuarts. In 1762 the *North Briton* used the reign of Edward II in order to attack the position of George III's favourite, Bute. It was a reign

> distinguished in history as the reign of *favourites*: to his un-abounded affection for them, may be ascribed the various mis-fortunes that afflicted this country at that time; and by those attachments, the affections of the Old Nobility were so alienated from his that he became involved in disputes which terminated with the loss of his crown and life.

The same paper contested the accuracy of the *Briton*'s claim that the history of Athens and of republican Rome indicated the danger of a commonwealth ruled by a mob. The transience of the Anglo-Spanish settlement of 1739, the Convention of the Pardo, was held up as a warning during the Falkland Islands Crisis of 1770–1. History also warned against standing armies and evil ministers, both old favourites, and allowing the French to construct a navy.[30] However in the second half of the century, although historical examples were used plentifully in the discussion of the virtues of particular policies, history did not tend to serve as the all-embracing means of conveying a message that Bolingbroke had employed in the *Craftsman*. This partly reflected the particular interests and skills of Bolingbroke, and partly the need in the 1720s and 1730s for the opposition Whigs to define their position.

Alongside the need of both ministerial and opposition Whigs to assume the mantle of true Whiggery, each group had to defend its particular course and assume contradictory positions on the definition and role of public opinion in the political system. This process was developed partly in one of the principal topics of debate, the press, and encouraged by the intoxicating pressures of newspaper rivalry. The ministerial press, those papers that consistently supported the government, whether subsidised or not, regularly deplored the extent of press comment. It was argued that this comment was seditious in both intent and effect. The opposition press was accused of spreading lies about government policy, and of encouraging faction, an imprecise term by which opposition could be castigated. Specific accusations included abetting domestic treason, namely Jacobitism, and harming British foreign policy by revealing secrets and encouraging an image of a divided Britain. The 'Hague Letter' episode of early 1731, when the *Craftsman*, in an item supposedly from The Hague, revealed secret Anglo-Austrian negotiations, encouraged a particularly marked revival in the ministerial newspapers of the theme of the dangers of press freedom, an issue that Jacobite conspiracy and newspapers had last caused to be extensively aired in the early 1720s. The success of the *Craftsman*, not only in circulation terms but in also becoming a talking point in the political world,[31] and its determination to make the freedom of the press an issue, was probably partly responsible for the degree of ministerial criticism, for at one level the struggle between ministerial and opposition press was fought as a debate over press freedom. Ministerial newspapers had to reply to the *Craftsman*'s claims that they had abandoned the Whig legacy, but they also probably found it convenient to defend aspects of government policy, particularly foreign policy, by using the arguments of mysteries of state and royal prerogative. The ministerial press based its constitutional arguments on the sovereignty of Parliament, denying that extra-parliamentary pressures should be heeded and claiming that most of these were manipulated and/or self-interested. The popular appeal of the opposition was not usually denied, but the populace was presented as fickle and foolish,[32] an argument that related to the view advanced in several ministerial newspapers that they should stick to their tasks and not open themselves to temptation by reading about the affairs of the world.

These arguments in the ministerial press have received little attention, but they help to explain why the *Craftsman* thought it worthwhile to use the issue of press liberty in order to cast doubt on the Whig credentials of the ministry. Given the ministerial harrying of the Jacobite press in the mid-1710s, it is not surprising that defences of such activity were produced:

In writing papers of public intelligence there seems to me to be a particular view which every man of right principles keeps before him, and by which he guides his steps in all he writes, and this is in short not only to give intelligence, but that all his intelligence be calculated for the public good.

It is on this foundation that Governments think themselves obliged to resent, and even to punish the telling public news in a manner injurious to the general tranquillity, and with evident testimonies of disaffection.[33]

In 1722 the *St. James's Journal* reprinted a sermon preached before the Commons by a Whig divine calling for legislative action and commenting on some of the tricks of the opposition press:

Among the many ways taken to poison the minds of the people, and to alienate their affections, the most dangerous and diffusive, has been that insufferable licence, which has been of late so scandalously taken of spreading seditious papers and libels thro' the Kingdom. This is at length advanced into a claim of right; and it is declared that no free people can subsist without them. Were men of low and needy circumstances alone concerned in this matter, the Government, for ought I know, might continue their indulgence; only taking care, that as they write for bread, so they should sometimes eat it in sorrow. But when men of great and plentiful fortunes shall abuse the leisure which their circumstances afford them; when men of parts and education shall prostitute their pens, in conveying weekly poison through the nation, it is constantly high time for those who are in authority to look about them, and prevent the growing evil. . . . shall not be deemed innocent, under the cover and protection of two or three words thrown in about former reigns and neighbouring Kingdoms. For as the case at present stands, the most bare-faced insults pass with impunity . . . if at the end of a virulent paragraph, full fraught with sedition, the writer can but persuade himself in a dull line or two to protest against fact . . . Seditious papers are the certain forerunners of public confusion; the tendency is natural; nor is it to be wondered at, that when some write upon the confines of treason, others shall act within them.[34]

The same paper argued that treasonable libels were printed in newspapers in order to increase their sales, whilst *Applebee's Original Weekly Journal* suggested that the most loyal subjects were those 'that meddle least in public affairs'. The *Whitehall Journal* dealt with liberty of the press by arguing that the liberty to purchase 'sulphur, nitre and arsenic' did not extend to using them for blowing up the Royal Family or mass poisoning. The paper called for 'the silencing of libellers', and condemned not only Tories but also 'grumbling malcontent scribblers', who sought to gain office. In 1723 the same newspaper complained that it could not use the tone it wished, because the opposition press had given up reason in order to win the people.[35] Other ministerial papers stressed the self-interest of opposition writers,[36] the impossibility of ministerial perfection,[37] the declamatory manner and appeal to the emotions of opposition writing,[38] and their creation of domestic division.[39] A series of subsidised papers bitterly attacked the freedom of the opposition press to encourage sedition and/or foreign enemies.[40] The *London Journal* citing Rome and Athens claimed that 'the Liberty of the Press is not essential to a free Government'.[41] Some stressed the mercenary nature of opposition writing, Henley claiming in 1732,

> The cry of the Liberty of the Press is nothing but their trade, which is of late years so overstocked and glutted with a disproportioned and imprudent number of apprentices that some followers of the profession have been obliged to recur to new methods of subsidence: Among which, inferior booksellers, in fortune and name, have found the scandalizing persons of any rank, especially the highest, and the ministry, the most remarkable.[42]

Others stressed political aspects. The government-subsidised *Free Briton* stated in 1732, 'The writing and publishing of the Hague Letter was an offence against the essential laws of human society.'[43] The vigour of the opposition press and the government's resort to legal action against it forced the ministerial press to define the reasonable limits of press freedom. Prosecutions led the general debate to become slightly more specific. The *London Journal* distinguished between calumny and accusation. The latter, 'an open, legal charge, to make out which it is necessary to produce witnesses, proofs and evidence', was acceptable, the former, lacking such supports, was not. The *Free Briton* praised 'the sacred rules of public enquiry', but found that the 'spreading of false news is no part of the freedom of the press', adding 'no honest man can defend prosecutions, where opinions offered upon national affairs are proceeded against as criminal; but representations of these affairs are very different points'.[44] Ministerial papers presented the opposition press as all too effective, both with foreign powers and with a populace 'eager to buy all virulent papers against their superiors'.[45] As a result they called for restraint on the press,[46] and stressed the absence of any constitutional role for it. The *British Journal* stated in 1727 that it was only reasonable to call a minister corrupt and evil after he had been condemned by Parliament. The *Daily Gazetteer* stressed the royal prerogative and the position of Parliament as the questioner of policy: 'To suppose that a point of this importance ought to be explained in public prints to every little fellow that asks it, is supposing our government dissolved, and the mob ready to sit in judgment on the legislature.' At the time of Walpole's fall the paper suggested 'that there is nothing more useful in a free country than general and moderate discourses on political subjects'.[47] The press had no constitutional role, it was representative only of profit or sedition, and though the ministry could combat its opinions it was not necessary to do so. Opposition claims of the corruption of parliamentary representation could be ignored,[48] or matched by questioning the integrity of politicians who sought to stir up the populace. One pamphlet asked, 'Have the authors of a two-penny weekly journal, a right to make a national inquiry?'[49]

These views were rejected by the opposition press, particularly the *Craftsman*. Stressing the liberty of the press as an issue helped to focus interest on the newspaper. This liberty was 'one of the greatest blessings of a free people', 'the chief bulwark and support of Liberty in general', 'a point of so essential a nature to the constitution of this Kingdom', 'this great bulwark of our Constitution'.[50] Those who sought to suppress it had sinister motives.[51] Claiming impartiality, the paper sought a political role as a defender of 'the public welfare'. There was a need to debate 'the great affairs of peace and war', and the *Craftsman*, 'a Pensioner of the People', venal because sold, had the independence to do this.[52] The ministerial press was written off as subsidised, 'a standing army of writers' that included the *British Journal*, *Daily Courant*, *Flying Post*, *Free Briton*, *Hyp Doctor*, *London Journal*, and *Weekly Register*.[53] Its political role rendered invalid by corruption it joined Parliament and the Court as an institution unsuited for the expression of free opinion and unable to advise the monarch. Opposition papers claimed that it was a characteristic of arbitrary states to keep the people in ignorance and prevent them expressing their opinions.[54] Discussing and contesting legal cases on the role of the press played a significant part in establishing the views of ministry and opposition on the nature of the political system and the role of public opinion in it. Much was doubtless dictated by the exigencies of government and opposition. The *Craftsman* could hardly do anything other than applaud the role of the press, just as its advocacy of a 'Country' opposition of Tories and opposition Whigs reflected the political opportunities of the period. It was natural for government to seek to keep the sensitive sphere of foreign negotiations confidential. It was also obvious that they should seek to censor publications when they were aware of the attempts of Jacobites and foreign powers to disseminate their opinions. No government worried about Jacobitism or concerned about the efforts of envoys, such as the Swede Gyllenborg in 1717, to insert material in the press would have accepted the argument advanced by several opposition writers during the century, including Junius in 1769, that 'if news papers are scurrilous, you must confess they are impartial. They give us, without any apparent preference, the wit and argument of the ministry, as well as the abusive dullness of the opposition'.[55] Once it was necessary for the ministerial press to defend the suppression of Jacobite material or that pertaining to foreign negotiations, and the bulk of press prosecutions and other actions against newspapers stemmed from these sources, then it is not surprising that the ministerial press developed a general theory hinging on the distinction between Liberty and Licence. Arguments for the restriction of press freedom were obviously related to those seeking to limit the role of newspapers and public opinion in the political system, for the more the latter was exalted the less plausible restrictions on press reporting could seem. Added force was probably given to these intellectual links, by evidence of the unpopularity of the Whig regime, particularly apparent in London,[56] and worryingly obvious to ministerial newspapers concerned about their sales. The relatively high circulation of the *Craftsman*, *London Evening Post* and papers produced by Mist would have fortified the opposition press in their feeling that they represented public opinion and encouraged ministerial writers to express doubts about the integrity of a readily manipulated public. The style of many opposition newspapers and the devices they employed to make their political message more appealing and comprehensible — verses, tales, epigrams — enhanced this impression. The tone of opposition newspapers often attracted criticism, and abuse was condemned. Such abuse was not essential to the message of opposition propaganda, though it often helped in making it more accessible and attractive to read. In 1763 the barrister Alexander Forrester wrote to the diplomat Andrew Mitchell, 'Faction, libelling without respect or control, and mutual revilings, have been our occupation. No wonder then if, as you say, we appear ridiculous to other nations.'[57]

In the second half of the century the same positions were adopted by ministerial and opposition newspapers. Ministerial papers claimed often that opposition politicians would adopt the habits of government as soon as they assumed office and these claims were on the whole justified. Successive ministries used government funds to subsidise the press and employed arguments centring on the need for limiting debate and the provision of information. The opportunism of opposition writers was discussed, the *Public Advertiser* pointing out in 1786 that the government was 'jeered by hackney writers when the stocks fall, and blamed when they rise'.[58] Defending George III's favourite, Bute, the *London Chronicle* printed a dialogue in 1762 that would not have been out of place fifty years earlier. Richard Candor, 'an honest tradesman in London', asked Henry Meanwell, 'Do'st thou think that Will Thimble the Taylor, and Ned Anvil the Smith, would not be much better employed in shaping a coat, and shoeing an horse, than in puzzling their own pates, and misleading others (ignorant as themselves) in matters vastly above their weak understandings?'[59] The *Ipswich Journal* published a letter two years later that employed the Liberty/Licentiousness dichotomy and called for 'the chastising hand of legal power' against those who transgressed 'the proper bounds, which Truth, Decency and Order' had set to the freedom of the press. In 1768 'Common Sense' in the *Reading Mercury* complained that excessive freedom of the press was leading Britain to become 'a nation of barbarians', whilst 'Cato' in *Lloyd's Evening Post* presented the press as the defender of Liberty and argued that libels were an inevitable evil. As with most political argument in the period 'Cato' employed an image to make his point:

> As to those who are for locking up the Press, because it produces monsters, they ought to consider, that so do the Sun and the Nile; and that it is something better for the world to bear some particu-

lar inconveniences arising from general blessings, than to be
wholly deprived of Fire and Water.[60]

The discussion of the role of the press in the 1760s and 1770s was
very similar to that earlier in the century. Grand claims for the role
and liberties of the press were advanced. It was 'the firmest
bulwark of the liberties of this country', and 'the chief bulwark and
support of Liberty in general', its printers 'Guardians to the
Public'.[61] Evil ministers sought to subvert it, because having
corrupted Parliament, only the press remained to challenge their
abuses. Junius dismissed the suggestion made by Sir William
Draper that the proper place for redress was Parliament, by
claiming that it was corrupt.[62] The politics of paranoia that characterised opposition attitudes also marked the press. There was little
suggestion of a genuine difference of opinion either existing or
being possible. Instead the entwined forces of corruption and
conspiracy were presented as suffusing the land. Such a threat
required a strident opposition. Thus the perception of a sinister
threat and the hyperbole of opposition rhetoric were mutually
reinforcing. The press was in no way unique in its rhetoric. However much newspapers might employ particular forms in order to
make their points, such as imaginary dialogues or papers from the
future,[63] their language and ideas were not unique, but were part
of the general public discussion of politics. Given the limited
journalistic resources of eighteenth-century newspapers, their
heavy reliance on reprinting items from other papers, and the
major role of foreign and later parliamentary news, it is not
surprising that there was little original political comment. Much
political comment came from summarising items in books and
pamphlets.[64] In some respects hyperbole was a substitute for hard
news, difficult to obtain because of the journalistic problems posed
by the relatively closed world of Court and country houses, and
the attendant legal prohibitions. In addition it is possible that
many readers preferred to read such items. From the point of view
of political agitation hyperbole was clearly of considerable value.
'An Old Consistent Whig', writing in the *Leeds Intelligencer* in
1767, complained that 'refined politicians think principles of no
further use to a party, than as the mere sound of words may serve
to attach men to their respective principles'.[65]

That the debate was repetitive did not necessarily indicate a
failure to comprehend the situation. Ministerial newspapers had to

face similar opposition attacks for most of the century. The situation confronting the opposition press was relatively unchanging. One of the principal theoretical problems facing opposition writers, who urged the importance of public opinion, was the difficulty of explaining the mechanism through which the voice of the public was to be heeded, particularly if Parliament was hostile. It was easy for foreign commentators to present Britain as a state ruled by a fickle public opinion, as the French envoy Chavigny did in the 1730s. In 1738 his Spanish counterpart Geraldino informed his colleague at The Hague that it was difficult to negotiate in Britain, where, he claimed, 'Reason and justice could not prevail, unless accommodated to the opinion of the people.'[66] However it was less clear how this opinion was to prevail. In February 1732 in the Commons debate over a ministerial proposal for a revival of the salt duty Edward Vernon claimed, 'Ninety nine in a hundred of the people would not bear the tax, and that he should expect if he voted for it, to be treated like a polecat and knocked on the head.'[67]

Such a method of enforcing the popular will had no influential supporters, and opposition publicists had to be very careful about advocating extra-parliamentary agitation. The conservative nature of political thought was amply illustrated by the frequency of references to an anticipated royal intervention, either by the Jacobites' current monarch or by future rulers, the Electoral Prince of Hanover (future George I) under Anne, the future George II during the Whig Split, Frederick Prince of Wales from the late 1730s until his death in 1751, the future George III thereafter. The list of often tenuous or unsuitable prospects closed with the future George IV. In one of its frequent allegories of British developments, made more interesting and legally safer by being located in the exotic Orient, the *Craftsman* presented the fictional Persian kingdom of Timbutan where the rule of an evil chief minister lasted 'till the complaints and cries of the people (which were now grown almost universal) reached the Court and pierced the ears of a most indulgent Prince'.[68] In 1769 Junius caused a sensation with a bold letter to George III claiming that the King had never 'been acquainted with the language of truth, until you heard it in the complaints of your people'.[69] Monarchs were aware to some extent of what was being printed,[70] but they did not appreciate their policies and ministerial choices being dictated by their ministers, let alone by the opposition press. This press was in one respect being realistic when it appealed to the monarch, present or future. The two biggest shifts in political fortune in the century, the ushering in of one-party Whig rule in 1714 and its destruction in the early 1760s, were due largely to the personal opinions of Georges I and III. Recent work on eighteenth-century political history by such scholars as Baxter, Blanning, Clark, Gregg, Hatton, Mackesy and Owen has stressed the political influence of the monarchs. There was little reason for them to listen to the 'cries of the people', however defined or communicated, and this posed a problem for the opposition press's discussion of its own position. The attack on a monarch misled by evil ministers could serve to excuse assaults on the royal prerogative, but a monarch and ministry supported by a loyal Parliament, however corrupt, was difficult to condemn without rejecting the political and challenging the social system. 'Radical' solutions, including an element of franchise reform, were advocated in some newspapers, but it was not until the French Revolution encouraged the discussion of 'radical' ideas in some quarters that a sustained attack on the existing system was launched in print.

It is important not to exaggerate the problem posed by the nature of the political system. Very few people sought to overthrow the existing social structure prior to the French Revolution, and the impact of the latter should not be overestimated. One French diplomat and journalist described Britain in 1792 as a country 'où la superstition du Royalisme est fondée sur le fanaticisme religieux'.[71] The vast majority of opposition politicians wished to gain office under the existing system, and the newspapers they were linked with supported these aspirations. The revolutionary government of France had placed high hopes on James Perry, owner-editor of the *Morning Chronicle*, who had gone to Paris in 1791 in the capacity of a 'deputy' of the English Revolution Society, in order to send back reports that would give the paper the edge in its coverage of the Revolution.[72]

The French were disillusioned after the September Massacres in 1792, when Perry claimed that it was no longer possible to trust France, and they became more anxious about British press coverage and increasingly convinced of the need to secure newspaper support in a hostile environment.[73] The papers that praised the early stages of the French Revolution did not tend to call for change in Britain. Similarly the unstamped newspapers of the early eighteenth century, illegal publications, such as the *Penny Post* launched in 1717, the *London Post*, launched for a ha'penny the same year and the *London News*, which began at the same price in 1718, that were produced in London for local sale, were not characterised by political radicalism. The *Champion* suggested that they were tolerated by the ministry in return for being politically neutral, but there is no evidence to support this claim, though clearly it would not have been prudent for them to excite attention. Their prime appeal does not appear to have been political. Mist's referred in 1726 to 'the works of the unknown authors, which are often cried about the streets on Saturday nights, and bear the title of six pennyworth of laughing for the price of a half-penny'. *Parker's Penny Post* of 22 November 1727 carried part of a serial, 'The Unfortunate Lovers', and details of Tyburn executions. The *London Farthing Post* of 1738–9 carried foreign news similar to that of stamped papers, printed a fair amount of London news, often relating to crime, and, instead of essays, carried stories, including a lengthy series devoted to Pyramus and Thisbe and items of general interest such as the life of Prince Eugene and a poem to a friend in the country.[74]

It was only the Jacobite printers who really wished to see a major change in Britain prior to the French Revolution, and it was they who bore the brunt of government legal action. For many other printers of opposition material profit played a large role in the decision to take a political stance, as it was generally accepted that this was more popular. Henry Sampson Woodfall, the owner- printer of the *Public Advertiser*, saw his sales rise substantially thanks to Junius.[75] Despite the hyperbole of their papers it is unclear that opposition newspaper figures envisaged any major change in the political system. They would have been foolish to think otherwise.

Notes

1. Reynolds to Grantham, 20 July 1773, Bedford, Bedfordshire CRO., Lucas papers. L30/14. On George III reading the press 'Veteran' (Junius), *Public Advertiser*, 28 Jan. 1772.

2. Wood to James Bland Burges MP, 23 Jan. 1789, Bodl. Bland Burges papers, 18 f. 40–1.

3. Beauchamp to William Eden, 27 Sept. 1770, BL. Add. 34412 f. 131.

4. *Flying-Post: or, The Post-Master*, 8 Jan. 1713; L. J. Colley, *In Defiance of Oligarchy. The Tory Party 1714–60*. Possibly the Cowper/Wharton opposition of the early 1720s, an underrated and relatively ignored episode, should be termed a Whig Split. The Whig Split of 1725–42 led directly into that of 1742–4.

132   The Press and the Constitution

5. *Whitehall Evening Post*, 29 Nov. 1718.

6. *Nonsense of Common-Sense*, 21 Feb. 1738; *North Briton*, 22 Aug. 1762; *London Chronicle*, 13 Jan. 1776.

7. H. T. Dickinson, *Liberty and Property* (1977); J. P. Kenyon, *Revolution Principles* (Cambridge, 1977).

8. Tilson to Chetwynd, 25 Nov. 1712, Stafford CRO., D649/8/7/1. On the remarkable infrequency of references to the *Monitor* in the Duke of Newcastle's correspondence, M. Peters, *The 'Monitor' 1755–1765: A Political Essay Paper and Popular London Opinion* (unpublished PhD thesis, Canterbury, New Zealand, 1974), p. 586; *Answer to . . . Second Letter to the People* (1755), p. 33.

9. Whitworth to Lord Cadogan, 3 Dec. (ns) 1717, BL. Add. 37366 f. 124.

10. Perceval to Charles Dering, 27 Mar. 1722, BL. Add. 47029 f. 110; Tilson to Whitworth, 8 May 1722, BL. Add. 37389 f. 20.

11. Lyttelton to Stephen Poyntz, 24 Feb. (ns) 1730, BL. Althorp Mss. E 4.

12. Harcourt to Rochford, 8 July, Rochford to Harcourt, 17 July 1772, PRO. 78/285 f. 282, 285.

13. De Löss to Count Brühl, 26 Feb. (ns) 1734, Dresden, 638 IIa f. 156, 160–3; Cambis to Amelot, French foreign minister, 11 Sept. (ns) 1738, AE. CP. Ang. 399 f. 146. French translation of *Common-Sense*, 16 Sept. f. 168–71.

14. *Daily Courant*, 4 Jan. 1734; *Berrow's Worcester Journal*, 9 Nov. 1769; *Flying Post; or Post-Master*, 15 Dec. 1730; *Common-Sense*, 8 Oct. 1737; *Champion*, 24 July 1740; Anon., *An Historical View of the . . . Principles, Characters, Persons etc. of the Political Writers in Great Britain* (1740), pp. 8–9, 23; J. Moore, *A View of Society and Manners in France, Switzerland and Germany* (1779), pp. 403–4; P. Cunningham (ed.), *The Letters of Horace Walpole* (Edinburgh, 1906) I, civ.

15. Cranfield, 'The London Evening Post, 1727–1744', *HJ* 6 (1963), p. 20; Cranfield, 'The London Evening Post and the Jew Bill of 1753', *HJ* 8 (1965), p. 19; *London Evening Post*, 24 Mar., 2 June 1743; *World*, 30 May 1791.

16. *Newcastle Journal*, 22 Aug. 1740; *Cirencester Flying-Post*, 22 Mar. 1742, 22 Aug. 1743; *Newcastle Courant*, 27 Oct. 1750, 9 Feb. 1751; M. E. Knapp, 'Political and Local Verse in the early years of *The Salisbury Journal*', *Hatcher Review*, 2 (1983); A. Collins, *Discourse Concerning Ridicule* (1729).

17. B. Rizzo '"Hail, printing!": the Commonwealthman's salute to the printed word in eighteenth-century England', *Transactions of the Sixth International Congress on the Enlightenment* (Oxford, 1983), pp. 258–9.

18. *London Courant*, 22 Dec. 1688.

19. [J.] A. Downie, 'The Growth of Government Tolerance of the Press to 1790', in R. Myers and M. Harris (eds), *Development of the English Book Trade 1700–1899* (Oxford, 1981), pp. 50–2.

20. J. Toland, *The State Anatomy of Great Britain* (3rd ed., 1717), p. 90.

21. P. Chapman, *Jacobite Political Argument in England 1714–66* (unpublished PhD thesis, Cambridge, 1983).

22. *Heraclitus Ridens*, 20 Feb. 1718.

23. Mist's *Weekly Journal*, 27 Jan., 2 Feb. 1728; *Fog's Weekly Journal*, 30 Aug. 1735; *Senator*, 5 Mar. 1728.

24. R. Browning, *Political and Constitutional Ideas of the Court Whigs* (Baton Rouge, 1982).

25. *St. James's Evening Post*, 26 June 1722; *Weekly Register*, 1, 8 Jan. 1732; Philip Yorke, Attorney-General, to — , 26 Mar. 1732, PRO. 36/26 f. 144.

26. Anon. mss. Anti-Cato. or the Political Letters in the London Journal Examin'd, BL. Add. 61707, p. 2; *Whitehall Journal*, 18 Dec. 1722; *Craftsman*, 11 May 1728; *Daily Courant*, 26 Aug., 30 Sept. 1734; *Jacobite's Journal*, 20 Feb. 1746.

27. On dealing with treason, *Englishman*, 15 July 1715; *London Journal*, 3 Nov. 1722; *Weekly Journal: or British Gazetteer*, 9 Mar. 1723; *Old England*, 31 Aug. 1745.

28. *Whitehall Evening Post*, 29 Nov. 1718; *Craftsman*, 18 Nov. 1727, 24 Oct. 1730; Mist's *Weekly Journal*, 17 June 1727, 2 Feb. 1728; *Hyp-Doctor*, 30 Oct. 1733; *Common-Sense*, 26 Nov., 24 Dec. 1737, 4 Feb. 1738; *Daily Gazetteer*, 22 Feb. 1738, 19 Sept. 1740; *Champion*, 24 Nov. 1739; *Daily Post*, 16 Aug. 1745.

29. *Whitehall Journal*, 6 Nov. 1722; *Weekly Journal: or Saturday's Post*, 21 Dec. 1723, 11, 18 Jan. 1724; *London Journal*, 20 Feb. 1725, 10 Oct. 1730; *Daily Courant*, 4 Jan., 21 Sept., 2 Oct. 1734; *Fog's Weekly Journal*, 30 Nov. 1734.

30. *North Briton*, 3 July, 9 Oct. 1762; *Briton*, 11 Sept. 1762; *Reading Mercury*, 28 Jan. 1771; *St. James's Chronicle*, 18 July 1772; *Daily Universal Register*, 12 Aug. 1786; *Newcastle Chronicle*, 10 Nov. 1787; *Whisperer*, 9 Mar., 27 Apr. 1771; *Monitor*, 10 May 1760.

31. It was the paper most frequently mentioned by foreign envoys between 1726 and the late 1730s, and it made an impact on them greater than any previous opposition paper.

32. *Whitehall Journal*, 4 Dec. 1722; *Northampton Mercury*, 28 Oct. 1723; Anon., *Liberty and the Craftsman* (1730), p. 5; *Daily Courant*, 5 Oct. 1734.

33. *Whitehall Evening Post*, 30 Dec. 1718.

34. *St. James's Journal*, 1 Dec. 1722; *St. James's Chronicle*, 8 Feb. 1766.

35. *St. James's Journal*, 1 Nov. 1722; *Applebee's Original Weekly Journal*, 17 Nov. 1722; *Whitehall Journal*, 13 Nov. 1722, 26 Feb. 1723.

36. *Pasquin*, 13 May 1723; *Northampton Mercury*, 7 Oct. 1723.

37. *London Journal*, 9 Feb. 1723.

38. *London Journal*, 1 Aug. 1724; *London Packet*, 6 Mar. 1789.

39. *Weekly Register*, 4 Sept. 1731.

40. *Flying Post or Post Master*, 21 Jan., 12 Aug. 1731; *London Journal*, 2 Aug. 1731; *Daily Gazetteer*, 24 July, 30 Oct. 1740; *Senator*, 5 Mar. 1728.

41. *London Journal*, 5 Oct. 1728.

42. *Hyp-Doctor*, 25 Jan. 1732; *Whitehall Evening Post*, 6 Jan. 1728.

43. *Free Briton*, 6 Jan. 1732.

44. *London Journal*, 12 Oct. 1728; *Free Briton*, 21 Jan. 1731; Anon., *Popular Prejudices Against the Convention and Treaty with Spain Examined and Answered* (1739), pp. 28–9.

45. *Nonsense of Common-Sense*, 21 Feb. 1738; Anon., *Observations on a Pamphlet, entitled, an Answer to one Part of a Late Infamous Libel, etc. In a Letter to Mr. P[ulteney]* (1731), p. 29; Anon., *The True Principles of the Revolution Revived and Asserted* (1741), pp. 4–5; *True Patriot*, 3 June 1746; *Jacobite's Journal*, 12 Mar., 4 June, 24 Sept. 1748; *Senator*, 26 Apr. 1728; *Con-Test* 30 Nov. 1756.

46. *Daily Gazetteer*, 9 Dec. 1737; *Jacobite's Journal*, 12 Mar., 28 May 1748.

47. *British Journal*, 9 Dec. 1727; *Daily Gazetteer*, 18, 29 Oct. 1740, 25 Feb. 1742; *Jacobite's Journal*, 28 May 1748; Anon., *Abstract of the reciprocal Duties of Representatives and their Constituents* (1756), pp. 62–3; *Con-Test*, 18 Dec. 1756.

48. Lord Hervey, Lord Privy Seal, 1 Dec. 1740, Cobbett, 11, 739; Hervey to Stephen Fox, 25 Nov. 1729, Earl of Ilchester (ed.), *Lord Hervey and his Friends* (1950), p. 40; *Hyp-Doctor*, 2 Jan. 1733.

49. Anon., *Letter to Mr. P.*, p. 44; Presentation of *Craftsman* and *Fog's* by Grand Jury for Middlesex, *Daily Courant*, 7 July 1731. *Fog's Weekly Journal* summarised the ministerial arguments, 20 Sept. 1735.

50. *Craftsman*, 9 Dec. 1726; 24 June 1727, 28 Sept., 2 Nov. 1728; Anon., *Memoirs of the Life and Conduct of William Pulteney* (1735), p. 33.

51. *Craftsman*, 16 Dec. 1726, 24 June, 23 Sept. 1727, 28 Sept., 26 Oct. 1728; *Old England*, 11 Feb. 1744.

52. *Craftsman*, 23 Sept. 1727, 9 Dec. 1726, 25 Nov. 1727.

53. *Craftsman*, 31 July 1731; *Monitor*, 14 Nov. 1761.

54. *Champion*, 1 May 1740; *Old England*, 11 Feb. 1744.

55. *Public Advertiser*, 29 July 1769; Wedderburn made the same point in the Commons, 6 Dec. 1770, Cobbett, 16, 1290.

56. N. Rogers, 'Aristocratic Clientage, Trade and Independency: Popular Politics in Pre-Radical Westminster', *Past and Present*, 61 (1973); Rogers, 'Resistance to Oligarchy: the City Opposition to Walpole and his successions, 1725–1747', in J. Stevenson (ed.), *London in the Age of Reform* (Oxford, 1977); Rogers, 'Popular Protest in Early Hanoverian England', *Past and Present* 79 (1978); L. Colley, 'Eighteenth-Century English Radicalism before Wilkes', *TRHS* 5th ser., 31 (1981); Rogers, 'Riot and Popular Jacobitism in Early Hanoverian England', in E. Cruickshanks (ed.), *Ideology and Conspiracy: Aspects of Jacobitism, 1689–1759* (Edinburgh, 1982); Rogers, 'The Urban Opposition to Whig Oligarchy, 1720–60', in M. and J. Jacobs (eds), *The Origins of Anglo-American Radicalism* (1984); H. T. Dickinson, 'Popular Politics in the Age of Walpole', in J. Black (ed.), *Britain in the Age of Walpole* (1984).

57. Forrester to Mitchell, 12 Sept. 1763, BL. Add. 30999 f. 16.

58. *Public Advertiser*, 16 Nov. 1786; *World*, 31 May 1791. On the opposition inventing the news, *Berrow's Worcester Journal*, 30 Nov. 1769.

59. *London Chronicle*, 21 Dec. 1762; *Test*, 18 June 1757.

60. *Ipswich Journal*, 18 Feb. 1764; *Reading Mercury*, 2 May 1768; *Lloyd's Evening Post*, 4 Nov. 1768.

61. *North Briton*, 5 June 1762; *St. James's Chronicle*, 14 Apr. 1769, 28 Dec. 1771.

62. *Public Advertiser*, 7, 13 Oct. 1769; *Reading Mercury*, 1 Jan. 1770.

63. *The Future Chronicle: or The Nova Scotia Intelligencer* printed in the *North Britain* of 17 July 1762 was a witty example of anti-Scottish propaganda. John Bull had died from swallowing a thistle.

64. *London Chronicle*, 13 Jan. 1776; *Newcastle Courant*, 23 Mar. 1776; *National Journal*, 8 Apr. 1746.

65. *Leeds Intelligencer*, 3 Nov. 1767.

66. Chavigny to French foreign minister Chauvelin, 3 Mar. (ns) 1732, 28 Apr. (ns) 1733, Anon. memorandum, 27 June (ns) 1739, AE. CP. Ang. 376 f. 258, 380 f. 132, Mémoires et Documents, Ang. 8 f. 202; Geraldino to St Gill, 1 July (ns) 1738, PRO. 94/246 f. 179.

67. Historical Manuscripts Commission, *Diary of the First Earl of Egmont* (3 vols., 1920–3) I, 220.

68. *Craftsman*, 6 Apr. 1728; *Old England*, 14 Sept. 1745; *Craftsman*, 17 Feb. 1770.

69. *Public Advertiser*, 19 Dec. 1769; *St. James's Chronicle*, 14 Jan. 1766.

70. Robert Trevor to Poyntz, 21 Dec. 1729, BL. Althorp, E 3.

71. François Noël to Lebrun, acting French foreign minister, 10 Sept. 1792, AE. CP. Ang. 582 f. 109.

72. Noël to Lebrun, 10 Sept., Lebrun to Noël, 28 Sept. 1792, AE. CP. Ang. 582 f. 109, 240. On Perry, I. R. Christie, 'James Perry of the Morning Chronicle, 1756–1821', in Christie, *Myth and Reality*, pp. 334–58; Asquith, *Perry*.

73. Lebrun to Noël, 28 Sept., Noël to Lebrun, 18, 22 Oct. 1792, AE. CP. Ang. 582 f. 240, 583 f. 12, 48; *Morning Chronicle*, 16 Oct. 1792.

74. *Champion*, 11 Nov. 1740; *Mist's Weekly Journal*, 22 May 1726.

75. Cannon (ed.), *Junius*, xv.

6 Controlling the Press: Censorship and Subsidies

> As soon as Government has any influence over a paper printed in this town, the sale of it decreases, and an Englishman will like no newspaper that does not shew him he is ill governed and on the brink of ruin.
>
> Anthony Chamier, Under-Secretary in the Southern Department, 1778[1]

> What friend of social order will deny, that *the Press* requires some strong control? And what control is more effectual than that which *the Press itself* can supply? Falsehood is best opposed by the promulgation of truth.
>
> *Anti-Jacobin Review and Magazine*, prospectus, July 1798

General considerations

The political impact that the press did enjoy may have owed much to the widely held belief that it either was or could be influential. This was a view widely expounded in the press. It was argued that newspapers spread information about developments, and that they were read for that purpose. 'Neuter', writing in *Lloyd's Evening Post* in 1768, complained that the prophecies of doom in the press were like tales told to frighten children,

> for as these terrify their fancies, and disturb their dreams with stories of ghosts, goblins, giants, and bloody-bones, so many a wise barber, grocer, and upholsterer, who go to drink their pot and smoke their pipe, return home . . . with dreadful tales of foreign war, domestic discord, loss of trade, breach of public credit, bankruptcies, famine, ruin, misery, and desolation.

W.C. claimed in the *Reading Mercury* in 1780 that without the press 'our country villages, the curate, the exciseman, and the blacksmith, would lose the satisfaction of being as wise as any first minister of state'.[2]

135

How far provincial readership of political material aroused concern is unclear. References to the pernicious impact of opposition
newspapers can be found in the correspondence of the provincial
agents of members of the ministry. In 1733 Dr Thomas Curteis,
rector of Wrotham in Kent, and an electoral agent of the Duke of
Dorset, complained about the impact of press attacks on one of
the ministerial candidates for county representation as a supporter
of the Excise Bill: 'The enclosed Canterbury newspaper (which is
dispersed over the county) will do us a great deal of mischief unless
the edge of it be taken off by something handsomely written on the
other side.'[3] At election time such material was clearly worrying,
but the lesser role of governmental intervention in the provincial
press, both in terms of legal action and of financial support,
suggests that it was only the metropolitan press that engaged
ministerial attention for most of the century. Legal action against
provincial opposition newspapers appears largely to have arisen
from the independent initiatives of local ministerial supporters, as
with the Norwich moves against Henry Crossgrove, the printer of
the *Norwich Gazette*, in the 1710s, 1720s and 1730s. A significant
exception, unrelated to any electoral considerations, was the decision by the ministry in 1726 to establish a system for the
surveillance of the provincial press. The Comptroller of the Post
Office was given funds to purchase all Irish, Scottish and provincial papers for the perusal of the Treasury Solicitor, Nicholas
Paxton, who appears to have played a significant directing role in
government intervention in the press. This system appears to have
led directly to the prosecution of Edward Farley in 1728, and John
White and Samuel Farley in 1731, printers respectively of *Farley's
Exeter Journal*, the *Newcastle Courant* and *Farley's Bristol Newspaper*.[4] These printers were prosecuted not for any comments on
local news nor for printing their own views on national events, but
for reprinting items from *Mist's Weekly Journal* and the
Craftsman, the Jacobite 'Persian Letter' of 1728 from the former
and the 'Hague Letter' from the latter, both of which had led to
prosecutions of the London paper. The moves against the provincial newspapers can therefore be seen as part of a campaign
against the leading opposition London newspapers. Restricting
their national influence by discouraging provincial reprints of
items might have been a good idea, but it was not followed
through, and after 1731 governmental intervention in provincial
cases lapsed, though the Comptroller was paid for the service until

1736. Cranfield suggested that this was due to the difficulties of securing a successful prosecution,[5] but, though such a step was indeed difficult, it was the initiation of prosecution, rather than its success, that was the principal threat to printers both provincial and metropolitan. In the summer of 1729 Edward Farley petitioned Queen Caroline from prison. Charged with High Treason, he had been kept in prison since September 1728 'loaded with irons'. He promised 'to behave as a dutiful subject as long as he lives' and complained that his wife and family had been 'reduced to extreme poverty'. Philip Yorke, the Attorney-General, recommended a pardon, but Farley died in gaol in 1729.[6]

Provincial printers were deterred by the fate of colleagues. In 1728 the House of Commons acted to prevent the reporting of its proceedings in Robert Raikes's *Gloucester Journal*, a York paper, commenting, 'The public cannot expect to have an account of the proceedings of the Hon. House of Commons in this or other newspapers, since the printer of Gloucester is taken into custody of the Serjeant of Arms for inserting the same.'[7] Rather than following Cranfield in treating the lapsing of central governmental action against provincial printers after 1731 as due to the limited effectiveness of their legal powers, one could suggest that it reflected a relative lack of interest by an overburdened and understaffed administration. Possibly it was felt that local control was better and that particularly heinous items would be referred by provincial agents. To a certain extent the attitude to the provincial press reflected that towards the opposition London press, for there was a diminution of direct ministerial legal action in London after 1731. However there was a distinct difference in attitude towards the metropolitan and provincial press, one recently noted by John Feather in the case of the *Cambridge Intelligencer*, a very widely circulated radical newspaper of the 1790s. In 1793 the Canterbury newspaper the *Kentish Herald* felt able to add *Assertor of the Liberty of the Press* to its title. In the same year the initiative for the idea of acquiring *Swinney's Birmingham and Stafford Chronicle* and thus depriving the 'violent supporters of Priestley and Paine' of control of a major paper in an important region came from a local JP, not from the ministry.[8]

It would be mistaken to argue that successive ministries were oblivious to provincial opinion. It was rather the case that they appear to have assumed that the most effective way in which they could easily limit the provincial dissemination of opposition material was by taking steps against the circulation of metropolitan opinion. In January 1733 *Wye's Letter* remarked;

> 'Tis remarked, that hardly any scheme ever met with a more general aversion throughout the nation than this for a new Excise, which is looked upon to be owing, in some measure to the *Craftsman*, and that he may be called to account for misrepresentations.

The instructions to the Post Office not to send out copies of the *London Evening Post* in 1733 and 1754, on the eve of general elections, represented the simplest method of pursuing this policy. It was claimed that newspapers were being 'taken out of the letters' in 1775.[9]

If successive ministries concentrated their attention, insofar as they paid any, on the metropolitan press, this reflected not only a belief that metropolitan opinion was more significant than that of the provinces, but also a correct assessment both of the greater importance and of the greater accessibility to government action of the London over the provincial press. The opposition press boasted of its influence, 'Domitian' in the *Public Advertiser* claiming that Junius had 'fairly hissed' the Duke of Grafton off the stage.[10] The first number of the *Universal Spy* claimed in 1732 that 'the great Mr. Mist, the patron of journals, has brought us to the democratical state of Athens, to be judges of treaties, and arbitrators of peace and war'.[11] Ministerial newspapers could scorn these claims, or stress the pernicious strengths of opposition newspapers. The *Flying Post*, replying in 1730 to the *Craftsman's* boasts of its importance, claimed, 'There has nothing happened in the affairs of Europe, but what would have happened if the law had had its effect, and D'Anvers been silenced 3 or 4 years ago . . . The fly upon the Chariot Wheel!'[12] The following year this fly was credited with possessing 'a murmuring trumpet, which blows a political rumour in a few minutes from Berwick to Cornwall', whilst Fielding quoted Lucretius to the effect that dripping water hollows a stone, when assessing the 'mischievous consequences of opposition propaganda'.[13]

Informed repeatedly that the people took their opinions from the press,[14] it was not surprising that politicians, both British and foreign, believed that the newspapers were powerful.[15] Given that historians are uncertain, with reason, as to the influence of the

press in the period,[16] it is understandable that many contemporaries chose to ascribe great influence to this unpredictable,
vociferous, constant, politically active and often politically linked
force about which, by modern standards, relatively little was
known as to ownership, finances, political linkage and intentions.
It was credible, given this lack of knowledge and the paranoia
characteristic of the period, that the sinister fictional Whig Sir
Thomas Double could claim on behalf of his party, 'We have
libels, songs and lists ready in the press, to defame and blacken all
different ranks of men; nay, we need but reprint what we have
heretofore published. Have we not the happy opportunity of
giving the Kingdom, for 20 years, wrong notions of men and
things?'[17] Steele presented 'some part of the species' as willing
victims of the press: 'What mere blanks they are when they first
come abroad in the morning, how utterly they are at a stand till
they are set a going by some paragraph in a news-paper.'[18] The
same theme was developed by several Whigs and Whig papers who
attributed the impact of the opposition press to the desire by 'the
vulgar' for scandal.[19] This argument implied that supporting
ministerial papers would not lead to a lessening of the effect of
opposition propaganda. Something more drastic was necessary to
protect both the ministry and the readers, for as William
Windham, in a strident call for action, assured the Commons in
1798, 'He never saw a man with a newspaper in his hand, without
regarding him with the sensation that he was taking poison.'[20]
George Tilson might feel that opposition propaganda would
'amuse coffee-house politicians, but make little or no impression
on people of sense',[21] but others were not so sure, though they
tended not to explain how popular attitudes, however defined or
quantified, would influence policy. After the fall of Minorca to the
French in 1756, the London lawyer Nathaniel Cole wrote, 'The
newspapers and pamphlets tend to raise an uneasiness among the
people and to point out a Militia law upon which much stress is laid
as the only thing to save the nation and from this disposition I
think such a bill must pass in the same session.' In 1770 Viscount
Harcourt gave a warning about Junius: 'The lengths he has
ventured to go are really amazing, and may in the end occasion the
greatest disorder, if the means taken by Government to stop the
career of that treasonable libel should prove unsuccessful.' In 1784
Philip Yorke claimed, 'The publication of the debates and
opposition speeches have lost America, and the fewer there are to

be published, the better the business will be done, if in good hands.'[22]

How far these attitudes influenced successive ministries is unclear. By the very nature of things the surviving sources tend to stress government intervention in the press. There are memoranda suggesting courses of action, evidence of subsidies paid to particular newspapers, records of legal action. In State Papers Domestic one does not expect to find preserved letters to ministers saying that newspapers could be ignored. There was no reason to send such letters, and, as to a great extent legal action reflected complaints from domestic informants or foreign envoys,[23] it tends to be evidence of such complaints that survives. There was no systematic reporting by a range of officials on the press that would have permitted accounts that there was nothing to worry about. The same was true of the private correspondence of ministers. A Warwickshire correspondent could urge Granville to take action against the press in 1756 and provide quotable passages about sounding 'the trumpet of rebellion'. There was no reason for someone to write in from Nottinghamshire to Granville to let him know that there was nothing to worry or write about.[24] By their very nature it was the most strident complaints that survive, and have been quoted. In a similar fashion the opposition press stressed suspicions of governmental subsidising of ministerial newspapers and criticised prosecutions. When subsidies and prosecutions lapsed or lessened this was not commented upon by contemporaries and has not attracted the attention of historians. As the political role of the press has been most fully discussed for periods of acute political tension such as the 1700s, it is not surprising that government intervention has been stressed. This also corresponds with the picture of an influential 'public opinion'. Much able work has been devoted to this subject, but the coverage hitherto has been patchy. More is known about the press of the 1700s, 1730s and 1760s than the newspapers of the late 1710s, the 1740s and the early 1750s. This division does not exactly match that of government intervention, which can be seen in each of the last three periods, the propaganda campaign of the Sunderland ministry being a topic in particular need of study. However it is true that the level and nature of government intervention in the press varied, even if these variations cannot be readily quantified from the available sources: there are no financial series stretching through the whole century for an eighteenth-century Ministry of

Propaganda, and the surviving material is often difficult to match. It is also true that the periods most thoroughly studied have been those when political intervention was most obvious, whereas the peacetime Pelham ministry (1748–54), in which serious press conflict was episodic, has not been studied from this angle. The Seven Years War (1756–63) did not see comparable press warfare, insofar as this can be assessed, to that of the Spanish Succession War, and there was a definite shift in 1762 noted by Bute, who wrote, 'War seems to be declared at home with the utmost virulence.'[25]

It is arguable that with time the political impact of the press, or at least ministerial concern about it, was lessened as politicians became more accustomed to newspapers. Newspapers legally selling in their thousands, carrying informed political comment, advancing party views and containing pieces by eminent politicians, were an innovation to the politicians of the 1690s, whose most recent experience had been the short lived, often hysterical pieces produced during the Exclusion Crisis. A series of innovations, principally the first daily newspaper, the *Daily Courant* (1702), the first evening paper, the *Evening Post* (1706), and the first provincial papers, probably encouraged a sense of developing possibilities. In 1695 the returns in the general election and the addresses in favour of supply were printed by the newly-founded papers.[26] Some politicians clearly sensed new opportunities,[27] and the medium of print was used with great effect to stir up feelings in a series of issues, such as the Sacheverell case and the conduct of Britain's Dutch allies.[28] The wishes of those who wished to turn the clock back to 1695 were ignored, and the press did not suffer excessively from Harley's Tory administration or its introduction of a Stamp Duty. The press was felt to be worth subsidising. Politicians and newspapers could, if they wished, seek to attribute some of the changes in ministry and policy that characterised the reign of Queen Anne to the influence of opinion 'out-of-doors', public opinion, the press, whatever term best summarised the sense that something outside the world of Whitehall, Westminster and Versailles had an impact on British politics. The degree of scepticism about the impact of the press is impossible to assess, as the sceptical were usually silent. Godolphin was not a great inspirer of printed propaganda. However, as one party sponsored a particular paper another felt it necessary to reply.[29] The personal political role of some writers such as Steele and the connections of

others such as Swift with prominent statesmen may have encouraged greater political commitment to the press. What is unclear is how many politicians shared the belief expressed in June
1711 that 'it is possible to scribble these men [the ministry]
down'.[30] Queen Anne herself could see opposition literature as
evidence simply 'that it was party and faction that was discontented and not the body of the nation'.[31]

Whatever expectations about the role of the press were engendered during the politically volatile reign of Anne, the experience of the succeeding two decades should have induced
caution. As the generation of politicians, such as Addison and
Steele, who had been active in the politics of Anne's reign and
often written pamphlets and other material, died, they were replaced by others whose experience was of Whig ministries enjoying substantial parliamentary majorities whose longevity made
the opposition press appear as a mere irritant. When Pulteney and
Bolingbroke founded the *Craftsman* in 1726 they hoped it would
play a role in the fall of the Walpole ministry rather than shine in
future textbooks on political thought. They had not envisaged
Walpole remaining in office until 1742. The *Craftsman* and *Fog's
Weekly Journal* might well have explained the mysteries of government 'to the Crowd'[32] (bearing in mind the use of such
terminology to describe the middling ranks of society), and this no
doubt helped them to sell copies, but in political terms they were
designed to do more and this they failed to do.

It may not be fanciful to suggest that from the mid-1730s
onwards there was a different ministerial attitude to the press. The
opposition[33] failure in 1733–4 to use the Excise Crisis either to
wreck Walpole at Court or in the general elections marked the
collapse of a sustained attempt to vilify the first minister. The
Country ideal collapsed as opposition Whigs and Tories clashed in
1734–6 over foreign policy and ecclesiastical issues, and its pro-
genitor Bolingbroke retired to France. These developments had
their echo in the press. The ministry consolidated its subsidised
press in 1735, closing down a number of famous titles. Mist returned to London in 1736 and made his peace with the ministry, an
attempt to keep *Fog's Weekly Journal* going as an opposition
paper under different ownership ending in failure. The
Craftsman's circulation fell and it headed towards internal division. The Earl of Stair complained to Sarah, Duchess of
Marlborough in February 1737 that the issues of the *Craftsman*

'have had nothing in them a great while'. Opposition opinion was still expressed in many papers, but to many it must have appeared marginal in its political relevance and it could be suggested that this was to remain the case substantially for at least two decades. Newcastle was uncertain as to what to do about answering opposition propaganda in the late 1750s, and John Brewer has referred to the fumblings and hesitations in their dealings with the press of 'Newcastle and the whig mandarinate' when they were forced into opposition in the early 1760s, and has argued that their reluctance to become involved in any newspaper war was inherited by the Rockingham Whigs. Hardwicke professed himself not well-informed concerning attacks on Bute. Lord Hervey in his unpublished tragedy *Agrippina*, written in about 1736, expressed his views through Pallas:

> The wise in silence therefore bear each pain
> or only where redress is sure complain.
> Content they seem with necessary ill
> and what they must submit to seem to will.
> Whilst babbling fools their discontent relate
> rail at the world, and murmur against fate.[34]

Pension papers

> It is no secret, that the St. James's Evening Post is what the printers call a Pension Paper, that is, it is obliged for its existence to a certain great man.
> *A Letter to the Craftsman from Eustace Budgell* (1730), p. 26

Why, if the press had relatively little direct political impact and a wider effect that was difficult both to assess and politically to exploit, did successive ministries use their powers to subsidise a government and prosecute the opposition press? An intuitive answer that may actually contain a lot of truth is that they did so because their predecessors had done so, they could do so, and might as well do so. The force of habit was extremely important in eighteenth-century government and once a practice was begun it was rarely discontinued. Any decision to discontinue ministerial intervention in the press may have been further discouraged by the difficulty of assessing the effectiveness of the government press. It was easy for opposition papers to claim that it was ineffective, the *Westminster Journal* stating in 1742 that the *Daily Gazetteer* may have done Walpole harm: 'The stupid apologies of his advocates in the Gazetteer have perhaps done him more harm than the witty invectives of the Craftsman or Common Sense.'[35] Such was possibly no more than the habitual taunting that characterised references to opposing papers.

A definite encouragement for ministerial intervention was Jacobite propaganda. Blatant examples could be prosecuted, but the resilience of Mist's papers suggested that this was not enough. Subsidising ministerial papers to counteract the effects of Jacobite propaganda could be readily justified: the latter represented a sinister ideological and political threat. In addition successive ministries were urged to take action by writers keen for subsidies, or supporters worried about the impact of opposition propaganda. In 1723 the invalid Josiah Hort, Bishop of Ferns, wrote from London concerning an issue of the *Weekly Journal or British Gazetteer* which he felt represented a particularly serious challenge by its use of Whig language for Jacobite ends, a charge that was later to be used against the *Craftsman*:

> You will find in it an affected panegyric on those who put King Charles the 1st to death. The author introduces his poem with a letter wherein he professes his zeal for his present Majesty, and for the memory of K. William. This is only to obtrude himself upon the world for a Whig, the better to work mischief under that character. But the father of it is plainly some Jacobite who begot this bastard in rancour, with a design to lay it at the door of the Whigs. It is evidently calculated to inflame peoples minds against the administration, and will captivate the multitude if no remedy be apply'd.[36]

Ministerial publications were not simply designed as a 'remedy' to influence the uncommitted. They were also seen as a means of keeping supporters informed. This was seen most clearly in the pamphlets that appeared before each parliamentary session and set out government policy. This was of great value to ministerial supporters providing as it did the cue for the sessions. Government papers at the beginning of the sessions tended to carry similar items, often extracts from the pamphlets. The *Original Weekly Journal* carried in 1718 'a large abstract of a famous pamphlet, said to be written by a certain noble Lord at the head of affairs, and chiefly levelled at Mr. W—, which is entitled, "The Defection Consider'd"'. The *Free Briton* specialised in summarising pamphlets in the early 1730s whilst *Wye's Letter* carried the message into the provinces,[37] where it was juxtaposed with opposition material, the *Suffolk Mercury or Bury Post* carrying on 9 July 1733 ministerial material from the *Daily Courant* and on 30 July over two columns from the *Craftsman* attacking the Excise.

The extensive use of pamphlet material indicates the continuity between different forms of propaganda that is a feature of the entire period. If newspapers are abstracted for purposes of study it must not be forgotten that they often acted as a medium for the dissemination of verses, magazines, pamphlets, books, sermons, plays, obituaries, announcements, speeches and poetry. Political opinion and information was not a specialised function of the press, particularly in the case of domestic news. Newspapers might possess an advantage in immediacy, but pamphlets could be printed speedily, and the amount of new domestic news that could be printed was limited. Opinion rather than events dominated the political news of those newspapers that specialised in politics. Instead of 'in depth reporting' there were discursive essays on general, particularly ideological, themes. This was a sphere in which newspapers had little advantage over pamphlets, unless they dispensed with lengthy essays in favour of shorter items often forceful or humorous. It was only in terms of foreign news, when there was a mass of fast-changing information to be reported, that the newspapers were at a distinct advantage.

The continuum in different forms can be seen in the case of government (and opposition) sponsored items. Particularly in the first half of the century pamphlets were central to political pro-paganda, and vigorous pamphlet controversies, with large numbers of Answers, Confutations and Replies, established the subject matter of controversy in particular years. Marie Peters has suggested that there was a diminution in the role of pamphlets in the second half of the century, a transition from pamphlets to newspapers,[38] but this argument has to be handled with care. The issue of the British response to the French Revolution led to a major burst of pamphleteering, and there was no shortage of pamphlets in the previous three decades, as the Eighteenth-Century Short Title Catalogue is making increasingly apparent. Brewer saw the Rockingham Whigs as producing a steady flow, though not a stream, of pamphlets in the 1760s. Pamphlets went on being extracted at length in the press, both provincial and metropolitan,[39] and newspapers continued to carry news items about them, the press serving as a means of publicity. The *Reading Mercury* carried in 1771 a London item announcing that 'Mr. Edmund Burke is preparing for the press, this ensuing winter, a political pamphlet, under the inspection of the Marquis of Rockingham; the subject of which, we hear, is "A plan for the Coalition of Parties"'.[40]

Though pamphlets and newspapers could carry the same information and be read by the same people, they tended to serve different markets if only for reasons of cost and circulation figures. Certain pamphlets enjoyed very large sales, but the average number of copies printed for a single edition by William Bowyer and William Strahan in London in the 1760s was 500.[41] Though this figure was not too different from that of certain low-circulation newspapers, and in particular subsidised essay-sheets, it represents a substantially lower figure than that of the envisaged circulation of a successful newspaper. Pamphlets were aimed at a smaller market and costed accordingly in order to ensure a profit.

In choosing to subsidise newspapers, politicians and ministries were therefore opting for a circulation that was, by the standards of the age, the widest possible.[42] Subsidised pamphlets were intended for distribution to a readership that was to a great extent already known and well-informed, such as parliamentarians, office-holders and British and foreign envoys, who, through being largely in London, presented minimal problems of distribution. In contrast newspapers were designed for a substantially unknown and unquantified readership, whose political awareness, susceptibility and impact could only be guessed. Copies of newspapers were sent to particular officials, politicians and connections of both. The only paper mentioned in the account for papers sent to Newcastle's correspondents in 1726–8 was the *London Journal*. Copies of the *Whitehall* and *St. James's Evening Posts* were distributed in 1725 from the Secretaries' of State offices.[43] Local officials, such as postmasters and customs officers, could be expected to aid in distribution. The *Craftsman* printed a letter in 1733 that referred to this distribution system:

> For some years we have had gratis at the Post House all the Daily Courants, the Free Briton, the London Journal and many pamphlets on that side of the question. Now the Corn Cutter's

Journal is added; and they are offered gratis at all coffee-houses
in the country.

Letter of Mr. J. B-ll GPO, 9 October 1733

I shall send you the inclosed papers gratis as oft as they come
out, and desire you will make them as public as you can. If there
be any coffee-houses in your town, or within your delivery,
where gentlemen resort to read the news, please to send me the
names of such coffee-houses, or the persons who keep them,
and I will furnish them likewise gratis with the same
papers . . .[44]

Clearly such subsidised papers did not have to worry about purchasers but, whether sold or not, those who subsidised the papers
still had little idea about the potential or actual readership or the
impact that such papers made. The decision to invest time, talent
and money in the process did not reflect any knowledge of actual
or potential benefits. Reasons for this activity have been suggested
in the previous section of this chapter, but they are simply
hypotheses. In the absence of detailed ministerial documentation
setting out what was expected to result from the subsidised press,
it is difficult to know how far its success can be, or could be,
assessed. Contemporary comments tend to be unhelpful and
mostly abusive, opposition papers claiming that prosecution only
increased sales and that subsidised papers were used as waste
paper.[45] Ministerial correspondence suggests that stating the government viewpoint was regarded as crucial, but the anticipated
result in terms of persuading readers is obscure. In 1723 Viscount
Townshend wrote to Walpole concerning 'the City, where matters
appear to be carried with a pretty high hand against the Government; and I fear the paper called the True Briton is chiefly
calculated to animate that ill disposition; however I make no doubt
but you will take care to keep the writer within bounds and to have
the fallacy of his arguments laid open'.[46] Whether Benjamin
Hoadly's 'Britannicus' essays in the *London Journal* persuaded
anyone not hitherto committed of the superior merits of the ministerial case is unclear.

A series of important works have established the details concerning government patronage during the century.[47] Several
features stand out. The sums expended by various ministers varied
greatly. The Pelham and Newcastle ministries in the 1750s spent

relatively little on the press, aside from some pensions to writers. William Guthrie received £200 annually from 1746, James Ralph £300 from 1753, both on the secret service accounts.[48] William Arnall, author of the *Free Briton*, received in contrast £6,000 in 1732–3, and Hanson suggested that opposition claims in 1731 that Walpole was spending £20,000 annually on subsidising the ministerial press were not far from the truth.[49] This sum was slightly more than the annual establishment of an infantry regiment in 1762, whilst the annual pensions (payments) to ministerial writers were less than the perquisites colonels could expect to receive. Arnall's pension 'of about £400 p.a. which convinced him of the goodness of the cause he wrote in' was a high one, and it compared very favourably with the full pay of a captain of foot: £182.[50]

Pensions were not only paid to authors to write; they were also paid to dissuade them from so doing. Alongside ministerial expenditure on the governmental press was expenditure designed to neutralise opposition publications, and it is arguable that this was a more effective weapon than prosecution. The *London Journal* switched in 1722 from being the platform for John Trenchard and Thomas Gordon's critical 'Cato's Letters' to that for Hoadly's 'Britannicus' essays as a result of government expenditure. The journal had had a major effect, making 'such a noise in all the public papers', but though Gordon and Trenchard transferred to the *British Journal*, that was overshadowed by the *True Briton*.[51] Gordon's eventual transfer to the ministerial side was not retarded by the availability of government patronage, as a Commissioner for the Wine Licences. The *Westminster Journal* satirised ministerial techniques by printing in 1742 a letter supposedly from Ralph Courteville of the *Daily Gazetteer*, who had become with Arnall's death in 1736 the principal regular government writer. The letter announced that Courteville had been instructed to neutralise the *Westminster Journal*,

> by entering the lists against you, or by a treaty of subsidy. You have a fine opportunity of making your fortune. A pamphlet to show the necessity of three kingdoms being above the expence of a million of money, to protect a foreign insignificant tract of ground, would, at this juncture, be fifty pieces at least. Could you prove the consistent inconsistency, or the paradoxical maxim of the mutability of ideas in patriosmic disquisition, any of the people lately come into power would be your friends. Or

had you Burgersdiscius or Heereborod enough to chop logic, and prove representations and instructions are the seeds of sedition, I don't know but you might get a prebendary.[52]

These accusations were far from absurd. William Guthrie, who had written for the *Englishman's Evening Post*, *Common-Sense* and *Old England*, was paid a pension in return for not writing against the ministry. James Ralph, who had attacked the Walpole and Pelham ministries in *Common-Sense*, the *Champion* (for which he had been sole editor from 1741 to 1743), *Old England: or, The Constitutional Journal*, which he founded with Guthrie in 1744, the *Remembrancer* (1747–51) and the *Protester* (1753), was paid for his silence.

It is possible that the extent of ministerial (and opposition) patronage of the press was exaggerated by contemporaries. This may have been due to the tendency to stress the venal character of journalists and the willingness of politicians to indulge them. The *Grub Street Journal* stated in 1731 that

the Province, or rather the States, of Grub-Street, like those of Switzerland, never enter into any alliance offensive and defensive with any one contending power, against another; but wisely keep themselves in an exact neutrality. At the same time, their private members are ready to engage on either side for good pay, without ever inquiring into the merits of the cause.[53]

This image of the role of the press ignored the role of commercial pressures,[54] and the willingness of papers to adopt a marked political stance for reasons of personal conviction or marketing strategy.[55] Thus the number of papers that Walpole's ministry was accused of subsidising was exaggerated.[56]

It is possible that the effect, as well as the extent, of subsidies has been exaggerated. Pointing out that most papers and writers who were in receipt of money from the Secret Service Fund in the 1780s and 1790s received less that £200 annually, Lutnick suggested that these amounts were too small to sway any newspaper's editorial viewpoint and that they were probably spent in order to ensure favourable coverage of a particular issue.[57] Christie has argued that despite Aspinall's extensive catalogue of papers influenced by ministerial inducements, the degree of control enjoyed by the ministry was always limited. The Secret

Service accounts for 1784 list sums of only £100 each for the *Morning Herald*, the *Public Ledger*, and the *Whitehall, London* and *St. James's Evening Posts*. Haig claimed that the continued existence of the *Daily Gazetteer* after the ending of its subsidy with the fall of the Walpole ministry indicated that it was capable of producing a profit without governmental assistance and suggested that the revenue from direct sales and advertisements alone may have been sufficient during the Walpole administration to justify its publication.[58] The increasing impact of the government on the fiscal position of the press as a whole, through increases in Stamp Duty that bore no relation to inflation and the elimination of the unstamped press, did not lead to any apparent increase in ministerial influence on the content of the press, and may have had the opposite effect.[59] The rising volume of advertisements represented, despite the duty they carried, a source of fiscal independence. Increased circulation had the same effect. In 1793 the profit on the *Morning Chronicle* was £6,000. Such profits were too large to be jeopardised by selling a paper's political loyalties and no ministry would have been prepared to pay the £40,000 that the *Morning Chronicle* was sold for after Perry died in 1821.[60]

However, such developments lay in the future in the 1780s, when most papers were still small-scale affairs, with circulations no larger than they had been in the first two decades of the century.[61] In such a situation it was possible for even small ministerial subsidies to affect the profitability of particular papers. In 1770 an anecdote appeared in the press that Lord North, 'being lately told by a friend that his administration could not possibly last long, as Junius and all the good writers were against him, he replied that was certainly his own fault, for that he could have them all on his side whenever he pleased'.[62] It was not that easy to buy committed anonymous authors, but it was easier to buy papers. The *Morning Post*, hitherto a supporter of the opposition, was purchased by the government in 1776. Ehrman has suggested that an active press policy by Pitt between 1784 and 1790, including a marked rise in subsidies, played a role in improving press coverage of the ministry.[63] Successive ministries from the 1760s onwards appeared determined to ensure favourable publicity by spending money. Bute was an active patron of the press and the Grenville ministry (1763–5) was described by a contemporary as 'indefatigable in their productions both in newspapers and pamphlets'.[64] Ministerial propaganda in the 1760s boasted such talent as John

Shebbeare, a prominent opposition writer in the previous decade, James Macpherson, James Scott, Smollett and Caleb Whiteford. Opposition journalists were gained: Hugh Kelly with a pension, William Knox with a post.[65] Lord North's ministry (1770-82) was actively defended in print. North persuaded Dr Johnson to write pamphlets against the Wilkites and in defence of his policy in the Falkland Islands crisis, a pamphlet said to have been written 'under the special direction' of the minister. When in retirement North was to tell the French Ambassador that he had never seen a British government strong enough to be able to ignore what was said in print, and that it was necessary for ministries to reply to printed criticism, failing which they would swiftly become unpopular.[66]

It could be argued that, given the generally agreed propensity of readers of political news to turn to opposition material, it was necessary for ministries to subsidise newspapers if they wished to ensure at least a degree of good coverage, and that the precarious financial state of most papers made this a worthwhile method. The government had more than money alone to offer. Thomas Bradshaw, who as Secretary of the Treasury had played a role in ministerial propaganda, claimed in 1773 that 'a newspaper can never be supported without the insertion now and then of a secret'. Samuel Buckley sought to obtain for the *Daily Courant* 'such foreign news as is proper to be printed; this indulgence would add much to the circulation of a paper calculated and carried on entirely for public benefit'.[67] Ministerial newspapers could hope to receive advertisements from departments of governments (two of the only six advertisements in the *Daily Courants* of 4 September and 9 October 1734), assistance at the Post Office, and benefits to other aspects of their business. An active searcher of government patronage, John Walter was appointed printer to the Customs Office in 1787, having failed to obtain the profitable printing contract for the Stationery Office.

Policing the 'venom of every day's defamation'[68]

> Take such immediate steps as your knowledge of the law, and the nature of the case will suggest to you as most proper to bring the printer or author of this paper, or both of them, to condign punishment.
>
> Viscount Weymouth to the Attorney-General, 1770[69]

We hear that Miles Burton Allen, Esq. met with Hugh Kelly on Thursday night by accident at Vauxhall, and gave him a severe beating for the lie he had given him in a newspaper.

Darlington Pamphlet, 3 July 1772

The Freedom of The Press is one of the essential components of the Anglo-American liberal inheritance, its virtues proclaimed, rather than analysed, in tome after tome, both constitutional and popular. The process by which this Freedom was achieved was treated as a heroic struggle by Whig historians, both British and American. The excellent works that set out the judicial bases of government regulation, the changes produced during the eighteenth century and the *causes célèbres* of the period were imbued with support 'for the basic freedom of expression', 'a new concept of the liberty of the press'.[70] There has been little attempt to understand the ministerial point of view, the motives that led governments to take action and the difficulties they faced. Current intellectual suppositions are scarcely favourable to such an approach. If the heroes of today are no longer the liberal judges and lawyers of the eighteenth century, such as Camden and Erskine, they are instead enterprising, classless newspaper printers, those who rejected the 'sedative rhetoric of constitutional liberty' or helped 'bitter populist hatred of ministries and monarchs [to force] its way to the surface'.[71] Largely meaningless modern fashionable phrases such as the need for an open society can lead to a strange perception of the attitudes and problems of the past. Most of the prosecutions of the press in the eighteenth century resulted from political conflict, not from any attempt to suppress the expression of any bitter 'populist hatred', or to subvert the growth of a radical press. The latter interpretation conforms to a model stressing the need for 'the regime of the great proprietors' to protect their position by suppressing opposition and persuading the populace of the majesty and rectitude of their position, in order to create a spirit of consent and submission.[72] Social stability in this analysis required both coercion and manipulation. Ministerial intervention in the press could be seen as using the former to achieve the latter, and, more to the point to prevent subversion, because the essential core of the analysis is of a defensive system resistant to change. However, recent work on the period has stressed the strength of the social system and of the conservative social and religious ideology of the period, and the

Literary devices
"(verses, tales,
epigrams)" (p127)
used to appeal to
the masses —

bel effect" p165

see p. 104 – 6 for
circulation figs
from 1704 – 1790
(plus p. 146)

p141
First Daily was Daily
Courant (1702), first
Evening was Evening
Post (1706)

In one of its allegories... made
self/ safer by being located in
"exp't.c Orat." p134

absence of any need for sustained coercion or manipulation.[73] There was criticism of abuses, political, social and religious, national and local, in the press. The bad milk served to prisoners in Leeds gaol was condemned in 1766, a dispute over the salary of the master of Alnwick school made public by advertisements in the Newcastle press in 1737.[74] Corruption, of institutions, manners and morals, was often attacked, both generally and specifically. The *Gazetteer and New Daily Advertiser* printed a letter from 'Another Spy' in 1770 asking it to 'inform the public' about 'an open market for the buying and selling of offices'.[75] There were many bitter attacks on aristocratic habits. Gambling was often denounced, and the fondness for foreign products, customs, servants and interests condemned. There were frequent attacks in the press on French fashions, food and hairdressers and Italian opera. An anonymous letter printed in the monthly the *Political State of Great Britain* in 1739 condemned the illegal importation of gold and silver manufactures from France 'to the indelible reproach of our nobility' whose 'impolitick and unnatural' preference helped Britain's enemy. These views were disseminated by London items in the provincial press, attacking the playing of French card games or the employment of French servants and drinking of French wine by 'the nobility and gentry'.[76]

Such criticism, pointed or general, did not tend to lead to prosecution. Instead of prosecutions responding to attacks on the social system they tended to be of two types. The first was prosecutions aimed at particular political statements and accusations, statements and prosecutions that often reflected rivalry within the governing elite between politicians, as with the campaign against the *Craftsman*. The second was action designed to deal with the expression of subversive opinion closely linked with a threat to the British system. In the first half of the eighteenth century this meant Jacobitism, in the 1790s radicalism, both closely related to threats from foreign powers. It was this aspect of press censorship that successive ministries tended to vaunt, for, far from being a secretive embarrassing activity, judicial action was regarded as both necessary and desirable, essential to protect society from factious or treasonable propaganda. The protective function of government and the law was often stressed, protective not only of themselves, but also of morality and religion, and indeed of the press itself, judged by many to be incapable of self-regulation and requiring supervision in order to prevent its excesses driving government to new legislation. The possibility of such a determination of the liberty of the press was mentioned by an anonymous essayist in 1782 who further argued that an 'inflammatory address' to the weaknesses or prejudices of the people was 'nothing better than a libel upon freedom itself'.[77] The oft-made distinction between licence and liberty, crucial to the discussion of much besides the press, provided a general justification for judicial regulation, whilst the subversiveness of Jacobite, and in the 1790s radical, propaganda represented a challenge requiring action. In addition the general tendency of opposition criticism to weaken the state by fomenting domestic discord and exacerbating relations with foreign powers was an argument that was used with conviction to justify judicial action, and the latter was a particular cause of prosecution and harassment. There was indeed justification for such action. From their excellent interception and deciphering system, the ministry discovered in 1716 that papers, particularly the Tory *Post Boy*, did not dare to print material offered by the Swedish envoy Count Gyllenborg, who sought to use the press to stir up opposition to Britain's Baltic policy. In February 1717 John Morphew of the *Post Boy* was indeed arrested for publishing an item on Anglo-Swedish relations.[78]

Ministers sought secrecy or favourable coverage for sensitive foreign negotiations,[79] and it is interesting to note that several officials who had been prominent in the conduct of foreign policy played a significant role in the ministerial supervision of the press. Delafaye, Weston and Burges are good examples. There were institutional reasons for this. The Secretaries of State were responsible until 1782 both for foreign policy and for matters of internal policing, including the supervision of the press. From 1741 the office of Writer of the *Gazette* was held for life by present or former officials of the Secretaries' offices. Knowledge of the detrimental or inconvenient consequences for British foreign policy of press criticism and of the openness of newspapers to the inducements of foreign envoys could hardly have encouraged those Under-Secretaries, such as Delafaye, who played a major role in instigating and conducting the supervision of the press, to adopt a tolerant attitude.[80]

It is therefore easy to appreciate why officials did not share the view of the *Craftsman* that 'the Freedom of the Press . . . was never restrained but in order to serve some bad design, in wicked reigns, or under corrupt administration'.[81] The willingness of opposition newspapers, even in wartime, to use any material they could safely print to harm the government, whatever the consequences, and the ability and willingness of hostile individuals, Jacobites, foreign envoys and domestic rivals, to supply this material, would have entailed calls for rebellion, the disclosure of secret information, such as the state of naval preparedness, and abuse without restraint or qualification. It would not only have been ministries that would have suffered. Private individuals would have enjoyed no legal protection. As it was, anonymous attacks were a major threat to the reputation of others, as William Hutchins pointed out in a letter of complaint to the *Reading Mercury* in 1771. The printer of the *Daily Journal* was prosecuted in 1728 for accusing an individual of stealing tiles and stones. According to Paxton the Tories themselves were ashamed by the *London Evening Post*'s attack on the late Sir Charles Gounter Nicoll.[82] The freedom of the press also entailed extraordinary abuse of groups or nations that were in no position to defend themselves. The antecedents of Bute and Mansfield led to vicious attacks on the Scots in the early part of George III's reign. Foreigneers, both individuals and nations, could not expect fair treatment. In 1781 the *Leeds Intelligencer*, a keen supporter of the North ministry's American policy, attacked 'national reflections' at the expense of the Scots.[83] The outburst of anti-semitic comment that accompanied the Jewish Naturalisation Act of 1753 was no more than a politically motivated instance of a style of reporting that was all too common. The concomitant of exuberant patriotism was an intense suspicion and virulent dislike of everything that was different, foreign and strange. In 1732 the accusation that London Jews had burnt to death a child produced by a mixed union led to anti-semitic acts and an appeal for legal intervention against the printer.[84] Given the amount of unjustified and vicious abuse that politicians and private citizens had to 'as usual wade through',[85] a modern reader of the press may be forgiven for wondering whether there was not too little censorship and legal retribution, and for regretting that the machinery of governmental supervision and judicial action was apparently of limited effectiveness.

The effectiveness of governmental action is in fact difficult to assess. The course of judicial activity can be followed and the State Papers Domestic provide some interesting correspondence concerning the suitability and likely success of action or the threat of

action, arguably the most significant resource the ministry possessed and one best conserved by only resorting to judicial action
occasionally. There is also very little information concerning
non-official action to prevent or punish reports in the press. The
extent of such action, both in London and the provinces, is
difficult to assess. Charles, Lord Mohun rewarded John Dyer for
his comments on him with a severe beating. The Duke of
Marlborough wrote to Harley in 1706 demanding protection from
the *Observator* and threatened that if none was forthcoming he
would have the printer's bones broken. In the following year the
printer John Tutchin did indeed die shortly after being attacked.
During and after the 1713 election William Thompson MP raged at
Abel Roper for writing in the *Post Boy* that his property was 'an
estate in parcels', and therefore insufficient to come within the
terms of the Landed Qualification Act. He demanded a published
retraction, threatening supposedly to cut Roper's throat if he did
not comply. Five years later Mist complained about an attempt to
intimidate him into retracting an article concerning the indecent
behaviour of some women in church. In 1719 'one Boyer, a French
News Writer, and Author of the Political State, having reflected
on the Earl of Dundonald, a gentleman corrected him very
severely in a coffee-house, the French man not offering to draw his
sword'. In January 1728 the printer of the *London Journal* was
beaten up as punishment for an advertisement. This led to a
remonstration from Z. Mercer who wrote to the *Evening Post*
complaining about the attack on Wilkins and adding that 'even in
cases of sedition, the Government proceeds only according to the
known rules of law, and with all possible regards to the liberty of
the subject'. In 1762 Wilkes had to fight a duel with Lord Talbot
following the *North Briton*'s attack on the latter's management of
the royal household. In 1770 the prospect of an attack on the
character of Louis XV led Batailhe de Francès, the French Minister Plenipotentiary, accompanied by two French army officers
then in London, to pay an evening visit to the printer of the
Gazetteer and New Daily Advertiser. On being informed that the
latter was not at home he gave the printer's servant a letter made
out in the form of an advertisement, signed by a French officer
which announced that if he printed any attack on Louis XV he
would be beaten to death. Francès reported that the officers
accompanied him in uniform in order to persuade the printer that
the threat was not an idle one, and he defended his action by citing

the slowness and weakness of the law and the inability of the magistrates to prevent such articles. Francès' threat did not remain secret, and it led to a severe reprimand from the French foreign minister Choiseul. The Sardinian envoy pointed out that any attempt to carry out the threat would have led to legal retribution and the probable execution of the officers. However, as Francès pointed out, there was no attack upon Louis XV in the newspaper. Henry Bate of the *Morning Post* fought duels on several occasions.

It was in no way necessary to offer to lay down one's life as the French were reported to have done in 1770. Following threats to the life of a writer, a misunderstanding at a masquerade in 1789 did not get into print as had been threatened.[86] An attack in the dark by some hired bullies could be both effective and safe. The frequency and effects of such action are unclear. They belong partly to the world of private action, one in which individuals paid both for puffs and to avoid attack, and to the world of political life, in which hired mobs could be employed for violence and intimidation on occasions such as elections. There is little evidence that ministries used violence to intimidate opposition writers. The *Daily Gazetteer* might suggest in 1738 that opposition satirists should be 'clubb'd or rather bastinadoed',[87] but governments preferred to use the legal violence of raids by messengers of the press rather than extra-legal methods. Resort to the latter might have been effective, but it would just as likely have created a storm and provided an emotive issue for the opposition.

Commenting on the 'venom' of the party papers, the poet Edward Young suggested in 1728 that 'a pen seems not a weapon proportioned to the anger of either side'.[88] The following year *Fog's Weekly Journal* reported,

> This week Mr. Hussey, a Printer of Ireland, acquitted himself in single Combat, as a Gladiator, at Figg's Amphitheatre with great Honour. We don't tell this News, as if we took it for an Omen of War, that a Man should thus turn from *Letters* to *Arms*; that we shall leave to the Astrologers; we only conceive Mr. *Hussey* to be a wise Man, for as the World goes, it seems necessary for all *Printers* to *practice* the *noble Science of Defence*.[89]

In reality printers in dispute with the ministry had to envisage imprisonment rather than brawls, to acquire patience, sureties and financial reserves, rather than pugilistic skills. The difficulties occasioned by arrest, seizure of papers, detention awaiting trial and legal costs were arguably as serious as the penalties incurred as a result of a successful prosecution. It was often argued that government action against publications led to publicity for the latter and increased sales, and both Mist and the *Craftsman* were able to continue profitable publication despite convictions.[90] Claims that the papers would be suppressed proved erroneous.[91] However, many found ministerial action a serious inconvenience even if it resulted in no conviction. Receiving notice of a trial, John Tutchin of the *Observator* offered in 1704 to write no more provided the case was dropped, and he was released accordingly on a legal technicality. In 1763 a new Wilkite weekly the *Moderator* was only published once, 'the author being threatened with a prosecution' for a libel on the Lord Chief Justice.[92] Political supporters could guarantee a printer against the costs and penalties of prosecution. Writers and printers continued their activities whilst in prison. However, legal action threatened the profitability of a paper for a variety of reasons. Imprisonment and the seizure of papers could disrupt the network of credit and debt within which papers operated. Punishment or the threat of punishment endangered the production and distribution of a paper. Hawkers may not have relished being whipped for crying opposition literature. In 1733 'several people were committed to the work house for hawking and selling a scandalous and seditious paper, called the Royal Oak Journal'. Shopkeepers and others who arranged wholesale and retail sales could not have appreciated imprisonment or other legal action.[93] The seizure of printers' papers must have been inconvenient,[94] whilst the sums they had to find as either sureties for their appearance in court or fines were often considerable. Thomas Payne of the *True Briton* was fined £400 in 1724 and sentenced to a year in prison. The previous year Delafaye had provided a catalogue of Payne's difficulties. Such treatment, even if it did not result in a conviction, was hardly to be welcomed. In addition the printer could face the arrest of his news gatherers,[95] and the arrest and possible suborning, by government or competitors, of his staff. In the attack on General Warrants inspired by the *North Briton* controversy one pamphleteer complained that there was nothing to prevent messengers from seizing whoever they thought proper and their papers, 'entering his house abruptly, alarming his family, keeping him in close custody; tumbling his most secret and confidential papers and deeds carelessly into a sack'.[96]

Such arrests could be very inconvenient. Mist found that his attack on the Protestants in the Palatinate, which resulted in a complaint in the Lords by the Bishop of Gloucester, led to serious problems:

> The concerns and distractions of my trial and subsequent sufferings, besides the attendant expences, disconcerted all my business, threw me out of my concerns with several booksellers, and gave an opportunity to another paper to creep into the houses of my customers . . . everybody that came near me entertained me with the comfortable prospect of Tyburn; my creditors took the alarm and showered down writs upon me . . . for it was time for them to look for their money when they thought a man was going to be hanged . . . I was committed close prisoner to Newgate; all commerce with my friends, or even my innocent books, being interdicted me. This strict confinement, during the hottest season of the year, created several disorders in my body, . . . my troubles having, one way or other, been above a thousand pounds out of my way.[97]

Such treatment did not prevent Mist from continuing his very profitable paper, but it may have helped to account for his relative moderation during the Atterbury trials. Ministerial action could keep particular papers off the streets. The *London Journal* suffered from the breaking of its presses and the seizure of an entire impression in 1721. The following year the entire impression of the nonjuror Mathias Earberry's *Monthly Advices from Parnassus* was seized by a messenger at the printers. No issue of *Mist's Weekly Journal* appeared on 7 September 1728 as a result of government action, and the imprisonment of the printer and publisher of the *Monitor* prevented its appearance on 13 and 20 November 1762.[98] Marie Peters has argued that the moves against the *Monitor* had little effect and that it maintained its stance though in a more subdued fashion.[99] It is true that the cases were not proceeded with, but the printers were first arrested, and then bound by recognisances to appear before the Court of King's Bench. The cases were dropped there and a release from the recognisances granted in June 1763, but the danger of conviction had hung over the printers for eight months. The judicial resources of the government appear to have had some effect in this case. The attack on Bute in the guise of the lover and favourite of Edward III's mother that was to have been carried in the issue of 19 June 1762 was omitted because Wilkes's patron Earl Temple thought it too dangerous. The printer of the paper, Jonathan Scott, refused to print a contentious item in October 1762 and produced his own rival paper. Wilkes's *North Briton* suggested that the attack on the *Monitor* was designed to prevent it attacking the terms of the Peace of Paris, but that there was no intention of prosecuting. Instead the *North Briton* suggested that the ministry hoped to cajole the paper into a secret treaty. It also commented on the impact on the *North Briton* of the steps against the *Monitor*, an interesting indication of the preventive nature of government action:

> Almost every man I meet looks strangely on me — some industriously avoid me — others pass me silently — stare — and shake their heads. — Those few, those very few, who are not afraid to take a lover of his country by the hand, congratulate me on being alive and at liberty. — They advise circumspection — for, they do not know — they cannot tell — but — the times — Liberty is precious — Fines — Imprisonment — Pillory . . . My correspondents likewise, those who seemed most sanguine in the cause, who were the most ready to encourage and assist me in my undertaking, are tainted with suspicion and fear; and those letters which used to breathe the genuine spirit of *Old English Liberty*, are become insipid, tame, and languid. Caution hath got the better of every public virtue, . . . This humour of suspicion seems to have taken its rise from the confinement of some persons concerned in the *Monitor*; but how doth that affect the *North-Briton*?[100]

Legal action, or the threat of it, had an effect on several papers. The second *Examiner*, launched in 1714, was brought before a Middlesex Grand Jury for sedition before it was a month old. It changed its printers twice, becoming general, relatively non-political and acceptable. A letter in the *Freeholder's Journal* in 1722 suggested that 'politics are become of late so dangerous a subject to handle' that discussion of them was limited. Delafaye was congratulated on the 'dullness of the True Briton' in 1723.

Two years later Mist announced that he would not print a letter he had received 'as there is a certain person in the world, at present, a little too strong for us', and Wharton, who had exchanged his writing for the *True Briton* for the role of Jacobite diplomat, informed the Austrian government that the cruelty shown so often to British printers had destroyed the freedom of the press. In 1730 Eustace Budgell could not find anyone to handle his anti-Walpole material, while Delafaye 'talked to our Whitehall letter man about his idleness in writing everything he has without better authority for it than towntalk, and he has promised me to be more cautious'. The following year the *Craftsman* felt unable to print a Spanish declaration critical of Britain and contradicting British ministerial statements 'as we are not yet furnished with sufficient proof to satisfy a Court of Justice that it was actually delivered'. In 1742 the *Universal Spectator* printed part of a letter before commenting, 'The rest of this Hague letter contains some very material advices from London, which we cannot with safety insert in our paper.'[101]

Such restraint might seem to justify opposition accusations that the Walpole ministry had crushed the Freedom of the Press. The *Craftsman* complained in 1728 that its circulation was restricted by the Post Office and claimed that the law of libel restrained the press:

I might add the manner of prosecutions in these cases as a farther restraint on this liberty. The dread of State Messengers, and Warrants, which commonly extend not only to the seizure of a man's person, but likewise his papers, even those, which concern his nearest interests and the most secret parts of his life, are sufficient to keep him within the bounds of the law; and, by intimidating booksellers, printers, publishers, etc. frequently deprive him of the fruits or design of his labour.

The following year, again on the eve of a parliamentary session, the paper added,

I must however call upon the world to judge whether warrants for seizing persons and papers, without distinction, and even breaking locks, in case of refusal to open them; whether strict examinations, commitments and confinement, without liberty of writing, or speaking to any friends in private; whether putting us to the trouble of running about town for bail, upon every taking up, and continuing us, upon divers recognizances (to a very great sum) for almost three years together; whether the expence of several trials, and of preparing for several others, which is near the same; not to say anything of intimidating booksellers, printers and publishers, by these means, and endeavouring to stop the propagation of our papers, by a particular prohibition at the Post-Office . . . the world must judge whether such methods of proceeding are properly marks of a passive disposition.

In 1733 a poem dedicated to Pulteney attacked the interpretation of innuendoes in order to establish guilt and condemned jurors for failing 'to stem the tide of oppression'. In 1740 the Earl of Marchmont thought it worth detailing the treatment of the press in his appeal to the electorate for the forthcoming general election:

If it so happens that a prosecution is resolved on, how is he then proceeded against? Not by a Bill of Indictment brought against him before a Grand Jury; by whom, if it was not found, he would be immediately acquitted without further cost, but by a novel, (and I will say a very oppressive) manner of proceeding. An Information is filed against him by the Attorney General, and, if ever so innocent, he must be at the expence of a trial, perhaps destructive to himself and family, as no costs can be given him where the Crown is made a party. Is not the former part of the foregoing instance an unwarrantable strain of power? Is not the latter, though pretended to be not illegal, extremely grievous, and liable to the most dangerous abuse? Will not a treatment of this kind be sufficient to deter a printer from venturing on the publication of any thing, which may thus expose him to the resentment of those in power? And will not the Public by these practices be most effectually deprived of all information, which by this means only can be conveyed to them?[102]

Thus alongside the resilience of Mist and the *Craftsman* must be placed the Opposition claim that governmental powers restricted their activities. Such powers did not prevent the development of new flourishing opposition papers, such as *Common-Sense* and the *Champion*, but they were used with success against a number of Jacobite papers. Tilson complained in 1722, 'Almost all our papers are poisoned with seditious stuff. We are not able to restrain it among ourselves',[103] but the relentless assault on government critics[104] of the mid 1710s seems to have been reasonably successful in dealing eventually with the Jacobite George Flint. Imprisonment in Newgate was followed by flight to France. Of the six Jacobite newspapers listed in *Thursday's Journal* in October 1719 only two remained three years later. The government campaign against the Jacobite press in the 1710s and early 1720s was reasonably successful.[105] Hoadly, who was critical of the prosecution of printers, doubting its success even if a conviction was obtained, excepted the case of High Treason.[106] There was reasonable confidence on the part of officials that the law gave them enough power to deal with Jacobite publications, even though they did not need to resort to accusations of treason in order to secure convictions. Delafaye was certain that the execution of John Matthews for printing the pamphlet *Vox Populi, Vox Dei*, a defence of James III's right to the throne, would be an example that would 'have the greatest influence upon those of his trade on deterring them from printing treason'.[107] Although Mist's paper was one of those which William Cowper in 1720 urged the Grand Jury of Westminster to have suppressed as seditious and treasonable,[108] its survival was not one that greatly upset the ministry. A spell in King's Bench Prison, 'this enchanted castle',[109] was followed by a cautious stance during the Atterbury Plot, and in 1723–4 the ministry was more concerned by Wharton's *True Briton* than by Mist.

Successive ministries possessed the determination and the means to deal with Jacobite papers. In 1746 the *National Journal or Country Gazette*, a tri-weekly launched in late March, ended in early June when the printer was removed to Newgate. Even Mist was forced to flee, and all his men tried in 1729 were found guilty 'tho' by a Tory jury'.[110] A lower rate of success attended moves against less clearly seditious papers, and the ministry found it difficult to cope with the succession of opposition papers, one title taking off on the same presses when another came to an end. The *Freeholder's Journal*, printed by Thomas Sharpe and published by Payne, was followed almost immediately by the *True Briton*, produced by the same team. However, when the latter came to an end Payne's penalties were probably responsible for the failure of the team to produce anything else. Payne asked the Lord Chief Justice for mercy, on the grounds that he had offered to reveal the identity of the author, but he was answered,

That a man may out of a petulent humour write the worst of libels, and, if he keeps them to read only for his own entertainment, they can have no ill effect but, if they are published, everyone knows the consequence; and that the printer and publisher therefore is the person that does the mischief.

Walpole and Delafaye had wanted to deny Wharton the publicity of a trial, the Sacheverell, Oxford (Harley) and possible Atterbury trials having induced a degree of caution over trying prominent individuals, and indeed there was little attempt to follow up judicially the identity of authors. This would have been difficult, but printers could have been persuaded to testify. Instead ministries chose to attack the printers and publishers.[111]

In dealing with less clearly seditious papers ministries were in a weaker position. It was not so easy to secure widespread support for legal action, and there were more doubts about the likelihood of securing convictions. Widespread support was important not simply from the point of view of juries, but because successive ministries wished to maintain their Whig credentials. Philip Yorke, as Attorney-General, was unsure of the value of bringing libels to the attention of the Commons, but suggested that an attack on William III and the motives of the Glorious Revolution would 'be an occasion wherein you would carry every whigg in the House along with you'.[112] There were few such issues and it is understandable that successive attorney-generals advised caution. The unsuccessful prosecution of Richard Francklin, the publisher of the *Craftsman*, in November 1729 was not an encouraging precedent, and though the problem of recalcitrant London jurors, which had played a significant role in the 1729 case, was remedied by the Juries Act of 1730, permitting judges to appoint special juries, the publicity the *Craftsman* had earned in 1729 was a warning against making it a *cause célèbre* for a second time.[113] A ministerial pamphlet of 1731 claimed that Walpole had

abused his power, in suffering a libel to be published weekly for near five years together, and dispersed with all imaginable diligence and industry, not only in all the counties and towns of England, but in several other parts of Europe, which was continually stuffed with the most gross and groundless invectives, the most daring and impudent falsehoods.[114]

It is possible that had the *Craftsman* avoided the sensitive area of negotiations in progress and maintained its more generalised criticism of government policy, the ministry would not have brought the paper to court again, as it did successfully over the Hague Letter of 1731.

The threat of prosecution forced newspapers to adopt an allusive style and an allegorical approach, rich in innuendo and code words and letters and 'so guarded that an information cannot be brought on any part of it'. The former Whig Lord Chancellor, Earl Cowper, predicted accurately that Mist would use this method.[115] To that extent it fulfilled one of the principal purposes of censorship, namely ensuring that pre-publication self-regulation avoided the need for costly and embarrassing government action. This, rather than occasional spectacular trials, was the essential element of the censorship system but it could not prevent a highly abusive opposition press. The Walpole ministry did not attempt to harass papers such as the *London Evening Post* or the *Craftsman* as they had harassed the Jacobite press, and Delafaye admitted in 1732, 'We can not govern authors and printers'.[116] There were occasional suggestions, probably produced by no more than irritation, that tougher action would be taken. In 1722 the *St. James's Journal* suggested that legislative action would be taken unless the press moderated itself. A poem of 1733 warned opposition writers,

At least, unless thou'rt crooked, have a care,
Huge-headed cudgels now in fashion are;
Remember Wilkins and his rueful fate,
Is thine a safe, more privileg'd a Pate?

The following year the *Daily Courant* carried a vague threat about the *Craftsman*'s treachery meeting 'that discipline which it deserves'.[117] There were accusations at the time of the introduction of the Stage Licensing Act in 1737 that the ministry intended to extend pre-publication censorship to the press, but these were unfounded. The publicity that several prohibited works enjoyed and the size of the editions of their scripts that were rushed into print were not a good advertisement for censorship, but on the other hand there was a surprising lack of opposition to the principle of censorship and by 1745 the theatre had largely withdrawn from politics, its opposition to the Act silenced.[118] However, it is unlikely that any such legislation would have been successful in the case of the press. Policing a small number of theatres was far easier than supervising the activities of a large number of presses, and the immediacy expected from news would have posed a major problem for any system of pre-publication censorship. There was simply too much to read too quickly. In addition, the difficulties that the French government had encountered in the early 1730s in seeking to suppress the illegal Parisian Jansenist newspaper the *Nouvelles Ecclésiastiques* was not a good augury. Burning by the common hangman was no substitute for the lack of a register of printing presses.[119] The introduction of pre-publication censorship would have increased the number of unstamped papers at a time when the ministry was becoming increasingly aware of them as a problem, and would have extended political, often aristocratic, patronage to such papers. In the mid 1720s opposition material had been printed on a press in the London house of the Duke of Bedford.[120] The prospect of raiding the houses of aristocrats such as the Duchess of Marlborough, the Duke of Argyll and the Earl of Chesterfield could not have appealed to any ministry. It would have violated an implicit principle of press regulation, namely that it entailed punishments for printers not politicians.

Such a policy would also have been a radical break from the Whig heritage, even the Whig ministerial heritage, justifying the *Craftman*'s attacks on their apostasy. Possibly Willes had as a young man during Queen Anne's reign been saved from the pillory for 'scribbling libels' by Carteret.[121] That would not have been any guide to his attitude later, but Yorke, ennobled as first Earl of Hardwicke and, as Lord Chancellor from 1737 to 1756, and a close ally of the Duke of Newcastle, the leading Whig legal expert, made clear his opposition to pre-publication censorship in 1739. A ministerial Whig apologist, Francis Hare Bishop of Chichester, a former writer of political works, recorded Hardwicke's speech in the Lords on the subject:

> My Lord Chancellor on this occasion made an excellent speech to explain the true meaning of the liberty of the press, which he said he found was not at all generally understood, that it was not a liberty to defame and libel, but that it was opposed to previous restraints put upon the press, as had been formerly done by licencers and other methods.[122]

Whatever the opposition claims, the ministry was not interested in increasing its legal powers over the press. Such an attempt would have been politically disastrous and alien to the essential conservatism of the government. That British ministries had less power than even their counterparts in the United Provinces, a country praised by many Whigs for its Protestantism and liberties, might irritate some,[123] and officials, such as Delafaye, would probably have preferred a stronger legal position. However, although Delafaye did not die until 1762, he was a figure of the past by the late 1730s, having retired as Under-Secretary in July 1734. His retirement symbolised a shift in the ministerial attitude to the regulation of the press. Delafaye's successor, Andrew Stone, and the senior Under-Secretary in the Northern Department from 1738 to 1746, Edward Weston, did not possess the same degree of interest, and the dominant official in relations with the press became Nicholas Paxton. Shifts in attitude are difficult to assess with accuracy, but it can be suggested that that of suppression, developed due to the challenge of Jacobite papers and associated with Delafaye, was replaced by a stress on subsidising a government press and only taking legal action when flagrant attacks on British or foreign ministries were printed. It may not be fanciful to associate this attitude with Paxton and Yorke and maybe with Walpole himself, who had shown little interest in the suppression of opposition papers in the 1720s apart from in 1723 when, as acting Secretary of State, he was responsible for moves against the *True Briton*.

There were frequent references in the press and in diplomatic correspondence of the 1730s to attempts by foreign powers to suppress printed works, and complaints from their envoys in London about critical references in British newspapers would have made ministers aware that a radically different attitude to the press was possible. However, such an attitude would have been regarded as alien. Reporting the French attempt to suppress the *Nouvelles Ecclésiastiques* the *Daily Post Boy* commented, 'What would some nations give for English laws and English liberties.'[124] The ministerial position in the last years of the Walpole government was as good as could be expected. The opposition were able to print vicious and inaccurate comments, as with their agitation for war with Spain in 1738–9 and their subsequent suggestions that the war effort was inadequate due to links between Walpole and the Bourbons, but it is doubtful that wider legal powers could have improved the situation. One of the Under-Secretaries, John Couraud, feared that a prosecution of the *Daily Post* would simply revive its sales and observed "tis difficult to know how to deal with those fellows'. The interceptor and translator of a letter of 1739 from the Dutch foreign minister Fagel to his envoy in London, both experienced commentators on British politics, would probably have agreed with the minister's argument.

> Certainly the manner in which he [Walpole] is abused, exceeds all bounds and is an abuse of the liberty of the press which ought not to be suffered, for many of those writings very much savour of sedition . . . can produce nothing but great hatred and divisions that cannot fail being prejudicial to the public welfare: However the remedy is not easy to be found out, because the evil is in the minds, and it seems passions have got the upper hand.[125]

'Inspired with the noble enthusiasm of liberty'[126] The position after the fall of Walpole

> The libellous papers are most provoking and infamous, and prosecutions will be very right, when you can see some probable prospect of success. In some glaring instances it may be prudent to take up the persons, though you don't intend to proceed to trial. Your Grace knows how the spirit of prosecution has been suffered to run down for many years past, for which one reason assigned has been the impossibility of getting Juries to convict. I wish that is not grown stronger now by this ferment of the people.
>
> Hardwicke to Newcastle, 1756[127]

Hardwicke's suggestion that the problems facing the ministry in 1756 in the regulation of the press owed something to a running-down of the spirit of prosecution over an unspecified period is a valuable one. Not only was there less judicial action against the opposition press after the fall of Walpole; there was also perceived to be less. There are probably several reasons for the lessened role of judicial action: the efficacy of outright purchase of opposition writers, the criticism that such action had brought the Walpole ministry, the weakness of Jacobite propaganda, a willingness to suffer opposition attacks, the lower prestige of the leading opposition papers. Hardwicke's suggestion that much was owing to the difficulty of securing a conviction is an interesting one. In 1752 George II, then in Hanover, was moved to fury by the acquittal of a printer 'contrary to evidence', launched into one of his customary 'declamations against our laws, that punished nobody' and condemned the independence of juries. Hardwicke however attributed the acquittal to particular features of the case that did not reflect upon the government. Juries had supported the ministry in prominent trials inspired by *Mist's Weekly Journal* and the *Craftsman* in 1729 and 1731 respectively. One writer claimed in 1740, 'I have known many an honest Englishman laugh, and extremely fond to read a paper, who, if he had been upon the Jury that was to try the author, would have voted for his losing his ears for his impudence.'[128] The Walpole ministry still felt able to issue warrants for arrests in its last years. In 1740 John Meres, the printer of the *Daily Post* and the *London Evening Post*, was arrested and then released with a warning about his conduct of the latter.[129]

It is therefore plausible to suggest that any shift in judicial action that occurred after the fall of Walpole was due not to so much to any weakness in the ministry's legal position, but to a different attitude on the part of government. The extent of this should not be exaggerated. Most of the relevant officials continued in place: Hardwicke, Ryder (Attorney-General until 1754), Newcastle and the senior Under-Secretaries. Opposition literature, particularly of a Jacobite inclination, was still subject to attention. In 1743 the London bookseller and publisher Jacob Robinson was bound over for £400 to appear in the Court of King's Bench for publishing a libel called *Old England's Te Deum*. William Guthrie was arrested for essays in *Common-Sense* and *Old England*. In 1746 Thomas Sherlock, Bishop of Salisbury and Lord Almoner, prepared a draft bill that included provisions to prevent 'the printing and sale of Catholic books'.[130] There were particular problems over the reporting of Parliament, an issue that should not have arisen after a Commons resolution of 1738. In December 1742 the *Westminster Journal* noted,

My last paper has produced a very strong representation against the liberty I have taken of inserting any proceedings of the

worthy society of INDEPENDENT SCALD-MISERABLE-
MASONS, but more especially against the impropriety of
publishing any speeches made to that august body.

Two years later Hardwicke, apparently on his own initiative, attempted, without success, to use the press in order to restrain the
reporting of parliamentary news. He sought to insert an
anonymous letter complaining of inaccurate reporting in the
magazines and warning 'that several members of the first distinction are determined to attempt the suppressing of this insolent
practice by authority of the legislature at their next meeting'.
However, his agent Thomas Harris could not get the letter inserted, even for ready money, the *Champion*, *Daily Advertiser*,
Daily Gazetteer, *Daily Post*, *General Evening Post*, and *Gazette*
all rejecting it, the last because it 'was not designed for controversial writings', the others because they did not wish to upset the
magazines.[131]

Hardwicke's lack of success revealed a disadvantage of having
disbanded the 'Gazetteer legion' of subsidised hacks in 1742. The
most significant action against press reporting of parliamentary
debates in the 1740s did not occur as a result of ministerial action.
Parliament appointed printers to print items such as the
Addresses, and in 1747 these printers, angry at what they regarded
as an illegal infringement of their privileges, instigated action by
the Lords against the printing of Jacobite treason trials conducted
by that house. The printers of the *Gentleman's* and *London
Magazines* were brought before the Lords and released on condition they did not repeat the offence. Action was taken against the
Ipswich Journal. The effect of these moves was to induce caution
into the provincial press, end parliamentary reporting in the
Gentleman's Magazine and end the attribution of speeches to
individual members in the *London Magazine*.[132]

Much parliamentary action in the eighteenth century was due to
the efforts of private individuals and groups and it is not necessary
to see the hand of government behind the printers' action in 1747,
though the fact that the year was one of a general election may not
be coincidental. The same year Henry Pelham responded to
suggestions that the Commons' act against reporting of their proceedings with the reported phrase, 'Let them alone; they make
better speeches for us, than we can make ourselves.' Fielding
pointed out the ministry's failure to use their available legal

powers: 'Is it not treason writ in our newspapers; and talked and sung and toasted in our taverns every day with impunity? And yet if you consult our law books, you will find there are very severe laws for the punishment of all these offences.' Indeed in 1746 Fielding turned this situation to his advantage, by predicting in his ministerial paper the *True Patriot* that the success of the Jacobites would be followed by 'a Bill proposed against the Liberty of the Press'. The following year the Earl of Sandwich, a prominent diplomat, was very concerned about the opposition exploiting any possible return of Cape Breton to France:

> The clamour that will be raised . . . will, I am certain, have very great weight in the nation, which fomented by those who we know are lying in wait for the first opportunity of doing mischief, must in the end rob the administration of their popularity; and I am clear in my opinion, that this Ministry cannot stand upon any other foundation.

In 1748 Newcastle complained about 'being pelted with pamphlets, and papers every day'.[133]

The ministerial position was not one of complete inaction, even if their stance scarcely justified opposition accusations that they were interested in restricting press freedom.[134] In October 1749 Ryder was willing to consider prosecutions to deal with the opposition attempt brought to his attention by Newcastle, to create a sense of uncertainty by suggesting that the elderly George II was ill. This was likely to be a far more certain way of harming the ministry than accusations of corruption, for the heir to the throne, Prince Frederick, was a supporter of the opposition and members of his entourage patrons of opposition propaganda, as they had been in the late 1730s. Ryder's letter revealed the concern for legality and uncertainty as to what the law actually was that characterised much ministerial judicial supervision of the press:

> As the publication of such false news of his Majesty, has a tendency to disquiet the minds of his subjects, hurt public credit, and diminish the regard and duty which they owe him, I think the doing it with such views is an offence punishable at Common Law, and for which an Indictment or Information can lye. And the frequency of such publications is evidence of such

wicked designs. But as every false report of this kind which may arise from mistake only cannot be charged as a crime, so it is very difficult to say how often it must be repeated in the same paper to make it criminal. . . . I don't know any method to prevent this practice, but by prosecuting the offenders when they are guilty.[135]

The following month the printer and publisher of the *Remembrancer* were arrested for their paper of 18 November accusing Newcastle and Pelham of corruption and manipulating George II, and the Duke of Cumberland of brutality in his administration of the army. However, there was none of the brutality that had characterised such action earlier in the century and nothing approaching a raid. The paper's patron George Dodington recorded, 'The Messenger us'd them with uncommon civility, touch'd nothing of their papers, presses or effects and took their words for their surrendering themselves the next morning.' The Prince of Wales's willingness to indemnify the printer and publisher limited the effectiveness of such arrests, though prosecution or the fear of it did play a role in preventing the *Remembrancer* printing an article by Horace Walpole and in persuading James Ralph to accept a pension in return for abandoning the *Protester*. It also led Thomas Cooke to offer in 1748 to turn the *Craftsman* into 'a paper of amusement . . . respectful to the ministry'. Furthermore Ralph's decision was made despite the fact that when the *Protester* was established he was assured that 'he should be thoroughly protected, and by those who would own him in both Houses . . . against all law prosecutions'. However, having used the *Protester* as a mouthpiece for the Duke of Bedford, Ralph asked for assurances of protection if the ministry took action against him. When these were not forthcoming the journalist changed sides hastily.[136]

The continued vigour of the opposition press clearly made some ministers uneasy, for while Pelham had opposed the idea of prosecuting Ralph in 1753, claiming that he was ineffective, Newcastle had supported action against him and in the following year was responsible for the successful prosecution of Richard Nutt of the *London Evening Post* for attributing the miserable state of the nation to the Glorious Revolution. This success did not prevent the paper from provoking Newcastle into considering another prosecution in 1756. The campaign against the Jewish

Naturalisation Act, particularly in the *London Evening Post*, described by Earl Temple as 'that Augean stable of filth and calumny', angered prominent ministerial Whigs because, on the eve of the general election of 1754, it created a climate of opinion in which they felt it expedient to repeal the Act. Horatio Walpole suggested in 1753 that action would have to be taken 'to correct the impudence' of the paper, though he advised waiting until after the election. Hardwicke told the Lords the same autumn

> that the only imbecility of the administration was in tolerating such libels; that the liberty of the press could not give liberty to print what a man may not write; that what a man could not justify to do, he could not justify to print; that he thought the libels on this bill ought to be prosecuted; that the Lords and Commons might trust themselves with looking into the license of the press.

In December 1755 Alexander Hume Campbell censured in the Commons 'the unlimited reflections that were daily thrown on the ministers; adding, that when people made charges on acts of state, they ought to be obliged to make them out . . . Hard would it be if that House might not resent unjust accusations of our *superiors*'. The following year the *Test* complained, 'A ministerial trumpeter dares openly attack the liberty of the press . . . dispute[s] with us our right of inspecting the conduct of our state pilots', and one of the Secretaries of State, the Earl of Holderness, pressed for action against a Yorkshire instruction printed in the *Public Advertiser* that he believed to be forged.[137] Such statements, mostly made in anger during the Jewish naturalisation agitation, are placed in perspective by the failure of the ministry, despite its overwhelming success in the general election of 1754, to introduce new legislation affecting the press. There was no change until the Second Stamp Act of 1757, a measure that was not apparently due to any desire to cripple the press, but reflected probably the exigencies of war taxation. The failure to alter the legal parameters of press activity reflected the cautious stance of the ministerial Whigs on most subjects and the particular difficulties of dealing with the press. Had the ministry wished to they could possibly have made life harder for the press, by restricting sales through substantially higher taxation, by ending postal privileges and by adding a supplementary duty on newspapers in public places, such as coffee-houses. No such legal attack on the stamped press followed that on the unstamped papers in the early 1740s. The ministry remained in a position where it was able to deal with conspicuously seditious items or papers, through purchase or legal action, largely because there were comparatively few of them, but relatively weak when faced, as over the Jewish Naturalisation Act, or the Byng case in 1756–7,[138] with a widespread press campaign reflecting the opinions of a determined political group and able to arouse substantial support.

It could be suggested that the failure both to change the legal parameters and to use exemplary judicial action, within the existing framework of the law, to deal with all the prominent opposition papers of the Pelhamite years helped to ensure that the press became a major topic of political and legal conflict in the 1760s and early 1770s. This was possibly as significant a legacy of the mid-century period as whatever impact can be attributed to the endless repetition of the critique of the Whig establishment as corrupt and sinister. Such articles must have lost all novelty. The Butite *Briton* attacked the vapid, repetitive character of the *Monitor* in 1762. Arthur Murphy's weekly *Gray's Inn Journal* claimed in 1753 that the ministry had usurped royal authority and 'set up their own private designs against the declared sentiments and repeated remonstrances of an entire kingdom'. The average metropolitan reader would have read such statements on numerous occasions. Repetition probably reinforced belief in them from those who were already convinced,[139] and made it easier to interpret new developments with reference to a strong set of suppositions, comprehensive because so many of its concepts were amorphous. The charge of endless repetition of the same themes can also be made with reference to ministerial propaganda and helps to give a somewhat tired flavour to many of the arguments advanced in the 1760s. Lord George Sackville claimed to be able to see development, if only in vituperation. In 1770 he told the Commons that even the famed issue 45 of the *North Briton* of 23 April 1763, which had attacked George III, was pallid by comparison with more recent papers:

> Libels and lampoons, audacious beyond the example of all other times, libels, in comparison of which the North Briton, once deemed the *ne plus ultra* of sedition is perfect innocence and simplicity. The sacred number 45, formerly the idol of the

multitude is eclipsed by the superior venom of every day's
defamation; all its magical and talismanic powers are lost and
absorbed in the general deluge of scandal, which pours from the
press.[140]

Sackville's statement must be seen in the context of parliamentary
debate in which he was seeking to establish a particular point. A
longer time-scale would call these views into question. Recent
work has shown that it is inaccurate to begin the history of
radicalism with John Wilkes, and that pre-Wilkite radicalism was
vigorous and sophisticated. It is also misleading to suggest that this
squinting anti-hero, the entrepreneur of faction, represented a
new departure in the history of the political press. Had the printer-
entrepreneurs of the early eighteenth century faced a succession of
short lived ministries, uncertain of royal support, and been able to
rely on the assistance of several sympathetic members of the legal
system, then it is likely that the legal battles fought in the 1760s
over the procedures of government regulation and intervention in
the press would have been fought earlier. There had been concern
over these procedures in the first half of the century, and they had
been discussed in the press with reference to general issues of
liberty. Thus a London item in the *York Courant* of 6 February
1739 announced,

> It is expected that the twelve Judges will this term give their
> opinions on that grand point relating to the Liberty of the
> Subject, whether a person apprehended on suspicion of being
> the author, printer, or publisher of a book or paper, being
> libellous, shall find security for his good behaviour, as well as
> for his appearance.

Issues of press regulation had always been seen as part of a
debate over the nature of the governmental system. In the 1760s
the political weakness of government, the relative lack of other
topics of comparable emotive interest, such as Spanish depredations, the Excise Bill or Jewish naturalisation, and the particular
features of the *North Briton* affair, helped to ensure that issues of
press regulation became symbolic of the essential public issues at
stake in the struggle between ministry and opposition. This was of
particular seriousness because the natural difficulties of regulating
the press and the specific problems of securing convictions were

exacerbated by judicial differences of opinion over the legal extent of government powers. These helped both to make the legal regulation of the press a major issue and to make a widely accepted solution of the issue difficult. The Sardinian envoy Scarnafis reported in 1771 that he had been unable to obtain an elucidation of the legal issues at dispute either from the Secretary of State, Rochford, or from several MPs and that the freedom of the press was very hard to determine. The American historian A. M. Schlesinger has suggested that the failure of the British government to tackle the issue of rebellious American views in the years before the War of Independence was probably due to their failure to control the domestic press.[141]

Two major elements of the challenge to the government's position were the difficulties of securing convictions and the willingness of the opposition to contest legally the actions of the Secretaries of State. Had the major newspaper trials been held outside London their course might have been different, for there was no doubt of the difficulty of securing convictions in London. Acquittals were obtained elsewhere, the Tory *Bristol Journal* being acquitted when charged with libel over its accusations of malpractice during the Bristol by-election of 1756. However, one significant aspect of continuity in the struggle over the regulation of the press was that all major cases were held in London and involved London newspapers. In 1756 Newcastle had sought legal opinion for a prosecution of the printer of the *London Evening Post* of 26 August. A letter signed Britannicus had asked 'Are not our rights, lives, and liberties, now brought into a very precarious situation by such unconstitutional measures, as introducing a foreign army, and neglecting our own militia?' Newcastle was advised that this was 'a direct and daring charge upon the Parliament of unconstitutional measures', but told that a prosecution was unwise because the paper had been printed in London and must therefore be tried before a London jury, who were very unlikely to convict: 'The temper of the times must . . . be consulted in prosecutions of this nature, and from all I have heard and been informed it is at present in too inflamed and convulsed a state to advise any prosecution of this kind.' As most of the 1760s were 'inflamed', at least insofar as the opinions of many London jurors were concerned, prosecutions remained a problem. William Guthrie might assure Bute in 1762 that had he or James Ralph when in opposition a quarter of a century earlier 'thrown out the half of that unguarded abuse which has been offered to your Lordship's person . . . we should both of us been sent to Newgate, in five hours after publication', but then he had not been reading past numbers of the *London Evening Post* or *Common-Sense*, whilst Bute, whatever his legal powers, could not create the perception that the situation was under control. Urging action on New Year's Day 1763, the *Briton* had thought it necessary only to execute the laws, not to legislate afresh and claimed that those who

> with equal malice and effrontery, published the weekly mess of slander and sedition, may be prosecuted either by indictment or information. Almost every page of their elegant lucubrations, exhibits a fresh libel against the g[overnmen]t, exclusive of paragraphs replete with the most malicious defamation . . . I would have the delinquents left to the authority of the law; to the equity of a fair trail; to the verdict of a British jury.

This method was to be tried with little success. Shortly after Lord Chief Justice Pratt had ordered Wilkes' release from the Tower, whence he had been committed whilst awaiting trial, on the grounds that his parliamentary privilege did not extend to the alleged breach of the peace represented by his essay in number 45 of the *North Briton*, Robert Ellison wrote from London that the agitation over the case had declined. He however added in his letter to his father that it would resume if Wilkes was prosecuted for seditious libel and that even if the government had proof that he had written the paper 'there are those who doubt, whether a London Jury would think it a libel'.[142] In 1770 the newspaper printers who had printed Junius's letters were all, bar one, acquitted, despite a major ministerial effort to secure convictions. The impact of Junius's attack on the king, which seemed also to provide an excellent opportunity for prosecution, can be gauged from the unprecedented number of printers charged: those of the *Gazetteer*, *Independent Chronicle*, *London Evening Post*, *London Museum*, *Public Advertiser* and *St. James's Chronicle*. Had these prosecutions all succeeded they may well have had a significant effect, at least in the short term, as the sole printer sentenced, John Almon of the *London Museum*, was forced to give sureties for two years. In the other cases the jurors either acquitted the printers or declared that they were 'guilty of printing and publishing only' and that the item in question was not a seditious

libel. 'Indignation', writing in the *Gazetteer*, greeted these decisions:

> The late decisions of the two very spirited London juries have
> given a mortal blow to the present despotic feeble, and un-
> principled administration. They had no chance to stand, but by
> keeping their actions, by the terror of law, a secret from the
> world. Now that an honest and indignant people have de-
> termined not to be longer the instruments of ministerial
> oppression, all men that can write will combine to expose the
> ignorant Goths in office.[143]

The paper was to be woefully inaccurate. The head ignorant
Goth, Lord North, received no such mortal blow and the political
consequences of the legal battles over the press were far more
limited than either successive ministries or their oppositions had
suggested. In 1774 the *Craftsman; or Say's Weekly Journal* printed
an essay from J.T. urging the need to defend the liberty of the
press and reported inaccurately, 'There has been for some time
past a report, that a project has been formed of laying some new
restraints upon the press.' An anonymous essay on newspapers
and the liberty of the Press, a popular topic in this period, claimed,
'It is a singular circumstance, but a real fact, that the Liberty of the
Press, has grown stronger from every attack on it; and that the
situation of newspapers has become more flourishing in proportion to the increase of the duties imposed on them.' Another
item in the same year, 1769, provided details to support its claim
that the press was better treated under George III than under his
two predecessors.[144] Freer and stronger the press may have been,
but it was to be no more influential in terms of having a direct
impact on policy. The Duke of Grafton dismissed in 1770 the idea
of making 'every impudent report, which may be circulated
through the channel of our newspapers' a matter of parliamentary
debate, and Lord North's ministry proved relatively impervious to
press abuse.[145]

One significant development of the period was the growth,
despite attempts to prevent it, of parliamentary reporting. In the
mid-1750s, when Richard Beckford had wished to practise
parliamentary oratory, he did so 'by studying magazines and
historical registers', rather than newspapers. The process by which
the newspapers entered this sphere has been well described by

Peter Thomas. Thomas concentrates on the metropolitan press,[146] and it is interesting to note that the development of parliamentary reporting underlined the influence of the metropolitan over the provincial press, as the latter eagerly devoted column after column to debates, taking its information from the London papers. The *Reading Mercury* obviously felt that this was what its readers wanted. Parliamentary items occupied a substantial portion both of the free sheets distributed occasionally with the paper and of the paper itself, notes on the front page drawing the readers' attention sometimes to such items on the back page.[147] It is interesting to speculate as to what the provincial press would have printed had they not had such items, particularly in peacetime. Possibly there would have been more items of local interest and even a development of local political news. Such an analysis would present parliamentary reporting as a prominent example of the metropolitan dominance of the provincial press. However, it is more probable that, in place of such items, the provincial papers would have printed material of general interest from the large number of London magazines then produced. There was no necessity to substitute one form of political news for another, and the general interest in parliamentary news that existed does not seem to have been matched by comparable interest in local politics. The *Town and Country Magazine* claimed in 1782, 'The speeches and debates, in both Houses of Parliament, are of such importance, as to ingross the greatest part of our newspapers, and necessarily become matters of the utmost consequence to all our readers.' Perry frequently widened the *Morning Chronicle*'s columns during the parliamentary session to ease the pressure on space caused by the fact he noted in 1794, that advertisements were most common in this period of the year. Nine out of the 16 columns of the *Courier* of 1 January 1795 were devoted to printing part of the Commons debate on the Address and the opposition paper provided a list of the Foxite minority and their constituencies. Four days later the *London Packet* printed a list of MPs who had abandoned support of the war with France.[148]

There were criticisms of some aspects of parliamentary reporting. Many debates did not seem to provide appropriate or attractive copy, but once newspapers had developed the practice of printing them during the session it was difficult to substitute other material speedily. In 1785 the first issue of the *Daily Universal Register* referred to readers facing 'long accounts of petty squabbles about trifles in Parliament, or panegyrics on the men and measures that he most disliked; or libels on those whom he most revered'. Two years later a London item in a Newcastle paper condemned the prime place of the Warren Hastings trial in the session, and made it clear that the writer felt that commercial considerations ought to be substituted for the repetitive rhetoric and ideological hyperbole of the trial:

> While the new commercial treaty with France, the convention with Spain, the renewal of our old alliances with Portugal, the continuation of our connexion and engagements with Russia, and many other matters of the first importance, call loudly on the attention of both Houses of Parliament, it must grieve every good Englishman to see the best and prime part of the sessions taken up, among the Commons, in futile discussions about Mr. Hastings and his Muny Begums.

The prospectus for the *Star* in 1788 stated, 'The debates in Parliament, being subjects of universal concern, claim a respectable portion of this paper; but dull and uninteresting prolixity will be as carefully avoided, as affected and unmeaning brevity.'[149]

Prolixity was not the only problem affecting parliamentary reporting. Accuracy was another difficulty. It was not easy for parliamentarians in hot and stuffy chambers to provide accurate reports of proceedings. Comparisons between different accounts often reveal major discrepancies.[150] Newspaper reporters were faced with additional problems. They were not allowed to take down notes until the 1780s and prior to that had to rely on their memories, William Woodfall excelling so far as to earn the name 'Memory' Woodfall. Reporters were not sure of a place, and from the back of the gallery they could not fully see the Commons. The gallery could be cleared whenever a Member on the floor of the House chose to 'spy Strangers' and in the 1770s this happened a lot. The clearing of the Lords in December 1770 aroused particular controversy.[151] The gallery was cleared automatically when a division was taken and then not reopened. In the 1770s there were no reliefs for the reporters and no comparison with the reporting of the National Assembly in Paris by the *Logographe* in 1791:

> That paper will make you as much master of everything which passes in the Assembly as if you were present; as there are

several men constantly employed, who, by each in turn taking down a sentence, are enabled to write as quick as speech and report even every exclamation and *bah, bah* that is pronounced.

The British situation improved in the 1790s, and the press was increasingly able to plan its reporting. The *Morning Post* of 4 January 1798 noted that its arrangements for reporting the debate of the previous night 'were made upon the supposition that Messrs. Fox, Pitt, and Sheridan would rise late, and we therefore reserved some of our reporters and a part of this paper for their speeches'.[152]

In 1787 the *Morning Chronicle* stated that 'the first aim of the reporter of parliamentary debates in this paper is, and ever has been, to evince the most unquestionable impartiality and fairness'. Despite this and similar claims there were many inaccuracies in the parliamentary reports, and some of these were even referred to in the press. As reports could be readily challenged papers had to seek accuracy. In January 1795 the *Oracle* declared:

The person who objects to our not having given Mr. Pitt's amendment on Mr. Grey's motion verbatim, will, however, feel, that our account contains the substance and purport of it, which are all that can be expected in a daily paper. The abridgment should by no means be attributed to the motives assigned.

Four years later the *True Briton* announced,

We have great satisfaction in having received from various quarters, and particularly from several Members of Parliament, who were present at the debate on Thursday night, the highest commendations of our report of it; and particularly of Mr. Pitt's speech. Our reporters were peculiarly attentive to his statement, as we thought it essential that both *Ireland* and this country should know what were the precise grounds upon which it was intended the Union should be established.

The paper also attacked the opposition press for exaggerating opposition strength in the divisions. All too few parliamentarians could expect disclaimers such as that in the *Reading Mercury* in 1771:

> We are well authorised to inform the public, that the article given in the papers called, The Duke of Richmond's Speech when he moved in the House of Lords to reverse its resolution of not impeaching directly or indirectly the judgment of the House of Commons in the case of the Middlesex election, is not genuine, and is evidently the second Protest which was entered last year by the Duke of Richmond, now turned into a speech.[153]

Some sent in copies of their own speeches. It could be suggested that some of those who regretted the freedom of the press in this respect, as in others, did so because of the partisanship and in-accuracies of much reporting, rather than the abstract idea of freedom itself. The former may have helped to make the latter an issue, to focus attention on what might otherwise have only been a subject of occasional dissent The role of such misrepresentations has been ignored. Robert Rea, whose account of the press and politics in the 1760s and early 1770s is easily the best, made his views clear. Having described the jurors who acquitted Henry Woodfall of the *Public Advertiser* in the Junius case of 1770 as 'twelve honest citizens', he introduced a chapter on the press and Parliament by declaring,

> The rights of electors, the rights of juries, the liberty of the press, all seemed destined to stumble upon the block of privilege upheld by a corrupt legislature supinely voting at the behest of its political managers and seeking to shield its actions from the public.

Many contemporaries would have been surprised by Peter Thomas's claim that political bias in the parliamentary reporting of the early 1770s was rare, and Thomas accepts that opposition papers 'often inserted partisan comments in their reports'. Robert Rea described the clearing of the Lords on 10 December 1770 'as the final step towards emancipation from the public',[154] without mentioning that the topic of debate was the state of Gibraltar and the navy at a time when war with France and Spain appeared imminent, and that the reason given by Earl Gower, the Lord President of the Council, was that he feared Spanish agents would listen to the debate. Action against, and the expression of fears concerning, the press tended to be in response to particular prob-lems, inaccurate reporting or fear of foreign consequences.

Colonel George Onslow was moved to demand action against parliamentary reporting in February 1771 by his anger about the misrepresentation of speeches. Under-Secretary Charles Fraser was concerned about the debates on peace with France in 1783: 'I only lament the language which will be held in both Houses from the consideration that it will be circulated in print.' William Grenville, one of the principal ministerial speakers in the Commons, informed the House, during the debate on Sir Elijah Impey's complaint about being attacked by the *Morning Herald* and *Gazetteer*,

> that the newspaper misrepresentations of the proceedings of that House had of late been very frequently complained of, and that possibly, unless some notice were taken of them, they would grow to such a head, that . . . it would not be in the power of the House to stop them.[155]

The absence of any defined, precise or public self-regulation by the press lent support to criticism of its inaccuracies. The sole restraint appeared to be the law and there proved to be little that politicians could do to ensure an accurate reporting of parliamentary news, if there can be such a thing when editorial selection necessarily introduces considerations of reader interest. The North ministry supported Onslow's attack on the printing of debates in 1771, but the refusal of City magistrates to co-operate led to a legal tussle and public storm from which the government wisely retreated. It is interesting to speculate as to what would have happened had the City officials handed over the printers who were in hiding, and supported the ministerial position. Those printers who were arrested did not suffer unduly.[156] The willingness to take action against six printers after the acquittals of the previous year suggest that they were not regarded as a bar to further action against the press, that ministerial figures may have seen some value in harassing opposition papers and that parliamentary privilege seemed a safer issue than seditious libel.

The difficulties encountered in the 1760s and early 1770s clearly encouraged a prudent attitude on the part of the ministers. The writer Frederick Dickens claimed in 1769, 'Informations having been so warmly exclaimed against, administration I believe are unwilling to have too frequent recourse to them.'[157] John Miller, the printer of the *London Evening Post*, suggested that the Earl of

Sandwich's prosecution of him in 1773 for publishing a letter accusing Sandwich, the first Lord of the Admiralty, of attempting the sale of an Admiralty commissioner's post, indicated 'that a resolution hath been taken by Government, to lay a restraint on the Freedom of the Press, by deterring all printers from daring to exercise the liberty of it for the service of the public, by the heavy punishment inflicted upon me'. There is no evidence to support this claim, which was made in order to assist the subscription formed to help pay the damages of £2,000 awarded to Sandwich. Sandwich himself wrote to Henry Woodfall before the trial asking for an anonymous letter to be inserted in his paper announcing that the action was being brought 'in order to vindicate his honour against the infamous falsehood contained in that paper'.[158] This claim appears a justified one, and, though there were prosecutions under the North ministry, these arose in response to particular cases and were sometimes due to the complaints of individuals. Such complaints were sometimes made directly to the newspapers in question, and such private, informal representation may have been effective, particularly with the provincial press. In the early 1740s Sir James Lowther tried to find out who was responsible for inserting anonymous items in the London press critical of Cumbrian trade. In 1780 William Lowther complained to the author of the *Cumberland Packet* about an article on the local elections. In 1742 the Earl of Hertford used the fear of parliamentary action to force the *Daily Advertiser* to retract an article about him.[159] However, private representations were as inadequate as the law for protecting government from inaccurate, malicious abuse and it is easy to see why informed foreign commentators, such as the experienced Bavarian envoy Count Haslang, could present Britain in 1778 as a country where it was impossible to protect the monarch from the press.[160] By eighteenth-century European standards this was a serious failing. It might not matter that readers in Edinburgh could rely on Woodfall for the parliamentary news,[161] but abuse of monarchs was a more serious matter, as was wartime criticism of ministries. It was partly because of the relatively free nature of the press in the 1770s and 1780s that the moves against radical newspapers from 1792 on appeared and could be made to appear a new departure.

The ministerial attempt to police the press in response to the growing radicalism of the British supporters of the French

Revolution did not represent a new departure. The Ochakov Crisis of 1791 had revealed how the press could be used by the opposition and a committed foreign envoy, the Russian Count Vorontsov, to seriously embarrass the ministry. Ministerial papers, such as the *World*, attacked the opposition claiming that their behaviour was treasonable. It would be attractive to argue that the ministerial divisions that arose over the prospect of war with Russia in 1791, and with Spain in 1739, were due to the impact of public opinion as evinced by the press. However, in both instances the divisions were long-standing, the points at issue during the crisis genuinely split the ministry, and the coincidence of the parliamentary session was very significant. The Ochakov Crisis did however show that the ministerial press was not strong enough. The diplomat Joseph Ewart wrote to Burges from Buxton, 'Opposition seems to be indefatigable in spreading their insidious reports in the country as well as in town, and I perfectly agree with you in thinking that something ought to be done to counteract them, and convey to the public some just ideas of the nature of the present crisis.' Furious about press reports concerning his resignation during the crisis, the Duke of Leeds turned, successfully, to Burges to have a rebuttal inserted.[162]

Clearly, a more organised ministerial press would be required to counter the domestic allies of revolutionary France, but it was not necessary to develop new techniques of press management. A comparison of the ministerial treatment of the press in the 1790s with that in 1714–28, the heyday of the Jacobite press, reveals more similarities than contrasts. The ministry sponsored new newspapers, Burges keenly supporting the *Sun* and the *True Briton*, founded in October 1792 and January 1793.[163] Despite public suspicion of links between the opposition press and the French envoy Chauvelin — 'Chauvelin pays the Morning Chronicle to write all manner of mischief'[164] — ministerial action against the opposition press was limited. Given the undoubted interest of the French in inserting material in the London press,[165] the actions of the ministry do not appear excessively repressive by eighteenth-century standards, however unpleasant they may have proved for the victims. The *Argus*, a paper that had defended such radicals as Tom Paine, and was content to link its fortune 'to the Revolution of France', was ended, its printer Sampson Perry having been outlawed when he fled to France to avoid trial for libel. The presses were used for the *True Briton*.[166] John Lambert and James Perry, as printer and editor of the *Morning Chronicle*, were tried in 1793 for seditious libel for publishing an address of a Society for Political Information in December 1792. The Attorney-General made clear what he meant by 'the Properly regulated freedom of the press':

> Did the mode in which the writers exposed what they considered as the abuses of the constitution, indicate a peaceable temper, or honest intentions, and a desire only to obtain redress by legal and constitutional means? . . . no man should be at liberty, without a specific object, to state truly or falsely what appears to him to be a grievance merely for the purpose of exciting a spirit of general discontent.

Thomas Erskine argued that it was necessary to prove a criminal intention in publishing, and the jury, despite being bullied by the Chief Justice, Lord Kenyon, supported him.[167] The *Morning Chronicle* might wonder whether it was still 'legal for a man to speculate in England upon the art of government', but it is unrealistic to talk of a 'Reign of Terror' affecting the press. Stamp duty was not raised again until 1797, and then only to a level that caused a temporary decline in circulation, and new legislation affecting the legal position of the press was not passed until 1798 and 1799. The former Act compelled the recording of the names and addresses of printers and publishers on every copy of a paper, prohibited the export of papers to enemy states and closed the oft-used loophole of permitting foreign newspapers to serve as a source for opposition reports. The following year a compulsory registration of printing presses was introduced. Gayle Pendleton's examination of the position with regard to pamphlets suggests a survival of the freedom of the press, a not very effective staunching of reformist literature and a ministerial record 're-markable for restraint and judgment'.[168] These steps did not prevent the expression of views severely critical of the war with France, and in this, as in so much else, the press at the end of the century continued the traditions of the previous hundred years, for criticism of British war aims and the war effort had characterised the preceding wars. Just as the *London Evening Post* had condemned the war in America and the *London Courant* regretted victories as likely to inspire a continuation of 'this mad war' so the *Courier* complained in 1795 about the continuation of 'a war, commenced with dishonour, and conducted with disgrace'. The following year the *Telegraph*, an opposition paper that printed short, sharp pieces, condemned French resistance to their republican government: 'LA VENDEE — Above 600,000 men are said to have perished there! And all for what? And who, moreover, will have to answer for the needless effusion of so much blood?' In 1797 the paper spread gloom about the possibilities of a successful French invasion of Ireland.[169] As had been the case in similar circumstances the opposition press was attacked on the grounds of disloyalty:

> The *Morning Chronicle* today, in its address to its readers at the commencement of the year, declaring that it must become *useful* to the country, by its rigorous inquiry after *truth*, when the multitude of falsehoods and misrepresentations contained in that Frenchified print are so notorious.

The *Morning Herald* was attacked for its 'Franco-Anglo Journalists', the *Morning Chronicle* for being hostile to Britain and criticising the conduct of the war. The *Star* and the *Courier* were also accused of being Jacobin. In a similar fashion the *Briton* had claimed in 1762 that opposition papers would have greeted defeats for Britain with delight.[170] Compared to the attempts to suppress radical opinion in other countries, such as Austria and Hungary, the efforts of the Pitt ministry appear modest. Possibly the experience of former attempts to subvert the opposition press induced caution. The government did not follow up the repressive suggestions of critics of the press such as Windham, who condemned parliamentary reporting in December 1798. Windham blamed such reporting for the naval mutinies of 1798 and argued that although it would not of itself produce Democracy it 'would essentially change the relations of the People with that House' as it gave

> the People an opportunity of sitting in judgment every day on the measures under discussion in that House, tumultuously to express this disapprobation or approbation — and favoured the propensity of all vulgar minds, perhaps also of minds of no mean endowments, to form premature and intemperate decisions upon the whole matter, long before the detail of its parts and the character of its principle could be discussed and unfolded by the Legislature.

The leader of the aristocratic Whigs, the Duke of Portland, suggested in 1793 that the public would benefit from the suppression of the radical press. A plan to regulate the press by a special 'screening committee' was submitted to Windham in March 1799 by John Adolphus.[171]

The traditional machinery of ministerial intervention was employed in the 1790s. It was largely metropolitan and opposition newspapers in the provinces, such as the *Bury and Norwich Post* which carried an often radical and Painite Norwich column and sympathetically reported the 1795 grain riots, that were allowed to continue. Richard Phillips's *Leicester Herald*, founded in 1792, was able to avoid prosecution for its radical pieces, and when it came to an end in 1795 it was due to fire not prosecution. Benjamin Flower's *Cambridge Intelligencer* flourished in the 1790s despite its radicalism.[172] Action was however taken against some papers that were closely associated with the radical Constitutional Societies. The printers of the *Manchester Herald* and the *Sheffield Register* fled abroad to avoid trial in 1793 and 1794 and their papers came to an end. James Montgomery, the conductor of the radical *Sheffield Iris*, was imprisoned for political libels in 1795 and 1796. The *Leicester Chronicle*, founded in 1792 by Thomas Combe, claimed to be of 'the party of the people' and its strong views led to a threatened ministerial prosecution which caused its dissolution in February 1793.[173] The Foreign Secretary, Lord Grenville, complained in the Lords that 'the conduct of Government was odiously misrepresented',[174] but there were no new acceptable solutions. Ministerial patronage could ensure that the government point of view was stated as fully as possible, but neither it nor the resources of the judicial system could or were designed to produce a monopoly for the ministerial viewpoint. However, if foreign commentators were surprised at the position in Britain they should have been aware that greater government powers did not prevent criticism elsewhere. In the mid-1770s Bréteuil, the minister responsible for the control of printers and publishers in Paris, was driven to conclude that existing French regulations for the suppression of critical material had failed and that a new approach was required.[175] The position was the same in Britain, even if the regulations were different, but in neither country was there any credible new approach.

Notes

1. Chamier to Sir Robert Murray Keith, 10 Sept. 1778, BL. Add. 35515 f. 15.
2. *Lloyd's Evening Post*, 21 Oct. 1768; *Reading Mercury*, 31 July 1780; *London Chronicle*, letter from 'Philomusus', 11 Feb. 1762; Anon., *An Impartial Enquiry into the late conduct of the City of London* (1733), pp. 36–7.
3. Curteis to Dorset, 29 Aug. 1733, Maidstone, Kent Archive Office, U 269 C148/2; Richard Buckner, estate agent of the Duke of Richmond, to Richmond, 25 Nov. 1728, Earl of March, *A Duke and His Friends* (2 vols, 1911) I, 165; Viscount Irwin to Lady Isabella Ingram, 28 Jan. 1734, J. F. Quinn, *Political Activity in Yorkshire, c. 1700–1742* (unpublished M.Litt thesis, Lancaster, 1980), p. 348.
4. Cranfield, *Provincial Newspaper*, pp. 143–6.
5. Cranfield, *Provincial Newspaper*, pp. 144–5.
6. Petition, Yorke to Newcastle, 14 July 1729, PRO. 43/79 f. 110–11, 113.
7. *Original Mercury, York Journal*, 2 Apr. 1728; for a similar response, *York Courant*, 13 Mar. 1739.
8. J. Feather, 'Cross-Channel Currents: historical bibliography and *L'histoire du livre*', *Library*, 6th ser., 2 (1980), pp. 12–14; J. Money, 'Taverns, Coffee Houses and Clubs: Local Politics and Popular Articulacy in the Birmingham Area in the Age of the American Revolution', *Historical Journal*, 14 (1971), p. 18.
9. *Wye's Letter*, 6 Jan., in *Derby Mercury*, 11 Jan. 1733; *London Evening Post*, 11 Oct. 1733; Richard Champion to the Marquis of Rockingham, 19 Aug. 1775, Wentworth-Woodhouse RI — 1592. On the *London Evening Post* having a rural impact during the Jewish Naturalisation Act controversy, Philip Yorke to Thomas Birch, 12 July 1753, BL. Add. 35398 f. 130.
10. *Public Advertiser*, 8 Dec. 1770. Cannon regards this as probably by Junius, Cannon (ed.), *Junius*, p. 468.
11. *Universal Spy*, 29 Apr. 1732.
12. *Flying Post*, 15 Dec. 1730; *Protestor*, 10 Nov. 1753.
13. *Norwich Mercury*, 13 Mar. 1731, reprinting item from *Daily Courant*; *Jacobite's Journal*, 24 Sept. 1748; *St. James's Post*, 6 Sept. 1717.
14. *London Journal*, 15 Sept., 6 Oct. 1722, Aug. 1724; I. Mauduit, *Considerations on the German War* (1760), p. 90; Anon., *A letter from a British Officer now in Germany* (1761), p. 1.
15. Mirepoix, French Ambassador in London, to Puysieulx, French foreign minister, 27 Sept. 1749, AE. CP.Ang. 427 f. 106; Anon., *Mémoire sur la France et l'Angleterre*, Sept. 1760, Paris, Bibliothèque Nationale, Nouvelles Acquisitions Françaises 10716 f. 8.
16. R. Munter, *History of Irish Newspapers* (Cambridge, 1967), p. x; H. T. Dickinson review of Downie, *Harley and the Press, Scottish Historical Review*, 40 (1981), p. 78; F. O'Gorman, 'Party in the later eighteenth century', in J. Cannon (ed.), *The Whig Ascendancy* (1981), p. 86; R. B. McDowell, *Irish Public Opinion 1750–1800* (1924), p. 263; S. Koss, *The Rise and Fall of the Political Press in Britain, I The Nineteenth Century* (1981), p. 3; J. Dinwiddy, 'Party Politics and Ideology in the early years of George III's Reign', *Historical Journal*, 20 (1977), pp. 988–9.
17. Davenant, *Sir Thomas Double at Court and in High Preferments* (1710), p. 108.
18. *Spectator*, 5 Mar. 1711.
19. Sir John Perceval to Philip Perceval, 26 Jan, 1715, BL. Add. 47028 f. 7; Transcript from a shorthand journal of Dudley Ryder, 25 July 1715, Sandon Hall. I would like to thank Earl Harrowby for giving me permission to consult these papers; *Whitehall Journal*, 4 Dec. 1722; *Comedian*, Aug. 1732, p. 33; Anon., *Dawley, D'Anvers, and Fog's Triumph* (1734), pp. 4–7; G. Shelton, *Dean Tucker* (1981), p. 84; *A letter to the Public Advertiser* (1764), p. 39.
20. *St. James's Chronicle*, 1 Jan. 1799.

21. Tilson to Waldegrave, 6 Jan. 1730, Chewton.
22. Cole to the Kent Landowner James Brockman, 12 Aug. 1756, BL. Add. 42591 f. 154; Harcourt to Charles Jenkinson, 6 Jan. 1770, BL. Add. 38206 f. 179; Yorke to Keith, 16 Dec. 1784, BL. Add. 35533 f. 101.
23. Paxton to Newcastle, 29 Nov. 1733, BL. Add. 32689 f. 58; Justice Foster to Newcastle, 11 Jan. 1750, PRO. 36/112 f. 17–18.
24. E.F. to Granville, 21 Aug. 1756, BL. Add. 35594 f. 164–7.
25. Bute to Sir James Lowther, 17 Nov. 1762, Carlisle, Cumbria R.O. D/Lons/L1/1: London Evening Post, 7 Jan., 15 June 1762.
26. H. Horwitz, *Parliament, Policy and Politics in the reign of William III* (Manchester, 1977), p. 157.
27. Harley to Godolphin, 9 Aug. 1702, L. Hanson, *Government and the Press 1695–1763* (Oxford, 1936), p. 93.
28. D. Coombs, *The Conduct of the Dutch. British Opinion and the Dutch Alliance during the War of the Spanish Succession* (The Hague, 1958). I find the claims of James Watson on behalf of the influence of the press exaggerated, *Four English Constitutional Principles and the Press, 1700–1707* (unpublished PhD thesis, West Virginia, 1980).
29. *Swift vs. Mainwaring. 'The Examiner' and 'The Medley'*, F. H. Ellis (ed.) (Oxford 1985), pp. xxiv, xlvi–xlvii.
30. H. Snyder, 'Arthur Maynwaring and the Whig Press, 1710–1712', in P. Haas *et al.* (eds), *Literatur als Kritik des Lebens* (Heidelberg, 1975), p. 127.
31. *Diary of Sir David Hamilton*, P. Roberts (ed.) (Oxford, 1975).
32. Anon., *Sir Robert Brass* (1731), p. 14.
33. The opposition to Walpole was of course composed of different elements and the term is only used for convenience.
34. Stair to Marlborough, 6 Feb. 1737, BL. Microfilm 687; Points for My Lord Chancellor, 15 Aug. 1756, Newcastle to John Roberts, 26 Dec. 1756, BL. Add. 35415 f. 247, 32869 f. 399; Brewer, *Party Ideology*, pp. 228, 233; Hardwicke to Newcastle, 29 July 1762, BL. Add. 32941 f. 94; BL. Egerton Mss. 3787, I,3.
35. *Westminster Journal*, 20 Feb. 1742; *Craftsman*, 31 July 1731; Anon., *Essay upon the Taste and Writings of the Present Times* (1728), p. 45, quoted in Hanson, *Government and the Press*, p. 108.
36. Hort to — , 1 Feb. 1723, PRO. 35/41 f. 137. He was referring to the issue of 26 Jan.
37. *Original Weekly Journal*, 18 Jan. 1718. *York Courant* of 21 Jan. 1729 carried a summary of the ministerial pamphlet *Observations on the Conduct of Great Britain* taken from *Wye's Letter* of 16 and 18 Jan.; Hanson, *Government and the Press*, p. 93.
38. Peters, *Monitor*, pp. 582–4.
39. Brewer, *Political Ideology*, p. 229; *Leeds Intelligencer*, 24 June 1766; *Berrow's Worcester Journal*, 14 Aug. 1766; *Reading Mercury*, 17 Aug. 1772.
40. *Reading Mercury*, 19 Aug. 1771.
41. Brewer, *Political Ideology*, p. 146.
42. Hardwicke to Newcastle, 29 Aug. 1756, BL. Add. 32867 f. 146.
43. Accounts, 22 May 1728, 22 May 1729, PRO. 36/6 f. 218, 36/11. On ministerial papers being sent to Ireland, John Lingen to James Payzant, Clerk in the Northern Department, 9 Jan. 1729, PRO. 63/390 f. 3; Lewis to James Payzant, 23 Mar., Mrs Markland to James Payzant, 16 Mar. 1725, PRO. 35/55; P. Forbes to Payzant, 9 Aug. 1723, PRO. 35/44.
44. *Craftsman*, 20 Oct. 1733. B–ll was Bell.
45. *Fog's Weekly Post*, 30 Jan. 1731, 15 Jan. 1732; *London Evening Post*, 3 Nov. 1733, 15 Sept. 1748.
46. Townshend to Walpole, 12 July (ns) 1723, PRO. 43/4 f. 75.

47. Hanson, *Government and the Press*; Downie, *Harley and the Press*; M. Harris, 'Print and Politics in the Age of Walpole', in J. Black (ed.), *Britain in the Age of Walpole* (1984); R. R. Rea, *The English Press in Politics 1760–1774* (Lincoln, Nebraska, 1963); L. Werkmeister, *The London Daily Press, 1772–1792* (Lincoln, Nebraska, 1963); Aspinall, *Politics and the Press*; E. Porritt, 'The Government and the Newspaper Press in England', *Political Science Quarterly*, 12 (1897).

48. L. Namier, *The Structure of Politics at the Accession of George III* (2nd ed., 1957), p. 229.

49. Hanson, *Government and the Press*, pp. 113, 109.

50. A. J. Guy, *Oeconomy and Discipline, Officeship and administration in the British army 1714–63* (Manchester, 1985), pp. 55, 154, 94; *Universal Spectator*, 5 June 1736.

51. Robert Freebairne to John Hay, 2 Sept. (ns) 1721, R.A. 54/144; Destouches, French envoy in London, to Dubois, French foreign minister, 21 Aug. (ns) 1722, AE. CP. Ang. 342 f. 206.

52. *Westminster Journal*, 4 Dec. 1742; *Select Letters taken from Fog's Weekly Journal* (2 vols., 1732), I, dedication.

53. *Grub Street Journal*, 12 Aug. 1731.

54. *Nonsense of Common-Sense*, 17 Jan. 1738.

55. This was less common in the provinces, particularly in the first half of the century.

56. Hanson, *Government and the Press*, pp. 114–15; *Grub Street Journal*, 26 Aug. 1731; *Champion*, 24 July 1740; *Daily Gazetteer*, 22 Feb. 1742.

57. S. Lutnick, *The American Revolution and the British Press, 1775–1783* (Columbia, Missouri, 1967), p. 19; I. Asquith, 'The structure, ownership and control of the press, 1780–1855', in G. Boyce, J. Curran, P. Wingate (eds), *Newspaper History* (1978), p. 111.

58. Christie, *Myth and Reality*, p. 328; A. Aspinall (ed.), *The Later Correspondence of George III* (Cambridge, 1962), I, 118; Haig, *Gazetteer*, p. 17.

59. G— to Newcastle, 17 Nov. 1757, BL. Add. 32876 f. 4.

60. Christie, *Myth and Reality*, pp. 345, 358.

61. Christie, *Myth and Reality*, p. 323.

62. *Reading Mercury*, 10 Dec. 1770.

63. Lutnick, *American Revolution and the British Press*, pp. 24–7; Ehrman, *Pitt*, I, p. 606.

64. K. Schweizer, 'The Origins of the "Press War" of 1762: A Reappraisal', *Notes and Queries*, 1978, pp. 47–50; Brewer, *Political Ideology*, pp. 221–6.

65. Rea, *English Press in Politics*, pp. 99, 133, 167; J. R. Foster, 'Smollett's Pamphleteering Foe Shebbeare', *PMLA*, 59 (1942), pp. 1053–1100.

66. Rea, *English Press in Politics*, pp. 218–19; *Public Advertiser*, 2 Apr. 1771; H. McGuffie, *Samuel Johnson in the British Press, 1749–1784: A Chronological Checklist* (New York, 1976); Luzerne to Montmorin, French foreign minister, 31 May 1790, AE. CP. Ang. 573 f. 202.

67. Bradshaw to Keith, 30 Apr. 1773, BL. Add. 35505 f. 220; undated memorandum, CUL. C(H) papers 75/19.

68. Lord George Sackville, 6 Dec. 1770, Cobbett, 16, 1283–4.

69. Weymouth, Secretary of State for the Southern Department, to William De Grey, 14 Aug. 1770, PRO. 94/184, referring to the *Gazetteer and New Daily Advertiser*.

70. Siebert, *Freedom of the Press*, p. 381; Rea, *English Press in Politics*, p. 224; R. E. McCoy, *Freedom of the Press, an Annotated Bibliography* (Carbondale, Illinois, 1968). For a teleological summary of 'the historical drama' and an interesting discussion of the nineteenth-century press as an agency of control, Boyce *et al.* (eds), *Newspaper History*, p. 51.

71. R. Porter, *English Society in the Eighteenth Century* (1982), pp. 130, 125.
72. Porter, *Society*, p. 130; D. Hay, 'Property, authority and the criminal law', in Hay, P. Linebaugh, and E. P. Thompson (eds.), *Albion's Fatal Tree*, p. 49.
73. G. Holmes, 'The achievement of stability: the social context of politics from the 1680's to the age of Walpole', in J. Cannon (ed.), *The Whig Ascendancy*; J. Cannon, *Aristocratic Century. The Peerage of Eighteenth-Century England* (Cambridge, 1984); I. Christie, *Stress and Stability in late Eighteenth-Century Britain* (Oxford, 1984); J. C. D. Clark, *English Society 1688–1832* (Cambridge, 1985).
74. *Leeds Intelligencer*, 18 Mar. 1766; *North Country Journal*, 14 May 1737.
75. *Gazetteer and New Daily Advertiser*, 11 Aug. 1770.
76. *Political State* (Jan. 1739), p. 38; *Newcastle Courant*, 16 Jan. 1742; *Caledonian Mercury*, 10 Dec. 1745; *Universal Journal*, 13 June 1724; *Grub Street Journal*, 16 Mar. 1732; *Universal Spectator*, 14 Dec. 1745; *Newcastle Journal*, 9 Dec. 1752.
77. *Town and Country Magazine*, 14 (1782), p. 95; *Whitehall Evening Post*, 30 Dec. 1718.
78. Gyllenborg to the Swedish minister Baron Görtz, 23 Oct., 4, 10 Nov. 1716, PRO. 107/1B f. 172–3, 210–11, 218; *Weekly Journal: or, Saturday's Post*, 2 Mar. 1717.
79. James Stanhope to Townshend, 18 Aug. (ns) 1716, PRO. 43/1 f. 36.
80. Delafaye received reports from agents in London, James Watson to Delafaye, 15 May 1728, PRO. 36/6 f. 203.
81. *Craftsman*, 16 Dec. 1726, 28 Sept. 1728.
82. *Reading Mercury*, 14 Oct. 1771; T. C. D. Eaves and B. D. Kimpel, 'Two Notes on Samuel Richardson', *Library*, 5th ser., 23 (1969), p. 245; Paxton to Newcastle, 29 Nov. 1733, BL. Add. 32689 f. 58.
83. *Leeds Intelligencer*, 5 June 1781.
84. *Whitehall Evening Post*, 11 May 1732; *Sheffield Advertiser*, 12 Feb. 1790.
85. Tilson to Waldegrave, 27 Jan. 1730, Chewton; *Scrutator*, 12 Apr. 1764.
86. J. Oldmixon, *History of England* (1730–5), II, 95; HMC, *Bath*, I, 105–6; *Weekly Journal: or, Saturday's Post*, 11 Oct. 1718, 4 Apr. 1719; *Evening Post*, 3 Feb. 1728; Francès to Choiseul, 17 Aug., Choiseul to Francès, 27 Aug. 1770, AE. CP. Ang. 492 f. 424–5, 456; Scarnafis to Charles Emmanuel III, King of Sardinia, 17 Aug. 1770, Turin, Archivio di Stato, Lettere Ministri Inghilterra, 76; *Gentleman's Magazine,* 40 (1770), p. 440, *Oracle*, 9 June 1789.
87. *Daily Gazetteer*, 27 Oct. 1738.
88. Young to Thomas Tickell, 5 Feb. 1728, *The Correspondence of Edward Young 1683–1765*, H. Pettit (ed.) (Oxford, 1971), p. 61.
89. *Fog's Weekly Journal*, 16 Aug. 1729.
90. Chammorel, French Chargé d'affaires, to Chauvelin, 27 Sept. (ns) 1728, AE. CP. Ang. 363 f. 178; *London Evening Post*, 17 Nov. 1733; Attorney-General Sir John Willes to Newcastle, 23 Dec. 1734, PRO. 36/33 f. 147; Anon., *An Historical View of the . . . Political Writers* (1740), p. 13.
91. *General Post Office Letter*, 11 Aug. 1722.
92. R. B. Patterson, *Robert Harley and the Organization of Political Propaganda* (unpublished PhD thesis, Virginia, 1974), p. 74; J. Parkes and H. Merivale (eds), *Memoirs of Sir Philip Francis* (2 vols., 1867) I, 87.
93. *Weekly Journal or British Gazetteer*, 20 Sept. 1718; *Worcester Post-Man*, 6 May 1720; *Norwich Mercury*, 13 Jan. 1733; Anon. note, CUL. Mss, papers 75/20; Petition of Elizabeth Nutt (1728), PRO. 36/161 f. 19; Warrant for Arrests, 9 Jan. 1731, PRO. 36/22 f. 12. Threats against the pamphlet-shops were used to try to prevent the sale of Budgell's books, Budgell, *Liberty and Property* (2 vols, 1732), II, 1.
94. *St. James's Journal*, 20 Sept. 1722; *Craftsman*, 30 Nov. 1728; Anon., *A Reply*

to the Defence of the Majority on the Question Relating to General Warrants (1764), p. 22.

95. Delafaye to Townshend, 6 Aug. 1723, PRO. 43/67; *Weekly Journal: or, Saturday's Post*, 9 Mar. 1717.

96. Anon., *A Defence of the Minority in the House of Commons, on the Question Relating to General Warrants* (5th ed., 1764), p. 35.

97. Mist, *A Collection of Miscellany Letters* (2 vols., 1722) II, viii–ix.

98. C. B. Realey, *The Early Opposition to Sir Robert Walpole* (Lawrence, Kansas, 1931), p. 95; *Northampton Mercury*, 24 Dec. 1722; Peters, *Monitor*, p. 48.

99. Peters, *Monitor*, p. 326.

100. Peters, *Monitor*, pp. 39, 41, 599–609; *North Briton*, 4 Dec. 1762.

101. R. J. Allen, 'William Oldisworth: the author of *The Examiner*', *Philological Quarterly*, 26 (1947), p. 175; *Freeholder's Journal*, 31 Oct. 1722; Poyntz to Delafaye, 25 Sept. 1723, PRO. 43/5; *Mist's Weekly Journal*, 12 June 1725; Wharton's memorandum, 23 Aug. (ns) 1725, Vienna, Haus-, Hof-, and Staatsarchiv, Staatenabteilungen, England, Noten 2; *Norwich Mercury*, 2 May 1730; Delafaye to Waldegrave, 19 Oct. 1730, Chewton; *Craftsman*, 17 Oct. 1730, 27 Feb. 1731; *Universal Spectator*, 6 Feb. 1742.

102. *Craftsman*, 30 Nov. 1728, 6 Dec. 1729; Anon., *The Wooden Age* (1733), p. 3, dedication, [Marchmont], *A Serious Exhortation to the Electors of Great Britain* (1740), pp. 20–1.

103. Tilson to Whitworth, 4 Mar. 1722, BL. Add. 37389 f. 8.

104. The description is that of I. N. Rothman, 'Defoe's *Family Instructor* in Glasgow: Dissent and the Schism Act', *Notes and Queries*, new series, 31 (1984), p. 386.

105. *Thursday's Post*, 8 Oct. 1719; Hanson, *Government and the Press*, pp. 64–6; Chapman, *Jacobite Political Argument*, pp. 185–7.

106. Hoadly to Lady Sundon, undated, *The Works of Benjamin Hoadly* (3 vols., 1773), I, xlviii.

107. Delafaye to Stanhope, 6 Nov. 1719, PRO. 43/63.

108. *Flying Post: or, Post-Master*, 4 Feb. 1720.

109. Mist, *Miscellany Letters*, I, preface; Chapman, *Jacobite Political Argument*, p. 187.

110. Delafaye to Poyntz, 27 Feb. 1729, BL. Althorp, E3.

111. *General Post Office Letter*, 19 May 1724; Walpole to Townshend, 28 June 1723, Delafaye to Townshend, 25 June, 26 July 1723, PRO. 43/4, 4, 66.

112. Yorke to —, 26 Mar. 1732, PRO. 36/26 f. 144.

113. Yorke to Newcastle, 14 July 1729, 29 June 1730, 15 Dec. 1733, PRO. 43/79 f. 110–11, 36/19 f. 102, 36/30 f. 345; Willes to Newcastle, 23 Dec. 1734, PRO. 36/33 f. 147; Hanson, *Government and the Press*, p. 67.

114. *Observations on a Pamphlet, . . . In a letter to Mr P—*, pp. 6–7.

115. Cowper to wife, 28 May 1721, Hertford CRO, Panshanger Mss, D/EP F 193 f. 90; Yorke to Newcastle, 15 Dec. 1733, PRO. 36/30 f. 345; Prince Kantemir, Russian Ambassador, to Tsarina Anna, 17 Apr. 1733, 15 Nov. 1736, R. J. Morda Evans, *Antiokh Kantemir. A study of his Literary, Political and Social Life in England, 1732–8* (unpublished PhD thesis, London, 1959), pp. 120, 84.

116. Delafaye to Waldegrave, 31 Mar. 1732, Chewton.

117. *St. James's Journal*, 1 Nov. 1722; Anon., *A Friendly Epistle to the Author of the State Dunces* (1733), p. 9; *Daily Courant*, 9 Oct. 1734.

118. A. D. McKillop, 'Thomson and the Licensers of the Stage', *Philological Quarterly*, 37 (1958), pp. 450, 452; L. W. Conolly, *The Censorship of English Drama 1737–1824* (San Marino, Calif., 1976), p. 10; V. J. Leisenfeld, *The Licensing Act of 1737* (Madison, 1984); *Champion*, 6 Mar. 1742.

119. *Daily Post Boy*, 29 Aug. 1730, 13 Feb. 1731.

120. Delafaye's notes on examination of James Watson, Mar. 1728, PRO. 36/5 f. 182.

121. *Craftsman*, 22 June 1728; Walpole, *Memoirs*, Brooke (ed.), I, 111–12.

122. Hare to son Francis Naylor, 15 Feb. 1739, HMC., *Hare*, p. 43.
123. Charles Holzendorf, Chesterfield's secretary at The Hague, to Tilson, 3, 7 Aug. (ns) 1731, PRO. 84/314 f. 31, 35; *Comedian, or Philosophical Enquirer*, Aug. 1732, p. 34. Robert Trevor benefited from the control of the press in the United Provinces when complaining about their coverage of Bonnie Prince Charlie, Trevor to Tilson, 12 July (ns), Trevor to Harrington, 16 July (ns) 1737, PRO. 84/366 f. 78, 84. Horatio Walpole referred to the contrast between the British and Dutch situation, Walpole to Trevor, 8 Apr. 1737, Aylesbury, Trevor Mss, Vol. 7.
124. *Daily Post Boy*, 15 Feb. 1731.
125. Couraud to Waldegrave, 4 Sept. 1738, Chewton; Fagel to Hop, 14 Apr. (ns) 1739, PRO. 107/26.
126. Description of John Glynn's speech in defence of Henry Baldwin of the *St. James's Chronicle*, *Reading Mercury*, 23 July 1770.
127. Hardwicke to Newcastle, 29 Aug. 1756, BL. Add. 32867 f. 146.
128. Newcastle to Hardwicke, 26 July (ns), 2 Aug. (ns), Hardwicke to Newcastle, 7 Aug. 1752, BL. Add. 35412 f. 184–5, 205–6, 209, 250; *Historical View . . . of the Political Writers*, p. 23.
129. Warrants, 15 July, 18 Oct. 1739, PRO. 44/82 f. 179, 183; Attorney-General Dudley Ryder to Harrington, 8, 18 Oct., examination of printer Dr Gaylard, 23 Oct. 1739, PRO. 36/50 f. 12, 14, 16–18; Notes of Ryder, 22 Sept. 1739, History of Parliament transcripts.
130. H. R. Plomer, *A Dictionary of the Printers and Booksellers who were at work in England . . .* (Oxford, 1932), p. 216; Sherlock, 'Heads of a Bill to prevent the Growth of Popery', mss in papers of Edward Weston.
131. *Journals of the House of Commons*, 23, 148; *Westminster Journal*, 11 Dec. 1742; Harris to Hardwicke, 12, 14, 28 July 1744, BL. Add. 35587 f. 263–4, 268–9.
132. Cranfield, *Provincial Newspaper*, pp. 163–5.
133. W. Coxe, *Memoirs of . . . Henry Pelham* (2 vols., 1829), I, 354–5; Fielding, *A Dialogue between a Gentleman from London . . . and an Honest Alderman of the Country Party* (1747), in W. B. Coley (ed.), *The Jacobite's Journal and Related Writings* (Oxford, 1974), p. 15; *True Patriot*, 7 Jan. 1746; Sandwich to Bedford, 29 Aug. (ns) 1747, Newcastle to Sandwich, 1 Apr. 1748, BL. Add. 32809 f. 210, 32812 f. 12.
134. *Daily Gazetteer*, 17 July 1747; *London Evening Post*, 1 Aug. 1747; *Old England*, 28 Nov. 1747; Anon., *A Critical Expatiatory, and Interesting Address to a certain Right Honourable Apostate* (1748), pp. 11–12, 22–3, cited Coley (ed.), *Jacobite's Journal*, pp. 159–60. Rebutted in *Jacobite's Journal*, 13 Feb., 2 Apr. 1748.
135. Ryder to Newcastle, 16 Oct. 1749, PRO. 36/111 f. 115.
136. *The Political Journal of George Bubb Dodington*, J. Carswell and L. A. Dralle (eds) (Oxford, 1965), pp. 27, 218; Hanson, *Government and the Press*, p. 121; D. Jarrett, *The Ingenious Mr. Hogarth* (1976), p. 163.
137. Hanson, *Government and the Press*, pp. 71–2; Sharpe to Newcastle, 28 Aug. 1756, BL. Add. 32867; T. W. Perry, *Public Opinion, Propaganda and Politics in Eighteenth-Century England. A Study of the Jewish Naturalization Act of 1753* (Cambridge, Mass. 1962), p. 132; Horace Walpole, *Memoirs*, (ed.) Brooke, I, 241, II, 96. On misrepresentation of the Act, *Public Advertiser*, 26 June 1753. *Test*, 11 Dec. 1756; Holderness to Rockingham, 28 Oct. 1756, Sheffield City Library, Wentworth Woodhouse Mss R1–85.
138. M. Peters, *Pitt and Popularity. The Patriot Minister and London Opinion during the Seven Years War* (Oxford, 1980), pp. 46–56, 67–8.
139. *Briton*, 24 July 1762; *Gray's Inn Journal*, 27 Oct. 1753; Forrester MP, 6 Dec. 1770, Cobbett, 16, 1282.
140. Sackville, 6 Dec. 1770, Cobbett 16, 1283–4; P. D. G. Thomas, 'John Wilkes and the Freedom of the Press', *Bulletin of the Institute of Historical Research*, 33

(1960). On these talismanic qualities, Brewer, 'The Number 45: A Wilkite Political Symbol', in S. B. Baxter (ed.), *England's Rise to Greatness, 1660–1763* (Berkeley, 1983).

141. Scarnafis to Charles Emmanuel III, 29 Mar. 1771, AST. LM. Ing. 77; A.M. Schlesinger, *Prelude to Independence. The Newspaper War on Britain 1764–1776* (New York, 1958), p. 311.

142. Shelton, *Tucker*, p. 157; Sharpe to Newcastle, 28 Aug. 1756, BL. Add. 32867; Guthrie to Bute, 2 Sept. 1762, quoted in J. B. Shipley, *James Ralph: Pretender to Genius* (unpublished PhD, Columbia, 1963), p. 370; Ellison to Henry Ellison, 10 May 1763, Gateshead, Public Library, Ellison Mss A12 No. 32; *Newcastle Journal*, 23 Jan. 1773.

143. Rea, *Press in Politics*, pp. 177–87; *Gazetteer*, 13 Aug. 1770.

144. *Craftsman*, 5 Feb. 1774; *Berrow's Worcester Journal*, 9 Nov. 1769; *St. James's Chronicle*, 4 May 1769.

145. Grafton, 5 Dec. 1770, Cobbett, 16, 1309.

146. Walpole, *Memoirs*, Brooke (ed.), II, 26; P. D. G. Thomas, 'The Beginning of Parliamentary Reporting in Newspapers, 1768–74', *EHR*, 74 (1959), reprinted in R. Mitchison (ed.), *Essays in Eighteenth Century History* (1966).

147. *Reading Mercury*, 25 Feb., 25 Mar. 1771, 22 Feb., 31 May, 21 June 1773, 21 May 1781.

148. *Town and Country Magazine*, 14 (1782), iii–iv; Asquith, *Perry*, p. 335.

149. *Daily Universal Register*, 1 Jan. 1785; *Newcastle Chronicle*, 10 Feb. 1787.

150. M. Ransome, 'The Reliability of Contemporary Reporting of the Debates of the House of Commons, 1727–41', *Bulletin of the Institute of Historical Research*, 19 (1942–3); Black, 'A Diplomat Visits Parliament: An unprinted account of the Army Estimates Debate of 1733', *Parliamentary History Yearbook* (1986).

151. Cobbett, 10 Dec. 1770, 16, 1318.

152. Ehrman, *Pitt*, I, 53; Francis Moore to Burges, 8 July 1791, Bodl. Bland Burges 45 f. 57; A. Aspinall, 'The Reporting and Publishing of the House of Commons Debates, 1771–1834', in R. Pares and A. J. P. Taylor (eds), *Essays to Sir Lewis Namier* (1956).

153. *Morning Chronicle*, 8 Jan. 1787; *Oracle*, 29 Jan. 1795; *True Briton*, 2 Feb., 23 Jan. 1799; Thomas, 'Parliamentary reporting', *EHR*, pp. 634–6; *Reading Mercury*, 27 May 1771; Anon. to John Almon, undated, BL. Add. 20733 f. 16.

154. Rea, *Press in Politics*, pp. 181, 201; Thomas, 'Parliamentary reporting', *EHR*, pp. 634–5.

155. Cobbett, 8 Feb. 1771, 17, 65–71; Fraser to Keith, 14 Feb. 1783, BL. Add. 35527 f. 286; Cobbett, 8 Feb. 1788, 26, 1429.

156. Rea, *Press in Politics*, pp. 205–6.

157. Dickens to Henry Woodfall, 9 May 1769, BL. Add. 27780 f. 11.

158. Letter from Miller to the printer of the paper, *Reading Mercury*, printed in latter, 21 Mar. 1774; Sandwich to Woodfall, 23 Feb. 1773, BL. Add. 27780 f. 21; *Noon Gazette*, 10 Dec. 1781.

159. Lowther to Spedding, 13 Dec. 1740, 29 Sept. 1743, Lowther to Sir James Lowther, 10 Oct. 1780, Cumbria RO D/Lons/L 1/1; Diary notes of Frances Lady Hertford, 1–15 Mar. 1742, Alnwick Castle, Alnwick Mss vol. 114.

160. Haslang to Baron Vieregg, 12 May 1778, Munich, Bayerisches Hauptstaatsarchiv, Gesandtschaft London 256. For similar comments by his counterpart in Vienna, Hallberg to Vieregg, 19 July, 3 Sept. 1786, Wien 728; *Newcastle Journal*, 30 Jan. 1773.

161. George to Patrick Home, 23 Apr. 1785, Edinburgh, Scottish Record Office, 267/1/10/47.

162. *World*, 9, 15 Nov. 1791, 27 Feb. 1792; Ewart to Burges, 5, 7 (quote) Apr. 1791, Bodl. Bland Burges papers, 34 f. 143, 144, 37, f. 34, 36; A. Cunningham, 'The Ochakov debate', *Middle Eastern Studies*, I (1964–5), pp. 209–37. Voronzov

had inserted articles previously, Barthelemy, French Chargé d'affaires, to Montmorin 4 Nov. 1788, AE. CP. Ang. 567 f. 104.

163. Burges notes, Bodl. Bland Burges 74, f. 22; Burges to Lord Auckland, 2 Feb. 1793, *Journal and Correspondence of William, Lord Auckland*, Bishop of Bath and Wells (4 vols., 1861–2), II, 494–5; François Noël, French agent, to Lebrun, French foreign minister, 22 Oct. 1792, Chauvelin to Lebrun, 19 Jan. 1793, AE. CP. Ang. 583 f. 47, 586 f. 187.

164. Richard Cambridge to Nathaniel Winchcombe, 3 Sept. 1792, Gloucester RO. D149 F41; Asquith, *Perry*, p. 50; L. Werkmeister, *A Newspaper History of England 1792–1793* (Lincoln, Nebraska, 1967), pp. 113, 186.

165. Noël to Lebrun, 23 Sept. 1792, AE. CP. Ang. 582 f. 210.

166. *Argus*, 6 Mar. 1792; Werkmeister, *Newspaper History*, p. 143; R. Rea, '"The Liberty of the Press" as an issue in English politics, 1792–1793', *The Historian*, 24 (1961).

167. *The Speeches of the Hon. Thomas Erskine . . . on Subjects connected with the Liberty of the Press* (3 vols., 1810), II, 406, 403, 406, 419.

168. *Morning Chronicle*, 30 Oct. 1792; Aspinall, *Politics and the Press*, pp. 18–19, 34–40; G. T. Pendleton, 'Radicalism and the English "Reign of Terror": The evidence of the pamphlet literature', *Proceedings of the Consortium on Revolutionary Europe* (1979), pp. 199–200; C. Emsley, 'An aspect of Pitt's "Terror": Prosecutions for sedition during the 1790s', *Social History,* 6 (1981). On the limited long-term impact of taxation, Brewer, *Political Ideology*, p. 220. For the use of the loophole, Newcastle to Townshend, 22 July 1729, PRO. 43/79 f. 163, *Newcastle Courant*, 26 July 1729.

169. *London Evening Post*, 6, 13 Jan. 1778; *London Courant*, 1 Jan. 1780; *Courier*, 2 Jan. 1795; *Telegraph*, 29 Mar. 1796, 10 Jan. 1797.

170. *St. James's Chronicle*, 1 Jan. 1799; *True Briton*, 3, 8 Jan., 14 Feb. 1799; *Briton*, 16 Oct. 1762; *Leeds Intelligencer*, 16 Jan., 6 Feb. 1781.

171. *St. James's Chronicle*, 1 Jan. 1799; Portland to Earl Fitzwilliam, 28 Sept. 1793, E. A. Smith, *Whig Principles and Party Politics* (Manchester, 1975), p. 155. I owe the information on Adolphus's scheme to Professor Rea.

172. G. Bage, *A Provincial Reaction to the French Revolution: Radical Politics, Social Unrest and the growth of loyal opinion in East Anglia at the end of the eighteenth century, with special reference to the county of Suffolk* (unpublished M.Litt thesis, Cambridge, 1983), pp. 5–6; D. Fraser, 'The Press in Leicester c. 1790–1850', *Transactions of the Leicestershire Archaeological and Historical Society* 42 (1966–7), p. 59; M. J. Murphy, 'Newspapers and Opinion in Cambridge, 1780–1850', *Transactions of the Cambridge Bibliographical Society* 6 (1972), p. 41.

173. W. H. G. Armytage, 'The Editorial Experiences of Joseph Gales', *North Carolina Historical Review*, 28 (1951), pp. 332–61; J. Wigley, 'James Montgomery and the *Sheffield Iris*, 1792–1825: A Study in the Weakness of Provincial Radicalism', *Transactions of the Hunter Archaeological Society*, 10 (1975), pp. 173–81; D. Read, *Press and People 1790–1850. Opinion in Three English Cities* (1961), pp. 69–73; Fraser, 'Press in Leicester', *Leicestershire Archaeological and Historical Society*, p. 59.

174. *St. James's Chronicle*, 5 Jan. 1799; C. Emsley, 'Repression, "terror" and the rule of law in England during the decade of the French Revolution', *EHR* 99 (1985).

175. Breteuil, 'Réflexions . . .', P. M. Conlon (ed.), *Studies on Voltaire*, 1 (1955), pp. 125–31; D. Echeverria, *The Maupeou Revolution* (Baton Rouge, 1985), p. 23. On the vigour of French 'libelling', Delafaye to Waldegrave, 18 Aug. 1732, Chewton, Poyntz to Delafaye, 10 Jan. (ns) 1730, PRO. 78/194 f. 9.

7   The Press and Europe

Poor S. Buckley will murmur at peace and quietness; since it quite starves his consumptive gazette, but an Irish Parliament, and a Swedish Diet may now and then afford a morsel.

George Tilson, 1723[1]

He surprised me by talking of the party disputes and adventures which have happened of late years in England, of which I found him minutely informed. Many people in Germany have the English newspapers and political pamphlets regularly transmitted to them . . . from these they often form very false and extraordinary conclusions with regard to the state of the nation.

John Moore on meeting with the heir to the Palatinate[2]

Modern readers of eighteenth-century newspapers tend to be most surprised by the small quantity of local news and the major role of foreign news. The latter has received relatively little attention, though there has been some good work by Graham Gibbs, and the present author has written on the subject.[3] Several interesting questions arise when considering the foreign news: Why was so much published? How accurate and sophisticated was it? What effect did it have, either on policy or opinion? How was the news related to the debates over foreign policy? How did the situation change during the century? What problems did regulating the news create? It is particularly difficult to answer these questions for the second half of the century, for although there has been much work on press treatment of Imperial themes,[4] there has been very little on reporting of European news prior to the French Revolution, bar Horn's chapter on newspapers in his too often overlooked brief work on public opinion and the first partition of Poland, and Schlenke's interesting study of public attitudes to mid-century Anglo-Prussian relations.[5] The close relationship between domestic politics and foreign policy in the first half of the century has no doubt encouraged work on the coverage of foreign news and often inseparable comment upon it in the press of that period.[6] However, this relationship remained true after the fall of

197

Walpole and yet scholarly attention for that period has been slight, particularly for the 1740s and the period after 1763.[7] This has made it difficult to assess changes during the century and to provide a full background for any study on the French Revolution and the British press. This chapter will seek to use material from both halves of the century, but it is inevitably weighted towards the first half, and it can only be hoped that new work will be undertaken on the decades after the fall of Walpole.

Quantity, organisation and accuracy

> The taking of Oczakow has attracted so much notice, that many of our readers may be desirous of knowing the exact situation of that place.
>
> *Felix Farley's Bristol Journal*, 24 January 1789

Quantity

The range and quantity of foreign news available to newspaper readers was staggering and this remained true throughout the century. It also remained true even when there were significant domestic developments. The *Newcastle Courant* was typical in being full of European news at the time of the fall of Walpole. There were certain papers that contained very little foreign news, but these tended to be essay papers, which contained very little news anyway, and whose definition as newspapers is open to discussion. Papers that printed news, whether they were London or provincial, dailies, bi- or tri-weeklies or weeklies, tended to contain a lot of foreign news, though there were some papers that appear to have made less of an effort in this respect and there were always issues of individual papers that contained very little foreign news,[8] often because of adverse winds. It is perhaps significant that in general when the newspapers sought to advertise their value and to obtain more readers they stressed the quality of their foreign news. The *Post Boy* in May 1728 drew attention to the quality of its printer's foreign news, and 'the extraordinary expense he is at in furnishing a Hague letter, which gives the best account we have of transactions in the different courts of Europe, the interests of Princes . . .'. Announcing that August plans to become a daily, it stated that the new paper would include, 'as usual, the Original Hague letter, confessedly superior to anything

extant of that kind: which has never fail'd to give general satisfaction, and which can be procured by none but the proprietors of
this paper'. In fact the paper's circulation appears to have suffered
in this period,[9] but other newspapers clearly regarded reports
about foreign affairs as of the greatest importance. The first
number of the *British Observer*, a London paper founded in
1733, proclaimed, 'Our constant care shall be to procure the best
foreign advices, to digest them into a proper method, and to cloath
them with a convenient style.' The *Daily Gazetteer* announced in
1735 that 'to render our paper still more generally entertaining, we
shall sometimes make a digression from politics, and insert essays
on miscellaneous subjects'. It is significant that this announcement, and the first such essay, one on politeness taken from an
Amsterdam periodical, appeared whilst there was a 'want of foreign intelligence'. Two years earlier the *General Evening Post* increased its size in response, so it claimed, to readers' letters asking
the proprietors to be more extensive in their relation of foreign
news, on account of the uncertain state of affairs in Poland.[10]

Most papers certainly provided as good 'foreign advices' as
possible. Assessing the contents of the previous day's papers, the
author of the *Grub Street Journal* of 12 December 1734 noted that,
'In the *Daily Advertiser* . . . there are but eleven lines of domestic
news; in the *Courant* and *Daily Post Boy* not one.' Given the
dominant role of items from the London press in the contents of
provincial newspapers, it is not surprising that numerous items of
foreign news appeared in the latter. Their source was clear: they
appeared under the heading London. The *Newcastle Journal* for
16, 23 and 30 January 1773 contained 76 items of foreign news,
approximately half the length of the London section of the paper.
This was at a time of domestic interest, namely the parliamentary
session, and a foreign situation that while not without events of
importance, such as the bankruptcy of several leading Dutch
banking houses, was in no way exceptional. Furthermore the items
carried displayed a great variety. The 24 items in the issue of 16
January included news of European bankruptcies and of international negotiations associated with the First Partition of Poland,
but they also comprised information concerning the new heavy
poll tax in Hanover, the new public library in Vienna, a fire at the
Hôtel Dieu in Paris, the Amsterdam mortality figures of 1772, a
mummy obtained in Tenerife by an English naval captain, the
submission of the Princes of the Blood in France, Iberian hostility

to the Jesuits, the despatch of a Tripolitanian envoy to Britain, the war on the Guinea coast between the Portuguese and the king of Benin, hostilities on Antigua and St Vincent between whites and non-whites and the discovery in Paris of a method of extracting a nutritious essence from barley. It is interesting to note the appearance of colonial news but it was still the case that this tended to take a distinctly secondary place to European items. In 1735 the *London Journal* had carried colonial items under a heading *News from the Plantations* announcing 'the British Colonies are of so much importance to the trade and commerce of Great Britain that we shall continue, (as we have begun a few papers since) to make a separate article, under which we shall present our readers with whatever comes to our hands of consequence, relating thereto'.[11] Such a practice did not however become common, and in general colonial items were mixed with those of European provenance, and in no logical order: news concerning French colonies did not follow news relating to France. Increased colonial news probably reflected not only the undoubted greater interest in the colonies, which can also be seen in the magazines of the period, but also the growing ease of providing such news, due in particular to the development of a colonial press. This provided a regular source for items of colonial news, reducing the significance of particular items provided by personal letters, often from travellers or merchants. It thus corresponded in its effect to the improvement in the network of British provincial newspapers. By the 1780s items were regularly appearing in British newspapers with acknowledgement to papers such as the *Calcutta Gazette*. In July 1781 the *Leeds Intelligencer* used the *St. Lucia Gazette* as a source of information for West Indian military news. On 27 September 1784 the *Leeds Mercury* reported the contents of the Antigua press which it had received from a ship arrived at Whitehaven. On 13 February 1792 the *Oracle*'s news from Jamaica was from 'the Kingston Newspapers'.

Organisation

How far foreign news was digested 'into a proper method' is open to question. In the absence of a well-developed headlining system one might nevertheless have expected foreign news to be separated from domestic news and the former to be arranged so that reports on the same topic could be found together. A modern reader might expect news to be differentiated from comment, and there was a clear distinction for many eighteenth-century foreign news items, for the news tended to relate what was happening abroad, whilst the comment discussed this in the light of current debates over British foreign policy. In practice there was little organisation of items and, although news and comment were usually, though not always clearly, distinct in tone, they were not always separated. Few papers went as far as the *London Observator or, Collins Weekly Journal* of 1723 which distinguished clearly between sections for news and 'remarks'. The *St. James's Weekly Journal: or, Hanover Post-Man*, a ministerial weekly that first appeared on 31 October 1719 announced, 'Our foreign news shall be taken from beyond sea by every mail; and all doubtful matters therein will be explained, with general remarks, without lessening one side, or magnifying the other, excepting upon very good ground indeed.' The paper accordingly printed after each item of foreign news a 'Remark' in a different type. Nor did many papers follow the magazines in grouping items together, the *Gentleman's Magazine* providing 'Foreign History', the *Town and Country Magazine* the 'State of Europe'. Some London papers did however group together types of news under the byline of coffee-houses associated with those interested in them. The *Freeholder's Journal* of 27 February 1723 printed foreign news under the Smyrna coffee-house, a poem under Burton's and religious news under Child's. The *Universal Journal*, a London weekly, in its issue of 29 June 1724, printed its foreign news under Tom's coffee-house, the court news under St James's coffee-house and legal news under Roll's coffee-house. The *Universal Spectator* of 30 October 1742 carried an item of foreign news under Slaughter's coffee-house, 'the resort of the most speculative politicians about foreign affairs', where the secrets of ambassadors were whispered. The basic organisation for the news in weekly papers, both metropolitan and provincial, remained that of separate posts and it was not until the following century that printers waited for an entire week's news before going to print. Items in later posts that superseded or contradicted those in the first post did not lead to the exclusion of the latter. This was unsatisfactory to some printers, the *Oxford Gazette* complaining in 1762, the *Ipswich Journal* introducing in about 1739 the practice of items in the earlier posts referring, when necessary, to those in later posts. This development, discussed in Cranfield's somewhat teleological 'Maturity' chapter,[12] was not however adopted by the majority of

London or provincial printers, suggesting that they regarded it as impractical or unnecessary. There is little evidence of complaints on this score. Andrew Hooke of the Bristol *Oracle* preferred a different system, but was in many respects exceptional among provincial printers, not least in his determination to remove the intermediary role of the London press in the reporting of foreign news, and it is not surprising that he remained an isolated figure. In the issue of the *Oracle* for 17 April 1742 Hooke announced at the start:

> Some of our readers, accustomed to the vulgar division of the news into Mondays, Thursdays and Saturdays posts, think it strange that we deviate from the common practice. To obviate this popular prejudice, therefore, we take the first opportunity to acquaint them that our manner of reducing every article under its proper general head is less confused, more laborious and more useful; that those who want to see the last advices from any quarter, need only consult the article of the latest date under its general head; that as all our foreign news is translated by ourselves for the press before it comes from London in the English papers, 'tis impossible for us to know what quantity of it will be retailed out every post, and consequently impracticable to comply with the general mode; that, as our intelligences are directly transmitted to us from abroad, we shall be able to pay more than an equivalent for this trifling innovation, by frequently obliging our customers with advices on Saturday that cannot possibly reach them any other way until the Monday following; and that to comply as far as we are able with the taste of all our readers, we shall, for the future, distinguish our foreign affairs as well by the mail that brings it over as by the particular country to which it appertains, and by this means we flatter ourselves we shall give universal satisfaction.

Newspapers often referred to the contradictory reports of various papers, British or European, and stressed the need for caution in evaluating reports from abroad. They appear however to have accepted that the necessity of printing items as they arrived would lead to error. There is little sign that readers objected to the intermingling of domestic and foreign news. Some London papers separated them, and Fielding's *True Patriot* of 1745–6 introduced his 'Foreign History' section with a short essay describing principal developments, before printing the items of foreign news. The *London Mercury: or, Great Britain's Weekly Journal* in its issue of 11 February 1721 printed all its foreign news under the heading 'Foreign Affairs' as a series of linked paragraphs that flowed well. Fielding's device was unusual and many papers did not maintain whatever distinction between foreign and domestic news they may have suggested in their headings. Thus foreign news often appeared under the London heading. This reflected the source of the news item rather than its subject, and this citing of news was also followed in the provincial press with foreign news items obtained from local sources. A good example of the location of news is provided by the *London Courant: or, New Advertiser* of 1 October 1747. The front page carried a lengthy item, over a column in length, including information on Russian, Prussian, Swedish, French and Dutch policy and developments, headed 'Extract of a private letter from Amsterdam', presumably a news-letter. This was followed by news under four headings, Home Ports, Scotland, Country News (Newcastle and York), and London, before the reader could turn to a poem on young Strephon and the beauteous nymphs. The London section lacked any internal differentation or subheadings, but it included three items of foreign news. There were no cross-references between these items and the letter from Amsterdam had nothing to indicate that such items could be found in the London section. The *General Evening Post*, a London tri-weekly, devoted the bulk of the first page of its issue of 30 September 1738 to an account of the war in the Balkans. In the London section on the second page, between the death of the master of the George and Vulcan Tavern in Cornhill and the fitting up of the royal apartments in St James's Palace, the printer printed an interesting paragraph discussing the Balkan situation. There were no cross-references between the paragraph and the news on the first page.

Not only was foreign news poorly differentiated from domestic items; in addition the differing types of foreign news were mingled without distinction or apparent organisation, other than by place of origin of news items. Thus crimes, accidents and details of the mischances of ordinary life could be interspersed with the details of court ceremonial, whilst reports from the capitals of two warring powers would not necessarily be found together. The *Newcastle Courant* of 13 August 1737 reported the arrest of a grocer of Lisieux for murdering his son in order to improve his daughter's chances of marrying a gentleman between items on insub-ordination in the Austrian army and the detention of some Parisians for keeping a private printing press. Items concerning the Balkan war were not juxtaposed.

There were few developments in the organisation of foreign, or any other, news during the century. The most noticeable was the increase in the number of headings. This was clear in the domestic section of the papers where parliamentary, court and theatre news was increasingly segregated with particular headings. It also took place in the foreign section. American news was often distinguished, and this distinction was maintained after independence. The French Revolution led to a marked increase in the importance and contro-versial nature of foreign news, 1789 forming an obvious contrast with 1788, and this was marked by distinguishing headlines, particularly for the lengthy reports of the National Assembly, which became a characteristic feature of the British press, as these reports were readily accessible, easier to print than other news from France, and exciting. Typical of the lengthy reports were the seven columns of the *London Chronicle* of 3 January 1792 devoted to the National Assembly.

Given the shortness of eighteenth-century newspapers and the fact that many were weeklies or tri-weeklies it might be suggested that it was not too much of an imposition to expect readers to read most of a paper in order to trace down all references to an issue, however inconvenient this may be for historians. What is particularly apparent is that there was relatively little alteration during the century in the organisation of the news, insignificant improvements failing to com-pensate for the increasingly small print of the press.

Accuracy

So much has been said of late, and so little understood, of *con-tinental connexions*, that one would imagine many writers had not travelled further than the Isle of Wight. Nevertheless they are so good [as] to dive into the cabinets of princes, unlock the politics of neighbouring states, and kindly divulge them to their good countrymen for their amusement, and to our ministers for their guidance.

London Chronicle, 23 February 1762

The account in some of the papers of Saturday, of the defeat of the Russians by the Turks, is altogether void of foundation, the date of the advice being a month older than that of the last account. The Russian army is near 300 miles farther than where they are reported to be defeated.

Gazetteer and New Daily Advertiser, 13 August 1770

Many eighteenth-century newspapers referred to errors in the press reporting of foreign news. Steele in number 18 of the *Tatler* predicted that newswriters of Britain would be worse hit by peace than the soldiers, 'considering that they have taken more towns, and fought more battles . . . They have made us masters of several strong towns many weeks before our generals could do it; and completed victories, when our greatest captains have been glad to come off with a drawn battle. Where Prince Eugene has slain his thousands, Boyer has slain his ten thousands'. In 1718 the author of the *Weekly Packet* reported,

I was one day sitting at the Rainbow, and listening to a sober tobacconist, while he read the news. In one article it was asserted, that the negociations between the Czar and the King of Sweden were certainly concluded, but that it wanted confirmation. In another article it was positively said that the same negociations were broken off; but that too wanted confirmation — How! says the tobacconist, (with great judgment) if we must neither credit true report, nor false report, why there's an end of all report.

The importance of foreign news in the politically sensitive debates over foreign policy that occupied most of the century, the partisan nature of most of the political press and the pervading reality of newspaper rivalry helped to make accuracy a subject of insult and controversy. The initial title of Defoe's *Review* was *A Weekly Review of the Affairs of FRANCE: Purg'd from the Errors and Partiality of News-Writers and Petty-Statesmen, of all Sides*. The *Flying Post* poked fun at the account of the British naval victory off Cape Passaro in 1718 printed in the *Daily Courant*, claiming that in its portrayal of Spanish bravery and British deceit it was comparable to Rabelais' Pantagruel, a reference that hardly suggests a wide popular readership for the paper. The same issue attacked the *Post-Boy* and the *Weekly Journal* for exaggerating Spanish naval strength. The *St. James's Evening Post* claimed that Jacobite writers invented diplomatic papers and memorials in order to serve their purposes, whilst 'Truth and Daylight', writing in the *Weekly Journal or British Gazetteer*, attacked Mist's accuracy, providing an example of the exactitude that controversies over accuracy could produce:

> Letters from Hamburg (says he, in his last paper) of the 13th confirm the account we had of the Treaty of Aland which goes on very well. Now in the first place, his paper is dated July the 5th, which with 11 days difference, makes it the 16th N.S. So that by this computation he has letters by Pacolet's Horse, from Hamburg to London in 3 days: he may well boast indeed, that nobody can have the same intelligence as himself, if he deals with the D-L, or some of the Lapland witches; when in reality there are no letters from Hamburg to London to the 5th of July, which day a Holland mail arrived, beyond the 8th or 9th N.S. and what is more, none that says the Treaty goes on well, but give a different account of it: Not that all which is written from Hamburg, or many other places, is to be esteemed Gospel; however, this is sufficient to show his ignorance.

The *Leeds Intelligencer*, an enthusiastic supporter of the North ministry and of its attempt to suppress the American rebellion, accused the opposition of spreading false news about enemy successes.[13] The opposition press replied in its turn with accusations of its own.[14]

It was not necessary to have political motives in order to criticise the accuracy of other papers. Simple incompetence, usually based on an absence of geographical knowledge, was sometimes alleged. In 1722 *Applebee's Original Weekly Journal* attacked reports that Peter the Great was gathering an army at Tobolski in Siberia in order to attack Georgia by pointing out how far apart these were. Thirteen years later the *Daily Journal* condemned the *Daily Post Boy* for suggesting that St Petersburg could be bombarded by a French fleet, and claimed that in fact the Neva was unnavigable for warships, due to sandbanks. Responding to an attack from his rival Farley, Hooke advised him to buy a dictionary, grammar, atlas and Moll's Geography:

> He will find that Hamburg is not in Denmark, where he places it, but in Germany . . . we hope, he will never afterwards be guilty of such an egregious blunder as to set the Russian fleet a

sailing on dry land, among rocks and mountains in Transylvania, in quest of the Swedish fleet in the Finnish Gulf.[15]

There were frequent condemnations of the accuracy of foreign reports and in particular foreign newspapers and newsletters.[16] Their contradictory nature was highlighted and the difficulties this created for the British press stressed.[17] Criticisms by British papers of the accuracy of their compatriots[18] were matched by the comments of diplomats and politicians. Du Bourgay wrote to Tilson from Berlin in 1724:

> As to what you observe that all the newspapers have it that I had an audience of the King of Prussia to declare the reconciliation, I must give you the same caution which Mylord Whitworth was pleased to give me some time ago in relation to the affairs at Cambray, not to believe one word that you will find in them.

The *Evening Post*'s reports about Spanish warships in Corunna in 1729 were dismissed as 'entirely false', and the *Craftsman*'s reports on Dunkirk suffered an identical fate the following year. A lengthy visit by the Spanish Ambassador to Horatio Walpole in 1732 led the press to jump to wrong conclusions, whilst four years later Tilson reflected that Britain was overrun with the weed of false news 'the growth almost of all countrys' and Robert Trevor complained from The Hague that the British press 'make me say and do abundance of absurd things'. In 1725 the Sardinian foreign minister told the British envoy that 'he did not doubt but I understood the world better than to give credit to a newspaper', in 1733 the British envoy in Paris remarked to the French prime minister that 'ministers of late had speeches oft made for them' and four years later the Earl of Morton informed his son that 'most part' of the newspapers 'are arrant lies', particularly the reports concerning a siege or negotiation over Gibraltar. In 1733 press reports concerning the despatch of a British squadron for the Mediterranean led Weston to comment, 'The Gazettes are for once in the right.'[19]

These comments can be endlessly repeated for the whole century and even beyond. An anonymous pamphlet of the early nineteenth century stated:

> We ought not to wonder at the ignorance of individuals, when even the *monitors* of the public, I mean the editors of newspapers,

propagate the most gross errors of the same kind. In several of our most popular papers it was lately stated, that the emperor of Russia was fortifying *Warsaw*; when they might have known that Warsaw not only belongs to the king of Prussia, but is nearly two hundred miles from the Russian frontiers.[20]

Inaccuracy was not the only criticism that could be and was directed at the press. There was at all times a strident xenophobia and militant patriotism that tended to ascribe sinister motives to foreigners, allies and enemies alike. Suspicion was accompanied by calls for eternal vigilance and by at times an earnest paranoia, a comprehensive world view that could link French naval preparations to ministerial corruption or find a fondness for French cuisine a sure sign of a fifth columnist. It is not surprising that in a recent work Professor Jones castigated the foreign coverage of the press as sensational, inaccurate, partisan and xenophobic.[21]

Such an analysis is less than fair to the efforts of newspapers to print accurate reports, to the difficulties of securing such reports and to the level of discussion of foreign affairs that could be anticipated. Papers frequently stressed the difficulties of obtaining reliable reports and the need for caution in assessing those in circulation.[22] This led to papers explaining why they were sceptical about particular items and these explanations may be regarded as part of the educational process that reading newspapers presented. The reader was often presented at the same time with the news, the information that it might prove an unfounded rumour, and the reason why the paper came to that conclusion. It is possible to suggest that this sceptical, qualifying stance, most marked necessarily in the reporting of foreign news, accorded more with the function of the newspaper as a medium for private consideration than with that of it as a source for public discussion or declamation. Many of these qualifications served partisan functions, particularly challenging favourable reports for the other side. During the War of the Quadruple Alliance the ministerial press challenged items favourable to Spain, while Tory papers questioned those setting forth the achievements of Britain's Austrian ally, the willingness of Tory papers, such as the *Weekly Journal* and the *Weekly Medley*, to applaud Spain, then the supporter of the Jacobites, providing the best evidence of their Jacobite sympathies. In 1717 the *Weekly Journal* doubted the Austrian claim that they had lost very few infantry in a Balkan battle: 'Everybody knows, that the weight of all that part of the work, viz. of attacking entrenchments, must lie on the infantry.' The following year the *Post Man* doubted reports of a Russo–Swedish peace, a development that would have been extremely inconvenient for the ministry, 'as the public has found by experience, that the reports about this mysterious negotiation prove commonly false, and designedly published to conceal the truth of the transactions on that side, and . . . private persons are forbidden to write any news from Sweden and Muscovy'. In 1727 *Mist's Weekly Journal* urged readers to question reports that the Austrians were willing to settle their differences with Britain, on terms satisfactory to the latter, with the reflection that 'such things are generally kept secret'. The reports were in fact correct. In 1762 the *Briton* queried the *Monitor*'s authority for its reports on Anglo–Austrian relations.[23]

Other comments were less obviously partisan. In 1717 the *Original Weekly Journal* questioned a report from The Hague that the Emperor Charles VI was dead, on the grounds that couriers from there had heard nothing about it. The *Whitehall Evening Post* was sceptical about favourable news of the fall of Messina to the Austrians in 1719, because it was ship news. The previous year the paper had commented on a Sicilian battle, 'Thus either side extenuate their own loss and exaggerate that of their enemy, both claiming the honour of the field; so that we must wait for a more particular and impartial account of this action.' The *Weekly Medley* questioned correctly reports of the death of Peter the Great in 1720, arguing that it 'would have made a much greater noise had it been true'. Commenting in 1722 on the report that the Russians and Spaniards intended to invade Britain, *Wye's Letter* claimed that 'a man may as well pretend to find out the longitude by the help of a candle and lanthorn in a dark night, as to affirm it for truth' and urged readers to wait for clarification by 'time and experience'.

The death of princes were a frequent cause of contradictory reports. In 1724 the *London Journal* queried reports of the death of Louis I of Spain as they were not corroborated from Paris. The following year the report in the *Utrecht Gazette* of the death of George I's brother, Ernst-August of Osnabrück, was challenged correctly and readers urged to wait for the arrival of fresh information. The *London Journal* was able to suggest the following week that Ernst-August had been confused with his brother Maximilian. In 1736 the paper announced,

The two following articles relating to the affairs of Corsica, will show that there is a difference in the accounts from thence; for which reason we cannot do better than to give both relations, and leave them to our readers to reconcile them, or make such observations thereon, as they shall judge proper.[24]

Other distant conflicts created difficulties for the press, for readers expected it to provide accurate reports on all wars. Having created an interest in Persian news, papers found it difficult to satisfy it accurately, the *Daily Gazetteer* printing a long account in 1737 after the comment, 'The intelligence we have relating to Kouli Kan is so contradictory, that we know not what to depend on.' Balkan conflicts presented similar problems of verification, the *Daily Post* commenting in 1737, 'There have been 5 times more Janissaries in the foreign prints within these 2 months, than are to be found in all the Ottoman Empire.'[25] Hostilities involving Britain led to a rise in interest for news, but also caused difficulties in ensuring reliability, particularly with naval and colonial hostilities.[26] The Turks and Caicos Island dispute with France in 1764 led the *Ipswich Journal* to confess that it was not sure which of the islands, rumoured to be at issue, were in fact in dispute. The paper added, 'We will not presume to determine precisely upon the subject, we would only beg leave to recommend a farther enquiry to such of our inquisitive readers as may have an opportunity for it.'[27]

The clash between speed and accuracy was handled with reasonable care. Most papers preferred to print whatever interesting information came to hand, but the willingness to include caveats transferred the responsibility for assessing the news to the reader. George James of the *Post Boy* pointed out in 1731 the difficulties faced by the paper: 'Les nouvelles étrangères de ce papier viennent de tant de differentes mains, et qu'elles sont envoyées à l'Imprimerie avec tant de precipitation . . .'[28] Comparatively few papers were willing to follow the *Weekly Miscellany*, in many respects an exceptional 'quality' paper of the 1730s, which declared in 1735 during the War of the Polish Succession, 'Why then should we anticipate what we shall have but too much occasion, (without a Providential interposition) in the course of our future advices, to take notice of with a greater degree of certainty than at present we are enabled to do?'[29]

It would be easy to quote a list of contemporaries on the unreliability of eighteenth-century newspapers and suggest that their foreign news was commonly ignored, particularly by those 'in the know'. However, it is equally possible to find many who were prepared to cite foreign reports. In 1734 the Earl of Chesterfield, a former diplomat, wrote to the Earl of Marchmont from London, 'You see in the public newspapers the wretched situation of our foreign affairs, as well as I could inform you.' Later that year John Drummond, London agent of the Earls of Morton, observed, 'There is no manner of news but what is in the evening post.' In 1745 Henry Fox, then a Lord of the Treasury, advised his brother,

> Order the *London Courant* to be sent you every day. It is wrote by Campbell, who used to write the Gazetteer. He has the Post Office's encouragement, and says he has the expresses an hour before the Duke of Newcastle, and by what I have hitherto observed may be more depended on than any newspaper ever could be.

The following year James Payzant wrote from the Secretaries of State Office in Whitehall, 'There is no news besides what is in the Daily Advertisers', and in 1789 George Aust, writing from the Foreign Office, expressed amazement that the press had obtained the news of the fall of Belgrade to the Austrians so rapidly.[30]

The difficulty faced by the press was essentially similar to that faced by diplomats: sorting out the truth from a mass of 'contradictory advices' and 'common reports.'[31] If their accounts of foreign, particularly distant, lands were sometimes ill-informed, prejudiced or prone to concentrate on the exotic this was also true of other works. The writer John Morgan, who had links with the press himself, exclaimed in 1728, 'What a monstrous load of gross lies and unsufferable absurdities . . . does not one fall in with immediately upon laying hands on any tract, treatise, history, memoir, dictionary geographical, historical, or critical, relating to Africa and its affairs!' As a result Morgan held a low view of the knowledge of Africa of 'the headstrong, conceited, partial and stupidly ignorant multitude'.[32] However, the press, in common with other literary works, books, magazines and encyclopedias, did provide a mass of information on the wider world, and the prejudice and xenophobia that continued to appear was increasingly well-informed. The drive for accuracy was possibly increased by a sense in some quarters that newspapers were journals of record, modern histories. Thus the *Flying-Post* felt it necessary in 1713 to print a second copy of the articles of a treaty, in both Latin and English, because their first copy had not been sufficiently exact.[33]

'Doubts, conjectures, and dark designs' might have been 'good for nobody but gazetteers' as George Tilson claimed in 1732,[34] but they were not easy to report. Scholars who have evaluated the accuracy of the reporting of foreign news have usually been favourably impressed by it. D. E. Clark's survey of several of the leading London papers for the period 1754 to 1763 indicated 'abundant and surprisingly accurate information' concerning American events. Though Nathaniel Wraxall was scathing about the accuracy of British press reports concerning Pugachev's rising in Russia, J. T. Alexander has concluded that those in the *Daily Advertiser* in early 1774 were on the whole moderate and accurate. The accounts of the events in the French Revolution were reasonably accurate, particularly allowing for the confusion surrounding some Parisian episodes, even if the reflections of the press on French developments were not always well-informed.[35] The level of accuracy may not satisfy those whom Lord Hervey termed 'history-bigots',[36] but it is difficult to see many of Hervey's contemporaries, however appreciative they may have been of the problems posed by 'the mists and clouds, with which prejudice and partiality industriously endeavour to obscure the truth of facts', accepting the argument of the *Weekly Miscellany* that it was necessary to 'prefer the truth before earliness of intelligence', to the extent of taking no notice of 'many particulars wherewith others abound'.[37]

Information of the wider world

> As we have often occasion to mention places in our papers that, perhaps, many of our readers may be unacquainted with, and as it will tend greatly to their better understanding what they are reading of, we shall take proper opportunities to oblige them.
>
> *Cirencester Flying-Post*, 8 November 1742

A rich *mélange* of information on foreign countries was presented in the press. There was great interest in curiosities, natural and manufactured. The *Weekly Journal* was sceptical concerning the sighting of a floating island near Gibraltar in 1718, but thought it worth discussing whether an island could float. 'Inflammation in the air' over Budapest or a strange New England serpent were worth reporting,[38] and a society that thought freaks and curiosities worth displaying in Britain was not going to stop at the Channel, particularly as more exotic and new specimens were likely to be found abroad. A strong interest in the Orient was a feature of the press, and contrasted with a relative lack of interest in Africa, which appeared by comparison to be uncivilised and lacking in wisdom. A wealth of background information was provided in order to aid understanding of this news. Much of this information reveals a facet of the newspapers that closely corresponded with the magazines. In 1723 the *Post Man* announced, 'Instead of troubling our readers with a tedious repetition of what they have already seen in other papers we think some account of the Sophi of Persia, who has lately made so much noise in the world, will be the more agreeable entertainment.' The following year the *Flying Post* offered the will of a Chinese Emperor, accompanied by explanatory notes, and the description of Yerevan recently taken by the Turks from the Persians accompanied by 'a remarkable story of one of the Kings of Persia', a tale of debauchery. In 1772 the *Darlington Pamphlet* provided a footnote to 'The Woman Justified — An Indian Tale', which spread over most of a page of the paper: 'The Kislar-Aga is the chief of the black eunuchs, who alone have the power to enter into the apartments of the Sultanas. The white eunuchs are appointed to guard the gates and doors of the harem, or place where the sultanas are shut up.'[39]

Most of the information provided by the press was more closely linked to the news, and much of it provided a geographical or historical context for political events. Other types of material were however provided, ranging from the Paris fashions[40] to brief biographies of prominent foreigners, such as the Russian Tsarinas, and the information printed was sometimes fairly detailed. The *British Mercury* announced in 1711:

> To enter into a particular discussion of the nature and management of the French finances, would require a larger treatise than the bounds of this paper will admit. But as there is no better way of judging of the circumstances of the enemy, with relation to the war, than that of drawing rational inferences from the state of their Treasury and public credit; and being

sensible, that the generality of English readers are but little acquainted with these affairs, we shall, in this scarcity of foreign news, make the following short observations, which will render this, and all other such edicts, more intelligible . . . We shall at the next opportunity of want of foreign news, give some farther account of the original of this, and such other French taxes, and of the past and present management and state of the revenue of that Kingdom, presuming that such a discourse will be more acceptable to the intelligent part of the world, than a tedious and useless repetition of stale news.[41]

If such items were not commonplace there was nevertheless a considerable amount of information supplied every month to explain items in the news. Much of this was very brief, often taking the form of a bracketed comment after the town at the head of an item explaining its location. This was particularly common in the provincial press. Constantinople was described in the *Northampton Mercury* of 30 April 1722 as 'one of the most famous cities of Europe, and the chief in Turkey', Cadiz as 'a strong, rich and famous city of Spain'. The *Oracle* used asterisks, and its launch in April 1742 made such locational descriptions necessary, as foreign news during the War of the Austrian Succession tended to arise from events in east-central Europe. Modern readers would require an explanation of where Selowitz and Donauworth are, both explained in the first number of the paper. The length of such comments varied. The *Bath Journal* described Vienna on 29 July 1745 as 'a stately city of Germany, subject to the Queen of Hungary, almost 730 miles from London' whilst the *Newcastle Courant* the following year simply placed the country in brackets after the town. Such explanations continued throughout the century, the *Oxford Gazette* describing such a prominent trading port in Leghorn in 1767 as 'a sea-port town of Italy, in the duchy of Tuscany'.[42]

Most descriptions in the London press were considerably longer, though they tended to be for places far less known than Leghorn or Paris. These descriptions reflected the site of hostilities and areas disputed in negotiations. The Spanish invasions of Sardinia and Sicily in 1717 and 1718 respectively led to a spate of descriptions of the two islands. A good account of the geography, inhabitants and agriculture of Sardinia printed in the *St. James's Post* in 1717 began with the announcement, 'The attention of the public being, at present, fixed to the invasion of Sardinia by the Spaniards, we shall supply the want of Dutch mails, by the following description of that island, which has been communicated by an English gentleman, who was an eye-witness.'[43] The Swedish invasion of Norway led to accounts of Trondheim, one of the scenes of conflict.[44] The rumoured forthcoming Turkish invasion of Malta in 1722, Anglo-French quarrels over St Lucia in 1723 and fighting in the Rhineland, northern Italy and at Gdansk in the War of Polish Succession all led to descriptions of the areas in dispute.[45] Balkan hostilities led to brief accounts of the position and history of Ochakov and Nis in 1737, whilst the outbreak of Anglo-Spanish hostilities in 1739 led the *Northampton Mercury* to offer first a brief account of Cartagena and Havenna and then a plan of the former.[46] The Austrian Succession War led to frequent descriptions of scenes of conflict,[47] as did hostilities or the threat of them in such places as Bukhara in 1741, India in 1752, the West Indies in 1760 and 1762, the Duchy of Berg in 1762, the Turks islands in 1764, Corsica in 1768, Moldavia in 1770 and 1788, Maastricht in 1748 and 1785, Belgrade in 1788, the Electorate of Trier in 1792, and Ceylon in 1796.[48]

There were also attempts to provide background information on European political news. A large number of documents were printed in translation: manifestos, memoranda, treaties and communiqués.[49] The *Flying Post* printed memoranda on the Tuscan succession in 1722, assuming that they would be acceptable, 'considering that the succession of Tuscany is likely to be one of the grand points of debate at Cambray, and that the reader will be best able to judge of the matter when he has seen the allegations on both sides'.[50] Much of the information made available related to disputes in which Britain was involved. Some were clearly partisan; the ministerial *St. James's Post* announcing in 1718,

> The differences between the court of Great Britain and that of Madrid, being the chief subject of debate at present; and because we have some amongst us unnatural enough to delight in represen-ting that affair as much as possible to the disadvantage of their own country, it may not be amiss to give the public a summary of the grounds thereof, as far as the materials yet come to our knowledge will enable us.

The printing of memoranda could be designed to serve partisan ends. The *London Evening Post*'s claim that British policy towards

France was pusillanimous was underlined in the issue of 30 August 1735:

> We have lately given the public some advices of the attempts of France to bring down the Turk upon Christendom; and as the following memorial from the Emperor to his allies is a full confirmation of those advices, and a complete picture of the French court, as to her present pacific protestations and underhand intrigues, we think it ought to be remembered by all Britons who have any regard either for liberty, or the honour, interest, or trade of their country.

Other news was less partisan. That Swedish women worked like labourers was one of the pieces of information contained in a newspaper article of 1717 that began, 'The difference between Great Britain and Sweden being now the chief subject of discourse among all people; we shall here give some account of the Swedes country.'[51] The backgrounds to conflicts that did not involve Britain were described. Having exhausted their 'stock of foreign intelligence' the *Daily Post* in 1722 sought 'to refresh the memory of some of our readers and to inform others, by giving them short historical descriptions of some of the countries and places, of which in our former papers we already had, and in our future shall have occasion to make mention'. It began with a description of Astracan, the Russian base for operations against Persia. The *Dublin News Letter* of 22 January 1737 provided a description of Jülich inspired by the byzantine Jülich–Berg dispute.[52] Most background information related to international tension and war, but domestic events in European states were not ignored. In 1722 the *Weekly Journal* announced 'the Doge of Venice being dead, we hope it will not be unacceptable to inform our readers of the manner of electing a new one'. Five years later the *Evening Journal* suggested that 'the present revival of the dispute in France concerning the constitution of Pope Clement XI, makes it necessary to refresh the readers memory with a general account of the rise and progress of that affair'. The *Newcastle Journal* offered first a geography of Spain and then one of Spanish America, but the paper stressed that the latter was designed for the particular needs of the press and of popular knowledge:

> We shall proceed in a manner very different from those authors who have digested their works systematically; not that we design

to lay aside all order and regularity; but we find the present posture of public affairs, and the desire and expectation of our readers, make it necessary for us to take a new course as to the form and method of our geography; which tho' it may possibly occasion the banter and reflections of some gentlemen, who are better versed in the rules and forms of schools than the tempers and manners of men; yet whatever we are convinced of be most entertaining to our readers, and best adapted to suit their inclinations, shall always be complied with as much as possible.

The *Leeds Intelligencer* devoted over a column in 1766 to the reasons for the Madrid insurrection of that year. Three years later the *St. James's Chronicle* followed a report of the troubles of the Sierra Morena in Spain with an account of the area, the latter placed in square brackets. Readers of the *Newcastle Journal* in 1752 were offered within five months a list of the ages of the crowned heads of Europe, a description of the office of Doge, an account of Java, and a geography and history of East Friesland, all items derived from the London press. Twenty-five years later another Newcastle paper supplemented its report of a disastrous fishing season in Greenland waters with an 'account of those dreary regions'. In January 1757 *Read's Weekly Journal* printed not only a description of Lima, but also an account of the Azores inspired by reports of a destructive earthquake. In 1779 the *London Chronicle* offered descriptions of Marie Antoinette and her mother.[53]

Some of these items were distinctly anecdotal and possibly space-fillers and their value for providing information to aid analysis of the news may be doubted. While the *London Chronicle*'s genealogical table of the Russian royal family was probably very useful to those seeking to follow Russian politics in 1762, 'the curious description of the City of Smolensko, where the Empress of Russia is to embark for the Crimea', of the *Daily Universal Register* in 1785 was of little value, beyond being easy to transcribe from the *Hague Gazette*. In 1727 the *Evening Journal* noted that the ages of the rulers of Europe had never been printed in any newspaper and proceeded to devote five issues to remedying this deficiency. Readers may well have been interested to know the age of the Emperor and the King of Prussia, but whether they felt the same about the rulers of Baden-Baden, Baden-Durlach and Bayreuth is open to question.[54] In 1734 the

Newcastle Courant provided its readers with an item of the sort of foreign information that was relatively common, one that included an element of 'human interest'. It noted that the combined age of the Austrian and French commanders of the Rhine was 134, that if 1600 was subtracted from their years of birth the latter combined equalled 134 and that two other permutations were of corresponding interest.[55]

Most foreign news was however far more serious, and the provision of detailed information, particularly documentation, provided readers with a wealth of material that could have enabled them to make up their own minds about events. Documents were usually printed with little if any comment, and in this the press differed from the major forms of oral culture. Furthermore press comment was often distinguished by being printed in italics, thus clearly differentiating news from comment. This method was used by newspapers such as the *London Evening Post* in the 1740s, the difference in type corresponding to one in tone and content. A large number of documents were printed in the press. Once available they had the great attraction of filling space with ease and their frequent appearance suggests that they were what readers wanted. Some of the documents were of direct relevance for Britain. The Convention of the Pardo, an Anglo-Spanish agreement by which the Walpole ministry sought to avert war, was widely printed in the press, enabling readers to assess the merits of opposition attacks on the agreement. It took up the whole of the first page and half the second page of the *Northampton Mercury* of 26 February 1739.[56] Other items were of less direct relevance, but their inclusion testifies to what was seen to be a strong interest in foreign news. One of the interesting items that led the *Reading Mercury* to produce a free supplement in September 1772 was 'A correct copy of the speech of the King of SWEDEN, addressed to the Counsellors of State assembled there on the 21st of August, 1772; with other interesting particulars, relative to the Revolution that lately happened in that Kingdom.'[57]

Sources of information

The wealth of background material printed in the press partially derived, as with the news, from foreign sources. The manifestos of warring powers had a continental provenance. However, judging from the sources mentioned by newspapers, many papers had access, either directly or indirectly, to an impressive range of books and other printed matter. Handbooks existed to provide basic information. In 1704 appeared the seventh, in 1732 the thirteenth edition of Laurence Echard's *The Gazeteer's or Newsman's Interpreter. Being a Geographical Index of all the considerable Provinces, Cities, Patriarchships, Bishoprics . . . Ports, Forts, Castles, etc. in Europe.* In 1704 the first, in 1732 the sixth edition of a similar work devoted to Asia, Africa and America was published. In 1759 *The News-Reader's Pocket-Book, or Military Dictionary* appeared. Many papers were far bolder in their search for information, a process no doubt aided by the close relationship, both in London and the provinces, between newspapers and bookselling. This often led to very interesting articles, some of which were not dissimilar to those that are more commonly associated with eighteenth-century magazines. In 1722 the *Flying Post* announced:

> The want of foreign mails gives us an opportunity to insert the following account of a very remote people little known to Europeans, but with whom 'tis presumed the readers will not take it ill to be better acquainted, especially considering their country is at present the chief, if not the only seat of war in the world, and that almost every post brings advices concerning them, true or false. The nations here intended are the Circassian, and the Daghestan or Highland provinces . . . The authors we are obliged to for it are Dr. Curll, Sir John Chardin and M. Tavernier.

Two columns were devoted to this item, which included information on the marital habits, dress, complexion, villages, government and economy of these people. The following year the *St. James's Journal* printed extracts from 'the Reverend Mr. Paschoud's Historico-Political Geography'. The issue of 23 March devoted over a page to the government, finances, law, army, clergy, religion and religious customs of Russia. Nathaniel Mist was one of the subscribers to Morgan's *Complete History of Algiers*. The *Daily Gazetteer* clearly owned a copy of Pöllnitz's *Letters and Memoirs*, with its detailed description of most European courts. In 1736 the paper announced:

> It being thought very consistent with the title of this paper, and conducive to establish it in the favour of the Public, to inform them now and then of the state of the foreign courts and cities from which

our intelligence arrives, and of the characters of the principal ministers and courtiers; we shall now venture upon an essay of that kind, to be continued, as room shall admit of it, in future pages.

The choice of the Duchy of Saxe-Gotha was doubtless dictated by curiosity over the provenance of the bride of the Prince of Wales. The account of the duchy's location and history was substantially derived from Pöllnitz. Three years later the same source was used for the account of the recently deceased Landgrave of Hesse Darmstadt and his heir. The heading for nearly five columns of the *London Chronicle* in 1762 was 'Of the Administration and Improvement of the Revenue of Spain. From Cardinal Alberoni's Political Testament'. The *Ipswich Journal* printed a note on the Russian succession in 1762, one on the Tortugas in 1764 and a description of Bengal the following year, citing as sources Campbell's *State of Russia*, Bowen's *System of Geography* and Helwell's new pamphlet, *Historical Events Relative to the Provinces of Bengal*. In 1767 the *Leeds Intelligencer* devoted nearly a column to 'An Estimate of the Manners and Principles of the Modern French. By Monsr. Helvetius'. Three years later the *Reading Mercury* offered nearly a column of 'An account of Falkland Island, taken from Guthrie's New Geographical Grammar'.[58]

There was a clear contrast in tone between such background pieces and the shorter, more pointed items that some opposition papers presented their foreign news in, but most foreign news items were printed without comment. The contrast can be seen in the *Newcastle Courant* in 1742 which printed both barbed items, taken on the whole from the *London Evening Post*, and others that were comment-free and politically neutral. There was an obvious attempt by most papers throughout the century to give form and meaning to the often apparently incomprehensible actions of foreign powers. This provided an opportunity for political partisanship by individual papers and a significant sphere for press controversy, but these attempts were on the whole intelligent and informed. Ministers rarely discovered things from the press, though the *Post Boy* prevented Walpole's attempt to keep Russian naval preparations secret in 1723 and Newcastle first heard the news of Washington's defeat at Fort Necessity in 1754 when he read the *London Evening Post*.[59] However the press was the principal means by which the rest of the political nation was informed of foreign affairs and it was partly for that reason regularly scrutinised by foreign envoys.

Diplomats and the press

> These envenomed accounts, which weaken the national reputation abroad more than can be easily imagined, keep those who wish us well in suspense and at a distance, and too much encourage the enemies of the present happy establishment.
>
> Whitworth to Townshend, 19 August (ns) 1715[60]

> There is perhaps nothing in the case of the Prince of Wales which ought to affect us more than the influence it will have on foreign nations. The London Gazette goes to every Court of Europe. What must be the feeling of every foreigner, when he sees the heir apparent of the British dominions advertising a dividend to his creditors of one shilling and ten-pence farthing in the pound!
>
> *Newcastle Chronicle*, 19 May 1787

The British press was regularly scrutinised by foreign diplomats concerned about the reporting of their own country and interested in creating, or more often sustaining, an interpretation of British politics. The former purpose tended to produce the disputes with British ministers or papers, the *démarches* of diplomats and the actions against newspapers, that are often best known, but it was the latter function that was possibly more serious for British ministers, and more significant evidence of the impact of the press. The problem is partly one of archival accessibility. State Papers Domestic, with its correspondence about action against the press, has been fully examined by newspaper historians. The despatches of foreign envoys have received far less attention. However, eighteenth-century British ministries were well aware of the problem, not least because of their excellent system of postal interception and deciphering. The same system also provided evidence of attempts by foreign envoys to influence the content of the British press. If it was difficult for British ministries to prosecute newspapers successfully at the behest of foreign envoys, it was harder still to prevent those envoys seeking to influence the content of the press, and it was well-nigh impossible to prevent diplomats from writing reports heavily influenced by the opposition press. The intractable nature of these linked problems probably helped to increase ministerial frustration concerning the opposition press, without providing any glimpse of a solution.

The freedom with which the British press discussed foreign powers was in no way unique. Attacks both on foreign powers and on foreign policy, the two usually inseparable, as with Mist's frequent assaults on the Anglo-Dutch alliance, characterised opposition newspapers throughout Europe. Manual Freyre's *Duende Crítico* of 1735–6 concentrated on attacking the French, and foreign powers took note of its contents, to the anger of the Spanish first minister Patino.[61] In the United Provinces diplomats had to deal with a legal press that was frequently critical. Nevertheless most European newspapers, particularly in the first half of the century, outside Britain, the Netherlands, Hamburg and Switzerland, were court gazettes, and opposition newsletters and newspapers were commonly illegal, and subject to government action. Envoys, concerned to maintain the dignity of their countries, and associating the respect paid to their masters with the public perception of their power, expected action from British ministries. Many of the complaints had no direct political relevance. In 1730 Hop 'exhibited a complaint against the accounts published in several English newspapers, relating to persons said to be guilty of sodomitical practices in Holland, etc. and praying, that the authors of them may be punished'.[62] However, as the prestige of a state was a matter of political importance, critical references to foreign monarchs or ministers could lead to complaints, Prince Eugene demanding the printing of a reply in one such case in 1731, the Palatine foreign minister Baron Wachtendonck demanding a recantation in another in 1759.[63] Other complaints were more obviously political in their nature. In 1786 William Eden, then negotiating a commercial treaty with France, was confronted with

> a French letter from some correspondent in England being apparently either the original or copy of various paragraphs which I see in the papers respecting the expediency of France insisting upon a free admission of brandies; my supposed intention to do nothing but amuse myself here for two years; and the Duke of Dorset's desire to thwart me even if I were better disposed. I treated the whole comme un recueil des Im-

pertinences et des sottises and advised him to have a better correspondent: He said that he perfectly agreed with me except as to the brandy paragraph which was pertinent enough.[64]

In private conversation between experienced negotiators press comments could be thus shrugged off, but they were often made the subject of official complaint, forcing British ministers to take action or to confess their weakness in this sphere. A defensive tone characterised the stance of successive British ministries in the face of actual or potential complaints. Promising action against the printer of the *Daily Post Boy*, who had angered the Dutch, Newcastle wrote to Horatio Walpole in 1735, 'Your Excellency is too well acquainted with the liberties, that are taken in the printed papers here, to be surprised, if our utmost endeavours to discover, or punish the authors of this scandalous libel should not meet with the desired success.'[65] Foreign envoys resorted to self-help or to impotent complaints. The *Evening Post* of 6 April 1732 printed an article discussing the failure of an alleged Russian attempt to promote a Russo-Prussian dynastic union. Prince Kantimer ascertained that the item had come from the *Daily Post Boy* of the previous day. He summoned the editor of the *Evening Post* to his lodgings and ordered him 'almost with menaces' not to publish such items in the future. The editor promised to be careful and on 17 June published a refutation written by Kantemir. The Russians took similar action in 1762, albeit with ministerial support.[66] Only a systematic survey of diplomatic papers can reveal how common such action was. Many other envoys displayed a more resigned attitude, accepting that there was little that could be done about press attacks. French diplomats often felt themselves obliged to do nothing. In 1724 the French and Spanish envoys ignored the printed songs abusing the Queen of Spain, a French princess, Broglie, the French Ambassador, commenting that in Britain even the monarch was not spared criticism. In 1739 Cambis sent the French naval minister Maurepas translations of the *Daily Post* for 5 and 6 October and the *Daily Advertiser* of the former date. The papers claimed that the French envoy mediating the Balkan conflict had been bribed by the Turks and that France was arming. Cambis claimed that they illustrated British hatred and fear of France, but that there was nothing that could be done about them due to the difficulties of securing justice. The previous year he had complained of the difficulties of prosecuting libels and urged a prudent silence or diplomatic representations rather than honouring the author with any attention.[67]

As with the ministerial response to press criticism, envoys had the options of prosecution, subsidisation and inaction. The first was not an easy alternative, as it depended both on the goodwill of the British ministry and on their ability to take action. Ministries were best placed to influence the contents of papers they subsidised, but it tended to be opposition papers that caused the most offence and against which it was most difficult to secure action. However in 1799 the editor, printer and publisher of the *Courier* were imprisoned for accusing Paul I of Russia of tyranny and inconsistency. Paying papers to insert particular items was no more than an extension of two normal activities. Many individuals and groups paid for items to be inserted as news, while foreign envoys frequently served as an acknowledged source of items. In 1724 the *Evening Post* carried an item beginning, 'The Swedish Minister Plenipotentiary Baron Sparre, having received orders from the King his master, to publish here the following regulations made by his Swedish Majesty'.[68] The insertion of material was most marked in wartime and during international crises. Diplomatic reports are usually vague as to how the material was communicated. In some cases diplomats saw newspaper figures, but in others they took advantage of the cosmopolitan milieu of London where a variety of shadowy figures, many foreign, lived on the fringes of the diplomatic world, sometimes enjoying privileges as nominal servants. This milieu has received very little attention. A prominent example from the 1720s to 1750s was Giovanni Zamboni, 'but a mean tradesman', who became the London agent of Baden-Durlach, Hesse-Darmstadt, Modena, Saxony and the government of the Austrian Netherlands, and was proposed for the posts of Russian Consul and Neapolitan agent. A speculator in books and paintings and a pimp, Zamboni certainly provided newspapers and pamphlets to interested foreigners.[69] He also cropped up in an obscure episode in 1726 when the ministry investigated an attempt to insert material in the press. On 27 May the Spanish Ambassador, the Marquis of Pozzobueno, presented a manifesto to George I and the Secretaries of State justifying the seizure of the recently disgraced Spanish first minister Ripperda from the home of the British envoy in Madrid. One Christopher Perry tried to get the manifesto published, but he met with refusals from the printers he approached 'as apprehending the government would call them to an account for it notwithstanding it should be true and countenanced by an ambassador'. Examined before Townshend and the Duke of Devonshire and shown the paragraph that had been seized from him by two messengers, Perry 'declared that it was put into his hands by a person who desired him to get it inserted in the newspapers. Being asked who that person was, he begged to be excused from naming him'. Perry admitted approaching George James of the *Post Boy* and Richard Nutt of the *Daily Post*. James testified that Perry had told him that the paper would be protected by Pozzobueno, an idea James had rejected as impossible. Nutt, offered the same protection, had demanded to see Pozzobueno and had been taken to see 'Mr. Samboni', whom he was told was an essential intermediary.[70] The possibility is that Zamboni was the source of the report, and it is certain that the general attitude of the British ministry to him was a hostile one. It is possible that diplomats used the news gatherers employed by papers such as the Mr Jones arrested in 1718 for communicating a letter that he claimed had been written by the Secretary of State James Craggs to the Spanish ambassador Monteleón. Earlier that year Monteleón himself had sought to make public his declaration to the British ministry that the arrival of a British fleet in the Mediterranean would be regarded as a declaration of war and would lead to a confiscation of British goods in Spain. Monteleón had hoped that he would be able to spread alarm among the public, and his declaration was soon reported in the press.[71]

Material inserted by diplomats was designed for two purposes. The first, as with Kantemir's activities in 1733, was intended to influence opinion favourably in a situation where the British ministry was either neutral or undeclared.[72] The second, as with Gyllenborg in 1716, Haslang in 1742 and Vorontzov in 1791, was designed to in some way counteract what was seen as a hostile ministerial policy.[73] There is however no evidence that envoys sought to buy up newspapers in any systematic fashion, no suggestion that they owned them, either directly or through intermediaries, and no apparent evidence that money was used to change the stance of any paper. After the Anglo-Spanish agreement of November 1729, the Treaty of Seville, *Fog's Weekly Journal*, in an allusive reference, announced, 'It is supposed by some politicians that the happy conclusion of this treaty will put an end to another, which was reported to have been made betwixt the

Court of Spain and the powers of Grub Street.'[74] In practice the newspapers that diplomats seeking to attack the ministry turned to were opposition papers, such as the *Post Boy* in 1716, which were only too willing to use issues of foreign policy in order to discredit the government. Vorontzov's expenditure on propaganda during the Ochakov crisis was only £250: there was no shortage of papers willing to attack the ministry.[75] However, one of the handicaps facing any diplomatic attempt to exploit the press was the general preference of opposition papers for much of the century for isolationist policies expressed in xenophobic terms. From the late 1730s onwards it was ministerial papers that tended to be less critical of Bourbon policy, and opposition papers that called for action, as in the Corsican crisis of 1768 and the Falklands crisis of 1770. The standard opposition critique offered few points of access for the views of any foreign power, as the blue water strategy was in the interest of none. In such a situation there were no obvious recipients for Bourbon patronage. In 1729 Chauvelin had thought that it would be possible to use propaganda to destroy the anti-French views of 'le gros de la nation'. Two years later Chammorel had blamed printed material for inflaming natural popular anti-French sentiments.[76] However there is no sign of a sustained French propaganda offensive, though as Joseph Klaits has shown, the French monarchy of the early eighteenth century was well aware of the possibilities of foreign propaganda.[77] Chavigny's links with Bolingbroke may have influenced the *Craftsman*'s reporting of British policy during the War of the Polish Succession, though there are no obvious signs of this, and the paper adopted the views that were to be expected. Thereafter the contracts between French envoys and opposition newspapers were fleeting until the revolutionary period.

Possibly the limited direct intervention of diplomats should be seen as an indication of an awareness of the limitations of their position as potential patrons of the press. Given the willingness of foreign powers, including Britain, to spend money in order to influence policy in other states with representative assemblies, particularly Poland and Sweden, it is possibly surprising that more was not invested for similar purposes in Britain, doubly so as the corruptibility of British public life was a frequent theme both of indigenous (ministerial and opposition), and foreign commentators.[78] Furthermore similar methods had been adopted in the late seventeenth century. Possibly there was felt to be no need to subsidise newspapers actively. Opposition papers could be relied upon to berate ministries anyway, and, as Gyllenborg and Perry discovered, there was little more they were willing to do, because of their fears of ministerial action. It is however difficult to see censorship as preventing the development of a diplomatic–press nexus. There rather seems to have been a lack of sustained interest on the part of envoys. As with Poland and Sweden, where foreign intervention in domestic politics was concentrated in periods of Diets, so in Britain the need for action was episodic. It was neither feasible nor in accordance with diplomatic practice to attempt a lengthy programme of influencing public attitudes in favour of a particular foreign country. There was not enough attractive copy for such a series even if a paper had been willing to run it, which was unlikely given the adversarial nature of the press. Foreign interest in press campaigns was episodic, linked to particular crises in relations with Britain and based on the idea of attacking ministerial policy, something that the opposition press could be relied upon to do anyway. This was true of Swedish and Spanish interest in the opposition press in the early years of George I's reign and of Voronzov in 1791.

It is possible that interest in diplomatic circles in intervening in the British press decreased during the century. This is an impression that is impossible to quantify, but could be linked to the increasingly isolationist nature of the press, to the unwillingness of Britain between 1763 and 1787 to adopt a significant interventionist role in European politics and to a possible sense of the limited political effectiveness of the press. In addition, although this has not been quantified, it could be suggested that envoys were sending fewer newspapers with their reports. The despatch of printed material by diplomats predated the development of the press. Barrillon sent printed matter to Louis XIV in 1687.[79] The growth of the press produced far more material than could be forwarded, and also posed the problem of selecting what items to send. In the first half of the century a large number of foreign powers received British newspapers regularly, including France, Saxony, Prussia and the United Provinces. In 1731 Waldegrave reported that the French army minister D'Angervilliers had a Jacobite officer constantly with him 'to translate the Craftsman, and Fogg, and other libels'. The previous year Edward Finch, envoy in Stockholm, wrote that his Prussian counterpart 'has had Mist's Journal and the rest of the infamous grey papers, published in London, regularly sent to him, and which he has been at the pains to have translated into French to distribute to those who would receive them, and to thrust upon others'.[80] Most of the papers sent abroad were opposition in sympathy,[81] and the *Craftsman* commanded European attention.[82] However, some ministerial papers, such as the *Daily Courant* and *Free Briton*, were occasionally forwarded.[83] The definite opposition bias can be seen in a sample of papers sent from February to June 1737 preserved in the French foreign ministry, a sample weighted towards papers such as the *Craftsman, Common-Sense* and the *Alchemist.*[84]

Newspapers continued to be sent abroad to foreign governments after the 1730s. Many of those found in foreign archives were clearly preserved, and possibly sent, because they made specific points. The *General Advertiser* of 15 August 1750 commented on the situation in Nova Scotia, the *London Chronicle* of 17 February 1763 accused the French of breaking treaties, the *Daily Advertiser* of 8 February 1769 commented on trade between the French West Indies and the British American colonies, the *St. James's Chronicle* of 13 February 1784 on commercial negotiations. Items on subjects such as the fall of Choiseul and the Falkland Islands dispute were forwarded.[85] There seems however to be less evidence of a regular forwarding of papers, particularly in the French foreign ministry archives. Many of those that survive, and the form in which they tend to do so is that of French manuscript newsletters, can be found instead in the archives of the French naval ministry. For example there are a large number of 'extracts from British papers' for 1772 in the latter, which seem to have been sent on a regular basis.[86] If fewer newspapers were sent to the French foreign ministry in the latter half of the century this may reflect the absence of any feeling of novelty in their discussion of foreign policy. No subsequent eighteenth-century paper acquired the European reputation of the *Craftsman.* The collapse of Jacobitism as an issue of international relations, a source of potential British weakness susceptible to external influence, may also have lessened diplomatic interest in those features of domestic politics that could be glimpsed, however imperfectly, through the press. The latter was a very poor guide to high-political struggles and ministerial feuds, and diplomats had access to better sources for these. Newspapers could be used to illustrate despatches, the *Morning Herald* of 31 August 1782 underlining the insolent francophobia of the population,[87] but their discussion of foreign affairs could provide little guide to ministerial policy.

This relative decline in diplomatic attention to the British press contrasted with a buoyant foreign interest in non-ministerial circles. Several of the periodicals of the early eighteenth century had had a considerable foreign impact, notably the *Spectator* and *Tatler*. British colonies provided an obvious foreign market, but there was considerable interest in Europe in the essay periodicals. Some European journals were clearly influenced by the British periodicals. The *Bee* announced in 1733 that a twice-weekly was appearing in Hamburg entitled 'Extracts from the English Bee'.[88] English newspapers were cited in the foreign press and could be purchased in several European centres, including towns without British diplomatic representation. Sir James Nasmyth found them at Frankfurt in 1782.[89] The interest of the foreign press in British items, usually taken from newspapers, could in turn be exploited by British papers. The London section in the *Leeds Intelligencer* of 17 May 1768 carried an item on the respectable behaviour of participants at a Wilkite ball in London taken from an undated report in a Brussels paper. An Amsterdam paper was the source of an account of Wilkite activities carried in the issue of 28 June 1768. In 1740 the *Champion* used a London report in a Utrecht paper to substantiate the idea that Admiral Vernon's exploits in the West Indies were being hindered by a ministerial failure to send troops. Such borrowings and in particular the use of London items in foreign papers, were open not only to manipulation for partisan reasons but also to the propagation of false reports. The *St. James's Chronicle* of 11 April 1769 carried a Parisian report reprinted from the *Leiden Gazette* claiming that Britain was ready to restore Canada to France for money. Thirty years earlier *Wye's Letter* had warned 'that some persons will not be wanting by means of their correspondents to raise jealousies and misunderstandings by spurious accounts from abroad'.[90]

The impact of the British press on the foreign perception of Britain is difficult to assess. Contemporaries were most interested in and concerned about the direct consequences in terms of the policy of foreign states, and devoted very little attention to the impression made in wider circles. British envoys were interested only in a small elite of decision makers, and pressed ministries to send papers or pamphlets for their benefit. There was little interest in inserting material in foreign papers and in 1732 the British ministry rejected the idea of setting up a French-language news-paper printed in the United Provinces and intended to exploit French domestic tension over religious disputes.[91] More typical of British interest was the suggestion made by the British envoy in Berlin in 1721 that British papers be sent to help the Princess Royal learn English.[92] British ministries complained of items in foreign newspapers,[93] and were prepared to voice the opinion that they should receive satisfaction in return for meeting foreign com-plaints about the British press.[94] However, particularly once the Jacobite threat had ended, British ministries displayed less concern than other powers. Judging from the diplomatic correspondence the French made more complaints about Dutch publications than the British. Most European newspapers were in truth less adventurous in their comments on foreign states than the British or Dutch press, and the more relaxed attitude of British ministries towards foreign publications may have sprung from an awareness of their vulnerability on the issue.

British ministers and diplomats were convinced that the press had an impact on foreign powers. Benjamin Keene wrote in 1731 'that upon the King of Spain's reading one of our *Craftsman* wherein it was said that we were to demand a certain district before that place [Gibraltar] . . . he fell into such passions'. The Earl of Shelburne was concerned about the effect of the press on his ministry's attempts to negotiate a satisfactory peace with France at the end of the War of American Independence, and complained about the *Morning Herald* and *Public Advertiser*.[95] Both comments on foreign policy and domestic criticisms of the ministry were held to have detrimental effects abroad.[96] British envoys felt themselves obliged to counteract the impact of the press, Waldegrave telling Fleury in 1736 that things seen at a distance were usually false, Stormont informing the French in 1774 'that whatever those may think who judge from popular clamour, and articles in the newspapers, all the sober thinking men in America, know that its salvation depends upon its union with Great Britain'. In 1730 Waldegrave replied to an Austrian com-plaint concerning the reprinting in an Amsterdam paper of material from English news letters by stating positively 'that the expressions found fault with were not taken out of the English Gazette . . . the only paper published by authority'.[97] The ex-ternal influence of the press varied in practice, much being due to the state of relations with particular powers and the attitudes of individual envoys. The newspapers whose influence was discussed tended to be opposition ones. In 1729 *Fog's Weekly Journal* contested the claim that 'the practice of the writers tends to expose us to the contempt and ill will of foreign states. What is this but to tell the world, that a pamphlet or a journal is more regarded in other countries, than the conduct of our able ministers?' Such statements did not prevent further ministerial criticism, the *Daily Gazetteer* announcing in 1740, 'The mighty service done our foreign enemies, by opening, as far as they have been able, all our secrets both in state and in trade, by the writers for the Opposition, is more than sufficient to teach me discretion.' In 1731 the Hague letter led to an outburst of such attacks. The *Flying Post* asked 'shall false facts be impudently imposed upon us under the title of foreign news? Shall every occurrence from beyond sea, be amplified or diminished by falsehoods, as may best serve the present turn?' The *London Journal* claimed that

> great misrepresentations of their actions, and abuse of their persons, naturally tend to weaken their hands and render them odious at home, and contemptible abroad . . . it keeps foreign powers, who are at variance with us, from complying with our measures, under a firm persuasion that a Ministry so hunted, so savagely used, so vilely traduced and ignominiously treated, cannot long stand their ground.[98]

At times of apparent ministerial instability it was understandable that foreign powers should seek information widely and that they were believed to consult the press.[99] Papers that were close to the ministry could be regarded as a source of evidence for government policy, the *London Journal* of 30 June 1722 being forwarded to Paris on the grounds that its essay was supposedly based on memoranda provided by the government and published at its instigation. In 1738 Cambis asked the ministry about Irish anti-Catholic legislation, because he had read a report about it in the *Daily Gazetteer*, 'ce papier étant de la Cour, et fait sous les yeux des Ministres'.[100] Diplomats, including those of friendly powers, were known to read the press. In 1792 one friendly envoy drew the attention of Burges to an advertisement for a pro-French meeting in the *Morning Chronicle* of 7 September.[101] It was the use of the press, particularly but not exclusively the opposition papers, for unfriendly purposes, that was the key problem. The point at issue did not have to be political in order to cause difficulties. In 1716 William Poyntz, envoy in Lisbon, asked his brother to press the Secretary of State to act:

> We find it extremely inconvenient that the writers of our news-papers should be suffered to insert . . . that the men of war and packet boats from hence import vast sums in gold: as for ex-ample the Gibraltar man of war that went lately from hence, our papers say she carried £200,000 sterling in gold (which is about ten times as much as she really had aboard). This was immediately transcribed into the Portuguese Gazette printed in this city.

Poyntz, sure that this would have serious consequences, wrote, 'It would be extremely convenient that strict orders were given to all the printers and writers of our news papers that they would forbear mentioning anything of that nature for the future.' Stephen Poyntz forwarded the letter to Robert Pringle, an Under-Secretary, suggesting that he 'may possibly have an opportunity to speak a word to some or other of our news writers who may impart it to the whole fraternity'.[102]

The episode illustrated both the manner in which foreign difficulties could lead to pressure for action to restrain the press and the willingness to suggest a resort to persuasion rather than legal coercion. The latter is more useful for the historian, as it provides documentary evidence, but could be politically dangerous for ministries. In 1738, when the opposition press was calling for action against Spanish depredations on British com-merce, the *London Evening Post* reported that the Spanish minis-try had complained to Keene 'of the little respect with which the English news writers express themselves whenever they make any mention of the Spanish affairs'. For the ministry to have acted to enforce respect would have been legally difficult and would have provided the opposition with a basis for political attack. Observing that 'a heap of translated scandal out of our public papers has been sent to this Court'. Keene commented, 'I find by experience that he who cannot despise noise is not fit for a public employment. But let him despise it as much as he pleases it must disgust him at the long run and make him weary of public business.' In 1776 Hugh Elliot, envoy in Munich and Regensburg, complained, 'The licentiousness of our own public writings and speakers translated with augmentations and improvements into all foreign languages, have raised such a hue and cry against England, that the ignorance of foreigners, which was formerly only insipid, is now grating.' In an undated letter sent after 1748 the British Consul in Algiers urged the Earl of Sandwich, first Lord of the Admiralty, to continue good relations with Algiers and to prevent Britain 'from joining in a general crusade against those Barbary States, however much such a measure may be puffed of and cryed up at present by weekly and political writers to mislead and prejudice the people'.[103]

The potential impact of opposition press criticism varied. In the case of Anglo-Spanish relations in the late 1730s or Anglo-French relations in the late 1760s opposition papers attacked the government for not being firm enough. They could serve to underline ministerial claims, as over the return of Gibraltar in the 1720s, that they could not yield for fear of domestic repercussions. In contrast claims that ministries were weak and unpopular and maintained simply by corruption, or that the fiscal system of the heavily indebted nation was close to collapse, could serve to provide evidence for ministers and diplomats, such as Chavigny, urging action against Britain. Opposition papers were cited by Jacobites and others keen to argue that governments were weak.[104] They could also be mentioned by diplomats more favourable to the ministry in power.[105]

Clearly the impact of the press on diplomats varied. Simolin, Russian envoy from 1779 to 1785, who won a successful libel action against the *London Courant* for suggesting he was a French spy, was accused by his successor Voronzov of providing in his reports merely edited versions of those in the press. Similar accusations to those of Voronzov were made about other envoys. His French counterpart Adhémar was less impressed by the newspapers. Referring to critical press comment he claimed that it was received with general scorn.[106] A similar contrast can be noticed more generally. Horatio Walpole could write of Fleury, 'A guess in a newspaper, or a speculation from an ordinary nouvellist will have sometime an effect upon him', but this was not true of all ministers, and it seems to have become less so as people became more accustomed to both the vociferousness and the impotence of opposition press campaigns.[107] Foreign commentators did not associate the physical growth of the press in the second half of the century, both in terms of new titles and in increased circulation, with any enhanced political role or significance. Their view may well have been an accurate one.

The debate over foreign policy

> Almost all the glorious advantages we had gained over our most restless and perfidious foe, our ministers have given away; and in consequence of this weakness, or of this treachery, the trade and commerce of *France* will soon be in a more flourishing state than in the most prosperous times since their monarchy began, and ours in the same proportion will decline.
>
> *North Briton*, 11 December 1762

In contrast to modern British governments, their eighteenth-century progenitors neither had massive legislative programmes nor assumed that the purpose of power was legislation. There were naturally some ministries that sought more changes than others. The Tory ministry of 1710–14 envisaged major alterations in the position of the Dissenters, while the Stanhope–Sunderland Whig ministry conceived in 1718–19 what was by contemporary standards a radical programme, including substantial con-stitutional and ecclesiastical changes. Walpole was interested in significant fiscal reforms, Pitt in major changes in foreign trade. However, most ministries, whether of long or short duration, had no interest in discussing, let alone using their parliamentary majorities to push through, substantial change. Most legislation was private and the parliamentary session, having begun just be-fore or after Christmas, rarely lasted long after Easter. The nature of the ministerial legislative programme created problems for opposition publicists. The paucity and general repetitiveness of the programme led them to attack nearly all new schemes, whatever their value. They had to be made to appear to characterise all the supposed vices and sinister intentions of the ministry and to be of fundamental significance. Thus relatively minor pieces of legislation, such as the Excise Bill and the Jewish Naturalisation Act, or unexceptional legal actions, became test cases of the liberty of Englishmen. The relative absence of new public political developments was possibly one reason for the serious attacks made on ministerial legal action against the press. Issues that could be made to appear crucial could be discussed long after the session was over, but with Parliament in recess for more than half the year and elections infrequent after the Septennial Act of 1716 there was a lack of political events to discuss. Ministerial disputes and high-political jockeying were not considered at any length, though brief reports of rumoured ministerial changes were carried. The political attitudes and actions of the Crown, central to ministerial politics, were not a safe topic for press discussion.

In domestic political terms there was a lack of events for the opposition press and they were forced to concentrate on general attacks on the supposed stance and methods of administration. This inevitably led first to attacks on alleged corrupt practices and attitudes, attacks that were easy to make and generally accessible in their message, an often felicitous mixture of wit and moral outrage. However, such attacks were both repetitive and lacking in much particular political focus, as it was uncommon for generalised attacks on corruption to be translated into a strong campaign for the redress of a particular grievance.

Foreign news had the major advantage of being a sphere in which information and speculation altered daily, at least as long as the posts arrived. Its real and apparent importance was magnified both by this constant provision of events and by the relative ease with which information concerning them could be provided. This constant availability helped to make British foreign policy a major issue in the press, for it was necessary to interpret the kaleidoscopic pattern of European events and it was essential for partisan papers to do so in a way that bolstered their position. Thus foreign policy was not solely a major topic of political debate within the high political sphere, both parliamentary and ministerial, but also a sphere that it was exciting and reasonably credible for the press to discuss. As an area for partisan struggle it had much appeal. Rich in historical connotations it provided opportunities for successive oppositions not only to claim, but also to attempt to demonstrate that successive ministries were betraying national interests. The *Whisperer* advanced at length in 1771 its claim that the ministry had covered up a conspiracy of British traitors and Catholics with France that had led to a fire at the Portsmouth naval base. *Felix Farley's Bristol Journal* attacked in 1787 a supposed ministerial plan to return Gibraltar.[108] Jacobite papers sought to show that British interests were being betrayed for Hanoverian ends, while all opposition papers challenged the competence of government, foreign policy providing them with a

constantly changing basis for this claim. Partisanship was revealed
not only in the discussion of events, but also in the selection of
items. The *St. James's Weekly Journal* described what it claimed to
be opposition tactics in 1717:

> Amongst the foreign news, make heroes and saints of all who
> are not in the interest of the present establishment, and give
> them conquest and success in all their enterprizes; and those
> who are in our alliance, treat either as petty powers, or des-
> igning, over-reaching, formidable neighbours, that in a few
> years will strip us of our trade and riches, and make this nation
> a province to a foreign power.[109]

Added edge was given to the discussion of foreign news by the
partisan exploitation of events in foreign countries in order to
make domestic political points. It was relatively common for an
item to be followed by an exegesis usually in brackets or another
type. It was not necessary for these points to have a partisan bias
or political content. *Felix Farley's Bristol Journal* ended an
account of Parisian aristocratic charity in 1789 with a bracketed
note, 'The above is an example worthy of imitation to our Princes
and Princesses, and the first families of rank and fortune.'[110]
Other items were treated in a partisan fashion, though the
approach was often allusive. The *Craftsman* used the fall of the
Russian first minister as the basis for an attack on corruption in
1728, Prince Menzikof serving as a continental counterpart for
Walpole, as the Papal first minister Cardinal Coscia was to do in
1730, and as a host of figures from the past, such as Sejanus and
Wolsey, did on numerous occasions. *Mist's Weekly Journal* praised
the Papal decision in 1728 to remain in Rome and not go on a trip
to Albano, a clear reference to the Hanoverian visits of the new
British dynasty. In 1742 the *London Evening Post* commented on
Transylvanian demands for government reforms while Austria was
at war: 'Britons may take warning by their example. Now is the
only time to obtain redress.'[111] The relationship between various
linked European states such as Saxony and Poland, Austria and
Hungary, Austria and Naples, Austria and Transylvania, served to
highlight alleged features in that between Britain and Hanover:

> From Vienna we learn, that the States of Hungary have refused
> to grant the subsidies required of them, because they think it

too much for the people to bear: But we don't find that either bribes or menaces have been used to influence them; such practices would be inconsistent with liberty, which they, poor people, fancy they enjoy; tho' we in England, know that no nation enjoys it but ourselves.

In May 1737 *Common-Sense* published an essay by the Jacobite academic William King, supposedly giving a plan for a new government in Corsica, but in reality providing Jacobite propaganda,[112] Corsica's geographical reality serving as a better basis for political fantasy than other locations that had been used, such as the Moon and Persia. In 1742, in a commentary on French news, the *General Evening Post* urged the British nobility and gentry to emulate the public spirit of their French counterparts. Three years later Denmark provided a warning about the loss of liberty for the *Westminster Journal*, while in 1772 the monarchical coup in Sweden was cited for similar reasons. In 1734 a Londoner, Stephen Monteage the younger, copied out of the *Daily Advertiser* a report of the punishment of the secretary of the Persian ruler for suggesting the sale of posts in the government and army.[113] International developments could also be cited as warnings. The *Caledonian Mercury* warned in 1768 that the French invasion of Corsica was a practice for a threatened invasion of Britain.[114]

If Europe was a stage depicting what could happen to Britain, British foreign policy provided marvellous opportunities for more direct attacks on ministerial policy. These were not the sole reason for the inclusion of foreign news. Much was of economic importance, the direct significance of seemingly unimportant items being often great:

We hear from Leeds, that the plague being at Messina, in Sicily, is likely to prove of bad consequence to the woollen manufactures in that county; and that the principal merchants there have already felt the effects of it, by counter orders from their correspondents; so that in all probability the clothiers, who have already laid in, or shall buy any quantity of wool, at the present high advanced price, will be considerable losers.[115]

The press both symbolised and was an active agent of the forces breaking down parochial interests, of both locality and social group. Foreign news was a significant stimulus of the process by which information was disseminated, one provincial paper reprinting a London item in 1745 that began, 'As the French News Writers have already carried our arms before *Quebec*, in hopes there may be some truth in this report, we shall insert a short account of the place from one of their own geographers.'[116] The education of the reading public by the press served commercial and political ends but was none the less significant for that. The extent to which newspaper reports of European affairs led readers to feel concern over the fate of co-religionists or those of apparent similar political beliefs abroad is unclear. The limited nature of foreign advertising helped to ensure that there was no parallel influence to that of metropolitan fashion. Nevertheless thanks to the press, the diaries of Derbyshire ministers and Somerset doctors could include references to European affairs, while the siege of Prague was 'the topic of the tea-tables' in 1742. In 1787 the *Leeds Mercury* claimed,

'tis next to an impossibility to stop the torrent of party zeal which almost generally flows in the human breast, (at least in this island, even amongst the lowest class). One of the *nail-making* tribe, in a market town in Warwickshire, went into a barber's shop to have the weekly produce of his chin taken off, and as these places are always the mart of politics, a conversation took place respecting our late armaments in support of the Stadtholder; words growing high, and the sable chinn'ed customer insisting upon the justice of the Stadtholder's cause, the free-born *Knight of the razor* refused to finish his operation, and obliged his half-shaved opponent to quit the premises immediately.[117]

The political nation became fairly well informed about the affairs of the greater world and the issues of British foreign policy. If this process did not regularly bear political fruit, it was nevertheless of great importance in the education of the political nation. Britons may have been xenophobic, but they were increasingly well-informed xenophobes.

Notes

1. Tilson to Delafaye, 1 Oct. 1723, PRO. 43/5 f. 94.
2. Moore, *View of Society*, I, 390.
3. Gibbs, 'Newspapers, Parliament and Foreign Policy in the Age of Stanhope and Walpole', *Mélanges offerts à G. Jacquemyns* (Brussels, 1968); Black, 'The British Press

and European News in the 1730s: The case of the *Newcastle Courant*', *Durham County Local History Society Bulletin*, 26 (1981); Black, 'Russia and the British Press, 1720– 40', *British Journal for Eighteenth-Century Studies*, 5 (1982); Black, 'The Press, Party and Foreign Policy in the Reign of George I', *Publishing History*, 13 (1983); Black, 'Russia and the British Press in the Early Eighteenth Century', *Study Group on Eighteenth-Century Russia Newsletter*, 11 (1983); Black, *British Foreign Policy in the Age of Walpole* (Edinburgh, 1985), pp. 160–72.

4. Lutnick, *American Revolution and the British Press*; J. P. Thomas, *The British Empire and the Press 1763–1774* (unpublished D.Phil thesis, Oxford, 1982); D. E. Clark, 'News and Opinion Concerning America in English Newspapers, 1754–1763', *Pacific Historical Review*, 10 (1941); P. Lawson, '"The Irishman's Prize": Views of Canada from the British Press, 1760–1774', *Historical Journal*, 28 (1985).

5. D. B. Horn, *British Public Opinion and The First Partition of Poland* (Edinburgh, 1945); M. Schlenke, *England und das friderizianische Preussen 1740–1763* (Munich, 1963).

6. J. J. Murray, 'British Public Opinion and The Rupture of Anglo-Swedish Relations in 1717', *Indiana Magazine of History*, 44 (1948); L. M. Orosco y Aragon, *France and Spain in the English Periodicals of Queen Anne's Reign* (unpublished PhD thesis, Minnesota, 1973).

7. R. D. Spector, *English Literary Periodicals and the Climate of Opinion during the Seven Years' War* (The Hague, 1966), needs to be matched by a study of newspapers.

8. *Fog's Weekly Journal*, 16 July 1737.

9. *Post Boy*, 7 May, 29 Aug. 1728; London *Evening Post*, 17 Dec. 1728, 25 Nov. 1729.

10. *British Observator*, 10 Mar. 1733; *Daily Gazetteer*, 24 Oct. 1735; *General Evening Post*, 17 Nov. 1733; Cranfield, *Provincial Newspaper*, p. 267.

11. *London Journal*, 23 Aug. 1735.

12. Cranfield, *Provincial Newspaper*, p. 261; *Weekly Remarks*, 3 Mar. 1715.

13. *Flying Post*, 14 Oct. 1718. The *Daily Courant* was that of 4 October; *St. James's Evening Post*, 31 Oct. 1718; *Weekly Journal or British Gazetteer*, 12 July 1718; *Leeds Intelligencer*, 29 May 1781.

14. *Weekly Medley*, 6 Sept. 1718; *Weekly Journal*, 4 Oct. 1718; *Weekly Remarks*, 3 Mar. 1715.

15. *Applebee's Original Weekly Journal*, 14 July 1722; *Daily Journal*, 15 Dec. 1733; *Oracle*, 21 Aug. 1742; *Corn-Cutter's Journal*, 23 Oct. 1733; *Westminster Journal*, 28 Aug. 1773.

16. *London Journal*, 3 Jan. 1726; *London Chronicle*, 2 Mar. 1762.

17. *Evening Post*, 13 Sept. 1720; *Wye's Letter*, 2 Oct. 1735.

18. *Craftsman*, 21 Oct., 2 Dec. 1727; *Old Whig*, 16 Dec. 1736; *True Patriot*, 5 Nov. 1745; *Old England*, 21 July 1744; *True Briton*, 4 Apr. 1799.

19. Du Bourgay to Tilson, 9 Dec. (ns) 1724, PRO. 90/18; Consul Parker to Delafaye, 18 Oct. (ns) 1729, PRO. 94/215; Lascelles, agent in Dunkirk, to Delafaye, 21 Dec. (ns) 1730, PRO. 76/4; Delafaye to Newcastle, 13 Nov. 1732, PRO. 36/28 f. 231; Tilson to Robinson, 6 Oct. (ns) 1736, BL. Add. 23799 f. 186; Trevor to Weston, 9 Oct. (ns) 1736, PRO. 84/359 f. 127; Molesworth to Newcastle, 10 Feb. (ns) 1725, PRO. 92/ 31 f. 422; Waldegrave to Newcastle, 28 Oct. (ns) 1733, BL. Add. 32783 f. 56; George Earl of Morton to James Lord Aberdour, 25 Jan. 1737, SRO. GD. 150/3476/75; Weston to Robinson, 23 Mar. 1733, BL. Add. 23788 f.1.

20. Anon., *General Remarks on our Commerce with the Continent* (1806?), pp. 50–1; *Political Cabinet*, July 1744 iii–iv.

21. J. R. Jones, *Britain and the World* (1980), p. 13.

22. *Flying Post*, 11 Oct. 1718; *Weekly Medley*, 14 Feb. 1719; *St. James's Weekly Journal*, 9 Jan. 1720; *St. James's Evening Post*, 1 Oct. 1720; *Englishman's Journal*, 1 Aug. 1722; *Mist's Weekly Journal*, 18 Mar. 1727; *Craftsman*, 11 Aug. 1739.

23. *Weekly Journal*, 7 Sept. 1717; *Post Man*, 16 Sept. 1718; *Mist's Weekly Journal*, 4 Mar. 1727; *Briton*, 12 June 1762; *Owen's Weekly Chronicle*, 25 Nov. 1758.

24. *Original Weekly Journal*, 19 Jan. 1717; *Whitehall Evening Post*, 13 Nov. 1718, 15 Oct. 1719; *Weekly Medley*, 9 Jan. 1720; *Wye's Letter*, 8 May 1722; *London Journal*, 5 Sept. 1724, 20, 27 Feb. 1725, 12 June 1736.

25. *Daily Gazetteer*, 2 Apr. 1737; *Daily Post*, 25 Aug. 1737; *British Journal*, 22 Sept. 1722; *Post Man*, 27 Sept. 1722; *Weekly Miscellany*, 15 Dec. 1733; *Gazetteer*, 2 Sept. 1770.

26. *Worcester Post-Man*, 9 Oct. 1719; *Weekly Courant*, 29 Nov. 1739; *Universal Spectator*, 23 Oct. 1742.

27. *Ipswich Journal*, 1 Sept. 1764.

28. James to Count Philip Kinsky, Austrian envoy, 13 Apr. 1731, PRO. 100/11.

29. *Weekly Miscellany*, 1 Mar. 1735.

30. Chesterfield to Marchmont, 27 Aug. 1734, *A Selection from the papers of the Earl of Marchmont*, G. H. Rose (ed.) (3 vols., 1831), II, 44; Drummond to Aberdour, 19 Nov. 1734, SRO. GD. 150/3474/40; Henry to Stephen Fox, 12 Dec. 1745, BL. Add. 51417 f. 184; Payzant to Robinson, 26 Dec. 1746, BL. Add. 23824 f. 23; Aust to Keith, 27 Oct. 1789, BL. Add. 35541 f. 324. The city surrendered on the 8th and the news was reported in the London press on the 27th.

31. Harrington to Dickens, envoy at Berlin, 31 Aug. 1733; Dickens to Harrington, 6 Feb. 1734; Harcourt to Secretary of State Viscount Weymouth, 25 Jan. 1769; Viscount Stormont, envoy in Paris, to Earl of Rochford, Secretary of State, 16 Feb., 25 May 1774, PRO. 90/35, 96/36, 78/277 f. 81, 78/291 f. 91, 78/292 f. 92.

32. J. Morgan, *A Complete History of Algiers* (2 vols., 1728, 1729), I, ii, vi.

33. *Flying-Post*, 6 Jan. 1713; S. Tucoo-Chala, 'Presse et Verité sous L'Ancien Régime', *Revue du Nord*, 66 (1984), p. 718.

34. Tilson to Waldegrave, 18 Aug. (ns) 1732, Chewton.

35. Clark, 'News and Opinion', *Pacific Historical Review*, p. 75; N. Wraxall, *Cursory Remarks Made in a Tour Through Some of the Northern Parts of Europe* (1775), p. 264; J. T. A. Alexander, *Autocratic Politics in a National Crisis* (Bloomington, Indiana, 1969), pp. 183, 122; R. E. Begemann, *The English Press and the French Revolution* (unpublished PhD thesis, Emory, 1973), pp. 47, 51, 63–4; Lutnick, *American Revolution and the British Press*, pp. 20–2.

36. Earl of Ilchester, *Lord Hervey and his Friends* (1950) p. 207.

37. *Weekly Miscellany*, 26 Jan. 1734; *Kentish Gazette*, 14 Dec. 1774.

38. *Weekly Journal*, 8 Mar. 1718; *Post Boy*, 9 Jan. 1720, 10 Sept. 1723; Horace Mann to Horace Walpole, 25 Oct. 1755; W. Lewis (ed.), *Mann-Walpole Correspondence*, IV, 505. Description of a Mexican eagle, *Post Boy*, 7 Sept. 1723.

39. *Post-Man*, 9 Apr. 1723; *Flying-Post*, 23, 25 June, 10 Dec. 1724; *Darlington Pamphlet*, 10 July 1772.

40. *London Chronicle*, 17 Jan. 1788.

41. *British Mercury*, 7 Feb. 1711; Cranfield, *Provincial Newspaper*, p. 68.

42. *Oxford Gazette*, 25 May 1767.

43. Sardinia: *St. James's Post*, 11 Sept. 1717; *Flying-Post*, 12 Sept. 1717; *St. James's Weekly Journal*, 14 Sept. 1717; Sicily: *Weekly Packet*, 20 Sept. 1718; *Weekly Packet, with the Price Courant*, 27 Sept. 1718; *Weekly Journal*, 4 Oct. 1718; *St. James's Post*, 13 Oct. 1718; *St. James's Evening Post*, 14 Oct. 1718.

44. *Weekly Journal*, 4 Oct. 1718.

45. *Flying Post*, 26 July 1722; *Daily Post*, 25 Dec. 1722; *Northampton Mercury*, 18 Mar. 1723; *General Evening Post*, 11 Apr. 1734, 19 June 1735; *Whitehall Evening Post*, 11 Apr. 1734; *London Journal*, 13 Apr. 1734; *Applebee's Original Weekly Journal*, 13 Apr. 1734; *Daily Post Boy*, 1 June 1734; *Weekly Miscellany*, 29 June 1734; *Norwich Mercury*, 20 July, 17 Aug. 1734; *London Evening Post*, 17 June 1735; *Daily Gazetteer*, 25 July 1735.

46. *London Evening Post*, 11 Aug. 1737; *Northampton Mercury*, 19 Nov. 1739, 19 May 1740; *York Courant*, 13 Oct. 1741; *Bee*, 16 Dec. 1777.

47. *Universal Spectator*, 6 Feb. 1742; *Cirencester Flying-Post*, 8, 22 Nov. 1742; *Cambridge Journal*, 20, 27 July 1745; *Newcastle Courant*, 28 June 1746.

48. *Craftsman*, 21 Feb. 1741; *Newcastle Journal*, 29 Aug. 1752; *London Chronicle*, 30 Mar. 1760, 3, 6 Apr., 20 May 1762; *Ipswich Journal*, 15 Sept. 1764; *Reading Mercury*, 22, 29 Feb. 1768; *Gazetteer*, 18 Aug. 1770; *London Chronicle*, 8 Jan. 1788, 10 Jan. 1792; *St. James's Chronicle*, 12 Jan. 1796.

49. *Evening Post*, 3 Jan. 1713; *Mist's Weekly Journal*, 9 July 1726; *Daily Gazetteer*, 11 Aug. 1740, 1 Oct. 1742; *London Evening Post*, 26 Dec. 1741.

50. *Flying Post*, 11, 16, 18, 20, 25 Jan., 6, 22 Mar. 1722.

51. *St. James's Post*, 29 Sept. 1718; *Weekly Journal or British Gazetteer*, 16 Mar. 1717. Accounts of the life of the Spanish chief minister Alberoni, *Flying Post*, 14 Oct. 1718, *Weekly Journal or British Gazetteer*, 18 Oct. 1718.

52. *Daily Post*, 7 July 1722. Nearly two columns of the *Weekly Miscellany* of 5 June 1736 was devoted to an explanation of the Jülich–Berg dispute.

53. *Weekly Journal*, 1 Sept. 1722; *Evening Journal*, 7 Dec. 1727; *Newcastle Journal*, 15 Mar. 1740; *Leeds Intelligencer*, 6 May 1766; *St. James's Chronicle*, 11 May 1769; *Newcastle Journal*, 7, 21 Mar., 25 Apr., 4 July 1752; *Newcastle Chronicle*, 14 June 1787; *Read's Weekly Journal*, 3 Jan. 1756; *London Chronicle*, 7, 9 Jan. 1779.

54. *London Chronicle*, 20 Feb. 1762; *Daily Universal Register*, 6 Jan. 1785; *Evening Journal*, 12, 13, 14, 15, 16 Dec. 1727; *Owen's Weekly Chronicle*, 22 Apr. 1758.

55. *Newcastle Courant*, 22 June 1734.

56. *York Courant*, 20 Feb. 1739.

57. *Reading Mercury*, 21 Sept. 1772.

58. *Flying Post*, 6 Oct. 1722; *Daily Gazetteer*, 14 May 1736, 6 Oct. 1739; *London Chronicle*, 19 Jan. 1762; *Ipswich Journal*, 6 Feb. 1762, 25 Aug. 1764, 31 Aug. 1765; *Leeds Intelligencer*, 24 Feb. 1767; *Reading Mercury*, 1 Oct. 1770; *Owen's Weekly Chronicle*, 20 May, 17 June 1758.

59. Walpole to Townshend, 30 July 1723, PRO. 43/4 f. 159; T. R. Clayton, 'The Duke of Newcastle, the Earl of Halifax, and the American Origins of the Seven Years War', *HJ*, 24 (1981), p. 590.

60. BL. Add. 37362 f. 72. Referring to the translation of a London newsletter claiming extensive support for Jacobitism.

61. T. Egido López, *Prensa clandestina española del siglo XVIII: 'El Duende Critico'* (Valladolid, 1968).

62. *Daily Post*, 4 July 1730.

63. Eugene to Kinsky, 3 Mar. (ns), 20 June (ns) 1731, HHSTA. Grosse Korrespondenz 94 b f. 68, 72; Wachtendonck to Haslang, 27 Aug. 1759, Munich, Bayr. Ges. London 235.

64. Eden to Pitt, 25 May 1786, CUL. Add. Mss 6958 No. 113. The Frenchman was Joseph Rayneval who conducted the detailed negotiations with Eden.

65. Newcastle to Horatio Walpole, 4 July 1735, 21 Dec. 1727, PRO. 84/344 f. 246, BL. Add. 32753 f. 502.

66. Evans, *Kantemir*, pp. 78–9; Earl of Halifax, Secretary of State for the Northern Department, to Weston, 17 Dec. 1762, Weston-Underwood papers.

67. Broglie to Morville, 3 Aug. 1724, AE. CP. Ang. 348 f. 179; Cambis to Maurepas, 5 Oct. 1739, AN. AE. BI 761; Cambis to Amelot, 11 Dec. 1738, AE. CP. Ang. 399 f. 310–13.

68. *Evening Post*, 26 Dec. 1724.

69. Zamboni to Saxon minister Manteuffel, 27 Jan. (ns), 3 Feb. (ns) 1730, Manteuffel to Zamboni, 1 Mar. (ns) 1730, Walther, Saxon minister, to Zamboni, 16 Aug. (ns) 1730, 3 Feb. (ns), 10 Aug. (ns) 1731, Bodl. Ms Rawl. 120 f. 94, 118 f.

311, 129 f. 215, 217, 219; Zamboni to Lagnasc, Saxon minister, 16, 23 Jan. (ns) 1731, Dresden, 637 f. 39, 41–3.
70. PRO. 35/62 f. 75, 77, 79, 81, 88; *London Journal*, 11 June 1726; *Mist's Weekly Journal*, 4 June 1726.
71. *Whitehall Evening Post*, 25 Sept. 1718; Black, 'Parliament and the Political and Diplomatic Crisis of 1717–18', *Parliamentary History*, 3 (1984), p. 87.
72. Kantemir to Harrington, 26 Aug. 1733, PRO. 100/52; *Daily Journal*, 27 Aug. 1733; Bunau, Saxon envoy, to Count Wackerbarth, Saxon minister, 24 July (ns) 1733, PRO. 107/14; De Löss to Augustus III, 27 Nov. 1733, Jan. (ns) 1734, Dresden 638 I, IIa; Evans, *Kantemir*, p. 74.
73. Petkum, Holstein envoy to Görtz, 14 Sept. 1716, PRO. 107/18 f. 93; Haslang to Grimberghen, Bavarian envoy in Paris, 4 May, reply 9 June, 1742, Haslang to Count Preysing, Bavarian foreign minister, 17 Feb. 1758, Munich, Bayr. Ges. London 379, 234.
74. *Fog's Weekly Journal*, 29 Nov. 1729.
75. Ehrman, *Pitt*, II, 26.
76. Chauvelin to Chammorel, 23 Jan. (ns) 1729, AE. CP. Ang. sup. 8 f. 72–3; Chammorel to Chauvelin, 15 Jan. (ns) 1731, AE. CP. Ang. 373 f. 16.
77. J. Klaits, *Printed Propaganda under Louis XIV: Absolute Monarchy and Public Opinion* (Princeton, 1977).
78. Palm, Austrian envoy to Charles VI, 13 Dec. (ns) 1726, CUL. CH. corresp. 1379; Chammorel to Morville, 30 Apr. (ns) 1725, Broglie to Chauvelin, 9 Feb. (ns) 1730, AE. CP. Ang. 350, 369; D'Aix, Sardinian envoy to Victor Amadeus II, 30 July (ns) 1727, AST. LM. Ing. 35; Anon., 'Situation de L'Angleterre', 27 June (ns) 1739, AE. Mémoires et Documents Ang. 8 f. 199.
79. Barrillon to Louis XIV, 13, 30 Oct. 1687, AE. CP. Ang. 162 f. 207, 240–1.
80. Waldegrave to Horatio Walpole, 12 Apr. (ns) 1731, Chewton; Finch to Newcastle, 24 June (ns) 1730, PRO. 95/55 f. 57.
81. For example, *Fog's Weekly Journal*, AE. CP. Ang. 369 f. 267, 371 f. 163–4, 374 f. 96, 375 f. 63–5; *Common-Sense*, AE. CP. Ang. 399 f. 323; Cambis to Maurepas, 2 Feb. (ns), 5 Mar. (ns) 1739, AN. AE. BI 761.
82. AE. CP. Ang. 371 f. 146–7, 372 f. 5–6, 27–8, 47–51, 373 f. 100–5, 374 f. 3–4, 375 f. 1–2, 25–6.
83. AE. CP. Ang. 371 f. 170, 376 f. 8–9, 22–30.
84. AE. Mémoires et Documents, Ang. 38 f. 6–106.
85. AE. CP. Ang. 428 f. 267–71, Mém. Doc. Ang. 59 f. 61–2; AN. AE. BI 429; AE. CP. Ang. 547 f. 262, 498 f. 3–4.
86. AN. Archives de La Marine, Pays Etrangères, 434.
87. AE. CP. Ang. 538 f. 113.
88. G. M. Baker, 'Some references to German Literature in English Magazines of the early eighteenth century', *Modern Language Notes*, 24 (1909), p. 113.
89. Nasmyth to Keith, 10 July 1782, BL. Add.
90. *Champion*, 8 July 1740; *Wye's Letter*, 21 Apr. 1739.
91. William Erskine to [Harrington?], 9 Aug. (ns) 1732, PRO. 78/308 f. 806–7.
92. Whitworth to Tilson, 6, 30 Dec. (ns) 1721, PRO. 90/15.
93. Robinson to Delafaye, 28 Oct. (ns) 1727, PRO. 78/186 f. 88; Walter Titley, envoy in Copenhagen, to Harrington, 27 Mar. (ns) 1731, PRO. 75/56 f. 106.
94. Harrington to Horatio Walpole, 7 Aug. (ns) 1735, PRO. 84/345 f. 172.
95. Keene to [Delafaye], 20 May (ns) 1731, PRO. 94/107; Shelburne to Lord Grantham, Foreign Secretary, 24 Oct. [1782], Bedford, CRO. L 30/14/306/19; Edward Finch, envoy in Stockholm, to Newcastle, 11 May (ns) 1739, PRO. 95/86 f. 21.
96. Countess of Hertford to Lord Beauchamp, 7 Nov. 1742, Alnwick Castle, Northumberland Letters, vol. 113, p. 45.
97. Waldegrave to Robert Walpole, 23 Oct. (ns) 1736, Chewton; Stormont to

Rochford, 7 Dec. 1774, PRO. 78/294 f. 170; Waldegrave to Tilson, 22 Mar. 1730, Chewton.

98. *Fog's Weekly Journal*, 25 Jan. 1729; *Daily Gazetteer*, 30 Oct. 1740; *Flying Post*, 21 Jan., 12 Aug. 1731; *London Journal*, 2 Aug. 1731; *Jacobite's Journal*, 29 Oct. 1748.

99. Parry to Thomas Rawlins, 7 Jan. 1742, Bodl. Ms. Ballard 29 f. 73.

100. Destouches to Dubois, 23 July 1722, AE. CP. Ang. 342 f. 104; Cambis to Amelot, 10 Mar. 1738, PRO. 107/21; Chavigny to Chauvelin, 29 Jan., 3 Mar., Chauvelin to Chavigny, 14 Feb. 1732, AE. CP. Ang. 376 f, 127–8, 279, 166.

101. Baron de Kutzleben to Burges, 8 Sept. 1792, Bodl. Burges 45 f. 121–3; Fagel to Hop, 19 Sept. (ns) 1730, PRO. 107/2.

102. Poyntz to Pringle, 13 Apr., William to Stephen Poyntz, 10 Mar. (ns) 1716, PRO. 89/24 f. 50, 52–3.

103. *London Evening Post*, 22 Aug. 1738; Keene to Waldegrave, 23 Mar. (ns) 1739, Chewton; Elliot to Eden, 3 July 1776, BL. Add. 34413 f. 58–9; White to Sandwich, undated, Chelmsford RO. Braybrooke Mss. D/By 054.

104. Tilson to Waldegrave, 23 Dec. 1729, Chewton; Robinson to Harrington, 18 Nov. (ns) 1730, PRO. 80/69.

105. Evans, *Kantemir*, p. 120.

106. A. G. Cross, '*By the Banks of the Thames': Russians in Eighteenth Century Britain* (Newtonville, Mass., 1980), p. 20; Marquis of Carmarthen, Foreign Secretary to Eden, 30 June 1786, *Auckland Journal*, I, 137. The Saxon Count Watzdorf stressed that he would not use the press as a source, Watzdorf to Marquis de Fleury, 26 Dec. (ns) 1730, Dresden, 2676 I, f. 98. Adhémar to Vergennes, 17 Feb. 1784, AE. CP. Ang. 547 f. 281. Chammorel was another sceptical envoy, Chammorel to Dubois, 4 June 1722, AE. CP. Ang. 341 f. 116.

107. Walpole to Waldegrave, 23 Feb. (ns) 1735, Chewton.

108. *Whisperer*, 5 Oct. 1771; *Felix Farley's Bristol Journal*, 24 Mar. 1787.

109. *St. James's Weekly Journal*, 26 Oct. 1717; *Scotchman*, 25 Jan. 1772.

110. *Felix Farley's Bristol Journal*, 10 Jan. 1789; *Newcastle Courant*, 18 June 1743.

111. *Craftsman*, 24 Feb. 1728; *Mist's Weekly Journal*, 23 Mar. 1728; *London Evening Post*, 4 Nov. 1742; *St. James's Chronicle*, 3 May 1766.

112. *Fog's Weekly Journal*, 16 Nov. 1728; D. Greenwood, *William King* (Oxford, 1969), pp. 77–9; *St. James's Chronicle*, 4 Dec. 1764.

113. *General Evening Post*, 16 Nov. 1742; *Westminster Journal*, 22 June 1745, 2 Mar. 1771. *Reading Mercury*, 21 Sept. 1772; Monteage diary, BL. Althorp Mss. E13 f. 2.

114. *Caledonian Mercury*, 6 July 1768.

115. *Newcastle Courant*, 30 July 1743.

116. *Newcastle Courant*, 7 Sept. 1745.

117. Black, *British Foreign Policy in the Age of Walpole*, p. 164; *Letters on Various subjects . . . to and from William Nicolson* (2 vols., 1809, cont. pag.), II, 435; *Cirencester Flying Post*, 23 Aug. 1742; Robert Douglas to Earl of Morton, 25 Aug. 1742, SRO. GD. 150/3485/8; Francis Lord Hastings to Earl of Huntingdon, 19 Feb. 1742, HMC., *Rawdon-Hastings*, III, 35; *Leeds Mercury*, 4 Dec. 1787; Diary of Dr Wilkes, London, Wellcome Institute for the History of Medicine, p. 47.

8 English Enlightenment or Fillers? Improvement, Morality and Religion

The ridiculous notion of witches and witchcraft still prevails amongst the lower sort of people, as the following account will sufficiently evince.

Reading Mercury, 15 March 1773

Among the middling and lower class of people some real hospitality yet exists — but in the higher order, nothing but vanity or avarice is consulted . . . at present the old substantials of the table are banished, and a nobleman cannot have an elegant dinner if there be a turkey, goose, duck, fowl, or any joint of mutton, beef, veal, or pork, visible on his table; all must be in disguise; and no man knows what he is going to eat, nor when he eats it, is he able to discover what it was, or the dish is unfashionable. With the banishment of the sirloin, buttock, and chine, hospitality took its farewell of great men's houses, and with the fripperies of French dinners came the parade of French nothingness, attended by cooks, hairdressers and valets . . .

Sheffield Advertiser, 1 January 1790, article on Christmas

The resurrection, and a general judgment, (essentials in the belief of a Christian) are the most awful ideas that can possibly occupy the human mind. How depraved and reprobate must the wretch be, who can sport with such sentiments! What tie can society have upon the miscreant who dares to jest with a subject at once so solemn, so interesting, and so sublime!

Leeds Mercury, 4 July 1795, beginning account of one such

Although political news, particularly that of foreign lands, was the dominant element of the eighteenth-century British press, both metropolitan and provincial, English and non-English, instruction was a recurrent theme. Instruction took many forms ranging from the literature of social manners, that drew heavily on periodicals such as the *Spectator*, to didactic religious material. Two features that clearly characterised the full range of this material were a didactic tone and a content that differed little, if at all, from that of other periodicals, particularly magazines. Much of this material was contributed by correspondents. It was most common in weeklies, both London and provincial, less characteristic of dailies and tri-weeklies. This reflected the differing nature of various types of paper. 'Philalethes', writing in *Applebee's Original Weekly Journal* in 1722, differentiated weeklies from 'common daily newspapers' and urged the former to insert material on the arts and sciences.[1] The weeklies approximated most closely to magazines in terms of content, and readers appear to have expected reflective essays or shorter pieces which were less common in papers that stressed their 'Advertiser' character. Conduct literature, such as the 'Babler' essays printed in *Owen's Weekly Chronicle* from 1763 to 1767, was uncommon in the dailies. The increased number of words in the papers of the end of the century, achieved by smaller print, larger size and more columns, ensured that instructive material was not sacrificed to the pressure of more advertising or economic, sport and theatrical reports. It also enabled papers to offer several brief essays or reflective items. It could be suggested that long parliamentary reports, with their lengthy accounts of speeches rich in righteousness and rhetoric, served as a partial substitute for political essays. There was no equivalent substitution for the moral essays.

The didactic tone of instructive items was in keeping with the tone adopted for political reflections. There was little suggestion of anything to be discussed. Most pieces displayed a certainty that reflected an attitude that the reader would share the suppositions and intentions of the author. Preceptive rather than persuasive, instructive items were directed not at rival views requiring intellectual challenge but at like-minded readers. The general thrust of the articles was on the need for action by those holding similar views. Many were appeals to sympathetic magistrates, and most were aimed at intractable popular beliefs and practices. These customs were not treated sympathetically. Moral righteousness, religious conviction and the quest for improvement combined to ensure that the people were defined as a problem and treated as an undifferentiated mass that clung to past habits through superstition, ignorance, irreligion, indolence and folly. Improvement could not be and was not regarded as a secular matter. Morality was central to the fight to coerce popular beliefs and accustomed practices. Enlightenment was religious in its rationale. The drive for improvement and reform entailed criticism of aristocratic excess, but it was not politically radical. Authority was necessary, the poor were the problem. Just as newspapers, both ministerial and opposition, differentiated clearly in the political sphere, until the French Revolution, between liberty and licence, the people, who were to be appealed to and their opinions sought, and the mob who had to be kept from the portals of power, so there could be no appeal to the populace for social reform. However corrosive print might be potentially as a medium for the transmission of social and political ideas, newspapers tended to be hierarchical and conservative in their assumptions. Suspicion of popular beliefs and customs and the feeling that they must be improved was very marked in newspapers produced in towns such as Sheffield and Leeds experiencing significant economic change in the last decades of the century. Industrialisation might produce social dislocation and a labour force that it was felt required moral discipline, but the instructive attitudes of newspapers at the end of the century were not new. They could be found throughout the century, reflecting the continuity of customs and beliefs that moralists and bigots felt required correction.

The press as an agent of instruction was not simply a medium of middle-class morality or a catechism for class-discipline. Different views were advanced. Social behaviour was a matter for discussion that was not always didactic. Nevertheless one of the more interesting developments in the press was that the growth of local material, both news and opinion, in the provincial press which is a characteristic feature of the second half of the century, provided an opportunity for, and may have reflected, growing local expression of instructive views. These views were not dependent on metropolitan opinion, though in the case of certain campaigns, such as that against the slave trade, there was an important element of national interest and stimulus. In carrying this material the provincial press developed an important facet independent of metropolitan control. The relatively circumscribed public nature of local political life and strong interest in national and international news which was still very largely obtained from the London press, contrasted with the increased possibilities for the provincial press of expressing opinion or printing that of correspondents on other aspects of local life. One of the crucial developments in the nineteenth century was to be the emancipation of the provincial press from the control, if not the influence, of London opinion and news, a change that can be seen forcefully by contasting newspapers of 1789, such as the *Leeds Intelligencer*, with their descendants a century later. The increase in instructive material printed in the provincial press of the last decades of the eighteenth century was an important preparation for this development. It is also worth considering and quoting as it buries for good the view of the provincial papers of this period as devoid of opinion, interested only in advertising and dependent for the rest of their contents on a scissors and paste approach to the London press.

Making the profane tremble: religion and the press

> We have an account of a very extraordinary instance of the Divine Vengeance that happened about a week ago, at Chalford. One Richard Parsons, a young man of that place, was playing at cards, and he most prophanely wished his flesh might rot, and his eyes never shut, if he did not win the next game. When he was going to bed he observed a black spot upon his leg, from which a mortification began . . . he died in a day or two, his flesh being quite rotten; nor could his eyes be shut, notwithstanding all the efforts of his friends to close them. The truth of this fact is attested by many of the neighbours who were with him — *Read it ye Prophane, and tremble*!
> *Berrow's Worcester Journal*, 20 March 1766

> To form an accurate and sublime view of the dispensations of Providence, we should at the same time consider the sovereignty of the Supreme Governor, and the free-agency of the instruments which he employs.
> Foreign News section of *Weekly Register*, 25 April 1798

The amount of space devoted to religious and ecclesiastical topics in the press was less than might be expected given the central importance of religion in terms of ideology and morality. Several reasons can be suggested for this contrast. Religious developments produced less newsworthy material and events than the world of politics. Legal and social restrictions inhibited much discussion as blasphemous. In 1718 Richard Burridge of the *Weekly Journal, or the British Gazetteer* and in 1729 James Pitt of the *London Journal* were charged with blasphemy. Religious controversies tended to be waged in pamphlets, their length and independence possibly more conducive for clerical authors. It was not the custom for newspapers to print theological speculation, and as the press proceeded to a great extent by emulation and plagiarism, this was probably of great significance. Readers did not apparently expect to read much religious material in their newspapers and papers did not expect to print it. Therefore it was less frequent than might otherwise have been expected.

Periodicals devoted to religious topics tended to be produced by nonconformists. There is little sign that Anglicans found it necessary or prudent to support newspapers adopting a particular line. They had no need to launch a newspaper war with other confessions. To do so would have entailed surrendering their powerful position for one of equality and dialogue. A strident defence of the Anglican position and assault on that of the Dissenters would also have been politically controversial. An acceptance of the legal position of Dissenters was part of the religious settlement forced upon the Church of England by Whig ministries after 1714 and maintained by detailed control over church patronage. Defence of the church and attacks upon Dissenters came largely from the Tory newspapers, which the bishops could not support. Mist claimed that 'the Whig News-Writers are the sole patrons of blasphemers'. The *Orphan*, a Jacobite paper of 1720, attacked the Dissenters. The *Loyal Observator* of 1722–3, a paper with clear Jacobite sympathies, devoted a lot of space to the church. Its primary purpose was to present the cause of the high churchmen in an entertaining manner, and it both ridiculed low-church Anglican clergy, who wished to unite with the Dissenters, and supported the attacks on the latter by Francis Atterbury. The paper also defended the church against attacks by other newspapers. Tory papers remained firmly opposed to giving more rights to Dissenters. Indicative of the committed attitude of George Hill, the printer of the *Cirencester Flying-Post*, in 1744 was his printing of a London item condemning any repeal of the Text Act:

> The well-wishers to the present constitution (who are one thousand to one, throughout the whole Kingdom) think there's no occasion to use any endeavours to defeat them of their

design; because they suppose the Legislature will be of opinion with a judicious author, 'that whenever the Toleration breaks in upon the Establishment, or the Establishment upon the Toleration, the peace of this Kingdom would be at an end'.[2]

In 1742 and 1743 Hill published editions of two theological works.

These views were not supported by papers of a different political persuasion. Attacking the Nonjurors in 1702 the *Observator* claimed,

> To argue with men who have abandoned reason, is but a fruitless labour; but such as have just notions of the happiness of England, must allow that the Church Establish'd can never subsist upon a better foundation, than on that of *Lenity* and *Temper* towards such as differ from her only in circumstantials of Religion.

In 1718 the *Whitehall Evening Post* argued the need to end laws against Dissenters, claiming that only Jacobites disagreed.[3] There was some Anglican interest in the press. In 1731 Thomas Sherlock, Bishop of Bangor, sought to have a speech he had made in Parliament published anonymously in the *Daily Courant* and 'in the evening papers, which go further into the country'. A year later an Anglican cleric William Webster, under the pseudonym of Richard Hooker, founded the *Weekly Miscellany*, an excellent paper whose essays were commonly devoted to religious topics often directed against the Dissenters. The paper lasted until 1741 when it was replaced by the *New Weekly Miscellany* which proclaimed political impartiality and an attack on 'irreligion, schism and enthusiasm'. Thomas Secker, who was appointed Archbishop of Canterbury in 1758, despite the fears of some Whigs that he was hostile to Dissenters, wrote pseudonymously for the press on religious topics.[4]

Most religious newspapers were non-Anglican. A leading London Dissenting minister Samuel Chandler founded the *Old Whig* in 1735 as a Dissenting newspaper. More common were essay publications lacking any news section devoted to politics. A series of Calvinistic Methodist journals were published between 1740 and 1745 under successive titles: the *Christian's Amusement*, the *Weekly History* and *An Account of the Progress of the Gospel*. Other papers were brought out by friends of George Whitefield.

William McCulloch produced a weekly in Glasgow in 1742 sold only to subscribers at a ha'penny, the *Glasgow-Weekly-History Relating to the Late Progress of the Gospel at Home and Abroad; Being a collection of letters partly reprinted from the London-Weekly-History, and partly printed first at Glasgow.* The *Christian Monthly History* (1743–4) was produced in Edinburgh and the *Christian History* (1743–5) in Boston, Massachusetts. The latter, a weekly, announced that it would 'be wholly confined to *Matters* of *Religion*, and no Advertisement inserted but of Books and Pamphlets or other Things of a religious Importance'. It appealed for authentic accounts of religious revival and interspersed them with religious writings. After two years it became a quarterly. In 1750–1 John Gillies, a leading Glaswegian evangelical minister, issued a weekly sermon, an *Exhortation to the Inhabitants of South Parish of Glasgow.* Another shortlived essay-paper was the London weekly *Man* of 1755. This offered morality and Christianity, rather than advertisements or news, and ended with the year: 'For the future it is thought more advisable to continue the design of these papers in pocket-volumes, occasionally, than in single sheets.' Arguably the newspaper was not the most suitable form for religious literature and it is significant that the Methodists, who were well aware of the value of print and produced a lot of tracts and serial material, displayed relatively little interest in founding newspapers. They were however adept at inserting material in the press.[5]

Sunday newspapers were not devoted substantially to religious topics. The first, *E. Johnson's British Gazette, and Sunday Monitor*, which began in about 1779, was in appearance and content like any daily paper with the exception of the first column of the first page which was headed 'For the Sunday Monitor' and provided religious instruction. The items in the first three issues of 1798 were headed 'Goodness proved to be a Divine Perfection', 'Moral evil consistent with the Divine Goodness', and 'The Creation of Mankind a Proof of the Divine Goodness'. A series of Sunday papers were founded in the 1780s and 1790s including *Ayre's Sunday London Gazette*, the *London Recorder, Sunday Chronicle, Review, Sunday Reformer, Observer, Bell's Weekly Messenger*, and the *Weekly Register.* The last, founded in 1798, and in some respect a counterpart of the *Anti-Jacobin*, announced in its first issue:

The late rapid and alarming spread of Infidelity and even Atheism, calls aloud for union of all serious Christians, on the most enlarged scale . . . The Press is certainly the most powerful engine which can be applied to the public mind; and, of all its productions, newspapers appear the most effective, because circulated to the greatest extent, and read by thousands with avidity, who scarcely ever read any other publication. That these are too generally employed in the cause of Scepticism, Vice, and Faction, cannot be denied: and to wrest this weapon from the hands of the enemy, and use it with energy in the cause of Religion, Virtue, and Social Union . . . show the harmony subsisting between the dispensations of Divine Providence and Scriptures. Occasional facts and observations will be introduced in favour of natural and revealed Religion . . . Ever cautious to guard the morals of the rising generation, we shall exclude the vain diversions of the Theatre, and every other source of mental dissipation: we shall endeavour to strip off the meretricious ornaments of Vice, to draw aside the gaudy robe of Pleasure and to show the worm that preys within. And when our Readers require entertainment . . . we shall point them to it in the various branches of useful and polite literature, in the progress of the Arts and Sciences, and, above all, in the Christian luxury of *doing good*.

In early issues the paper rejected a contributor's love song as an unsuitable kind of item, printed part of the Bishop of Durham's charge to his clergy against infidelity and, attacking novels as likely to lead people away from the Bible, urged writers to fear divine punishment and to destroy them.[6]

Religious material was not confined to papers with such a didactic purpose. W. A. Speck has discerned a shift away from religion as the prime concern of polemicists after about 1720.[7] The revelation by the Eighteenth-Century Short Title Catalogue project of numerous printed works hitherto unstudied may lead to some reassessment of this view, though it is true that in terms of the subjects of the leading essays of newspapers in any given year of the century politics was clearly dominant over religion. Lady Wortley Montagu complained about printers being uninterested in moral papers.[8] There was however a large and varied amount of religious material in the press. Very little was doctrinal or theological and most of it could serve the purposes of any denomination. The letter in the *Leeds Mercury* of 1795 on the integrity of Moses was less typical than the Sabbatarian article eight years earlier warning of the dangers of bathing rather than attending Sunday School.[9]

A certain amount of the religious news was confessional. The continued perception of Catholicism as a political, moral and religious threat which was such a marked feature of eighteenth-century British public discourse was reflected in the press. 'A Protestant' writing in the *General Advertiser* warned in 1780, 'Popery retains all her anathemas and her terrors, and only waits a proper opportunity to resume her power of prosecuting and oppressing mankind.' Anti-Catholicism was in many respects the prime ideological commitment in Britain, and though it was not incompatible with good relations with individual Catholics and peaceful relations with the Catholic community, it was marked in the press, particularly in discussion of the plight of Protestants abroad. The sufferings of the Huguenots in France were reported in considerable detail.[10] In 1752 the press was used to spread information about a new society for helping Huguenots to emigrate to Britain.[11] It was only in the late 1780s, prompted partly by a liberalisation of French policy towards the Huguenots, that support was expressed in the British press for more rights for Catholics. Intolerant towards Catholics, the press also served for the pursuance of Protestant feuds. Methodists were often mocked, particularly in anecdotes revealing them as the dupes of lascivious preachers. The *Leeds Intelligencer* carried a story in 1767 about a comedian passing himself off as a preacher.[12] Tithes and other privileges of the Church of England, as well as the behaviour of Anglican clerics, provided material for abuse and disputes.[13] The Anglican Feathers Tavern petition for relief from the 39 Articles appeared in many provincial as well as London papers.[14] There was considerable press interest in the position of the Dissenters and in particular their campaigns against the Test Act. In 1772 the committee of the Dissenting ministers pressing Parliament were driven to advertise in the press because of a false report about them in the *Public Advertiser*. Far from the press supporting the cause of reform, many newspapers were hostile, or printed hostile material, sometimes for political reasons. In 1787 the *Morning Chronicle* warned, 'The Dissenters will do wrong to push matters to an extremity. They should remember, that an over active zeal may be apt to excite a similar spirit in the opponents of their schemes of reform, as they are pleased to call their innovations.' The *Leeds Intelligencer* in

March 1790 published several letters attacking the repeal of the Test. One, from A.B. of Leeds, noted,

> Since last year, a reinforcement of *reasons for laying all things open* has been imported from France, and we are reproached with falling so far short of the *liberality of sentiment* displayed in that kingdom. I love liberty as well as any man, but not that particular species of it, which allows only seven minutes to prepare for death, before one is hanged up by fish-women at a lamp iron; and though superstition be a very bad thing, I hope never to see the British National Assembly possessed by the Spirit of Voltaire.

The paper also printed letters from both points of view, including an attack on Joseph Priestley for Socinianism. Most of these letters were clearly paid for, 'the terms of admission to all pieces on the subject of controversy'.

The attack on the privileges of the Church of England had a clear radical component and an obvious appeal to opposition political elements at the time of the French Revolution. The *Argus* declared itself a friend 'to the Civil and Religious Liberties of Mankind . . . to Religious as well as Political Freedom'.[15] This definition of progressive behaviour for a newspaper was not accepted by most papers. Just as most papers condemned political corruption and the excesses of conspicuous consumption without seeking constitutional reform or social revolution, so many pressed for a clearer moral attitude, based on a religious framework, towards life, without concerning themselves excessively with ecclesiastical politics or theological issues. Far from being a force corrosive of conservative values, or in some way marginal to the traditional beliefs of the bulk of the population, the press was novel largely only in its form. As with many new or expanding developments of the century, ranging from the circulating library to the subscription concert, the magazine to the Assembly rooms, it is important not to mistake the novelty of the form for an altered perception of life. The newsmen who distributed the *Cirencester Flying-Post* in the Cotswolds in 1742 also carried 'the works of Tillotson, Stackhouses' History of the Bible, Dr. Clarke's sermons, Burkitt on the New Testament'. Providing a scientific explanation of a recent meteor, 'Thunder-Bolt' was nevertheless anxious to locate it in the divine plan:

. . . why must God's Goodness and Mercy any more than his Vengeance and Justice be tied up, so that he cannot make use of such Things as these when he thinks fit, as well as to warn and foretell what the World are to expect from Him if they change not their wicked courses; we see His Power uses them to chastise the World . . . Had the Hand of Heaven no Influence to guide the Flash that set those Places on Fire? . . . Let us . . . not take such pains to remove these appearances out of the Disposition of Providence.

An essay on the earth's structure printed in the *Leeds Intelligencer* in 1766 claimed that earthquakes were best avoided by leading 'a life conformable to the gospel'.[16]

Such a life was also pressed by many newspapers and their correspondents. Aside from printing admonitory tales on such topics as 'Almighty vengeance for profane swearing and violation of the Sabbath',[17] associating God with Britain's political situation[18] and finding providence at work in the harvest,[19] papers also preached moral behaviour with direct reference to scriptural precepts. Charity and fortitude were enjoined, Sabbatarianism praised. 'One of the first charities in the gospel is visiting prisoners', observed 'Benevolus' in the *Sheffield Advertiser* in 1787 and he urged readers to follow this precept. Concerned about the grain shortage the *Leeds Mercury* preached restraint in 1795: 'As men we should bear with resolution, and as Christians, with cheerfulness and submission, the transient evils of the day.'[20]

It was possibly in providing this moral perspective on instruction and enlightenment that religious considerations had their greatest impact on the press. Daniel Baugh has recently suggested that one of the distinctive features of early eighteenth-century English Christianity was its inclination to incorporate secular wisdom wherever possible.[21] This could be rephrased to stress the absence of any perception of necessary division between the secular and the religious. The strength of lay piety, Anglican as well as Dissenter, and the importance of philanthropic education, ensured that newspaper readers perceived social issues from a moral viewpoint. Many of the poorer readers would have been educated in charity and Sunday schools, schools applauded by the press. In 1789 the *Leeds Intelligencer* praised the parish of Hornbury for building a Sunday school in thanks for the recovery of George III, 'a more *rational* instance of thanks to God, and of loyalty to the best of Kings, than the Bacchanalian slaughter of a thousand sheep on a thousand hills'. Two years earlier a quarter of a million children were attending Sunday charity schools.[22]

'These are not the days of Superstition', proclaimed the *World* in 1792 when the crown slipped on George III's head. In some circles this may have been true, but that did not necessarily make religious faith any less strong, and alongside 'West-End' papers that concentrated on fashionable society and had little to say about morality, London also produced in the late 1780s new periodicals such as the *Family Magazine*; *or a Repository of Religious Instruction and Rational Amusement-Designed to counteract the pernicious tendency of immoral books*, a new monthly launched in 1788. Felix Farley of Bristol was a keen supporter of the Wesleys, while Robert Raikes the Younger, owner of the *Gloucester Journal*, was active in the Sunday School movement. In such a context it was most appropriate for the press to adopt a moral stance derived from religious norms. Britain was still a Christian society in 1800, and though the evangelical movement might have little direct contact with traditional practices, the resilience of the latter, even when despised, ensured that the evangelical character of many newspaper contributions was not as marginal as their embattled tone might suggest. An unsympathetic report in the *Leeds Intelligencer* of 1790 was a testimony of the strength of traditional moral beliefs:

A carrier, between Aldstone and Penrith, lately had some goods stolen out of his waggon. In order to detect the thief, he made a *pilgrimage* to Rumbles Moor near Skipton in Craven, to consult the *Wise Man* who resides there, and who, having received the carrier's *offering*, dismissed him with the *consolatory* assurance, that if the thief did not restore the property before a certain day, — 'it should be *worse for him*!' — The carrier's reports of these *oracular* words had a wonderful, and as it happened, a beneficial effect on his neighbours . . . they having *wisdom* enough to know that in order to effect this the *Wise Man* must inevitably *raise the devil*, — and the devil, through vexation, would most probably *raise the wind*, — they loaded the thatched roofs of their houses with harrows, etc. which prevented the fatal consequences of a violent hurricane that came on in the night, and was felt in most parts of the kingdom. There can be no doubt that this circumstance will add considerably to the high opinion already entertained of *The Wise Robin* of Rumbles-Moor.[23]

The drive for a well-ordered society

A correspondent at Banbury in Oxfordshire, has sent us a most shocking account of a *Bull-baiting*, which we find annually takes place there at Michaelmas. After the poor animal has been baited for several hours, it was dragged round the town with ropes, amidst the shouts of a barbarous (barbarous in every sense) multitude . . . What are the magistrates and what are the clergy about on such occasions? If the latter would but use their influence to humanize the lower classes it would do more good than all their philippics against French Atheism, etc.

Item from *Cambridge Intelligencer* in *Iris*, 2 November 1798

Much of the instruction printed in the press was not didactic in tone. Humour was often used as a means of persuasion, as in the *Universal Spectator* (1728–47) or the *Connoisseur* in 1754. There was no sharp break between instruction and information, and the press, particularly the weekly papers in the second half of the century, was not short of the latter. There was no shortage of material, provided largely by correspondents but also available from books. Printing of such material helped to lessen the differences between papers and magazines. An anonymous essay in *Berrow's Worcester Journal* in 1769 claimed 'almost every newspaper is now a magazine'. A lot of informative material was scientific, with a particular interest in astronomy.[24] A wide variety of topics was covered, with a clear stress on the spectacular. Readers could expect accounts of the discovery of uncorrupted flesh in a quarry near Hartlepool and the dissection of an Egyptian mummy, the analogy between animals and vegetables and 'singular instances of subterraneous fires'. The general aim of the items was explanatory, providing logical, clear accounts of natural and man-made phenomena, such as the Question and Answer dialogue technique used in 1783 by the *Reading Mercury* to explain balloons, one of the great interests of the period.[25] In 1742 the *Newcastle Courant* reprinted an item from a London paper explaining one such phenomenon:

We hear from Canterbury that last Friday, about noon, a large ball of fire was seen to pass over that city, which was follow'd by a storm that broke almost all the windows in the town; and next morning three suns appeared in the sky, attended with a rainbow inverted, which lasted from nine till twelve to the astonishment of the inhabitants.

The item continued in a different type, 'But these phaenomena, after such sultry summers as the last are frequently to be met with in Historians, and are as natural and innocent as a comet, or an Aurora Borealis.' Evidence of public interest came in the form of replies to mathematical problems. In July 1743 the *Newcastle Courant* printed a controversy between two mathematicians offering their problems to the public. That December 'The Lilliputian' wrote to the paper, 'Your mathematical correspondents grow so numerous of late, that unless some task be assigned them, we shall know no end to their debates.' In 1788 a question printed in the *Leeds Mercury* attracted several replies.[26] The literary coverage of the press also permitted a response by readers in terms of purchasing books or going to see plays. Interest was not restricted to British works, the *Flying-Post* of 1723 offering extracts from the Bibliothèque Germanique, the *Weekly Miscellany* printing regular accounts of new European books in the 1730s. Some periodicals specialised in literary matters. In 1734 *Cotes's Weekly Journal: or, The English Stage-Player* appeared providing both news and plays. However, generalist journals were more common than specialist works in the eighteenth-century periodical world, both newspaper and magazine. This was particularly the case with theatrical news which became a regular feature of the press. Newspapers did not hesitate to tell their readers what they ought to think of particular plays and of the purposes of theatre. In 1787 the *Morning Chronicle* criticised the production of the tragedy *Julia*: 'On Saturday evening, it was half an hour after nine o'clock before the curtain dropped, after the Epilogue was delivered; nine o'clock ought to be the period of conclusion.'[27]

Instructive information was also provided in the case of health. The wealth of medical advertising was supported by accounts of cures in the news sections of the press. Newspapers and their correspondents offered remedies for every possible illness, some making a regular feature of such items. In 1742 the *Newcastle Journal* extracted 'for the benefit of the public' possible cures for rabies contained in 'a letter from an ingenious correspondent in Bishop Auckland'. The *Remembrancer* inserted cures for the stone in 1748 'for the general information, and benefit of Mankind'. The *General Advertiser* ran a regular medical column, with features such as 'Advice to the Asthmatic', in 1780 and provided prescriptions at the newspaper office. In 1743 the *Newcastle Courant* printed an account of a successful trepanning of the skull in Garstang, ending 'this shows the usefulness of the trepan'. The frequency with which cures for illnesses, both human and animal, were printed reflected a popular interest in health, a supply of plentiful material for the newspapers and a belief that this was an acceptable function for the press. Cures were printed in large numbers in both the London and the provincial press, though they were less common in the first three decades of the century than thereafter. It could be suggested that they benefited from the increase in the size and diversification of the contents of individual papers. In reporting matters of health provincial papers were not as dependent on the metropolitan press as in matters of politics. Typical of both the interest in curious cases and the increased extent to which provincial papers took their items from each other, with or without London intermediaries, was the account taken from the *Ipswich Journal* of a recently deceased person with extremely weak bones printed under a London byline in the *Newcastle Chronicle* in January 1787.[28]

Health and literary judgements were not the only spheres in which the press provided advice, advice offered commonly without any suggestion that an alternative existed. Newspapers warned of the dangers of deadly nightshade and gunpowder accidents, of bathing where there were weeds, of the need for precautions against fires and for rails along the river at Reading, of the dangers of eating too many hazel nuts, 'hard of digestion, clogging to the stomach, and hurtful to the breath', and of firing pistols near barns.[29] They also called for action, the banning of begging and the moving of the poor to workhouses, 'useful necessary and elegant' urban improvements, such as those 'A Lover of Useful and Elegant Improvements' urged on Reading in order to induce 'several families of rank' to live there, the setting up of schools 'for instructing indigent blind persons' for useful employment while paying 'the strictest attention' to their morals, and the adoption of a new method of baking bread for the army that would be of 'general utility'.[30] Not all the advice was humourless. 'Rebecca Lightfoot' made her point about London chairmen jostling women so that their stockings were splashed in an amusing fashion, and the use of an open umbrella to scare off ferocious bulls could also be advocated. Many moral essays continued to adopt a traditional pattern modelled on those of the *Spectator*, frequently treating the same subjects, adopting the same approach and taking the same tone. The essay by 'The Gallant' on women following fashion printed by the *London Packet* in 1787 could easily have been written seventy years earlier. 'Lucretia' in the *Reading Mercury* of 1767 returned to another traditional theme with her attack on men marrying for money.[31]

However, the press took seriously, at the very least to the extent of printing numerous pieces by contributors, its self-proclaimed function of, as the *Hull Packet* put it, improving the mind, as well as conveying early and useful information.[32] It is clear from the pieces sent in to many newspapers, and possibly inserted by the printers themselves using pseudonyms, that there was in some circles a pressure for social reform. This was most marked in the press of the 1780s and early 1790s. Pressure for the reformation of society and manners deriving partly from Anglican lay piety had also been a feature of the early decades of the century, but the widespread expression of these views in newspapers depended on the growth and diversification of the press. It could be suggested that it was also related to political developments. The 1760s, 1770s and early 1780s were a period of domestic political strife and conflict in America which provided plenty of interesting copy for the press. From 1793 on Britain was at war with revolutionary France and political and popular attention was devoted to this conflict. Newspapers reflected this by extending their coverage of European news, improving their sources, stressing the speed and superiority of their news and using devices to increase excitement such as headlines and announcements that they had stopped the presses to insert late items. The intervening period was one of political stability in Britain, lesser concern about European developments, particularly in the mid-1780s, a more sympathetic attitude to the idea of reform in some quarters, and the expression of evangelical views on social questions such as the slave trade. The latter was the most significant instance of the manner in which campaigns on such questions provided interesting material for the press. As political campaigns, such as that for economical reform in 1780, had shown, petitions, demonstrations, public meetings, dinners, instructions and addresses could provide an interesting variety of material based on newsworthy events that all tended to the same end and produced a cumulative impression that this represented the general will of all reasonable people. In terms of making social issues interesting in the press, events, whether the calamities of the reprobate or the resolutions of meetings of the godly, were of greater value than general moral reflections, and this was well appreciated by many late eighteenth-century papers, and their correspondents. These writers benefited from the existence of a campaigning attitude, that in some cases, as with slavery, extended to an organisation. The press could serve a variety of purposes. In 1777 'Benevolus' wrote to the printer of the *Reading Mercury*, 'The methods used by the Society formed at Amsterdam, for the benefit of the drowned, being little known to the public, and more general knowledge of them being likely to conduce to the preservation of many lives . . .'. He instructed him to print a thousand copies of the methods suitable for framing and to deliver them free where the paper was circulated. Newspapers could encourage charitable subscriptions,[33] and discourage potential lawbreakers by providing information of likely penalties. In 1789 Sir John Riggs Miller MP sent a circular letter to magistrates and newspaper printers seeking information and instructions to support his campaign for a uniform national standard of weights and measures. Two years later the High Bailiff of Birmingham published in the local papers the names of tradesmen using false measures.[34]

Slavery excited a lot of interest in the press. Most of the material printed was opposed to the slave trade and provided details of the campaign against it. Meetings and subscriptions were announced and reported. Some letters supporting the trade were however published. The *Oracle*, under the heading 'SLAVE TRADE' printed one such in 1792 after the announcement:

Opinions on this subject deserve attention, in proportion to the fair opportunities of forming them, without interested designs, or from motives of prejudice; we therefore give the following extract of a letter, written by a young gentleman, the son of a dissenting clergyman in the North of England, who was sent not long since to the West Indies, under the patronage of an eminent banker in London.

A fortnight later the *Argus* proclaimed that Wilberforce's campaign against slavery could 'calculate on success, for Reason and Truth want but to be exhibited in their proper lights, to force conviction on the most reluctant mind'. This confidence was misplaced as the trade was not to be abolished until 1807, but there is no doubt that the skilful use of printed propaganda helped to achieve widespread publicity for the cause throughout the country and to make it an issue of conscience for those inclined to adopt a religious perspective on national issues. In 1789 the *Leeds Intelligencer* reported the collection of £18 for supporting the application to Parliament for repeal 'raised by voluntary contributions in a small part of the high end of Wensleydale . . . The contributors (being chiefly farmers) were informed of the injustice and inhumanity of the slave trade by pamphlets circulated previous to the collection'.[35]

Drink was another evil castigated in the press. General attacks were joined with stories 'of the fatal effects of intemperance'. Parliamentary action was demanded 'to correct a malady that affects the very vitals of the State — that preys on her industry — dissipates her wealth — and renders her people debilitated, vicious and miserable'. Aside from the obvious moral problems and the manner in which drink lubricated the fall into profanity, atheism, crime, sensuality and a host of other signs of indulgent individualism, alcohol was also attacked for causing dearth. 'Atticus Police', a regular contributor to the *Public Advertiser*, linked defeat and dearth to drink in 1757. Condemning the use of grain in alcohol for causing famine and mass poisoning he asked 'what hopes may not the French flatter themselves with, when they are to fight against Englishmen who are scorched in the womb by spiritous liquors and who suck gin from their mothers instead of milk'. In 1795 *Leeds Mercury* used capitalisation and large print to drive home its message that dearth was due to 'drinking too much spiritous liquors'.[36]

Popular pastimes were also condemned. The *Leeds Intelligencer* called for action in 1787 against 'bull-baiting, and cock-fighting, and such other diabolical practices' and suggested that 'the masters of alehouses who permit or connive at them, ought to be punished with the greatest severity'. Four years later a correspondent of the paper attacked bull-baiting, 'a disgrace to a civilized people' that produced depraved manners rather than amusement: "Tis pity, then, but those who make this a practice merely from *custom* would reflect upon the cruelty of it, and, by substituting any harmless diversion in its stead, do themselves a most permanent credit, and render a true service to the rising generation.' Boxing was not regarded with favour either: 'The blackguard entertainment of *boxing* is reviving a little: probably the bill "to enable magistrates to apprehend all disorderly persons, etc." may effectually *knock it down.*' A story underlined a point made in the *Leeds Intelligencer* in 1789:

> There is a practice but too common, and very dangerous, especially at this season of the year — we mean the cruel custom of fastening a tin can to the tail of a dog, from the pain of which the animal runs as long as he has strength, and often till he is in a state of madness. An instance of this lately occurred in London, which may perhaps induce those who have hitherto considered the operation as a *joke*, to reflect upon the consequences it is likely to produce.

The *Oxford Gazette* supported its condemnation of gambling by a salutary instance in 1767 and urged gamblers to donate winnings to the poor. The *Leeds Mercury* castigated the shooting of street lamps for fun and the *Sheffield Advertiser* warned that the sale of wives, frequent 'particularly among the lower class of people', was illegal.[37] Dogs were seen as a problem in Leeds and their taxation urged as a means to lessen the worrying of sheep and the consumption of food. The denial of parish relief to dog owners was suggested.[38]

Popular recreations were not the only activities that received attention. Relatively little concern was shown for poor women despite the extensive magazine-type literature devoted to women and social manners, and the growth in the number of women readers of the press. 'Civis''s articles on prostitution which appeared in the *London Packet* in 1787 dealt with a topic that received very little attention. 'Civis' urged the need for compassion, condemned infant prostitution and seducers and pressed for 'some plan to prevent this evil from growing greater, to reclaim those who are already involved, and perhaps, by the assistance of the legislature, to prevent seduction from being so very easy a crime as rakes and profligates find it to be, as to punishment'. More typical was the item in the *Leeds Mercury* eight years later that began, 'The following is given as a caution to young women, against the too frequent practice of their following private soldiers.'[39] Vagrants also received very little sympathy. Their removal to workhouses was supported and they were blamed for crime. Pedlars and hawkers were condemned as receivers of stolen goods or sellers of inferior products, and the need for dealing with disorderly people at fairs was stressed. The press-ganging of gypsies was suggested.[40] Anti-social behaviour was castigated. Cruelty to animals was condemned, the *Newcastle Chronicle* announcing 'mercy to beasts is a duty'. The mistreating of hired horses was attacked in the *Sheffield Advertiser* and the *Leeds Intelligencer* in March 1790, only one example of what appears to have been a sharing of news by the two papers.[41] The parading of stallions through crowded market places, the taking of stone from old buildings, public dinners at times of dearth, and calumnies, were condemned, and the salutary effect of whipping the idle and disorderly applauded.[42] A letter in the *Westminster Journal* of 18 September 1773 recommended the beating of children for swearing. The justification for such exhortations varied. At times there was clear reference to self-interest, as in a piece in the *Leeds Intelligencer* in 1791:

It now becomes necessary to remind the public not to throw pea and bean shells, or other offal of greens, upon the foot pavement; a practice which is productive of many fatal accidents — Masters and mistresses would do well to look strictly into the conduct of their servants. — No one knows who may be the sufferer through such carelessness.

This was not too dissimilar from certain medical injunctions,[43] and was not combative in tone. Very different was a piece in the same paper four years earlier:

A correspondent observes, that it must give an heart-felt satisfaction to every honest man, every lover of peace and good order, to see magistrates, peace officers, and principal inhabitants in many parts throughout this riding, persevering in the laudable resolution of supporting the law of the land by every proper exertion . . . they must of course have a troop of enemies to contend with, some prompted by interest, or ignorance, others actuated by their own depraved notions, and not a few from mere *opposition only*:- but in God's name, what is all this for? What else but to discredit those who are solicitous only to make mankind happier and better? — to oblige disorderly persons to stay at their own *homes*, and there to be honest and industrious:- to punish irregular alehouse-keepers, tiplers, and sabbath-breakers:- in short, to bring offenders of every kind to public justice.[44]

Thus in some papers a combative tone emerged on social matters similar to that which already characterised political debate in most of the press. It was not limited to papers produced in areas of industrialisation, as the *Reading Mercury* showed, and can tentatively be linked to a moral stance based on religious attitudes that encouraged a universalising approach to social problems and not one of judicious compromise, as much as to any sense of social tension engendered by economic change. It would be foolish to argue that the latter was irrelevant but it is the moral, rather than the economic, background to the attitudes expressed in such papers as those produced in Leeds, Newcastle and Sheffield that is most notable. The paternalist nature of the views and notices published in the press, with their frequent stress on charitable acts by the fortunate, is readily apparent. Newspapers devoted much favourable coverage to the cause of inoculation against smallpox. The account printed in *Read's Weekly Journal* in 1756 of how James Buller MP had himself and his family inoculated and encouraged his tenants and neighbours to follow was typical of the social arrangements extolled by the press. Paternalism grounded in moral behaviour and religious attitudes rather than economic dominance was the justification of the social policing required for the well-ordered society that was a necessary moral goal. In 1795 the *Leeds Mercury* noted,

It gives us peculiar pleasure to read in accounts from all parts of the country, of the liberal benefactions voluntarily bestowed upon the poor during the late inclement season, by those whose situation in life enables them to diffuse happiness; and we deem such conduct the best refutation of their arguments, who would persuade the lower class of society, against their interest, that exclusive rank and title are but political engines, tending to hold them in a state of abject dependence, subjection, and misery.[45]

The perception of social tension

The following anecdote may be depended on. Some time ago Lord Pomfret called at a bookseller's in the City, who takes in advertisements for one of the papers, to give in one for the sale of some lands. The bookseller (who did not know his lordship) seeing some grammatical errors in the advertisement, took up a pen, and was going to alter them, when his lordship stopped him short, with his *usual vehemence*: 'Come, come, Sir, print that as you see it; that's the style of a *gentleman*, not of a *mechanic*; my name is Pomfret, sir!' The bookseller made his best bow, dropt his pen, and the advertisement appeared new morning *with all the usual marks of quality*.

London report in *Newcastle Journal*, 16 January 1773

Newspapers were owned, produced and written by men who were neither part of landed society nor generally members of the urban oligarchies that governed most towns. Though read by men of wealth and position, most newspaper readers and advertisers were of unexalted social background. Britain was a society with gross economic, social and political inequalities, where mobility into the elite was very restricted. Over some issues, such as the free trade of grain, it was possible to oppose rural and urban interests. The unearned effortless political position of the landed orders with their seats in the Lords, influence over urban parliamentary constituencies, their mode of political operation, intensely personal, often dominated by considerations of patronage and within a small world in which everyone knew everyone else, contrasted with the position and mode of newspapermen, a public world in which individuals struggled for attention on behalf of causes that were stridently advocated.

Critical attitudes towards the landed orders were often expressed in the press. In a powerful attack in 1725 the *Plain Dealer* condemned the idea that trade debased lineage, an idea it claimed that was believed by 'the Indolent, and Unthinking, *Part* of our *Nobility* and *Gentry* . . . To the just, and lively, Observation, that a merchant ought to be qualified for a minister of state, I will add this wish, of my own, — that we may, never have a minister of state, who is not qualified for a merchant!'

Aristocratic recreations and activities were often lambasted, particularly if they entailed a costly preference for foreign imports or customs, such as Italian opera, Catholic dancing-masters, hairdressers and footmen, French eggs and turkeys and imported ice.[46] Luxury and conspicuous consumption were condemned. The *Connoisseur* attacked the vacuity of aristocratic gambling at White's in 1754. In 1791 the *Leeds Intelligencer* criticised a duel between two Cambridge students, an 'idle and unpardonable abuse of the word *honour*'. The following year under the headline

'Senators on a Holiday!' the *Gazetteer* painted an unedifying picture of the activities of parliamentarians not usually mentioned by political historians:

> There being no ballot, yesterday, in the House of Commons, some of the members, upon their return from thence, were inclined, as they could not have business, to find play. Accordingly, Colonel LENNOX, and seven or eight others, might have been seen in Cockspur-Street, pelting two of their friends in a hackney-coach, with a *composition* of dirt and snow made in the hand.

In 1795 a correspondent of the *Leeds Mercury* pressed for taxation 'to limit the number of lazy footmen', rather than 'to the inconveniency of small private families', and the following year the *Sun* hoped 'that the prosecutions to be instituted against the fashionable Gaming-Houses, at the west end of the Town, will be conducted with a degree of vigour, equal to the importance of their object'.[47]

Individual aristocrats could expect criticism. In 1788 the Duke of Bedford was condemned for departing from traditional charitable acts and preferring to spend £22,000 on new kennels at Woburn. Three years later the *World* announced, 'The Duke of Clarence's succession to the West-India station, has given much joy to his *petit jolie fille*. The applicants for Promotions are all to be addressed to this Lady.' Behaviour that departed from the paternalist image, such as that of the Duke of Bedford, was castigated. Commenting on the poor state of the economy, the *Leeds Mercury* noted in 1788, 'There are people cruel and inhuman enough to add horror to misery. A gentleman on the borders of Lancashire . . . has, at one time laid a distrain for rent on eighty of his tenants, who were incapable, from recent misfortunes, to make regular payment.'[48]

Individuals and what they represented were criticised, and many newspapers clearly differentiated between luxury and desirable social behaviour. The *Newcastle Courant* devoted a wartime leading essay to an attack upon luxury in 1747. 'Reflector', in another wartime piece in the *London Evening Post* of 1762, condemned 'that ruinous prevalence of following the fashions of the court which now infects the citizens of London'. Five years later an item in the *Public Advertiser* discerned one law for the rich and another for the poor, so that the cook must be sober, though her lady loves liquors. She must read her Bible and go to church, though her ladyship studies Hoyle and plays cards on Sundays. She must keep the commandments though her lady don't know one from t'other; and she must love and fear God though her lady never thinks at all about him.[49]

It is difficult to discern much of a chronological pattern in the social criticism that was printed. John Money has suggested that it was the food riots of the mid-1760s 'which first brought opinion at large to recognise that relationships between the different parts of English society which had hitherto been accepted as constant were already in the process of fundamental and irrevocable alteration'. John Brewer saw the 1760s as a crucial decade for the establishment of 'an alternative structure of politics'.[50] These judgements cannot be matched by any discernible development in social criticism in the press as a whole. The bitter attacks upon certain economic practices in the mid-1760s that appeared in the press can be linked to a rise in food prices. Attacks upon luxury were most common in periods of dearth when they represented an infringement of paternalist codes of conduct. To a certain extent the press of the 1760s had to reconsider the problem of political content. From 1738 to 1762 war and international relations dominated the press and provided the prime subject of domestic political debate. The latter was no longer true after 1762, and both the larger size of individual papers and the need to provide issues that could be used to make political points helped to lead to diversification in the political content of the press. It is interesting that so relatively little social criticism was printed, other than with reference to the dearth of 1766, and in this respect the 1760s were very similar to the 1770s and 1780s. The press was not of course designed as a recorder of social tension for the convenience of future historians, but reading the papers of the 1770s and 1780s it is easier to appreciate the social background against which first North and later Pitt rebuilt ministerial stability. Political stability had arguably never been lost, for the central political problem of the 1760s was a managerial rather than a structural one, the difficulty of finding a minister who would both enjoy royal confidence and control Parliament. The accession of a new monarch who dismissed his predecessor's ministers usually led to a period of ministerial instability as politicians tested their power. This was customary in European monarchies and had affected British

politics in 1714–21 after the accession of George I. The relative
ease with which North governed the country was a testimony to
the basic stability of the system. In 1781 the *Leeds Intelligencer*
claimed, 'If unanimity in Parliament is a just criterion of a minister's popularity, Lord North is certainly more popular than any of
his predecessors, since Lord Chatham went out of office.' North
and Pitt essentially fell, as Walpole and Newcastle had done, due
to external factors, war and imperial problems proving more intractable than domestic governance.

It was an external factor, the example and encouragement of
French political, social and religious radicalism, that helped to put
social tension on the political and newspaper agenda in the 1790s.
Newspapers that adopted a radical position were willing to express
criticism of aspects of British society. The *Argus* was particularly
blunt:

> We repeatedly read in the *mercenary* newspapers, that 'The
> King hunts today and to-morrow Lord Grenville gives a
> splendid dinner to all the Cabinet Ministers.' When shall we
> hear, that to-morrow His Majesty sits in Council, with a select
> number of experienced men, among his Privy Counsellors, to
> devise means for meliorating the hard condition of the poor, or
> making them more satisfied with their lot? and next day — the
> comfortable effects of their consultation will be made known to
> that *valuable*, because laborious, class of people, through the
> channel of the *Argus*.

The paper argued that good government would come from fear
of popular action, not paternalism:

> It is obvious to every discerning eye, that to obtain redress of
> any public grievance, Ministers must be stimulated by the
> vigilance of Opposition, and goaded on by apprehension of
> popular resentment.

The *Argus* saw the press as being involved in a struggle to bring
knowledge to the people that would enlighten them as to their
plight, and declared triumphantly in 1792,

> However strenuously the Ministerial Papers may labour to keep
> John Bull in ignorance, it is certain he begins to look about him,

and to ask the *why* and the *wherefore* of many things, which appear unnecessary and oppressive.

More typical of the non-ministerial press was the *Telegraph*, a London daily which called for official action on many fronts. It pressed 'the necessity of . . . a radical reform in the Commons' and 'legislative enquiries into the misfortunes of the country' and attacked the game laws. Its general tone was however hostility towards the abuses of power and privilege, rather than towards power and privilege themselves:

A New Crime — A Gentleman travelling lately in Suffolk, observed painted boards put up all round the premises of a great Loan Contractor, (Mr. Thellusson, of Kendlesham in that country), who has amassed hundreds of thousands during the present cruel war, offering rewards for the discovery of any person who should disturb the game.

The bread we daily eat has so much allum, to make it look white, and so many other pernicious ingredients, to save the flour, and defraud the public, that we eat poison instead of the staff of life. How many wholesome laws do our books teem with, and yet how shamefully are they neglected. Why don't those Lord Mayors, who are always altering and realtering the assize of bread, punish the millers and bakers who gradually destroy their fellow creatures.

Posting-Imposition. In Yorkshire the gentlemen have resisted an attempted combination of innkeepers to raise the price of post-horses to 14d a mile! — and resisting, they have overthrown it. — A pretty good hint this to the people, what may be done by union, to abolish impositions, much more insufferable than can be from any exertion as to post-horses.[51]

Papers such as the *Telegraph* were ambiguous about change. They called essentially for action for the redress of grievances, but these grievances usually entailed the reform of institutions and the reformation of morality, rather than any substantive change of the hierarchical social system. In November 1792, at a time of serious ministerial concern over domestic radicalism, the author of the *Country Spectator* declared,

I myself am a staunch friend to *Democracy*. It is not necessary that I should give my particular reasons for having espoused the cause of the people, since nine authors out of ten have done the same, and since it seems perfectly natural that they all should do so. If a declaimer can by his eloquence persuade the people that they are oppressed by their governors, and can incite them to take the power into their own hands, he may surely hope to be rewarded for having meliorated their condition.[52]

These claims were inaccurate. Nine out of ten authors did not espouse the cause of 'Democracy', and indeed the article in question was to be the last political one in a journal that ended six months later. Inciting 'the people . . . to take the power into their own hands' did not fit comfortably with the traditional distaste of what the author of the article later called 'the mob' and the traditional ambiguity concerning the appeal to the populace. Rather than that, opposition newspapers of the 1790s tended to follow the usual practice of opposing ministerial policy, particularly when it entailed change. Possibly a more radical approach was nipped in the bud by the legal action that ended the *Argus*, and the xenophobic response to French developments that accompanied the drift towards war. It was change, whether the new experiments in war taxation or the Union, that excited most criticism, and it was easy to oppose these developments without making reference to social issues. Socio-economic criticism was essentially traditional in its content, as with the dearth of the mid 1790s. In January 1795 the *Leeds Mercury* observed,

As we had a very plentiful corn harvest last year, the two ways to account for the immoderate rise in that necessary article are either a *clandestine exportation* to France, or a *monopoly* at home. This matter requires the most serious investigation, as well as a strict enquiry into the monopoly of *sugars*, an evil loudly complained of.

Three months later the paper was in no doubt about the remedy for food riots:

These disturbances, we find, particularly at Plymouth, have risen from the nefarious practices of *forestallers*, and not from an advance of price by the farmers. To prevent that common, but most unjust and injurious practice, should at this time be the particular care of those whose department it is in every

> market throughout the kingdom . . . we must look to the
> humanity and policy of Parliament for such measures as may
> place on more stable foundation than the will of forestallers or
> monopolizers, the existence of the poor.

The following year the *English Chronicle* ended a monthly report
on agriculture with the claim that

> notwithstanding the general plenty, and reduced price of bread
> corn, flour is suffered to be retailed by the millers through all
> parts of the kingdom, at extortionate prices, to the great dis-
> tress of the people, and reproachful to the policy of a country,
> either for not having, or not exercising the powers of correcting
> a nuisance so widely oppressed.[53]

Newspapers called for moves by the relevant authorities rather
than condoning popular action. Responding to the grain riots of
1795 the *Leeds Mercury* commented,

> The benevolent exertions that have been made by the opulent
> throughout the kingdom, have in some places experienced gross
> ingratitude; led on by the vicious and abandoned, the people
> have committed those acts of outrage and violence which can
> only tend to increase the distresses of which they complain, and
> heap calamity on their heads.[54]

Sympathetic to popular distress but opposed to popular action,
newspapers displayed little interest in any significant change in the
hierarchical nature of society, whatever their views on changes in
France might be. The response to the social changes in France by
the press was largely political. Papers that opposed the war with
France and praised aspects of her social changes did not urge
revolution at home. Instead the press continued to provide tales of
the munificence of the great and a considerable amount of news
about their social activities and those of royalty. The births,
celebrations, marriages and deaths of the members of the landed
orders were reported regularly and a large amount of space was
devoted to court news, whether royal trips or court celebrations.
The dresses worn on occasions such as the Queen's birthday were
described at great length, by papers such as the *Telegraph* as well
as in the ministerial press. In the same issue in which it claimed

that 'the rising spirit of liberty makes all the tyrants tremble', the *Argus* reported the arrival of the Duke of Marlborough in London in order to attend a family wedding.[55]

It could be suggested that the limited amount of social radicalism advocated in the press and the tendency for social criticism to adopt a conservative stance reflected a society in which shared assumptions bound landed society and urban opinion together, particularly in the face of external threat. It was not a society based on tolerance towards or understanding of the problems of those who only inadequately shared in its benefits. However charitable its social policing may have been, the practice of paternalism entailed a condescending and assertive attitude towards the bulk of the population, as in 'Z' 's article in the *Leeds Intelligencer* of 1789:

At this period, when the attention of the higher ranks is happily directed to the improvement of the lower class in general, and particularly in the article of *cleanliness*, some of your benevolent readers may be glad to learn the result of my experience in removing that deplorable consequence of filth and scorbutic humour among the children of the poor, a *Scald Head* . . . Were the poor taught to wash the heads of their children regularly with soap and water, instead of depending entirely on the comb, which they seldom use effectually, the disease of the scald-head might in general be prevented.[56]

Notes

1. *Applebee's Original Weekly Journal*, 10 Feb. 1722.
2. *Weekly Journal*, 15 Mar. 1718; A. S. Limouze, 'Dr. Gaylard's Loyal Observator Revived', *Modern Philology*, 48 (1950), pp. 100–1; *Cirencester Flying-Post*, 16 Jan. 1744; *Westminster Journal*, 1 Oct. 1774.
3. *Observator*, 20 May 1702; *Whitehall Evening Post*, 30 Dec. 1718; Broadsheet, *An Elegy on the Death of the late Famous Observator*.
4. Sherlock to Weston, 1, 8 May 1731, Weston-Underwood; *New Weekly Miscellany*, 18 July 1741. In 1738 Webster claimed that the *Weekly Miscellany* was opposed by 'the several Enemies of Religion and the Church of England', 21 Apr.
5. *Man*, 31 Dec. 1755; J. L. Althoz, 'The First Religious Magazines', *Notes and Queries*, 230 (1985), pp. 223–4; *Country Tatler*, 3 Sept. 1739; *Leeds Intelligencer*, 27 Apr. 1790.
6. *Weekly Register*, 11 Apr., 9, 16, 30 May 1798.
7. W. A. Speck, 'Political Propaganda in Augustan England', *Transactions of the Royal Historical Society*, 5th ser. 22 (1972), p. 21; J. Feather, 'British Publishing

in the Eighteenth Century: a preliminary subject analysis', *Library*, 6th ser. 8 (1986); *Westminster Journal*, 6 Aug. 1774.

8. *Nonsense of Common-Sense*, 17 Jan. 1738.

9. *Leeds Mercury*, 11 July 1795, 10 July 1787.

10. *General Advertiser*, 15 Jan. 1780; *Newcastle Weekly Journal*, 11 May 1723; *Whitehall Evening Post*, 14, 28 Apr. 1752; J. Black, 'The Catholic Threat and the British Press in the 1720s and 1730s', *Journal of Religious History*, 12 (1983), pp. 364–81; *Owen's Weekly Chronicle*, 3 Nov. 1764.

11. *Newcastle Journal*, 16 Sept. 1752.

12. *Leeds Intelligencer*, 3 Nov. 1767; *Morning Herald*, 5 Apr. 1787; *Mercury*, 28 Apr., 26 May, 9 June 1777; G. Shelton, *Dean Tucker* (1981), pp. 24–5.

13. *Leeds Mercury*, 13 Nov. 1787; *Sheffield Advertiser*, 4 June 1790; *World*, 15 Nov. 1791; *Oracle*, 20 Feb. 1792.

14. I owe this information to Grayson Ditchfield.

15. J. Stephens, 'The London Ministers and Subscription, 1772–1779', *Enlightenment and Dissent*, 1 (1982), p. 55; *Morning Chronicle*, 16 Apr. 1787; *Sheffield Advertiser*, 26 Feb. 1790; *Argus*, 15 Nov. 1791, 29 Feb. 1792; *Public Advertiser*, 26 Oct. 1766.

16. *Cirencester Flying-Post*, 10 May 1742; *Weekly Journal*, 18 Apr. 1719; *Leeds Intelligencer*, 25 Nov. 1766; *Westminster Journal*, 19 June 1773. For doubts re lightning, *St. James's Chronicle*, 3 May 1766.

17. *Leeds Mercury*, 4 Dec. 1787, 7 Oct. 1788.

18. *Newcastle Courant*, 23 Apr. 1748; *Oracle*, 26 Jan. 1795.

19. *Leeds Mercury*, 5 Sept. 1795.

20. *Sheffield Public Advertiser*, 2 May 1772; *Newcastle Chronicle*, 22 Sept. 1787; *Sheffield Advertiser*, 7 Sept. 1787, 8 Jan. 1790; *Leeds Mercury*, 18 July 1795.

21. D. A. Baugh, 'Poverty, Protestantism and Political Economy: English Attitudes toward the Poor, 1660–1800', in Baxter (ed.), *England's Rise to Greatness*, p. 94.

22. *Leeds Intelligencer*, 31 Oct., 28 Nov. 1786, 7 Apr. 1789; *Reading Mercury*, 27 June 1785; *Sheffield Advertiser*, 31 Aug., 7 Sept. 1787; M. G. Jones, *The Charity School Movement* (1964), p. 26.

23. *World*, 12 Mar. 1792; *Leeds Intelligencer*, 16 Mar. 1790.

24. *Berrow's Worcester Journal*, 9 Nov. 1769; *Parker's London News*, 11 May 1724; *London Chronicle*, 7 Jan. 1779; *Leeds Mercury*, 23 Dec. 1788; *Star*, 25 Apr. 1798; *St. James's Chronicle*, 29 Mar. 1764; *British Apollo*, 30 June 1708.

25. *Newcastle Chronicle*, 17 Mar. 1787; *Newcastle Courant*, 2 Jan. 1742, 12 Apr. 1788; *Lloyd's Evening Post*, 12 Jan. 1791; *London Chronicle*, 12 Jan. 1792; *Reading Mercury*, 29 Dec. 1783; *Daily Gazetteer*, 22 July 1738.

26. *Newcastle Courant*, 23, 30 July, 17, 24 Dec. 1743, 21 Jan. 1744; *Leeds Mercury*, 2 Dec. 1788; *St. James's Chronicle*, 10 Apr. 1766: translations sent in of French epigram published in paper.

27. *Cirencester Flying-Post*, 19, 21 Sept. 1723; *Morning Chronicle*, 17 Apr. 1787; *Protestant Intelligence*, 26 Dec. 1724: book extract.

28. *Newcastle Journal*, 30 Jan. 1742; *Remembrancer*, 5 Mar. 1748; *General Advertiser*, 15 Jan. 1780; *Newcastle Courant*, 29 Oct. 1743; *Newcastle Chronicle*, 27 Jan. 1787.

29. *Weekly Worcester Journal*, 23 July 1742; *Penny London Post*, 13 Jan. 1749; *Public Advertiser*, 13 Jan. 1757; *Reading Mercury*, 4 Jan., 15 Feb. 1768; *Leeds Mercury*, 16 Sept. 1788; *Star*, 25 Aug. 1795; *Craftsman*, 2 June 1781.

30. *Newcastle Courant*, 18 June 1743; *Reading Mercury*, 16 Apr. 1770; *Leeds Intelligencer*, 1 Mar. 1791; *Star*, 25 Apr. 1798; *Middlesex Journal*, 21 Oct. 1783.

31. *Gray's Inn Journal*, 19 Jan. 1754; *Leeds Intelligencer*, 5 Oct. 1790; *London Packet*, 23 Apr. 1787; *Reading Mercury*, 21 Dec. 1767.

32. *Hull Packet*, 1 Jan. 1788.

33. *Reading Mercury*, 17 Nov. 1777; *Leeds Mercury*, 15, 22 Aug. 1738.

34. *Leeds Intelligencer*, 7 Apr. 1789, 22 Feb. 1791; *Leeds Mercury*, 20, 27 Nov. 1787.

35. *Sheffield Advertiser*, 27 Sept. 1787; *Leeds Mercury*, 4 Dec. 1787, 8, 22 Jan., 11 Nov. 1788; *Newcastle Courant*, 2 Feb., 22 Mar. 1788; *Oracle*, 20 Feb. 1792; *Argus*, 3 Mar. 1792; *Leeds Intelligencer*, 7 Apr. 1789.

36. *Plain Dealer*, 19 Feb. 1725; *Public Advertiser*, 12 Jan. 1754; *Leeds Intelligencer*, 4 Jan. 1791; *Leeds Mercury*, 20 June, 22 Aug. 1795.

37. *Leeds Intelligencer*, 6 Feb. 1787, 26 May 1789, 15 Nov. 1791; *Leeds Mercury*, 25 Apr. 1795; *Oxford Gazette*, 20 Apr., 18 May 1767; *Leeds Mercury*, 25 Dec. 1787; *Sheffield Advertiser*, 19 Feb. 1790; *St. James's Chronicle*, 25 Nov. 1762.

38. *Leeds Intelligencer*, 5 May 1789, 4 May 1790, 22 Feb. 1791; *Leeds Mercury*, 1 Nov. 1794, 20 June 1795; *London Evening Post*, 16 Feb. 1762.

39. *London Packet*, 27, 30 Apr. 1787; *Leeds Mercury*, 7 Mar. 1795; A. S. Collins, 'The Growth of the Reading Public during the Eighteenth Century', *Review of English Studies*, 2 (1926), pp. 430–2.

40. *Newcastle Courant*, 16 Oct. 1742; *Leeds Intelligencer*, 22 Dec. 1772, 7 Nov. 1786, 20 July, 2 Nov. 1790; *Leeds Mercury*, 29 Jan. 1788, 18 Oct. 1794; *Owen's Weekly Chronicle*, 17 Nov. 1764; *St. James's Chronicle*, 25 Dec. 1764.

41. *Newcastle Chronicle*, 8 Sept. 1787; *Leeds Intelligencer*, 9 Mar. 1790; *Sheffield Advertiser*, 12 Mar. 1790; *Leeds Mercury*, 27 Sept. 1794.

42. *Leeds Intelligencer*, 17 May, 29 Mar. 1791; *True Patriot*, 10 June 1746; *Oracle*, 1, 24 July 1795; *Sheffield Advertiser*, 22 Jan. 1790; *Leeds Mercury*, 4 Dec. 1787; *Owen's Weekly Chronicle*, 10 Nov. 1764.

43. *Leeds Intelligencer*, 28 June 1791; *Newcastle Courant*, 24 Sept. 1743.

44. *Leeds Intelligencer*, 9 Jan. 1787.

45. *York Chronicle*, 17 Dec. 1779; *Read's Weekly Journal*, 3 Jan. 1756; *Leeds Mercury*, 28 Feb. 1795.

46. *Plain Dealer*, 11 Jan. 1725; *Cirencester Flying-Post*, 3 May 1742; *Newcastle Journal*, 23 Jan. 1773; *Sheffield Advertiser*, 18 June 1790; *Westminster Journal*, 9 Jan. 1773.

47. *Connoisseur*, 31 Jan. 1754; *Leeds Intelligencer*, 6 Dec. 1791; *Gazetteer*, 23 Feb. 1792; *Leeds Mercury*, 7 Mar. 1795; *Sun*, 3 June 1796; *Sheffield Advertiser*, 16 Apr. 1790; *Westminster Gazette*, 23 Nov. 1776.

48. *Leeds Mercury*, 11 Nov. 1788; *World*, 9 Nov. 1791; *Leeds Mercury*, 1 July 1788; *Westminster Journal*, 30 Jan. 1773; *Westminster Gazette*, 24 Dec. 1776.

49. *Newcastle Courant*, 12 Dec. 1747;: *London Evening Post*, 8 Apr. 1762; *Public Advertiser*, 23 May 1767; *Citizen*, 19, 22 Mar. 1757; *St. James's Chronicle*, 22 Mar. 1766.

50. Money, *Experience and Identity*, p. 246; Brewer, *Party Ideology and Popular Politics*, pp. 267–9.

51. *Leeds Intelligencer*, 17 July 1781; *Argus*, 5, 7, 15 Mar. 1792; *Telegraph*, 14, 17, 19, 20 Jan. 1797, 29 Mar. 1796.

52. *Country Spectator*, 6 Nov. 1792.

53. *Leeds Mercury*, 10 Jan., 18 Apr., 24 Oct. 1795; *English Chronicle*, 11 Oct. 1796; *London Packet*, 19 June 1795.

54. *Leeds Mercury*, 15 Aug. 1795.

55. *Leeds Mercury*, 6 Nov. 1787; *Oracle,* 5 June 1789; *London Packet*, 21 Jan. 1795; *Telegraph*, 19 Jan. 1797; *Argus*, 6 Mar. 1792.

56. *Leeds Intelligencer*, 26 May 1789; '. . . . there is now a serious Intention of putting a speedy and effectual End to an old Grievance: I mean, the driving Cattle about the Streets of this Metropolis, at a Time when they are full of

People, passing through them on their necessary and honest Occasions. This is one of those Reformations, which, as you have more than once observed, we owe to our News Papers; therefore, whenever it is accomplished, I shall set it down in a List, that I have formed of the Benefits derived to the Publick, from the Liberty of the Press', letter in *London Evening Post*, 16 Feb. 1762.

9 Conclusion: A Changing Press Altering Society?

Play-houses and players are become the general topics of coffee-house politicians, and the houses of Austria and Bourbon are left to take care of their own interests.

Grub Street Journal, 17 April 1735

When we hear every day of Lords and Lordlings, and Baronets, and Esquires, talking of *their* boroughs, and of how many members *such a one* sends to Parliament, what are we to think? Is it not an insult to the common sense and common feelings of Englishmen?

Argus, 2 March 1792

A few interested men may be averse to an Union between this country and Ireland, and *Faction*, we know, is ever clamorous and loud . . . but we should as soon gauge the loyalty of the People of England by the drunken orgies of a few noble, honourable, and not honourable Democrats, as we would determine the sober opinions of a nation by the precipitate and intemperate proceedings of a tumultuous meeting.

True Briton, 3 January 1799, with reference to the claim in the *Morning Chronicle* of 26 December 1798 that the Irish were opposed to the Union

A changing press?

A report was yesterday afloat in some of the higher circles, of a small French force, aided by a disaffected part of the garrison, having possessed themselves of the Cape of Good Hope, where, in four days after, a strong British armament arrived, and commenced so powerful a siege, by sea and land, as to encourage strong hopes that a surrender would be the consequence. This account is said to have come through a private channel, by way of Holland, but there was no possibility of tracing it to its original source.

Star, 25 August 1795

There were significant changes in some aspects of the eighteenth-century English press. Those in size and appearance were obvious. Prior to the first Stamp Act papers were two or four pages long, the distinctive newspaper of the 1700s being single leaf with two columns to the page. The failure of the Act of 1712 to consider papers consisting of more than one sheet encouraged the appearance of longer papers that were registered as pamphlets and paid a lower duty. From 1712 to the second Stamp Act many London and all provincial papers were six pages or longer. The 1725 Act ended this loophole and thereafter most papers, in both London and the provinces, stuck to four pages, although, as the Acts had failed to establish a standard size for a sheet of paper, printers were able to treat increasingly large four-page papers as half-sheets. The basic physical appearance of papers was therefore set in 1725, although in the 1750s a variation was made with the appearance of tri-weekly 'Chronicles', in eight smaller pages, such as the long-lasting *London Chronicle*. The essential stability of the form established in 1725, which was not to be broken until the following century, was a testimony to the role of commercial considerations and possibly to the inherent conservatism of the newspaper world, as much as to the determining constraints of taxation. The 1725 Act did not prohibit the production of papers of more than four sheets, it simply made them more expensive. One interesting feature of the press was the unwillingness of papers to deviate from the price charged by other papers of the same type, and, after the unstamped papers were dealt with in the early 1740s and the penny tri-weeklies disappeared a decade later for reasons that are unclear, to vary in price to any significant extent. In the second half of the century the press, particularly the London press, offered a variety of products at similar prices and in similar forms. As very little is known concerning the internal arrangements of papers it is unclear whether different approaches were considered regularly, but the essentially static physical nature of the press at a time when there was no shortage of additional material and when, particularly for tri-weeklies and weeklies, it would have been easy to print longer papers, suggests a conservative attitude to the issue of size. Given the money spent on magazines, which were more expensive, it is difficult to believe that a market did not exist for weekly newspapers combining the news with magazine-type articles and costing more than most papers because they were longer.

Larger columns and smaller print enabled more material to be printed, an aspect of the press that definitely changed. In 1796 *Bell's Weekly Messenger* hoped that 'the readers of this paper, who complain of the smallness of the print, will at least give us credit for our motive. By this mode of printing, we are enabled to afford more interesting information than is contained in any other *two newspapers*'.[1]

An increase in the amount of material printed can be noted throughout the century but a definite shift can be discerned in the 1760s with more papers adopting four columns per page. This increase was not automatically accompanied by an improvement in the organisation of the news and in the layout of the paper, and in many papers neither of these can be said to have improved until the 1790s. *Bingley's London Journal*, a weekly, had very poor headlines in 1779. In the issue of 23 January information from the *Gazette* on bankrupts was not consolidated into one item, while the heading London occurred seven times. That October an account of a meeting of the Middlesex freeholders was printed as an undifferentiated item, without a headline in the London news of the *St. James's Chronicle*.[2] By the 1790s the position had improved with good headlining in papers such as the *Argus*, *Evening Mail*, *Oracle*, *Star* and *Sun*. This was accompanied in some papers by a system of sub-headlines that helped to define the organisation of the news. This often followed the traditional pattern by which items appeared under the source of the news report. In the *Oracle* of 14 November 1791 the sub-heading 'Insurrection in St. Domingo' appeared under the Paris heading, 'India News' under London. Not all the newspapers of the 1790s matched the clear layout of papers such as the *Sun*. The *London Packet* had poor headlining, while in the 1 January 1795 issue of the *Courier*, a paper with good headlining, news from Guadeloupe was printed alongside the report of a powder mill explosion, both doubtless for some readers a relief from the 'Ode for the New Year' that took up over a column of the front page. Most papers by the 1790s resorted to leading and the use of rules across the columns to differentiate between major items, though *Bell's Weekly Messenger* disapproved of this fashion, announcing,

It has of late been the custom in newspapers to distinguish the most prominent articles by leaving greater space than usual between the lines, which is called giving them *lead*. The proprieter of the MESSENGER, however, wishing to afford his readers as much information and amusement as possible, means to put as little *lead* as may be, in his paper. He trusts that their taste and discrimination will enable them to find out of themselves which is the most interesting part of his Miscellany.[3]

Among the items differentiated were those appearing under new headlines. The one-time largely amorphous mass of news was increasingly organised into new categories, and the introduction of the latter both enabled newspapers to appear to be providing new types of news and to stress aspects of their news that they felt to be especially good or peculiar to them. In 1789 the *Oracle* offered its readers a speech of the American President to Congress under the heading 'United States', followed by the claim that

these original, authentic, and important papers, thus early communicated to the Public by means of the Oracle *alone*, will show the extended sources of intelligence which are peculiar to this print. The New World is now opening scenes and subjects for great political speculation, wherein the interests of Europe may be deeply concerned. It behoves Great Britain carefully to attend to their progress. It shall be the object of the Oracle to report the rising consequence of the American states, whenever circumstances may challenge the attention of statesman, or the contemplation of a politician. We have assurances of constant communication with persons high in confidence, and of the most unimpeachable integrity.

Six years later 'The Field of Mars' appeared as a headline for the first time and the paper's explanatory notice stressed the mutually reinforcing relationship of a specific readership and good advertising potential, a facet of the attempt by all papers to boost their appeal to crucial advertising revenue by increasing their readership:

Under this head, all communications respecting military affairs will be arranged in future. Gentlemen of the army are requested to favour the Oracle with every information which they may think beneficial to the service. Such articles, as well as any others of an interesting nature, will be the most respectfully attended to. From the extensive sale which this paper has now established in the military circles, all advertisements respecting the army will be read with advantage. They will be received by the agents at the different camps, who are appointed to distribute this paper, or at the Oracle's office.[4]

Many newspapers increasingly offered a distinct editorial. Lucyle Werkmeister suggested that the spurious *Star* in 1789 was the first paper to present a well-developed editorial. She discerned a definite shift between the expression of opinion in short paragraphs or letters from real or invented correspondents and the example of the spurious *Star* which offered a daily commentary for which it took the credit itself, located in the central column of the third page, where it would attract the most attention.[5] It could be suggested that Werkmeister exaggerated the contrast between the short paragraphs of earlier papers and the spurious *Star*, but it is clear that in the 1790s most London papers had clearly defined editorial sections. These however contained material that could be found in papers prior to 1789. The editorial section of the *Express* of 5 April 1796, with its comments on the authenticity of the accounts of war news in German and Parisian papers, would not have been out of place 80 years earlier. Provincial papers essentially continued their practice of making comments in the local section of their news, though some, such as the radical *Manchester Herald* (1792–3), published clear editorials. The credit for first publishing editorial articles in the provincial press has been given to two Unitarian reformers of the period, Benjamin Flower of the *Cambridge Intelligencer* and Joseph Gales of the *Sheffield Register*, though, as with the London press, it is difficult to define what an editorial was. It is interesting to note however that provincial papers were as far advanced in some cases as the London press.

Many features of the press changed, ranging from improved distribution to larger staff, which permitted greater differentiation in function, from the foundation of Sunday papers to the increase in the country section of London newspapers, with many papers such as *Bell's Weekly Messenger* making provincial news a regular feature. The amount of local news in the provincial press also increased. On 13 April 1723 the only items of Newcastle news in the *Newcastle Weekly Mercury* were the price of butter and the departure of ships. On 16, 23 and 30 January 1773 the *Newcastle Journal* printed two and a quarter, nearly two, and one and a half columns of news under the Newcastle byline. To some extent this was a deceptive indicator of the importance of local news in a paper then offering 16 columns weekly, for the byline included many items from other towns. On 16 January pieces from Edinburgh, Appleby and Durham and an explanation of the bankruptcy of the Cliffords banking house of Amsterdam appeared. Items from Edinburgh, Norwich, Wakefield and York were among those under the Newcastle byline on 23 January, Edinburgh and Glasgow featuring a week later. The local byline referred to items the printer had received from local sources. Most of the Newcastle news in January 1773 fell within traditional categories of local news, particularly the reporting of crime, deaths and the weather. The increase in local news in the provincial press was general, but it was largely a development of the last quarter of the century. J. J. Looney, who has studied the leading Leeds and York papers for the sample years 1720, 1741, 1760, 1784 and 1807, noted an appreciable increase between 1760 and 1784, but dated the substantial increase to the 1784–1807 period. This period emerges repeatedly in his study as the crucial one for a number of developments, and it is greatly to be regretted that he did not have the time to introduce another sampling year for statistical analysis or to read the papers of the period in order to spot important shifts.[6] The development of local news in the Sheffield press was very slow. William Ward's *Sheffield Advertiser* carried no Sheffield news at all in its issue of 26 May 1761 and used very simple headlining. The *Sheffield Public Advertiser* of 17 May 1770 devoted one third of a column of the 16-column paper to local news, including deaths, an accident and a crime. The issue of 22 September 1770 contained no Sheffield news, that of 15 February 1772 only three items: a suicide, the death of a woman as a result of bruises inflicted by a relation, and the coming of age of the Marquis of Carmarthen. Local news did not become a significant item until the 1780s.

Alongside the development of new features the continuance of many old ones can be noted, some the natural result of the technological constraints of assembling the news and producing a paper, others the consequence of the conservative nature of the newspaper world, in which well-tried methods that produced successful results were maintained by men whose conception of the potentialities of print was based on experience. The criticisms that Arthur Murphy in the first issue of the *Gray's Inn Journal* directed against the *Craftsman* when he broke with it in 1753 were unfair to some extent and unduly dismissive about periodicals interested in news, but they could have been repeated a half-century later:

> . . . instead of aided by my connexions with that paper, I rather found myself clogged with incumbrances, which, like the heavy baggage of an army, served only to retard my progress. By this I would be understood to mean, the additional articles of news collected out of the daily historians, from all which, I never could conceive, what kind of advantage can redound to a rational creature, who can neither receive instruction or entertainment, by reading that Mr. *Such-a-one* died at his country house, when perhaps the gentleman is in perfect good health; and if *Squire Rent-Roll* is arrived in town with a grand retinue, I apprehend it in no way interesting to any man breathing, except his tailor . . . dull letters from the *Hague* and fictitious advices from the *Swede* and *Turk* . . . I do not think it decent to hand up advertisements to a gentleman's wife or daughter, which are only fit for an hospital or a brothel.[7]

The papers of the 1790s, lacking a corps of journalists, still actively encouraged correspondents to send in items. The first number of the *Oracle* asked 'Ye Moralists, ye Poets, Historians, Philosophers, and Politicians! Ye Artists and Men of Commerce, send therefore your communications hither'. Nine days later the paper was able to comment on 16 contributions, three of which were rejected for 'venom', one for libel and one for blasphemy.[8] Numerous contributions were not the sole reason why newspapers in the 1790s faced the same problems of selection that had confronted their predecessors. The four-page format created the essential problem but it was exacerbated by the lifting of restrictions upon the reporting of parliamentary news, the growth of economic, theatrical, sporting and provincial news and Britain's entry into war in February 1793. Whereas the previous war involving Britain, the War of American Independence, had largely taken place at a distance and posed problems of securing reports, the war with revolutionary France created far too many reports for the press to cope with. In the American war Britain had not been involved in continental hostilities with France and there had been no active French press to serve as a source of reports. From 1793 the British press had to decide whether to allow the British war effort to swamp other news. Newspapers frequently referred to having to choose what material to insert. In 1795 the *Courier* noted, 'We have received a great number of letters, and of Dutch, German, and French papers, of which the extreme length of the debate in the House of Commons prevents us at present from entering into detail.'[9] Reporting the early stages of the war created problems for the press similar to those in the earlier wars of the century. The use of foreign correspondents was very rare. Most foreign news came from traditional sources, the foreign press and the British government. Rather than seeking the news themselves, newspapers continued to be derivative, competing for primacy in government information, as the *Times* and the *True Briton* did, or struggling to obtain copies of the French papers as speedily as possible. The latter was a source of great rivalry, and papers prided themselves on their late news, the *Oracle* proclaiming in 1792, 'As a proof that the *Oracle* still retains its boasted superiority in point of continental intelligence, yesterday's paper contained two entire days of the proceedings of the National Assembly later than any of our contemporaries.' According to the *English Chronicle* in 1796, 'The ministerial papers, however they may like the design of the *City Gazettes* do not much approve their earliness.'[10] Newspapers remained dependent on the continental mails, with the concomitant problems of delayed information and uncertain news. Commenting on reports of a battle between the Austrians and the French on 1 June 1796, the *Sun* of 14 June announced, 'We wait, with the most anxious impatience, for the arrival of the two Hamburg mails that still remain due, from which alone we can expect to derive any authentic intelligence on the subject.'

Similar problems concerning the speed and verification of news also affected the provincial press. There was no sign in 1800 of the changes that were to follow the widespread introduction of such technological innovations as steam-powered transport and the telegraph. Competing provincial papers stressed the speed with which they obtained the news from London, just as they had done 80 years earlier. In 1787 the *Sheffield Advertiser* declared,

This paper is published about 8 o'clock in the morning of every Friday, and contains the most important intelligence from all the

London and other papers, and the last post from the Wednesday evening London papers (Lloyd's and London Packet) which arrive at Sheffield late on Thursday night; and it is impossible to publish a paper in this town, on any part of the day on Friday, to have the last day's news or postscript of the St. James's, the General, the Whitehall, the Chronicles, or any other of the Thursday evening's London papers, as they are not published till Thursday evening in London, nor do they arrive here earlier than by the mail coach on Friday night. This is what is usually understood to be Saturday's Post.

This account, part of a rebuttal of the claims of a rival to publish fresher news,[11] indicated both the continued importance of London news for the provincial press and the traditional methods by which it was transmitted. Although there was no difficulty in filling newspapers with material, it was still relatively difficult for both the London and the provincial press to fill their columns with unique items of news. At the end of the century the need to obtain news from other publications still encouraged both London and provincial papers to use plagiarism on a large scale, and this in turn limited the development of particular journalistic styles for individual papers. The borrowing of items from other British papers was particularly marked in the case of tri-weeklies and weeklies, both London and provincial, less so for morning dailies. In 1798 the *Weekly Register* commented,

> As the Weekly Register will not be a mere selection, *servilely copied*, as is the usual manner from the public prints; but contain a great variety of original articles, and the whole be entirely recomposed, it is hoped it may preserve a consistency, both of style and fact, not very usual in a newspaper, and be found worth the inspection even of gentlemen who are in the habit of perusing the daily papers.

This aspiration was as unusual as the determination to devote the profits of the paper 'to charitable and religious purposes'.[12] It was not common practice to rewrite borrowed items, and a consistency of style was not the goal of most of the press, with the important exception of the essay-papers.

Stanley Morison, Ian Christie and Michael Harris all detected an increasing standardisation in the style of all newspapers from the mid-century, and linked this to the growing ownership of London papers by groups of booksellers. In the 1690s and 1700s most London papers were established and controlled by individuals, usually printers. Many newspapers were named after their printers, men such as Appleby, Gaylard, Mist and Read. However, by 1720 a significant number of conventionally priced newspapers were owned and controlled by groups of shareholding booksellers. This remained the pattern until towards the end of the century when there was a move towards ownership by an individual or small partnership. Harris has suggested that the growth of group ownership was an ambiguous development for the press. The injection of capital and the creation of an administrative framework probably encouraged significant internal developments, such as the employment of specialist staff and the emergence of an editor with overall control of content. On the other hand Harris argues that the booksellers were interested in investment returns, not innovation, and that the creation of a 'newspaper establishment' produced stagnation. The editorial, as opposed to financial, organisation of the press is a subject for which very little material survives. It is not therefore surprising that Harris's important argument is largely conjectural. He cites the *National Journal* and *True Patriot* of 1746, both newly established papers, which claimed that the existing newspaper proprietors sought to prevent the development of new papers.[13] This was doubtless true. In 1754 Arthur Murphy claimed that 'when a set of booksellers are concerned in a newspaper, a *Monthly Review*, or a *Magazine*, they take every opportunity in the said productions of praising the works, in which they have a property themselves, and of decrying every thing that may prevent an increase of their own sale'. He also complained about the difficulties that confronted him as author of the *Gray's Inn Journal* for which he lacked 'the advantages enjoyed by some of my brother writers. I have not had the happiness of being puffed in any of our common newspapers, nor have I stood well enough with the conductors of our magazines, to be admitted to the honour of furnishing them with an essay once a month'.[14]

However, new papers had encountered resistance from established rivals before bookseller control became established. It was not necessary to have group ownership by shareholding booksellers in order for established papers to fear the loss of readers and advertisers to new competitors. The charge of stagnation is an interesting one. In 1751 the first number of the *London Advertiser*, concerned, as all opening numbers were, to denigrate the existing press, complained that 'the papers of intelligence, so numerous as they are at present, are all on so similar a plan, that they appear but as transcripts of each other'. Harris has suggested that bookseller pressure 'probably . . . squeezed the legitimate cut-price papers out of existence by mid-century'.[15] If the evidence for conspiracy is lacking, that for stagnation is problematic. The mid and late 1740s, which Harris thus briefly depicts, may appear uninteresting, compared to the heroic ages of Mist and the *Craftsman* or Almon and Junius, and there was a failure to produce new types of newspaper, but the reasons for the ending of the cut-price papers are unclear, and many of the newspapers of the period, such as the *London Evening Post*, were still vibrant. The 1750s witnessed a spate of new papers, essay-papers, that were predominantly political, such as the *Test* and the *Con-Test*, or social, such as the *Connoisseur*, weeklies such as the *Universal Chronicle* and *Owen's Weekly Chronicle*, and more regular papers, such as the *London Chronicle* and *Lloyd's Evening Post*. The contrast between the late 1740s and the late 1750s, a period when several papers were founded, may reflect not any 'stagnation' caused by group ownership, but rather the contrast between a period of Pelhamite ministerial stability and international peace (1748–54) and one of ministerial instability and a drift towards war. As a result of peace the number of provincial papers fell from 43 in 1748 to 32 in 1753. In the former period it could be suggested that magazines provided effective competition to the conventionally priced papers and that the reading public's interest in magazine-type material was shown by the foundation of essay papers or essay series in conventional papers devoted to this material, such as the *Connoisseur, Adventurer, World, Gray's Inn Journal*, and *Rambler*. In the latter period war and ministerial change placed a premium upon the political news that newspapers could best provide. The *Test* drew attention to the strength of public interest in political news in 1756:

> The life of an author has been called a state of warfare upon earth; but of all authors there is not one who has so much reason to subscribe to the maxim as the political writer, because each of his readers is either a patriot, or an old-ministry-man, or a new-ministry-man, or a whig, or a tory, or, in short, of some

party or other, and very unreasonably expects that a writer is to conform to the passions and prejudices, that have already taken root in his own mind . . . it is impossible for the author of the *Test* to please our British statesmen of all denominations.

Five years later George Colman, whose essay-series 'The Genius' was carried in the *St. James's Chronicle*, stressed the value of war to the press:

During the time of war, a battle in Germany, a fort stormed in the West-Indies, or a Nabob created in the East, is worth forty shillings to every paper, that reprints that particulars from the Gazette Extraordinary: nay a town taken or a town lost is equally to the advantage of these half-sheet historians; and the perpetual curiosity kept alive by the public anxiety, sells off whole quires of deaths, marriages, and bankruptcies. How great then must be the dread of the consequences of peace to the proprietors of the swarm of Advertisers, Gazetteers, Ledgers, Journals, Chronicles, and Evening Posts? A peace, which will lie heavier on their papers than the double duty on the stamps! My good friend Mr. H. Baldwin of White Friars has already exprest to me his fears on this occasion. He fairly tells me to my face, that though the Genius were to stand in the front of his paper three times a week, the public attention would flag without great incidents and alarming paragraphs.[16]

This explanation is hypothetical, but it is no more so than the suggestion that group ownership caused stagnation. It is also necessary to allow for shifting public interests, both in terms of the type of news that was sought and the form in which it was desired, and that is a subject about which very little is known.

If one discernible shift in the development of the press may have occurred as a result of the growth of group ownership another has been detected at the end of the century. It has been suggested that the growth in the advertising revenue of certain important papers enabled them to become independent of political sponsorship and was the most important factor in enabling the press to emerge as the fourth estate of the realm. Christie discerned significant changes, including the development of higher editorial standards. H. R. Fox-Bourne was impressed by the rise of the Sundays. Looney detected an appreciable increase in advertising in the

Yorkshire press after 1784 and signs that the metropolitan dominance of advertising was coming under challenge. In an important recent work, which has much of interest for newspaper historians, John Feather has drawn attention to the growth in the expression of radical opinion in the provincial press and suggested that in 1800 'the age of the provinces was about to begin'.[17] These shifts are certainly more significant than any detected in mid-century, and yet caution is necessary in evaluating the idea of a major discontinuity. It is not so much that there is much about the Victorian press, recently discussed so ably by Lucy Brown, that is surprisingly familiar to the readers of eighteenth-century papers.[18] It is rather that many of the changes dated to the later Georgian age were more in evidence after 1800 than before it. The marked increase in the circulation, capital value and profits of the leading London papers discussed by Christie largely occurred after 1800, and this is also true of the development of an important radical provincial press. Despite excellent work on individual papers such as the *Times* and the *Morning Chronicle* relatively little is known about the bulk of the London press in this period, still less of the provincial papers. It is important not to judge the whole press from a few prominent papers. Though the *Daily Courant* was founded in 1702 no other daily appeared until 1719. In a similar fashion the advertising profits of the *Morning Chronicle* were unusual. Until more research can be carried out it is best to adopt a cautious response to the dating and assessment of the significant changes that can be found in the press, both London and provincial, of the later Georgian age. Relatively little is known about the nature of the readership in the period. Raymond Williams has pointed out that despite the rapid development of 'the print-culture, . . . it was still at almost all levels a minority culture'. C. B. Jewson has been dismissive of the appeal of the *Cabinet*, a radical periodical produced in Norwich in 1794–5.[19] The content of the press in the last decades of the century changed relatively little, suggesting that it was still serving essentially the same market, one possibly defined by an interest in national politics, as much as by literacy or wealth. The *Telegraph*, considering in 1797 how to improve its appeal, adopted the same solutions as other papers, noting,

> The late arrangements made in this paper have enabled us to add to our more important articles of information, a miscellany

of observations and remarks which we hope will add considerably to the interest of the paper, and contribute to soften the too serious details which the unfortunate situation of public affairs compels us so frequently to give.[20]

One of the characteristic features of the eighteenth-century British press was that the general growth in the circulation of the press seems to have permitted most newspapers to go on offering more of the same. The figure of close to 7½ million papers sold in 1750 could be nearly doubled only thirty years later. It is possible that much should be attributed to a feature Lucy Brown noted of the Victorian journalists, a 'tendency to accept established news values uncritically', stemming from long professional experience.[21] Given the limited circulation per paper, which does not seem to have increased for the successful London papers during the century, it might have been expected that papers would alter in order to obtain a greater market share. They did indeed stress particular features, especially in terms of topics covered and supposed earlier access to better political news, and innovative papers appeared at new times, tri-weeklies on the non-post days in the 1710s, and evening, noon and Sunday papers. This may appear to represent a considerable variety, but, particularly after the disappearance of the cut-price papers, most papers were very similar. The extent of the similarity is partly a matter of perception. Unique features stressed by papers in the past that may appear of little significance to the modern observer may well have struck eighteenth-century readers as important. Papers that appear very similar today had widely varying fortunes. Much of the similarity was however inevitable given the limited resources in terms of staff and access to individual sources of news that particular papers possessed. Though the number of staff employed by successful London papers appears to have risen at the end of the century, the increase was limited. In the early 1780s no printing house employed more than one parliamentary reporter. Despite the proximity of the European theatres of war and British interest in them, foreign correspondents were exceptional figures in the 1790s. Christie has suggested that it was only in the 1810s and 1820s that the increasing financial resources of the major newspapers began to be used for a significant expansion of the regular reporting staffs.[22] Given this situation it was difficult for them to develop particular strengths, and that may be more significant in explaining any supposed stagnation than the nature of newspaper ownership.

An appreciation of the essentially conservative nature of the London press, in terms of the organisation and contents of news-papers, helps to place in perspective the contempt sometimes voiced for the provincial press as if it was merely derivative of the London press. Provincial papers retained many traditional features at the end of the century. Despite the increase in the number of post days the news was still grouped in the papers of the 1780s in three sections. In the *Reading Mercury* of 1784 it appeared under Wednesday's, Friday's and Saturday's post. Traditional methods of organisation did not however prevent papers, such as the *Leeds Intelligencer* at the time of the American War of Independence, from expressing par-ticular political points of view. The provincial press at the end of the century is a subject that still awaits detailed attention, but further study of it, as of the London press, will require a consideration of what changes it would have been reasonable to anticipate. It is too easy to simply note the growth in the number of and total sale of newspapers and to avoid the problem of assessing the fundamental continuity and indeed conservatism of the organisation and content of the press.

The press and society

Lord Bute was furiously hissed in the City and the Mob called out Pitt for ever, but no great stress can be laid upon that, the Lord Mayor would have thought the whole parade incomplete, if the day had passed without proper hisses and huzzas.

Lady Charlotte Watson-Wentworth, 1762[23]

I send you the inclosed list of pensioners, printed by a late order of the House of Commons in Ireland; your publication of it in your paper, may perhaps convince Britons, that unless some expedient can be hit upon, to put a stop to the growing evil, of granting Irish pensions to English M——s, B——n may be more effectually conquered in Ireland, than America was in Germany.

A.R. in *Gazetteer*, 10 November 1763

I am much edified by the account in the papers of your reception in Yorkshire with the address of the manufacturers etc . . . You are really beating the late Great C[ommone]r [Pitt] at his own weapon, and receiving those eulogiums which his *Puffs* have hitherto supposed, that nobody was *entitled* to but himself.

Hardwicke to Rockingham, 1766[24]

The extent to which the press was increasingly used by significant political and economic groups was a testimony to their realisation that it represented an effective way of conveying a message to those interested in national concerns. In 1779 the independent freemen of Okehampton advertised their desire for 'two Patriotick English Gentlemen' to offer to stand for Parliament in the *London Evening Post* and the *Sherborne Mercury*. A decade later the Halifax and Bradford addresses thanking Pitt for his stance over the Regency Bill were printed in the Leeds, York and London press. Effectiveness in conveying a message was not of course identical with successful persuasion, but in many instances the intention was rather to preach to the converted than to convert the opposition. A classic instance of this was the widespread printing of addresses, instructions and similar material by political and economic groups. This was intended to encourage the initiation of similar action, to maintain morale and to create the sense of a powerful and popular interest. The instruction of the City of York to their MPs printed in the *Newcastle Courant* of 6 November 1742 noted, 'We have seen and perused those excellent instructions given by the City of London to their Members in Parliament for their conduct in the ensuing session.'[25]

The use of newspapers to popularise the idea of the representative nature of MPs was but part of a significant theme in the press, the public discussion of issues of policy. This was as much a feature of ministerial papers as of their opposition counterparts. It contrasted with the simple manifesto or declaration of policy without any suggestion of debate that characterised the court gazettes of eighteenth-century Europe, in some countries the only form of newspaper in the first half of the century. The British press kept its readership in contact with the activities of politicians, including those of local MPs. The lengthy publication of parliamentary reports was an important development in this process. The *Country Spectator* claimed that without the press few would 'know that our representatives are acting in Parliament, nor should we be able to gain any genuine political information, unless from the *Rights of Man*, and one or two other good books, which are sold cheap . . . for the benefit of the poor'.[26] Public criticism led to debate; few were prepared to suffer attacks in silence. In 1785 the *Leeds Intelligencer* printed one letter beginning, 'Much has lately been said respecting the water-works in this town — and since my conduct has been blamed, I take this method of laying the following state of the business before the public.' In 1742 George Minty felt it necessary to deny rumours that he had created a disturbance at Stourbridge New Chapel by wearing a hat and other practices, and a sustained controversy began in the *Weekly Worcester Journal*.[27] The newspaper became an accepted means in some circles for the pursuance of disputes, possibly contributing to both a more peaceful and a more public means of conducting political, social, economic and religious disagreements. The willingness of most provincial papers to publish material from both sides of a quarrel, albeit often paid for, was an important factor in this development. The *Leeds Intelligencer* of 17 February 1789 published advertisements claiming that the Halifax address to Pitt was well and poorly supported. This practice often reflected an interest in eliciting contributions and encouraging readers concerned about a particular dispute to turn to the paper. Thus the *Weekly Worcester Journal* informed readers in 1742 that they could expect to read more of the Minty controversy, and the *Argus* announced in 1791:

> To demonstrate our impartiality upon all subjects, and on all occasions, where the good of the country is concerned; we readily insert the following letter from a LOYAL BRITISH OFFICER, upon the concerns of Canada, though it is not calculated to forward a plan, of which we have the highest opinion. Indeed we consider the well colonizing of Canada of so much real consequence to the future revenue and prosperity of this realm, that we shall be glad to print the sentiments of any well-informed writers thereon, with a view to excite a full and satisfactory discussion.[28]

The willingness of individuals and interests to present their case in the newspapers and the need of the press, devoid of any large staff of reporters and of significant funds for editorial and reporting activities, to accept this material with the minimum of explanation or abbreviation, helped to make the papers a willing agent for the spread of opinion. Newspapers solicited items. The

Centinel, a weekly London essay-sheet, asked in 1757 for 'any detached essay, whether humorous or moral; any spirited criticism on books, men or things; any poetical morsel, either ode, elegy, epigram or epistle'. Not everything of course was accepted. In 1747 *Old England* announced

> The letter relating to the uncharitable Treatment and Ill-manners a certain brutish Aesculapian, from the suburbs, bestows on the poor Out-Patients, which a most noble Endowment, not far from Smithfield, consigns to his care, will have a better Effect if turn'd into a Petition of Complaint, and laid before the Governors.[29]

However, the need for a constant supply of material, coupled with the limited editorial intervention that it could anticipate, encouraged the provision of opinion or information by those who wished to supply it. The press was both an agent and a participant in this process, but the limited material surviving for the internal organisation and editorial conduct of the press makes it difficult to assess these functions. When newspaper comment is closely linked to material contributed by others, whether paid for or not, it is difficult to establish the pattern of causality and to determine whether the comment reflected outside pressure. In 1790 the *Leeds Intelligencer* published an advertisement inserted by the York hatsellers listing resolutions they had recently passed urging compliance with stamp duty on hats and pledging themselves to act against all offenders. The fourth of these was 'that these resolutions be printed and advertised in all the York papers, the Leeds Intelligencer, Sheffield Register, and Yorkshire Journal — and a copy affixed in some conspicuous part of each of our shops'. The paper supported the cause, not least by drawing attention to the advertisement. Its editorial comments may have been due to inducements, but they also reflected the general hostility of the paper to free enterprise in defiance of the law and its strong support for self-help:

> The resolutions entered into by the hatters of York, (see an advertisement in the preceding page) do them great credit, and we hope will be followed by similar associations in this county, by which the fair dealer may be protected, and the interests of the revenue secured. The attempts to evade the duty on hats

and gloves are perhaps more justly chargeable on the buyers than the sellers, great numbers of the former being shameless enough to insist on having these articles delivered without stamps, and to ensnare the well-meaning shopkeeper, by threatening in case of his refusal, to deal with some other who is less conscientious. But a compact like the present, by which tradesmen come forward and pledge themselves to the public and to each other to resist such proceedings, will be the surest way to defeat them; as the illicit purchaser will have fewer resources, and the shopkeeper who with-holds his assent in the hope of such customers, will by that means expose himself to the suspicion and discountenance of his neighbours.[30]

A fortnight later the paper reported convictions in Chester and Shropshire for buying and selling unstamped hats with the caption 'A Caution'. The public shaming of the reprobate was part of the social as well as the political morality of the press, and was central to the frequent use of accusations of corruption by the opposition press. However, it is important to note that such accusations were also used by ministerial, in the sense of pro-government, papers, such as the *Leeds Intelligencer*, just as many devices of the opposition press that are, largely as a result of work on the 1760s, traditionally identified with it, were also features of ministerial papers. This was true of the reporting of celebrations, with their rituals such as toasts and bonfires. Just as opposition celebrations, for example those following the defeat of the Excise Bill or associated with Wilkes, were reported by some papers, so the same was true of ministerial occasions, such as those inspired by victories, for example Cape Passaro and Dettingen, in wars that were politically contentious. The same was also true of stylistic devices. The use of humour for political purposes and the favourable presentation of controversies by the use of familiar analogies was not restricted to opposition papers. The intro-duction to a collection of essays in *Common-Sense* published in 1738 claimed that 'all the wit and good sense . . . appeared on the side of Liberty', but this was not the case. Discussing the essay papers founded to debate the Peerage Bill in 1719 Mist claimed that they were

drawn up in warlike order on both sides, to carry it on, even as far as one penny is to be got by it, which, by the way, is the chief end of the strife. These dreadful combatants . . . are all armed with satires, invectives, sarcasms, retorts, replies, false history, wrong quotations, and the devil and all of ribaldry and nonsense.

Other ministerial papers used the same techniques. The *Test*, founded in November 1756 to defend Henry Fox against the *Monitor*, printed the very funny 'Proceedings of the Patriotic Junto'. The *Briton* was very skilful in its use of readily understood analogies in order to associate politics with everyday life. It also used imaginary dialogues and histories. Such techniques were not restricted to the ministerial London press. Mocking the petitioning movement, which it was consistently opposed to, the *Leeds Intelligencer* announced:

We are informed that a committee of fish-women is appointed to meet at York . . . to debate *upon a redress of grievances* — to petition his Majesty to give directions to his Ministry, — that mackerel may be brought to market at Christmas instead of summer, as they keep best in cold weather — that oysters may open of their own accord — and that sprats may be as big as herrings.[31]

The use of humour in political pieces and the attempt to make political discussions more interesting can be viewed as an effort to make them more accessible. This can also be seen in the use of lists, such as that of national grievances printed in the *Argus* in 1792, or the five simple reasons why peace with the French was impracticable, published in the *London Packet* in 1795.[32] 'The Political Dictionary for 1797', which defined words in a way that criticised the ministry and was printed in the *Telegraph*, was another instance of the same method, as were ostensible future newspapers and accounts of imaginary machines, such as North's 'modern Political Perspective'.[33] How far the attempt to make the news more accessible and interesting was intended to widen the social range of readership is unclear. It could be suggested that this material, like the sensational serials printed in the cheap London papers of the second quarter of the century, such as the story of cannibalism on the high seas carried by the *Penny London Morning Advertiser* in July 1744,[34] represented an attempt by some papers to move away from the largely middle- and upper-class readership of books[35] and magazines towards the much larger, but less exalted readership of chapbooks and ballad sheets. In an interesting recent article, Susan Pedersen has suggested that the strength of popular literature lay in its ability to amuse. Several papers stressed their willingness to adopt an 'easy style', Arthur Murphy asking in 1754,

> Why may not a person rather choose an air of bold negligence, than the obscure diligence of pedants, and writers of affected phraseology? For my part, I have always thought an easy style more eligible than a pompous diction, lifted up by metaphor, amplified by epithet, and dignified by too frequent insertions of the *Latin* idiom. I am therefore inclined to flatter myself that my expression has been natural and unambitious; and that my arrangement has been grammatically just, unperplexed and clear . . .[36]

If an attempt to extend the social range of readership existed it was neither shared by most of the press nor obviously successful: *Old England* announced in 1747 'This Paper is not for the Canaille, nor carry'd on by mercenary Hands.' The cut-price London papers of the second quarter of the century came to an end and were neither succeeded by new papers, nor matched in the provinces. Despite the massive rise in the total annual sale of stamped papers from over 14 million in 1780 to 85 million in 1851, per capita consumption in that period only increased significantly after 1836. Even though per capita consumption appears to have risen during the eighteenth century there was no massive growth in popular readership, particularly outside London. It is worth noting that the distribution and sale of chapbooks grew considerably in the course of the century.[37] An examination of the literary or theatrical news or the bulk of the advertisements in the London and provincial press does not suggest much of an effort to cater for and thus create a mass readership, and the bulk of the claims made for its existence related to London. If E. P. Thompson's distinction between polite and popular culture is to be adopted, and there is need for considerable caution in this sphere, then the press was clearly a facet of the former. The limited readership of the press puts a perspective upon the claims that have been made for the creation of a national political culture. The experience of civil war and violent political change in the seventeenth century, as well as the state-directed religious changes that had characterised that and the previous century had forced the regions of Britain to take note of national politics, and they, coupled with the two wars in the period 1688–1713, arguably played a larger role in the development of national political awareness than any events in the eighteenth century. Such an issue is a matter largely of personal impression, but correspondingly it could be suggested that the interpretation of the eighteenth-century press as a successful modernising force is one based on a teleological, progressive interpretation of the century and requires cautious evaluation. Some recent work has suggested a limited impact for the press. Detailed studies have led to a sceptical view of the value or use of the press as a medium for the diffusion of agricultural information.[38] Much has been made of the role of advertising in creating a national market for goods and services, Mist publishing a letter in 1719 condemning quack advertisements:

> At present, these people disperse their lies, under your protection, to every part of the nation; and spread death and desolation, by your assistance, through every corner of the island. Were they to keep to their stage, and only harangue the gaping crowd, from an eminence eight or ten foot high, their voice would not be heard very far, and some parts of the Kingdom would escape their infection: or, were they only to publish their shams on little billets, they might still be innocent, in spite of all their physick; their papers being usually converted another way, upon the very next occasion. But, as it is, your journal supplies the defects of both those methods, it carries them through town and country, gains admittance for them at coffee-houses and tea tables, and gives them opportunity of prating to all qualities, ages, sexes, constitutions and parties.

However, a more cautious approach might appear justified by Walker's work on the London press in the first half of the century and Looney's work on the Yorkshire press. Walker concluded that most goods were never or only rarely advertised and that even luxuries were advertised irregularly after they ceased to be novelties. Looney found that most goods and services were not advertised and that advertising in the provincial press by London tradesmen outside of the medical and print trades was comparatively rare for most of the century. He suggested that Neil

McKendrick made George Packwood and his advertising campaign on behalf of his shaving goods appear more typical than was in fact the case. An examination of papers produced in a number of provincial centres, including Newcastle, Reading, Sheffield and Worcester lends support to Looney's suggestions.[39]

Naturally the press spread information, particularly as provincial papers continued to print much London material, and as London papers increasingly circulated in the provinces, over 4½ million being sent out of London by the post in 1790, as opposed to just over 1 million 26 years earlier.[40] However, the extent to which the press was an agency for the transmission of London news and opinion is difficult to assess. The transmission of information about market prices throughout the country, with *Bell's Weekly Messenger* devoting the whole of its front page to information about prices in May 1796, may have encouraged the free movement of goods and the erosion of 'local' economies, but there is little evidence of this and it is difficult to believe that the press was the sole or crucial means by which information about prices was transmitted. The press spread cultural news and opinion, mostly from London to the provinces, but also in the reverse direction, as with the Edinburgh theatrical news printed in the *General Advertiser* of 15 January 1780. The *Country Spectator* suggested in 1792 that the provinces had become less rustic though it did not attribute this to the press:

At the time, when periodical papers were first issued into the world, refinement and a taste for reading had scarcely found their way into the country. The capital itself having but lately emerged from ignorance to civilization was as yet the sole abode of wit and learning . . . Soon, however, the manners and taste so conspicuous in the metropolis began to enlarge the sphere of their existence: the greater convenience and dispatch in travelling, wealth and polished life quitting the busy scene of the Town for the shade of retirement, a noble spirit of emulation in those, who disdained inferiority, and, not least, the striking improvements, which the present age has introduced into the system of female education, are causes which have concurred to aid the progress of refinement, to obliterate those habits, which had been stigmatised with the appellation of *rusticity*, and to raise the Provinces to a level with the metropolis in the love of letters and the pursuit of science!

George Colman had made similar claims in 1761.[41] The extent to which this process had taken place may be questioned, not least on the grounds that the nature of the rural elite thus discussed may well have been a relatively limited one. The rise of professional groups charted so ably by Geoffrey Holmes was largely a metropolitan and urban phenomenon, and although these groups may well have become more attuned to metropolitan trends, Britain in 1800 was still, for the bulk of the population, a matter of scattered dwellings, villages and very small towns.[42] The 1801 census revealed a population of nearly 9 million in England and Wales, of whom 70 per cent did not live in towns of 2,500 inhabitants or more, a figure that still excludes many living in fairly small settlements. What the press or urban culture meant for these groups is still unclear. It is too easy to assume that rural society responded evenly or rapidly to urban developments and to extrapolate national developments from the culture of print. Newspapers of course circulated widely in rural areas, but it is difficult to believe that these areas were not still in 1800 securely located in the realm of oral culture. Looney suggested that the rise in newspaper advertising 'involved a real shift in the balance of power between oral and written culture, rather than a mere change in technique within the latter', and that 'a more impersonal society' arose.[43] However, Robert Houston, in an important recent study of illiteracy and society in northern England and Scotland in this period, has stressed the continuing importance of oral culture. In such a world newspapers perforce remained marginal, not because of limited literacy, but because the impact of literacy on the mental world of early modern people was neither immediate nor total. In 1789 the people of Saddleworth and its neighbourhood in West Yorkshire heard Pitt's answer to their address in church, when it was read out by the vicars. For them as for others the press would only have been one source of information.[44]

The press may well have served to transmit metropolitan news and opinion and, in the process, further the already existing national perspective of the regional elites that would have encouraged them to seek such news, but there is little sign that it substantially increased interest in such news among groups that had not previously shown much of a regular or detailed interest in national politics. Interest among all groups in national news probably increased at times of war, which was an important source of economic change and dislocation. This situation predated the growth of the press and, as in many other fields, the preponderant amount of news concerning war and international relations printed in the newspapers reflected the extent to which they represented, rather than shaped, reader interests. It is probable that during the century the press became for some groups a more significant source of information and even of opinion. Newspapers may have encouraged in these groups a more individual and independent response to the news. It is true that newspapers were often read or read aloud in public places, such as coffee-houses, where the individual response may well have been guided by that of the assembled company, and where the reading of the papers may have been only part of the public discussion of matters. In 1702 the *Observator* attacked false war news, invented by the Jacobites and spread by Dyer's newsletter, and called for government action, adding,

'Tis an easy matter to pull down pallisades, to attack half-moons, bastions, and counterscarps, in the coffee-houses of *London* and *Westminster*, and to bomb citadels and castles with quart bottles of wine in a tavern, where there is seen no smoke but that of tobacco, nor no shot felt but when the reckoning comes to be paid.

Carrying the supposed account of an American Indian visitor to London, the *Universal Spectator* printed under 'coffee-houses':

Politicians who come to read certain papers, and afterwards talk, commend, or disapprove, arguing on the whole subject with great zeal and seeming sagacity: Every coffee-house has a set of these people; they settle the affairs of powerful and mighty Kings and Nations; They examine the conduct of their chiefs; they say how they ought to be governed at home, and how to govern others abroad.

The following year the paper referred to coffee-houses as 'the Schools of Town Politics'. Attacking 'the weekly mess of slander and sedition', produced by the opposition press in 1763, the *Briton* complained that 'some individuals . . . have, in public coffee-houses . . . harangued by the hour upon such dangerous topics'. Twelve years later the *Country Spectator* praised the news-rooms springing up 'in almost every market-town' as excellent schools 'for young students in the art of oratory. I lately visited one of these places . . . where a politician was holding forth with exultation on the Duke of Brunswick's inglorious retreat'. In 1795 the *Leeds Mercury* complained about a man called Parkes who had

> for some months past been prophesying in many of the public houses about Birmingham, and terrifying the ignorant by pre-dicting disasters; the numbers that have resorted to hear his sybillic rhapsodies are astonishing; but, as his grand prediction, the landing of the French army, in this country, before the end of February, has failed, we suppose he will lose the appellation which he has hitherto possessed, 'the Birmingham Prophet.'[45]

To some extent the press was therefore only part of the public discussion of news, and readers were influenced by the circumstances in which they read the news, just as their views were guided by the papers themselves, most adopting a markedly didactic tone. How-ever, it would be mistaken to assume that public places were the only ones in which newspapers were read. Because coffee-houses were an exciting development and a subject of discussion, in newspapers, plays and other printed works, they have possibly received excessive attention, as in general the public discussion of news may have done. Because less is known about the private reading of the press that does not mean that it was inconsequential. 'Mr Kilmister, one of the four Ale-Conners of London', who died 'in his chair, reading a news paper', or the elderly sitting in their houses and reading papers with their spouses, mentioned by the *Oracle* in 1789, were among the private readers who, judged by such criteria as the distribution networks of provincial newspapers, must have been the largest category of newspaper readers.[46] Furthermore, it is unlikely that all public places of readership, such as taverns or coffee-houses, witnessed public discussion of the news. The *Country Spectator* claimed that, whereas in the countryside people were happy to listen to such discussion, in London coffee-houses 'orators' were inter-rupted by others who wished to read, not to listen.[47] Thus the press was both part of a public world in which news was discussed aloud and stuck up to be read in public places and a private world in which individuals chose what to read and made their own assessments of it. This contrast was in no way unique to the press, being a general condition of printed works, but it makes it harder to assess the impact of newspapers.

Contemporary accounts of discussion of the news in coffee-houses stress the political nature of such discussions. Whether this was equally true of private consideration is unclear, as is the general issue of the extent of public interest in politics, local, national and international. For obvious reasons the press operated on the assumption that a certain level of interest existed, though the increased willingness, during the century, to print non-political news and items suggests an appreciation of a limited public interest in political news and a demand that newspapers avoid a concentration upon it and become more like a miscellany, as the magazines had succeeded in doing. Fielding declared in 1746 that 'in Politics, every man is an adept, and the lowest mechanic delivers his opinion, at his club, upon the deepest public measures'.[48] Such a view was understandable for a metropolitan commentator at a time of Jacobite insurrection and British participation in a major international crisis, but it is possible that it was an exaggeration of the position even then.

The extent of public interest in politics is a subject for which the surviving material is patchy and difficult to assess. Most of it, as with comments in newspapers or reports of demonstrations, supports an interpretation of widespread interest, but for obvious reasons a lack of interest did not tend to produce much evidence. The general direction of scholarly interest in eighteenth-century popular politics has emphasised radicalism, modernity, secularism and widespread support. A note of caution may however be introduced. Much of this work has been metropolitan or restricted to the larger towns and relatively little is known about the attitudes of the bulk of the population. Alongside the view that presents a populace deprived of the franchise by a corrupt oligarchy, eager to divest their minds of inherited 'silly prejudices',[49] seething with new ideas, keen to gain the vote and unwilling to accept the continued dominance of the old order, may be placed a contrary model that stresses deference, conservatism, religious belief, and the 'mental chains' that the *Argus* claimed 'arrogance and insulting power' held 'the mass of the people in'.[50] Important scholarship has been devoted to developing both of these interpretations and at present no consensus exists on the subject. This poses problems for the scholar interested in eighteenth-century newspaper history. The rise of the press has often been associated with political reform, both being attributed to that great *deus ex machina*, the rise of the middle class. By suggesting a limited popular interest in change a reinterpretation of some aspects of newspaper history is permitted. Just as many who enjoyed the franchise did not choose to vote so it could be suggested that many who could afford to purchase newspapers did not do so, and that this, rather than taxation, was the principal restraint on the growth of press readership. Richard Altick has stressed the distinction between those who could and those who did read. Instead of the system being maintained by the monopoly powers of the Church of England, restrictions on the franchise and taxes on the press, there was little demand for ecclesiastical or franchise reform or for a free press. The last was certainly true as far as parliamentarians and newspapers were concerned, and there is little evidence of popular interest in the subject. The failure to maintain the London cut-price press and develop a provincial counterpart may therefore reflect a limited market for such products.

However, the press did grow in the eighteenth century, particularly towards its close. The number of papers did not rise exponentially or regularly, and there tended to be failures after periods of wartime interest, but the general trend was upwards. In 1723 there were about 24 provincial newspapers in existence, in 1753 32, in 1760 35, in 1782 about 50 and in 1808 over 100.[51] The growth was less than the spate of new titles might suggest, as many papers failed, but the general trend, both in London and the provinces, in England, Scotland and Ireland, was for a rise both in the number of titles and in total sales. This may seem to conform more to a model of a changing rather than a conservative society, but just as that is too crude a dichotomy, so it is essential to remember that the press was not necessarily a radical force. The *Country Spectator* claimed that 'the reputable and independent prints nobly display the corruptions, which disgrace our Church and State' and 'teach us to despise the slavish restraints, which all governments impose', but it also noted the existence of papers that affected 'to speak with reverence of the Ministry and our glorious Constitution'.[52] Individual papers pointed in different directions and the amount of radical opinion printed in the press was very limited, particularly prior to the 1790s. In the case of long lasting opposition papers, such as those of Mist and the *London Evening Post*, it is possible that reader interest was maintained by the varied nature and accessible style of the papers, as much as by their political attitudes. The basic political stance of the press was not adversarial in terms of suggesting the existence of incompatible social interests. By calling for national unity and suggesting that bad government was due to corruption, differing political groups to ambition, folly or malice, and opposing the thinking people to the unthinking 'mob', the press sustained an ideology that made consensus a goal. In 1702 Tutchin wrote in the *Observator*,

> I know 'tis impossible to write a paper of this nature without the censure of most, if not all parties; but the author of it professing himself to be an Englishman, writes only to such; that is, to such as love their dear country, its ancient rights and privileges, and the known laws and customs of this our realm; he does not write to foment divisions or increase discording parties, but would endeavour by cogent reasons and demonstrations from matter of fact, to persuade Englishmen to be on their own side, and to endeavour the support of his beloved country and the present settlement.

Sixteen years later Mist attacked party distinctions: 'We should unite in the interest of the nation . . . and as there can be but one way of safety, which the reverse of it can never give, so every person, (all prejudice first banished,) would accord in that one way.'[53]

Many of these arguments were used to serve political ends as when 'Lucius' called for national unity during the War of American Independence.[54] They are, however, evidence of the tendency to discuss political issues in political, constitutional, ideological and historical rather than socio-economic terms. It is important not to push this argument too far, as real and alleged socio-economic differences between Whigs and Tories played an important role in political discussion in the early years of the century and were also significant in Bolingbroke's attempt in the 1730s, to define politics around a court/country polarity.[55] Nevertheless the dominance of 'political' interpretations of political differences is a reminder of the need for caution against any analysis of the century that aggregates changes in different spheres in order to produce a common chronology and pattern of development. The press was not isolated from society, but it is dangerous to treat its growth as in some way related to and therefore somehow due to other changes. Newspapers presented a variety of opinions on the political issues of the day. The growth in their numbers and sales was not marked by any appreciable change in their methods or intentions. This work has sought to strike a note of caution about the tendency to treat the expansion of the press as in some way symptomatic of wider social changes. It is not the case that all was static and at different points in the book the stress has been on development and change on the part of newspapers. However, the overall impression that reading and studying a large number of London and provincial newspapers throughout the century has given this author is of a press that developed far less and was substantially less influential than is commonly believed. Others will not share this view and if the appearance of this book encourages a debate one of its principal objectives will have been attained. This work has sought to encourage a more critical evaluation of the eighteenth-century press and a more probing examination of assumptions about its influence. Hopefully it will lead more scholars to read the newspapers of the period and to consider their significance.

Notes

1. *Bell's Weekly Messenger*, 12 June 1796.
2. *St. James's Chronicle*, 14 Oct. 1779; for cross-referencing by asterisk, *ibid.*, 22 May 1764.
3. *Bell's Weekly Messenger*, 1 May 1796.
4. *Oracle*, 11 June 1789, 1 July 1795.
5. Werkmeister, *London Daily Press*, p. 255; Read, *Press and People*, pp. 69, 71.
6. J. J. Looney, *Advertising and Society in England, 1720–1820: A Statistical Analysis of Yorkshire Newspaper Advertisements* (D.Phil thesis, Princeton, 1983), pp. 37–9.
7. *Gray's Inn Journal*, 29 Sept. 1753.
8. *Oracle*, 1, 10 June 1789.
9. *Courier*, 6 Jan. 1795; Devon RO. 63/2/11/1/46.
10. *Oracle*, 14 Feb. 1792; *English Chronicle*, 11 Oct. 1796; *World*, 1 Jan. 1791.
11. *Sheffield Advertiser*, 7 Sept. 1787; *Ayre's Sunday London Gazette*, 7 Apr. 1793.
12. *Weekly Register*, 11 Apr. 1789.
13. S. Morison, *The English Newspaper* (Cambridge, 1932), pp. 143–50; I. Christie, *Myth and Reality*, pp. 316–17; Harris, 'Structure', in Boyce *et al.* (eds), *Newspaper History*, pp. 94, 97; Harris, 'The Management of the London Newspaper Press during the Eighteenth Century', *Publishing History*, 4 (1978); I. Asquith, 'The structure, ownership and control of the press, 1780–1855', in Boyce *et al.* (eds), *Newspaper History*, pp. 102–3.
14. *Gray's Inn Journal*, 4 May, 21 Sept. 1754.
15. *London Advertiser*, 4 Mar. 1751; Harris, 'Structure', in Boyce *et al.* (eds), *Newspaper History*, p. 94.
16. Cranfield, *Provincial Newspaper*, p. 21; *Test*, 18 Dec. 1756; *St. James's Chronicle*, 13 July 1761.
17. I. Asquith, 'Advertising and the Press in the Late Eighteenth and Early Nineteenth Centuries: James Perry and the *Morning Chronicle*, 1790–1821', *HJ*, 18

(1975), p. 721; Christie, *Myth and Reality*, pp. 311–58; H. R. Fox-Bourne, *English Newspapers* (2 vols., 1887), I, 289; Looney, *Advertising and Society*, p. 278; J. Feather, *The Provincial Book Trade in Eighteenth-Century England* (Cambridge, 1985), p. 124. For an interesting discussion of the press towards the end of the century, K. Schweizer and J. Klein, 'The French Revolution and Developments in the London Daily Press to 1793', *Publishing History* 18 (1985).

18. L. Brown, *Victorian News and Newspapers* (Oxford, 1985).
19. R. Williams, 'The press and popular culture: an historical perspective', in Boyce *et al.* (eds), *Newspaper History*, p. 45; C. B. Jewson, *The Jacobin City. A Portrait of Norwich 1788–1802* (Glasgow, 1975), pp. 59–60.
20. *Telegraph*, 2 Jan. 1797.
21. Brown, *Victorian News*, p. 100.
22. Christie, *Myth and Reality*, p. 322.
23. Watson-Wentworth to Rockingham, [Nov. 1762], Sheffield, RI–327.
24. Hardwicke to Rockingham, 24 Aug. 1766, Sheffield, RI–679.
25. *London Evening Post*, 9 Dec. 1779, *Leeds Intelligencer*, 17 Feb. 1789; *Western Flying Post*, 7 Jan. 1793. There is little mention of the press in the otherwise very interesting treatment by Paul Kelly, 'Constituents' instructions to Members of Parliament in the eighteenth century', in *Party and Management in Parliament 1660–1784*, ed. C. Jones (Leicester, 1984).
26. *Darlington Pamphlet*, 19 June 1772; *Leeds Intelligencer*, 15 May 1781; *Leeds Mercury*, 11 Dec. 1787; *Country Spectator*, 6 Nov. 1792.
27. *Leeds Intelligencer*, 15 Nov. 1785; *Weekly Worcester Journal*, 9, 16, 30 July, 6, 20, 27 Aug., 24 Sept. 1742; *London Evening Post*, 14 Jan. 1777: re a lottery.
28. *Weekly Worcester Journal*, 13 Aug. 1742; *Argus*, 15 Nov. 1791.
29. *Centinel*, 6 Jan. 1757; *Old England*, 25 July 1747.
30. *Leeds Intelligencer*, 20 July 1790.
31. *Common-Sense* (1738), p. vi; *Weekly Journal*, 11 Apr. 1719; *Test*, 18 Dec. 1756; *Briton*, 5 June, 29 Aug., 4 Sept., 20 Nov., 18 Dec. 1762, 12 Feb. 1763; *Leeds Intelligencer*, 13 Feb. 1781, 13 July 1790.
32. *Argus*, 3 Mar. 1792; *London Packet*, 5 Jan. 1795; *Country Spectator*, 6 Nov. 1792.
33. *Telegraph*, 5 Jan. 1797; *London Packet*, 4 Apr. 1787; *Newcastle Journal*, 6 Feb. 1773; *London Evening Post*, 8 Jan. 1778; *London Courant*, 5 Jan. 1780.
34. *Penny London Morning Advertiser*, 6–9 July 1744.
35. Feather, *Book Trade*, p. 42.
36. S. Pedersen, 'Hannah More Meets Simple Simon: Tracts, Chapbooks, and Popular Culture in Late Eighteenth-Century England', *Journal of British Studies*, 25 (1986), p. 113; *Gray's Inn Journal*, 21 Sept. 1754.
37. *Old England*, 30 May 1747; Asquith, 'Structure', in Boyce *et al.* (eds), *Newspaper History*, p. 100; V. Neuburg, *Popular Literature* (1977), pp. 103–7.
38. E. P. Thompson, 'Patrician Society, Plebeian Culture', *Journal of Social History*, 7 (1974), p. 397; S. Macdonald, 'The Diffusion of Knowledge among Northumberland Farmers, 1780–1815', *Agricultural History Review*, 27 (1979), p. 32; J. R. Walton, 'Mechanization in agriculture', in *Change in the Countryside*, ed. H. S. A. Fox and R. A. Butlin (1979), p. 34; P. Horn, 'The Contribution of the Propagandist to Eighteenth-Century Agricultural Improvement', *HJ*, 25 (1982), p. 317.
39. *Weekly Journal*, 31 Oct. 1719; Walker, 'Advertising', pp. 124–5; Looney, *Advertising and Society*, pp. 142, 205, 257–8; McKendrick *et al.*, *Consumer Society*, pp. 146–94, esp. pp. 191–2.
40. Harris, 'Structure', in Boyce *et al.* (eds), *Newspaper History*, p. 90.
41. *Country Spectator*, 9 Oct. 1792; Colman, 'The Genius', *St. James's Chronicle*, 6 Aug. 1761.

42. G. A. Holmes, *Augustan England Professions, State and Society, 1680–1730* (1982).

43. Looney, *Advertising and Society*, pp. v, 114, 155.

44. R. A. Houston, *Scottish Literacy and Scottish Identity* (Cambridge, 1985), pp. 193–210, esp. pp. 204, 209; *Leeds Intelligencer*, 24 Feb. 1789. The significance of changes in literacy is a difficult subject. Relevant works include R. S. Schofield, 'The Measurement of Literacy in pre-industrial England', in *Literacy in Traditional Societies*, ed. J. R. Goody (Cambridge, 1968); L. Stone, 'Literacy and Education in England, 1650–1900', *Past and Present*, 42 (1969); R. M. Wiles, 'Middle-class Literacy in Eighteenth-Century England: Fresh Evidence', in *Studies in the Eighteenth Century*, ed. R. F. Brissenden (Canberra, 1968), and 'The Relish for Reading in Provincial England Two Centuries Ago', in *The Widening Circle*, ed. P. J. Korshin (Philadelphia, 1976); M. Sanderson, 'Literacy and Social Mobility in the Industrial Revolution in England', *Past and Present* (1972).

45. *Observator*, 10 June 1702; *Universal Spectator*, 16 Jan., 6 Feb. (quote) 1742, 25 June 1743; *Briton*, 1 Jan. 1763; *Yorkshire Freeholder*, 10 Feb. 1780; *Country Spectator*, 6 Nov. 1792; *Leeds Mercury*, 14 Mar. 1795; *Weekly Journal or British Gazetteer*, 1 Nov. 1718; *Weekly Packet*, 13 Dec. 1718; *Genius*, 13 July 1761; J. Miller, *The Coffee-House* (1737), pp. 3–6; Shorthand diary of Dudley Ryder, 10 Sept. 1716, Sandon Hall; Sutherland, 'Circulation', p. 124; *Senator*, 15 Mar. 1728; *Weekly Comedy, As it is Dayly Acted at most Coffee-Houses in London*, 17 May 1699; *Flying Post*, 25 May 1731.

46. *Northampton Mercury*, 18 Nov. 1723; *Oracle*, 11 June 1789.

47. *Country Spectator*, 6 Nov. 1792.

48. *True Patriot*, 11 Mar. 1746.

49. *Country Spectator*, 6 Nov. 1792.

50. *Argus*, 29 Feb. 1792.

51. R. D. Altick, *The English Common Reader* (Chicago, 1957), p. 30; Cranfield, *Provincial Newspaper*, pp. 19, 21; Read, *Press and People*, p. 59.

52. *Country Spectator*, 6 Nov. 1792.

53. *Observator*, 3 June 1702; *Weekly Journal*, 26 Apr. 1718.

54. *Leeds Intelligencer*, 23 Jan. 1781.

55. W. A. Speck and G. A. Holmes, *The Divided Society: party conflict in England 1694–1716* (1967); I. Kramnick, *Bolingbroke and His Circle* (Cambridge, Mass., 1968). H. T. Dickinson's *Liberty and Property. Political Ideology in Eighteenth-Century Britain* (1977) is the best introduction to the issue of ideology. Recent works include Clark, *English Society* and the unduly neglected J. A. W. Gunn, *Beyond Liberty and Property* (1983).

Bibliography

For reasons of space only a select list of sources consulted has been given.

Manuscript sources

Bedford	*Bedfordshire Record Office*
	Lucas papers.
Bury St Edmunds	*West Suffolk Record Office*
	Grafton, Hervey papers.
Cambridge	*University Library*
	Cholmondeley Houghton papers.
Carlisle	*Cumbria Record Office*
	Lonsdale papers.
Chewton Mendip	*Chewton Hall*
	Waldegrave papers.
Gateshead	*Public Library*
	Ellison papers.
London	*British Library*
	Almon, Althorp, Blenheim, Brockman, Caryll, Hardwicke, Holland House, Newcastle, Robinson, Wilkes, Woodfall papers.
	Public Record Office
	State Papers Domestic, Foreign, Regencies.
Oxford	*Bodleian Library*
	Bland Burges, Firth Tanner papers.
	Queen's College
	Minute book of the proprietors of the *Grub Street Journal*.
	St. John's College
	Rawlinson papers.
Paris	*Quai d'Orsay, Archives du Ministère des Affaires Etrangères*
	Correspondance Politique Angleterre.
Reading	*County Record Office*
	Additional Trumbull papers.
Windsor	*Royal Archives*
	Stuart papers.

Newspapers

Newspapers held in the British Library, the municipal libraries of Birmingham, Bristol, Bury St Edmunds, Chester, Cirencester, Colchester, Derby, Gateshead, Gloucester, Hereford, Hull, Ipswich,

Kendal, Leeds, Newcastle, Norwich, Preston, Reading, Sheffield and York, the university libraries of Cambridge, Durham, Leeds, Newcastle, Oxford and Reading, the library of All Souls, Oxford, the Guildhall Library in London, the Polytechnic Library in Newcastle and the Minster Library in York, have been examined. In addition newspapers have been found in various manuscript collections. For purposes of comparison French and Dutch papers in the Bibliothèque Nationale, the Bibliothèque de L'Arsenal and the Archives Nationales were examined.

Secondary works

For reasons of space not all works cited in the footnotes have been mentioned a second time.

R. J. Allen 'William Oldisworth: the Author of *The Examiner'*, *Philological Quarterly*, 26 (1947)

J. D. Alsop 'New Light on Nathaniel Mist and Daniel Defoe', *Papers of the Bibliographical Society of America*, 75 (1981)

—— 'Defoe and his Whig Paymasters', *Notes and Queries* (1981)

R. D. Altick *The English Common Reader* (Chicago, 1957)

A. Andrew *The History of British Journalism* (1859)

W. H. G. Armytage 'The Editorial Experiences of Joseph Gales', *North Carolina Historical Review*, 28 (1951)

A. Aspinall *Politics and the Press c. 1780–1850* (1949)

I. S. Asquith *James Perry and the 'Morning Chronicle' 1790–1821* (PhD thesis, London, 1973)

R. Astbury 'The Renewal of the Licensing Act in 1693 and its Lapse in 1695', *Library*, 5th ser., 38 (1978)

B. Bailyn and S. B. Hench (eds) *The Press and the American Revolution* (Worcester, Mass., 1980)

J. Barrell *English Literature in History 1730–80* (1983)

E. S. De Beer 'The English Newspapers from 1695 to 1702', in *William III and Louis XIV*, ed. R. Hatton and J. S. Bromley (Liverpool, 1968)

L. Bertelsen 'Have At You All: or Bonnell Thornton's Journalism', *Huntington Library Quarterly*, 94 (1981)

J. Black 'Manchester's First Newspaper: The Manchester Weekly Journal', *Transactions of the Historical Society of Lancashire and Cheshire*, 130 (1981)

—— 'The British Press and European News in the 1730s: The Case of the Newcastle Courant', *Durham County Local History Society Bulletin*, 26 (1981)

—— 'Russia and the British Press, 1720–40', *British Journal for Eighteenth-Century Studies*, 5 (1982)

—— 'The Challenge of Autocracy: The British Press in the 1730s', *Studi Settecenteschi*, 3–4 (1982–3)

—— 'The Catholic Threat and the British Press in the 1720s and 1730s', *Journal of Religious History*, 12 (1983)

—— 'The Cirencester Flying-Post, and Weekly Miscellany', *Cirencester Archaeological and History Society Annual Report*, 25 (1983)

—— 'Press and Politics in the Age of Walpole', *Durham University Journal*, 77 (1984)

—— 'Political Allusions in Fielding's Coffee-House Politician', *Theoria*, 62 (1984)
—— 'The Political Impact of the Eighteenth-Century British Press', *Journal of Newspaper and Periodical History*, 1 (1985)
—— 'Eighteenth-Century Journalism in the North-East: the *Darlington-Pamphlet* of 1772', *Durham County Local History Society Bulletin* (forthcoming)
—— 'A Missing Northampton Paper', *Northamptonshire Past and Present* (forthcoming)
—— 'Russian Intervention in the British Press: an Example from 1762', *Study Group on Eighteenth-Century Russia Newsletter* (forthcoming)
—— 'An Underrated Journalist: Nathaniel Mist and the Opposition Press during the Whig Ascendancy', *British Journal for Eighteenth-Century Studies* (forthcoming)
D. H. Bond and W. R. McLeod (eds) *Newsletters to Newspapers: Eighteenth-Century Journalism* (Morgantown, 1977)
R. P. Bond (ed.) *Studies in the Early English Periodical* (Chapel Hill, 1957)
R. P. Bond *Growth and Change in the Early English Press* (Lawrence, 1969)
S. Botein, J. Censor and H. Ritvo 'The Periodical Press in eighteenth-century English and French Society: a cross cultural approach', *Comparative Studies in Society and History*, 23 (1981), 464–90
J. Brewer *Party Ideology and Popular Politics at the Accession of George III* (Cambridge, 1976)
L. E. J. Brooke *Somerset Newspapers 1725–1960* (1960)
P. S. Brown 'The vendors of medicines advertised in eighteenth-century Bath newspapers', *Medical History*, 19 (1975)
—— 'Medicines advertised in eighteenth-century Bath newspapers', *Medical History*, 20 (1975)
T. N. Brushfield 'Andrew Brice and the early Exeter newspaper press', *Report and Transactions of the Devonshire Association*, 2 (1888)
P. M. Chapman *Jacobite Political Argument in England, 1714–1766* (PhD thesis, Cambridge, 1983)
I. Christie *Myth and Reality in Late-Eighteenth-Century British Politics and other papers* (1970)
D. Clare 'The local newspaper press and local politics in Manchester and Liverpool, 1780–1800', *Transactions of the Lancashire and Cheshire Antiquarian Society*, 73 (1963)
T. R. Cleary 'Henry Fielding and the Great Jacobite Paper War of 1747–49', *Eighteenth-Century Life*, 5 (1978)
T. N. Corns, W. A. Speck and J. A. Downie 'Archetypal Mystification: Polemic and Reality in English Political Literature, 1640–1750', *Eighteenth-Century Life*, 7 (1982)
D. H. Couvee 'The Administration of the *Oprechte Haarlemse Courant* 1738–1742', *Gazette*, 4 (1858)
M. E. Craig *The Scottish Periodical Press 1750–89* (Edinburgh 1931)
G. A. Cranfield *The Development of the Provincial Newspaper, 1700–1760* (Oxford, 1962)
—— 'The London Evening Post, 1727–1744', *Historical Journal*, 6 (1963)
—— *The Press and Society* (1978)
D. Cressy *Literacy and the Social Order* (Cambridge, 1980)
R. Davies *A Memoir of the York Press* (1868)
K. S. Dent *The Informal Education of the Landed Classes in the Eighteenth Century* (PhD thesis, Birmingham, 1974)
J. A. Downie 'Mr. Review and his Scribbling Friends: Defoe and the Critics, 1705–1706', *Huntington Library Quarterly*, 41 (1978)
—— 'An Unknown Defoe Broadsheet on the Regulation of the Press?', *Library*, 5th ser., 33 (1978)

F. H. Ellis (ed.) *Swift vs. Mainwaring. The Examiner and The Medley* (Oxford, 1985)

C. Emsley 'Pitt's "Terror": prosecutions for sedition during the 1790s', *Social History*, 6 (1981)

—— 'Repression, "terror" and the rule of Law in England during the decade of the French Revolution', *EHR*, 99 (1985)

W. B. Ewald *The Newsmen of Queen Anne* (Oxford, 1956)

P. Fabel 'The Patriotic Briton. Tobias Smollett and English Politics, 1756–1771', *Eighteenth-Century Studies*, 8 (1974–5)

H. R. Fox-Bourne *English Newspapers* (1887)

D. G. Gallop *Chapters in the History of the Provincial Newspaper Press 1700–1855* (MA thesis, Bristol, 1954)

G. C. Gibbs 'Newspapers, Parliament and Foreign Policy in the Age of Stanhope and Walpole', in *Mélanges offerts à G. Jacquemyns* (Brussels, 1968)

J. J. Gold '"Buried Alive": Charlotte Forman in Grub Street', *Eighteenth-Century Life*, 8 (1982)

B. Goldgar *Walpole and the Wits: The Relation of Politics to Literature, 1722–1742* (Lincoln, Nebraska, 1976)

——'Fielding, Periodicals and the Idea of Literary Fame', *Journal of Newspaper and Periodical History*, II, 1 (1985)

W. Graham *English Literary Periodicals* (New York, 1930)

A. Gregory *Robert Raikes: journalist and philanthropist* (1877)

R. L. Haig 'The Last Years of the *Gazetteer*', *Library*, 5th ser., 7 (1952)

—— *The Gazetteer* (Carbondale, 1960)

L. Hanson *Government and the Press 1695–1763* (Oxford, 1936)

—— 'English Newsbooks, 1620–1641', *Library*, 4th ser., 18 (1937–8)

M. Happs, 'Sheffield Newspaper Press, 1787–1832' (Oxford Thesis Blitt 1973)

M. Harris 'Figures Relating to the Printing and Distribution of the *Craftsman* 1726 to 1730', *Bulletin of the Institute of Historical Research*, 43 (1970)

—— *The London Newspaper Press, c. 1725–1746* (PhD thesis, London, 1973), to be published as *London Newspapers in the Age of Walpole. A Study in the Origins of the Modern English Press* (1986)

—— 'Newspaper distribution during Queen Anne's reign. Charles Delafaye and the Secretary of State's Office', in *Studies in the Book Trade*, ed. R. W. Hunt, I. G. Philip and R. J. Roberts (Oxford, 1975)

—— 'London Printers and Newspaper Production in the first half of the eighteenth century', *Journal of the Printing History Society*, 12 (1977–8)

—— 'Journalism as a Profession or Trade in the Eighteenth Century', in *Author/Publisher Relations during the Eighteenth and Nineteenth centuries*, ed. R. Myers and M. Harris (Oxford, 1983)

—— 'Print and Politics in the Age of Walpole', in *Britain in the Age of Walpole*, ed. J. Black (1984)

M. Harris (ed.) *The Press in English Society from the Seventeenth to the Nineteenth Centuries* (1986)

F. J. Hinkhouse *The Preliminaries of the American Revolution as seen in the English Press 1763–1775* (New York, 1926)

D. B. Horn *British Public Opinion and the First Partition of Poland* (Edinburgh, 1945)

T. Horne 'Politics in a Corrupt Society: William Arnall's Defence of Robert Walpole', *Journal of the History of Ideas*, 41 (1980)

L. S. Horsley 'The Trial of John Tutchin, Author of *The Observator*', *Yearbook of English Studies*, 3 (1973)

—— '*Vox Populi* in the Political Literature of 1710', *Huntington Library Quarterly*, 38 (1974–5)

—— 'Rogues or honest gentlemen: the public characters of Queen Anne journalists', *Texas Studies in Literature and Language*, 18 (1976)

F. K. Hunt *The Fourth Estate* (1850)

K. L. Joshi 'The London Journal 1719–1738', *Bombay University Journal*, 9 (1940)

J. Klaits *Printed Propaganda under Louis XIV: Absolute Monarchy and Public Opinion* (Princeton, 1976)

M. E. Knapp 'Political and Local Verse in the early years of the *Salisbury Journal*', *Hatcher Review*, 2 (1983)

I. Kramnick *Bolingbroke and his Circle* (Cambridge, Mass., 1968)

C. R. Kropf 'Libel and Satire in the Eighteenth Century', *Eighteenth-Century Studies*, 8 (1974–5)

P. Langford 'William Pitt and Public Opinion, 1757', *English Historical Review*, 88 (1973)

W. T. Laprade 'The power of the English Press in the Eighteenth Century', *South Atlantic Quarterly*, 27 (1928)

—— *Public Opinion and Politics in Eighteenth-Century England to the fall of Walpole* (New York, 1936)

P. Lawson '"The Irishman's Prize": Views of Canada from the British Press, 1760–1774', *Historical Journal*, 28 (1985)

A. S. Limouze 'Dr. Gaylard's Loyal Observator Revived', *Modern Philology*, 48 (1950)

T. Lockwood 'New Facts and Writings from an Unknown Magazine by Henry Fielding', *Review of English Studies*, n.s. 35 (1984)

J. Loftis 'The Blenheim Papers and Steele's Journalism, 1715–1718', *PLMA* 56 (1951)

J. J. Looney *Advertising and Society in England, 1720–1820: A statistical analysis of Yorkshire newspaper advertisements* (PhD thesis, Princeton, 1983)

H. M. Lubasz 'Public opinion comes of age: reform of the libel law in the eighteenth century', *History Today*, 8 (1958)

S. Lutnick *The American Revolution and the British Press 1775–1783* (Columbia, Missouri, 1967)

N. McKendrick, J. Brewer and J. H. Plumb *The Birth of a Consumer Society* (1982)

R. L. Merritt 'Public Opinion in colonial America: Content Analysing the Colonial Press', *Public Opinion Quarterly*, 27 (1963)

G. Midgley *The Life of Orator Henley* (Oxford, 1973)

J. Money *Experience and Identity. Birmingham and the West Midlands 1760–1800* (Manchester, 1977)

J. R. Moore '"Robin Hog" Stephens: Messenger of the Press', *Papers of the Bibliographical Society of America*, 50 (1956)

S. Morison *John Bell, 1745–1831* (Cambridge, 1930)

—— *Ichabod Dawks and his news-letter* (Cambridge, 1931)

—— *The English Newspaper* (Cambridge, 1932)

C. Morsley *News from the English Countryside 1750–1850* (1979)

J. G. Muddiman *The King's Journalist 1659–1689* (1923)

B. Munter *History of Irish Newspapers* (Cambridge, 1967)

M. J. Murphy 'Newspapers and opinion in Cambridge, 1780–1850', *Transactions of the Cambridge Bibliographical Society*, 6 (1972)

J. J. Murray 'British Public Opinion and the Rupture of Anglo-Swedish Relations in 1717', *Indiana Magazine of History*, 44 (1948)

T. F. M. Newton 'William Pittis and Queen Anne Journalism', *Modern Philology* 33 (1935–6)

G. Nobbe *The North Briton* (New York, 1939)

L. M. Orosco y Aragon *France and Spain in the English Periodicals of Queen Anne's Reign* (PhD thesis Minnesota, 1973)

P. B. Patterson *Robert Harley and the Organization of Political Propaganda* (PhD thesis, Virginia, 1974)

H. A. Peacock *The Techniques of Political Controversy in early eighteenth century periodicals with particular reference to the Craftsman* (MA thesis, London, 1951)

T. W. Perry *Public Opinion, Propaganda and Politics in Eighteenth-Century England: A Study of the Jew Bill of 1753* (Cambridge, Mass., 1962)

M. Peters 'The *Monitor* on the constitution, 1755–1765: new light on the ideological origins of English radicalism', *EHR*, 86 (1971)

—— *The Monitor 1755–1765: A Political Essay Paper and Popular London Opinion* (PhD thesis, Canterbury, New Zealand, 1975)

—— *Pitt and Popularity: The Patriot Minister and London Opinion during the Seven Years' War* (Oxford, 1980)

—— '"Names and Cant": Party Labels in English Political Propaganda', *Parliamentary History*, 3 (1984)

C. Press 'The Georgian Political Print and Democratic Institutions', *Comparative Studies in Society and History*, 19 (1977)

M. Ransome 'The Press in the General Election of 1710', *Cambridge Historical Journal*, 6 (1939)

R. Rea 'The North Briton and the Courts of Law', *Alabama Lawyer*, 12 (1951)

—— 'The Earl of Chatham and the London Press, 1775', *Journalism Quarterly* (1954)

—— 'Anglo-American Parliamentary Reporting: A Case Study in Historical Bibliography', *Papers of the Bibliographical Society of America*, 49 (1955)

—— 'The "Liberty of the Press" as an Issue in English Politics, 1792–1793', *The Historian*, 24 (1961)

—— *The English Press in Politics 1760–1774* (Lincoln, Nebraska, 1962)

D. Read *Press and People, 1790–1850. Opinion in Three English Cities* (1961)

C. B. Realey 'The London Journal and its Authors, 1720–3', *Bulletin of the University of Kansas Humanistic Studies*, vol. 5 (1935)

P. Rétat (ed.) *Le journalisme d'Ancien Régime* (Lyons, 1983)

I. Rivers (ed.) *Books and their Readers in Eighteenth-Century England* (Leicester, 1982)

N. Rogers *London Politics from Walpole to Pitt* (PhD thesis, Toronto, 1975)

—— 'Popular protest in early Hanoverian London', *Past and Present*, 79 (1978)

—— 'The Urban Opposition to Whig Oligarchy, 1720–60', in *The Origins of Anglo-American Radicalism*, ed. M. and J. Jacob (1984)

L. Rostenberg 'Richard and Anne Baldwin, Whig Patriot Publishers', *Papers of the Bibliographical Society of America*, 47 (1953)

K. W. Schweizer 'The Origins of the "Press War" of 1762: A Reappraisal', *Notes and Queries* (1978)

L. G. Schwoerer 'Propaganda in the Revolution of 1688–89', *American Historical Review*, 82 (1977)

—— 'Press and Parliament in the Revolution of 1689', *Historical Journal*, 20 (1977)

R. Sedgwick 'Horace Walpole's Political Articles 1747–49', in *Horace Walpole, Writer, Politician and Connoisseur*, ed. W. H. Smith (New Haven, 1967)

M. A. Shaaber *Some Forerunners of the Newspaper in England, 1476–1622* (Philadelphia, 1929)

J. B. Shipley *James Ralph: Pretender to Genius* (PhD thesis, Columbia, 1963)

M. Shugrue 'Applebee's Original Weekly Journal: an index to eighteenth-century taste', *Newberry Library Bulletin*, 6 (1964)

F. S. Siebert 'Taxes on Publications in England in the Eighteenth Century', *Journalism Quarterly*, 21 (1944)

—— *Freedom of the Press in England 1476–1776* (Urbana, 1965)

Q. Skinner 'The Principles and practice of opposition: the case of Bolingbroke versus Walpole', in *Historical Perspectives*, ed. N. McKendrick (1974)

D. N. Smith 'The Newspaper', in *Johnson's England*, ed. A. S. Turberville (Oxford, 1933)

H. Snyder 'The Reports of a Press Spy for Robert Harley', *Library*, 5th ser., 22 (1967)

—— 'The circulation of newspapers in the reign of Queen Anne', *Library*, 5th ser., 23 (1968)

—— 'Arthur Maynwaring and the Whig Press, 1710–1712', in *Literatur als Kritik des Lebens*, ed. P. Haas *et al*. (Heidelberg, 1975)

W. A. Speck 'Political Propaganda in Augustan England', *Transactions of the Royal Historical Society*, 5th ser., 22 (1972)

R. D. Spector *English Literary Periodicals and the Climate of Opinion During the Seven Years' War* (The Hague, 1966)

M. Spufford *Small Books and Pleasant Histories. Popular Fiction and its Readership in Seventeenth-Century England* (1981)

B. M. Stearns 'Early English Periodicals for Ladies 1700–1760', *PMLA*, 48 (1933)

A. Sterenberg 'The spread of printing in Suffolk in the eighteenth century', in *Searching the Eighteenth Century*, ed. M. Crump and M. Harris (1983)

M. M. Stewart 'Smart, Kenrick, Carnan and Newbery: New Evidence on the Paper War, 1750–51', *Library*, 6th ser., 5 (1983)

W. P. van Stockum *The First Newspapers of England Printed in Holland, 1620–1621* (The Hague, 1914)

L. Stone 'Literacy and Education in England 1640–1900', *Past and Present*, 42 (1969)

J. Styles 'Sir John Fielding and the Problem of Criminal Investigation in Eighteenth-Century England', *Transactions of the Royal Historical Society*, 5th ser., 33 (1983)

A. Sullivan (ed.) *British Literary Magazines: The Augustan Age and the Age of Johnson, 1698–1788* (Westport, Conn., 1983)

J. R. Sutherland 'Circulation of Newspapers and Literary Periodicals, 1700–1730', *Library*, 4th ser., 15 (1934)

D. B. Swinfen 'The American Revolution in the Scottish Press', in *Scotland, Europe and The American Revolution*, ed. O. Edwards and G. Shepperson (Edinburgh, 1976)

J. P. Thomas *The British Empire and the Press 1763–1774* (D.Phil thesis, Oxford, 1982)

P. D. G. Thomas 'The Beginning of Parliamentary Reporting in Newspapers, 1768–1774', *English Historical Review*, 74 (1959)

—— 'John Wilkes and the Freedom of the Press', *Bulletin of the Institute of Historical Research*, 33 (1960)

S. Tucoo-Chala 'Presse et Verité sous l'Ancien Régime', *Revue du Nord*, 66 (1984)

S. Varey *The Craftsman 1726–52* (PhD thesis, Cambridge, 1976)

—— 'Printers as Rivals: The Craftsman, 1739–40', *Library*, 6th ser., 2 (1980)

S. Varey (ed.) *Lord Bolingbroke's Contributions to the Craftsman* (Oxford, 1982)

J. Walker 'The Censorship of the Press during the reign of Charles II', *History*, 35 (1950)

R. B. Walker 'Advertising in London Newspapers, 1650–1750', *Business History*, 15 (1973)

—— 'The Newspaper Press in the Reign of William III', *Historical Journal*, 17 (1974)

J. A. Watson *Four English Constitutional Principles and the Press, 1700–1707* (PhD thesis, West Virginia, 1980)

R. K. Webb *The British Working Class Reader* (1955)

L. Werkmeister *The London Daily Press 1772–1792* (Lincoln, Nebraska, 1963)

—— *A Newspaper History of England, 1792–1793* (Lincoln, Nebraska, 1967)

J. Wigley 'James Montgomery and the *Sheffield Iris*, 1792–1825: A Study in the Weakness of Provincial Radicalism', *Transactions of the Hunter Archaeological Society*, 10 (1975)

R. M. Wiles *Serial Publication in England before 1750* (Cambridge, 1957)

—— *Freshest Advices. Early Provincial Newspapers in England* (Columbus, Ohio, 1965)

—— 'Middle-Class Literacy in Eighteenth-Century England', in *Studies in the Eighteenth Century*, ed. R. F. Brissenden (Canberra, 1968)

—— 'The Relish for Reading in Provincial England two centuries ago', in *The Widening Circle*, ed. P. J. Korshin (Philadelphia, 1976)

J. B. Williams 'The newsbooks and letters of news of the Restoration', *English Historical Review*, 23 (1903)

C. Winton 'Steele and the fall of Harley in 1714', *Philological Quarterly*, 37 (1958)

Index of Titles